MONEY
AND BANKING

**CONTEMPORARY PRACTICES,
POLICIES, AND ISSUES**

MONEY AND BANKING

CONTEMPORARY PRACTICES, POLICIES, AND ISSUES

TYRONE BLACK, Ph.D.
Professor of Economics
University of Southern Mississippi

DONNIE DANIEL, Ph.D.
Associate Professor of Finance
University of Southern Mississippi

1981

BUSINESS PUBLICATIONS, INC. Plano, Texas 75075

Irwin-Dorsey Limited Georgetown, Ontario L7G 4B3

To Dianne, Leanne, and Doug
and to
Jody, Joel, and Noel

© BUSINESS PUBLICATIONS, INC., 1981

ISBN 0-256-02420-0
Library of Congress Catalog Card No. 80–70312

Printed in the United States of America

1 2 3 4 5 6 7 8 9 0 D 8 7 6 5 4 3 2 1

Preface

This book grew out of the classroom trials and tribulations of the authors over several years of teaching courses on money and banking and on bank management. Our criteria for selecting texts in the courses we have taught have influenced the preparation of this volume. We believe that a college textbook should have four basic characteristics: (1) it should contain an accurate and up-to-date coverage of the subject area involved; (2) it should be comprehensible to students at the level at which it will be used; (3) it should be capable of generating and holding student interest in the subject; and (4) it should be organized so that most instructors find it adapts reasonably well to their presentation of the course material. We feel that the absence of a dominant money and banking text is primarily due to the third factor, and we believe that this text addresses that important point successfully.

Basically, human beings are problem-solving creatures. Much of the educational process is designed to make the student a better problem solver by either teaching new or more efficient methods of solving problems or by providing information that has proven useful in solving certain recurrent problems. It is our belief that relating classroom and textbook information to relevant problems is the primary ingredient in generating interest in that material. With this in mind, we have tried to create a text in which the material will seem current and relevant to the student.

There is no shortage of interesting problems in the field of money and banking. To be able to grapple with these problems intelligently, students must necessarily absorb a considerable amount of what some may consider to be "dry" material; but often material is considered dry and uninteresting because it is not seen in the context of problems that are themselves interesting. Thus a successful money and banking text must present the course material so that it appears pertinent in a problem-solving context. It is also our belief that the approach we have taken in this book—an approach that has proven successful in our classroom teaching—accomplishes this objective to a considerable extent.

v

In putting this philosophy into practice, we have used several techniques. One involves the phrasing of each major section heading in the form of a question. This procedure makes the material presented in that section immediately relevant to a key question that money and banking students should be able to answer, and students seem to pick up central ideas better under this approach. A second technique is to preview the chapter at its beginning. This procedure helps by giving the student an idea of the content and development of the chapter.

Familiarity with key terms is essential if issues in the news are to become understandable and hence more meaningful. We have included a glossary of important new terms at the beginning of the chapter in which the terms are introduced. Thus the student is assured of being familiar with a key term when it is encountered in the text; moreover, an alphabetical listing of all these terms and their locations precedes the index.

Each of the five major sections of the book contains a chapter on current issues relating to topics covered in that section. Some professors may prefer to cover selected topics in these chapters as they treat related sections of other chapters; others will prefer, as we do, to postpone the current issues chapter until all topics in a given section have been covered.

It is our contention that an undergraduate text should communicate with students. Consequently, we have attempted to deal with the intricacies of theoretical issues which abound in the areas of monetary theory and policy at the level of the student for whom the text is intended. At the same time, however, our objective has been to provide a foundation for understanding more advanced treatments if a student's interests and career objectives call for it. Finally, since some instructors prefer not to devote the time necessary to discuss the IS-LM model, Chapter 15 can be omitted with minimal loss of continuity.

There are several important ways in which this book is distinctive. First, it has two full chapters on the problem of inflation. Second, there are three chapters on the international aspects of the monetary economy; in particular, the international section covers the realities of floating exchange rates, OPEC, SDRs, Eurodollars, the recycling problem, and other current developments. Third, the book is also up to date in its coverage of recent developments in the financial system. NOW accounts, share drafts, the new measures of the monetary aggregates, and the provisions of important new legislation such as the Depository Institutions Deregulation and Monetary Control Act are given extensive treatment. Fourth, the book also treats the monetarist-Keynesian controversy in a balanced, up-to-date, but thorough manner with particular emphasis on the policy implications of the different positions. Finally, the money supply process is presented logically by integrating Federal Reserve policy, the monetary base, and the money multiplier.

Acknowledgments

The authors wish to acknowledge the many helpful comments of Michael L. Butler of the University of North Alabama and Walter L. Johnson of the University of Missouri—Columbia. We also want to thank Frank Whitesell and Colleen Cameron, both of the University of Southern Mississippi, for their suggestions on specific chapters. We greatly appreciate Lynn Cochran's efforts in typing the manuscript and Kathy Pope's work with the figures and tables. Finally, we are indebted to John and Jan Logan and their firm, Data Processing Consultants of Hattiesburg, for generously permitting us access to word-processing equipment for use in preparation of the manuscript.

Tyrone Black
Donnie Daniel

Contents

States. The central banking hiatus, 1837–1914. Why was the Federal Reserve System formed? What are the Federal Reserve's major functions? What is the organizational structure of the Fed? *The Board of Governors. The Federal Open Market Committee. The 12 Federal Reserve banks and their 25 branches. The member banks.* Who controls the Federal Reserve System?

What is the trade-off between inflation and unemployment? What measures have been tried in the fight against inflation? Can inflation be controlled? *The choices before us. The outlook.*

Why do monetarist and Keynesian macroeconomic policy prescriptions differ? *The classical (pre-Keynesian) approach. The Keynesian approach. The monetarist approach.* Should the discretionary powers of macroeconomic policymakers be limited? Can supply-side economic policy revitalize the U.S. economy? *Causes of declining productivity growth. The Laffer curve. Supply-side solutions.*

PART V
INTERNATIONAL TRANSACTIONS IN THE MONETARY ECONOMY

What is the balance of payments and how is it measured? *The U.S. balance of payments. Balance of payments problems.* How are payments made in international transactions? *The exchange of currencies in international transactions. Exchange rates.* How do international transactions affect domestic economic activity? *The workings of the international gold standard. Current account transactions and economic activity: Some direct effects. Effects of international capital flows. Official intervention and domestic economic activity. Domestic effects of flexible exchange rates.*

What is the International Monetary Fund? *Background and functions. Performance and problems.* Will special drawing rights solve the international liquidity problem? *The international liquidity problem. Special Drawing Rights.* What is the Eurodollar Market? *Origins and nature of Eurodollars. Eurodollars and escape from Regulation Q. The Eurodollar market and the exchange value of the dollar. The Eurobond market.* How are Federal Reserve operations influenced by international monetary developments?

Should Eurocurrency markets be regulated? *The safety of Eurobank operations. Eurobank operations and exchange rate instability. The*

Euromarkets and domestic monetary policy. Prospects. Can the monetary economy cope with the petrodollar crisis? The recycling problem. The wealth transfer problem. The market power problem. What does the future hold for the international monetary economy?

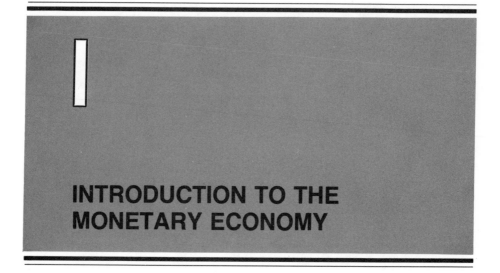

INTRODUCTION TO THE MONETARY ECONOMY

1

Money and economic activity: A primer

WARM-UP: *Outline and questions to consider as you read*

What is a monetary economy?
Why is a monetary economy more efficient than a barter system?
How closely related are money and economic activity?
Are there maladies in a monetary economy?
How are theories and models useful in solving the problems of a monetary economy?
How can the interrelation of money and economic activity be better understood?

NEW TERMS

Barter: a type of exchange which involves trading one commodity for another.

Commodity money: monetary items which have uses other than as a means of payment.

Credit money: money whose value depends on its general acceptability in exchange since it has little or no value otherwise.

Economic theory (model):   a simplification representing the essence of a more complex economic relationship; the term *economic*

3

model is commonly used when several cause and effect relationships are combined into a unified system.

Federal Reserve System (the Fed):   the agency which is responsible for regulating the United States' supply of money and credit.

Fiscal policy: the use of federal government spending and tax collections to influence the level of aggregate (total) economic activity.

Gross National Product (GNP):   the dollar value of a nation's total production of new goods and services during a given time period.

Inflation and hyperinflation: inflation is the process of a rising general level of prices, and hyperinflation is an extremely high rate of inflation.

Keynesians: a term applied to economists who tend to agree with and utilize the analysis and policy prescriptions of the late British economist John Maynard Keynes.

Macroeconomics: the analysis of the total (aggregate) economy with particular emphasis on aggregate output (Gross National Product), aggregate employment, and the general level of prices.

Microeconomics: the analysis of relatively small economic units such as households and business firms.

Monetarism: an approach to macroeconomic theory and policymaking that focuses on monetary influences and that is associated with the American economist Milton Friedman.

Monetary economy: an economy in which money is the commonly used means of payment.

Monetary policy: the manipulation of money, credit, and/or interest rates to influence the level of economic activity.

Numéraire: the unit of measurement used to express the value of all goods and services.

Stagflation: the simultaneous occurrence of sluggish economic growth and inflation.

Advanced economic systems are characterized by an elaborate structure involving production, distribution, exchange, and consumption of goods and services; the monetary framework within which these functions are performed is the focus of this book. This introductory chapter is called "Money and economic activity: A primer," and the main objective in the following pages is to familiarize the reader with the essence of the material covered in the remainder of the text. Therefore, we are primarily interested in providing an overview of the framework of the monetary economy, and in the process we hope to whet the reader's interest to know more about the operation of the economic system of the United States, particularly its monetary aspects.

WHAT IS A MONETARY ECONOMY?

The development of a monetary economy is a natural and inevitable outgrowth of economic specialization and the resulting higher levels of production. When an economy is primitive and economic units are small and largely self-sufficient, exchange of goods and services occurs infrequently and is confined to a few items; therefore, little or no need for money exists. But as people begin to perform specialized tasks in the quest for greater productivity, they must exchange their output for a variety of goods and services.

As exchanges become more and more commonplace, a particular commodity, one that is traded frequently, typically becomes a standard of value or common denominator. This means that the value of various commodities is often expressed in terms of the number of units of the standard of value which could be obtained in exchange. The adoption of a standard of value simplifies trade. For example, if a trader wishes to trade an ox for horses, the exchange will be simplified if both parties use a common standard of value to establish an appropriate trade ratio. If wheat is a commonly traded good, then it is likely that the ox owner will have observed a recent trade of an ox for, say, 200 bushels of wheat; likewise, the horse owner may know that a horse presently is worth 100 bushels of wheat. Thus the basis for a trade is set, and the ox/horse exchange ratio is one ox for two horses. Even though wheat may not be used as the means of payment, it can still serve as a useful standard of value.

The foregoing illustration demonstrates how the adoption of a standard of value simplifies the process of determining a good's worth, thereby facilitating exchange. In a 20-good barter economy with no standard of value, the combinations formula can be used to calculate that there are 190 separate exchange ratios.[1] However, if one of the goods evolves as the standard of value or the numéraire, then there are only $n - 1$ (in this example, 19) exchange ratios.[2]

The adoption of a standard of value is the first step in the progression toward a monetary economy. If the standard of value has certain desirable characteristics, it may eventually come to be a commonly used means of payment (money). Desirable characteristics of money include relative scarcity, divisibility, portability, durability, safety, and convenience. If one or more of these characteristics are absent, it

---

[1] The number of exchange ratios involving 20 goods is

$$\frac{n!}{n!\,(n-2)!} = \frac{20!}{2!\,(20-2)!} = 190,$$

where n is the number of goods being traded.

[2] There are $n-1$ rather than n exchange ratios because there is no need to express the value of the numéraire in terms of itself.

is unlikely that the commodity will be widely adopted as a medium of exchange.

Eventually, however, it is probable that some standard of value possessing the necessary properties of a medium of exchange will come into use. Then barter will give way to an exchange process that involves exchange of goods for the medium of exchange and subsequent use of the medium of exchange to obtain other goods and services. Once a particular item is in general use as a medium of exchange, by common definition, it is money, and the economy can be considered a monetary economy. Early monetary economies used commodity monies such as bronze and gold, while modern payment systems are based primarily on credit monies such as paper currency and checking accounts. The evolution from commodity to credit money is covered in the next chapter.

WHY IS A MONETARY ECONOMY MORE EFFICIENT THAN A BARTER SYSTEM?

In the previous section we suggested that specialization increases the necessity for trade, making it more likely that first a standard of value and eventually a medium of exchange will evolve; otherwise, a considerable amount of resources will be expended consummating barter exchanges. Compared to a barter system, a monetary economy can be said to be more efficient if it uses fewer resources to generate a given level of economic activity. The resources thus freed can be employed to increase the level of production, and/or there may be increased leisure time; in any event, the standard of living will have risen. The use of money—if in fact it is more efficient than barter— can be likened to application of a lubricant that permits the wheels of commerce to turn more rapidly and smoothly.

Armen A. Alchian argues that the costliness of obtaining information about goods available for exchange provides the impetus for transforming a barter system into a monetary economy.[3] According to Alchian, barter is costly because it necessitates that traders be "experts" about both the good offered for trade and also the good that will be received in the exchange. Thus if Jones wishes to trade his oxen for Brown's horses, Jones must acquire knowledge about oxen and horses, and the same is true for Brown. Obviously the cost of becoming an expert in a multitude of commodities would be very high, and the existence of high information costs therefore discourages exchange. Further, use of money reduces the time required to complete a transaction, thereby lowering the cost of the exchange.

---

[3] Armen A. Alchian, "Why Money?" *Journal of Money, Credit, and Banking*, vol. 14, pt. 2 (February 1977), pp. 133–40.

For instance, it may require considerable time and effort to locate someone who is willing to trade horses for oxen.

High information costs encourage the proliferation of middlemen who are experts on one or perhaps a few goods. Competent middlemen earn the public's trust by building a reputation for being knowledgeable, honest, and dependable—traits necessary for their occupational survival. In our oxen-for-horses example, exchange cost is lowered for Jones—who desires to trade oxen—if there are middlemen who trade in horses. Exchange costs are reduced since by relying on the middleman's expertise there is no need for Jones to become an expert in horses. Of course, the exchange would be even less costly if the middleman dealing in horses were also an oxen expert. It is very unlikely, however, that such combinations would be commonplace, particularly if the variety of goods traded is fairly large.

To extend the example one step further, assume that some commodity—gold, for instance—is traded so commonly that almost everyone is a gold expert; that is, most of the populace are readily able to evaluate the quality of gold. In this situation, the costliness of trade will be diminished in the following manner. Jones can now trade his oxen to a middleman specializing in oxen. In return, Jones will receive gold, and since there are a large number of gold experts, it will be easy to trade the gold for horses and a variety of other goods as well, again probably dealing with middlemen who are experts in each of these products. Consequently, the use of a common means of payment makes trade less expensive to accomplish.

To summarize, a primitive barter system usually involves the costly situation of a nonexpert dealing with another nonexpert, and under these circumstances it is expensive for the parties involved to assay the quality of goods offered for exchange. As exchange becomes more commonplace, middlemen who are experts on one or several goods begin to market their expertise, thereby tending to lower exchange costs. Next some commodity which is traded frequently is likely to evolve as a standard of value. If that commodity possesses the desirable properties of money, it will amost certainly come to be a commonly used means of payment. Then a monetary economy will exist; exchange will be simpler and less costly; and economic efficiency will have been enhanced.

HOW CLOSELY RELATED ARE MONEY AND ECONOMIC ACTIVITY?

In the previous section we saw that, at the microeconomic level, money is an "efficient" alternative to barter, providing lubrication that helps the economy function smoothly. In this section we focus on the relationship between money and the macroeconomy.[4] Actually, there is a fairly wide range of opinion among economists regarding money's influence on macroeconomic activity, though there is more agreement now than a few years ago.

From the 1930s until fairly recently, mainstream macroeconomic theory relegated monetary policy to a secondary role, favoring tax and government spending changes (fiscal policy) as the primary means of economic control. The extreme version of this position can be summarized as "money doesn't matter"—though in fact few economists believed that money was incapable of influencing the economy.

Actually, it is more accurate to characterize the widely held view of the relation between money and economic activity as "money doesn't matter much" or at best "money matters." This assessment of the influence of money was based on the interpretation of John M. Keynes' pathbreaking work, *The General Theory of Employment, Interest, and Money*.[5] Keynes wrote his famous book during the midst of the Depression of the 1930s, and his analysis raised the possibility that monetary policy might be weak or even completely ineffective during periods of very low levels of economic activity. Keynes, however, did not argue that money is powerless in normal times, and some recent reinterpretations of *The General Theory* draw more optimistic conclusions about the usefulness of monetary policy during bad times. Nonetheless, the view that the impact of monetary policy is likely to be weak and/or unreliable prevailed during the 1940s and 1950s.

By the early 1960s a quite different view of money's influence on the economy was being advocated. Led by Milton Friedman at the University of Chicago, a group of economists who came to be known as monetarists developed an alternative to Keynesian analysis and argued that "money matters very much." On occasion some monetarists even seemed to be saying that in the short run "money alone matters."

There followed a period of considerable controversy regarding the efficacy of monetary policy; positions taken ranged from "money doesn't matter" to "money alone matters." While only a handful of economists was at either end of this spectrum, the gap separating Keynesians and monetarists was quite large. The decade of the 1970s was a period when some convergence of opinion occurred regarding

---

[4] Microeconomic analysis deals with small economic units such as the household, the firm, or an industry; macroeconomics is a study of the aggregate (total) economy.

[5] John M. Keynes, *The General Theory of Employment, Interest, and Money* (New York: Harcourt, Brace & World, 1936).

the relation between money and economic activity. Yet at the beginning of the 1980s, disagreement still exists concerning the relative strengths of monetary and fiscal policy, and economists continue to debate how monetary influences are transmitted through the economy and how monetary policy should be implemented. However, some issues have been resolved, thus narrowing considerably the range of disagreement about the influence of money on economic activity and the proper role of monetary policy.

ARE THERE MALADIES IN A MONETARY ECONOMY?

All economic systems yet devised by Man have deficiencies. Primitive societies are faced with subsistence living standards because a lack of specialization and other economic, political, technical, and social problems keep productivity and output at low levels. As development occurs, specialization brings rising standards of living but not without generating some new difficulties. Exchange must be accomplished as people have to trade their specialized output for a variety of goods and services. Some of the problems associated with a barter system have been discussed previously.

The evolution to a modern, monetary economy brings gains in efficiency and opens up the possibility that proper monetary control can promote the macroeconomic goals of high levels of production, full employment, and price stability. In Chapter 12 we shall review the performance of the U.S. economy with respect to these goals, and in doing so it will become apparent that there have been and are still many economic bright spots, not the least being the high standard of living enjoyed by most Americans. For 40 years we have escaped an economic decline of the magnitude of the Great Depression of the 1930s, and, except for the Confederacy of the Civil War South, the United States has never suffered the ravages of extremely high rates of inflation (hyperinflation).

Nevertheless, our economy has experienced and continues to experience numerous problems. In the 1970s, for instance, macroeconomic performance was unsatisfactory in several respects: Inflation seemingly became endemic, averaging over 7 percent annually; the average annual unemployment rate was above 6 percent; and sluggish labor productivity growth hampered the expansion of inflation-adjusted (real) Gross National Product. The lack of vigor of the U.S. economy accompanied by debilitating inflation has been given the rather inelegant albeit descriptive label *stagflation*. A recurrent topic of this text is consideration of how the monetary framework can be better structured in order to provide the advantages of a monetary economy while avoiding the attendant problems.

HOW ARE THEORIES AND MODELS USEFUL IN
SOLVING THE PROBLEMS OF A MONETARY ECONOMY?

Facts and information about the economy provide an impression of the real world. Based on this impression, one must then select what are perceived as the most important relationships. Selectivity is essential because available information about the economy is overwhelming; it would be impossible to digest and utilize all of the mass of facts relating to our economic system. Therefore, it is necessary to study the institutional structure of the economy carefully and to sift through the available empirical information. This selection process is the basis for the construction of a simplified version of how the economy or one of its components functions.

A simplified or condensed version of an economic relationship is known as an *economic theory*. In a similar vein but at a somewhat more formal level, the term *economic model* generally is used when several cause-and-effect relationships are combined into a unified system. Because they are generalizations, theories and models always have their exceptions; ideally, though, they can reduce complex systems to manageable proportions, thereby creating a framework for formulating better policy, making reasonably accurate forecasts, and providing enhanced understanding of the economic world.

Economic generalizations become more useful as they are made more specific. It is one thing to argue that aggregate spending of households and aggregate household income are related. But the usefulness of this relationship is obviously enhanced if we also know the direction of influence of income on consumption—that is, whether income and consumption are positively or inversely related to one another. It is even better if the income-consumption relationship is specified from empirical observation so that the level of consumption can be predicted given certain levels of income. Thus more effective solutions to economic problems are achieved by formulating theories and models, by using and verifying them, and by refining, reformulating, or discarding them according to their reliability. Figure 1-1 illustrates the economic methodology discussed in this section indicating the relations among facts, the use of these facts to formulate models and theories, and the uses to which models and theories can be put to solve economic problems.

Models may generate inaccurate forecasts or unproductive policies for a variety of reasons. Faulty or insufficient data may give a misleading impression, providing a distorted image of the economy. Moreover, the selection of "important" economic relations is difficult, and model builders are constantly discovering that some

FIGURE 1-1
Economic methodology—the role of economic theories and models

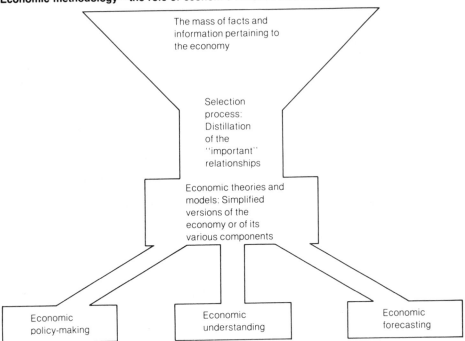

The mass of facts and
information pertaining to
the economy

Selection
process:
Distillation
of the
"important"
relationships

Economic theories and
models: Simplified
versions of the
economy or of its
various components

Economic
policy-making

Economic
understanding

Economic
forecasting

relevant relations have not been included. Finally, poor logic at the model-construction stage may affect the model's validity and usefulness.

HOW CAN THE INTERRELATION OF MONEY AND ECONOMIC ACTIVITY BE BETTER UNDERSTOOD?

The key to understanding the monetary economy is contained in the previous section on theories and models. Economic understanding requires the systematic application of economic methodology in order to reduce the real world to manageable proportions. The format of this text is a utilization of this approach to problem solving.

The first three sections of the book cover money, the financial sector, and the Federal Reserve System, respectively. In these parts a considerable amount of statistical and institutional information is presented; knowledge of such facts and information is vital because they provide our first impression of the monetary economy of the United States. However, as we indicated earlier, the large volume of available information is unmanageable without some simplification, so there must be a distillation process with the distillate consisting of (perceived) key relationships.

Thus we turn in Part IV to the formulation of economic theories and to the construction of models of the macroeconomy. These models indicate the more important causes of rises and falls in the level of short-run economic activity. Furthermore, they show how monetary and fiscal policy can be used to moderate cyclical fluctuations in output, employment, and prices. Our models are simple and therefore are imprecise in many respects; nonetheless, they are quite useful in portraying the fundamental nature of the macroeconomy.

The final section of the text covers an important aspect of our present-day monetary economy—international economic relations. Throughout most of the text we simplify the analysis by assuming that ours is a closed economy; that is, that there is no international trade. But in the final three chapters the advantages and problems of international exchange are discussed.

One other matter needs to be noted before concluding this primer on the monetary economy. A glance at the Table of Contents will indicate that we have devoted a great deal of attention to current trends, issues, and problems. Within every chapter there are topics that have implications for our economic well-being. Noteworthy examples include the evolution of new means of payment such as electronic funds transfers, fierce competition among the various financial intermediaries, policy actions of the Federal Reserve, inflation, unemployment, and international exchange problems. To underscore the relevance of the subject matter of this book, we have concluded each of the five major sections with a current issues chapter. These chapters relate the preceding material to many of the more pressing issues presently facing the citizenry of the United States.

SUMMARY

This chapter has been a primer on money and economic activity. A monetary economy evolves because utilizing a system of exchange with no standard of value and no medium of exchange requires that each trader be an expert on the quality and value of all goods traded. Considerable resources are therefore expended acquiring information. Adopting a commonly traded commodity as a standard of value and eventually utilizing a common means of payment (money) reduces costs and provides a more efficient exchange system than barter.

There is a fairly wide range of opinion about how money and short-term economic activity are related; the extremes run from "money doesn't matter" to "money alone matters." However, the controversy between Keynesians, who have traditionally emphasized fiscal policy, and monetarists, who stress the strength of monetary policy, has diminished in recent years. Today few economists would argue that monetary policy is incapable of influencing the level of short-run economic activity, and it is likewise true that few would assert that monetary forces are the sole determinant of the status of the economy.

Economists rely on economic theories and models to understand and attack problems. By first gathering and analyzing facts and becoming familiar with the institutional structure of the economy, economists obtain a feeling about the general nature of the system. The complex, real world is then reduced to a set of simplified relationships that constitute a theory or model. Economic theories and models are useful for formulating policy, making forecasts, and/or enhancing our understanding of how the economy functions.

REVIEW QUESTIONS

1. How does money help an economy function more efficiently?
2. Explain why each of the following items would or would not be likely to become a commonly used means of payment (money)?
   a. Bananas.
   b. Diamonds.
   c. Chickens.
   d. Cigarettes.
   e. Toothpicks.
   f. Checking deposits.
   g. Bricks.
3. True or false: Economists agree that money is the main determinant of the level of aggregate economic activity. Comment on your answer.
4. Why do economists use economic theories and models? What is the alternative?
5. What do you presently consider to be our most serious economic problems? How many of these problems seem to be related to money and the financial sector?

SUGGESTIONS FOR ADDITIONAL READING

Alchian, Armen A. "Why Money?" *Journal of Money, Credit and Banking,* vol. 14, pt. 2 (February 1977), pp. 133–40.

Burns, Arthur R. "Before the Introduction of Coins." *Money and Monetary Policy in Early Times.* New York: Gentry Press, 1965, pp. 1–36.

National Science Foundation. "Looking Before You Leap." *Mosaic,* vol. 3, no. 2 (Spring 1973), pp. 24–30.

Redford, R. A. "The Economic Organization of a P.O.W. Camp." *Economica,* vol. 12 (November 1945), pp. 189–201.

2 Money

WARM-UP: *Outline and questions to consider as you read*

What is money?
What constitutes the money stock of the United
  States?
What are the functions of money?
How has the nature of money evolved?
How is the value of money measured?
What is the velocity of money?

NEW TERMS

Automatic transfer service (ATS) deposits: deposit accounts in commercial banks which earn interest but are automatically converted to demand deposits when the depositor's checking account is reduced to a specified level.

Central bank: a bank that typically supervises the commercial banking system, serves as banker for the federal government, and regulates the nation's supply of money and credit; the Federal Reserve System is the central bank of the United States.

Certificates of deposit (CDs): time deposits issued by banks and thrift institutions which have a face value, a stated interest rate, and a maturity date.

14

Consumer Price Index (CPI): a measure of the general price level of a market basket of goods and services purchased by a representative sample of consumers.

Demand deposits: deposits (checking accounts) that are payable on the demand of the depositor and may be used to make payments to third parties.

Functional definition of money: functional money consists of anything that is commonly used as a means of payment.

Functions of money: money can be used in a monetary economy to perform the following functions:

> **Macroeconomic-control function:** the use of money to influence the level of aggregate economic activity.
>
> **Medium-of-exchange function:** the use of money as payment in transactions.
>
> **Standard-of-value function:** the use of money as the basis for measuring and expressing value.
>
> **Standard-of-deferred-payment function:** the use of money to express liability in debtor-creditor transactions.
>
> **Store-of-value function:** the use of money as a form of holding wealth.

Liquidity: the characteristic of some assets that permits them to be converted into a spendable form at short notice with little or no loss of value.

Monetary aggregates: the measures of money reported by the Federal Reserve System which include the following:

> **M-1A:** currency plus demand deposits at commercial banks.
>
> **M-1B:** M-1A plus other checkable deposits at all depository institutions.
>
> **M-2:** M-1B plus savings and small-denomination time deposits at all depository institutions, money market mutual fund shares, and other relatively minor components.
>
> **M-3:** M-2 plus large-denomination time deposits and other relatively minor components.
>
> **L:** M-3 plus other liquid assets not included elsewhere, such as bankers acceptances, commercial paper, and Treasury bills.

Money market mutual fund: a company that sells shares in itself and invests the proceeds in short-term, highly liquid securities.

Negotiable order of withdrawal (NOW) accounts: accounts at banks and savings and loan associations from which funds can be transferred to third parties by way of a checklike instrument called a negotiable order of withdrawal.

Policy definition of money: liquid assets closely related to short-run economic activity and controllable by the monetary authorities.

Share draft accounts: accounts at credit unions similar to NOW accounts.

Thrift institutions: depository institutions (other than commercial banks) such as saving and loans, credit unions, and mutual savings banks.

Time and savings deposits: deposits that earn the depositor an interest return and for which the depositor may be required to wait a specified period of time before withdrawing funds.

Velocity of money (V): the rate of turnover of the money stock to purchase goods and services, or how many times, on average, a unit of money is used in a given time period.

In the first chapter we presented a bird's-eye view of a monetary economy. Our overview (1) explained the nature of a monetary economy, (2) showed why a monetary economy is more efficient than a barter system, (3) discussed the fact that there are divergent opinions about the strength of the relation between money and short-run economic activity, (4) suggested that a monetary economy is subject to certain maladies, (5) noted the role of theories and models in economic problem solving, and (6) pointed out what must be done to enhance one's understanding of how the monetary economy functions. This chapter is a continuation of the introduction of money and the monetary economy, and the following pages focus on the element that makes an economy a monetary economy—money.

WHAT IS MONEY?

Defining money might seem at first glance to be a relatively easy task. For most of us money is an important part of our lives—we spend it; we save it; we borrow and loan it. Surprisingly, however, when people are asked for a definition of money, the answer requires a good deal of thought. There is a temptation to list those items that seem to be money, but this procedure puts the cart before the horse. Before it can be said whether something is or is not money, a definition must be formulated. Then an item is or is not money depending on whether or not it fulfills the terms of the particular definition. Therefore, we begin by presenting two definitions of money; subsequently, there is a discussion of the present composition of the money stock of the United States.

The functional definition probably best expresses the prevalent concept of money. Money, functionally defined, consists of those things that are commonly used as a means of payment; therefore, the functional concept emphasizes money's use as a medium of exchange. If there are particular items—oxen, wheat, gold, paper currency, or whatever—that are in general use for making payments, then these items would be money according to the functional definition which says in effect, "what serves as money is money." On the other hand, if exchange generally involves barter of one commodity for another, there is no common means of payment, and money does not exist according to the functional definition.

A difficulty associated with the functional definition of money is reaching an agreement about the meaning of *commonly* in the phrase "commonly used as a means of payment." In some cases there is no question that certain items are money according to the functional definition. In the United States, currency is certainly commonly used for transactions purposes and is therefore money. On the other hand, an item may be very similar to something that is clearly money, yet be used in only a small proportion of all transactions.

Share draft accounts offered by credit unions since 1974 provide a good example of the difficulty of deciding whether something is or is not functional money. Share draft accounts are similar to commercial bank checking accounts (also known as demand deposits) in that both can be used to make payments to third parties; however, checking accounts are used extensively as a means of payment, while share drafts are a minor component of the payments system in the United States.[1] Furthermore, demand deposits do not earn interest, but holders of share draft accounts are paid interest on their deposit balances. While credit union share draft deposits are used as a means of payment in a small proportion of transactions and are similar in some other respects to bank checking accounts, there are obviously differences between the two. There is no question that checking accounts should be classified as money according to the functional definition, but in the case of share draft deposits, the matter is debatable.

A second definition of money is related to its use in managing the level of economic activity. In Chapter 1 it was pointed out that most economists believe there is a relation between money and the level of short-run economic activity; that is, changes in the money supply

---

[1] Commercial bank checking accounts are also known as demand deposits since they are payable on the "demand" of the depositor.

influence such things as the unemployment rate, the level of aggregate output, and the amount of inflation. If such a relation exists, then it is appropriate to define money in such a way that monetary policy will be effective. In keeping with this objective, the following is a policy definition of money: Money consists of those liquid assets that are controllable by the monetary authorities and are closely related to the level of economic activity.

If the money stock is to be managed for policy purposes, it should be obvious that unless the central bank is able to control its size and growth, effective monetary policy is impossible. As shall be shown in Chapter 9, the Federal Reserve System has reasonably firm control over the nation's supply of currency, bank demand deposits, and bank savings and time deposits.[2] The Federal Reserve also can influence the level of savings and loan deposits, mutual savings bank deposits, and credit union accounts. However, the Fed's control over such other financial instruments as stocks and bonds is considerably weaker.

Selecting those items that are closely related to the level of economic activity from the list of things under Federal Reserve control is an empirical matter. Changes in the money stock defined in alternative ways can be correlated with changes in the level of economic activity, and the monetary measure that is most closely correlated with economic activity is the "best" one. However, economic relationships are rarely simple, and as we shall see in the next chapter, choosing a policy definition of money is a matter of considerable complexity and controversy.

The requirement of the policy definition that money possess a high degree of liquidity is related to the other requirements. The items over which the Federal Reserve can exercise reasonably firm control do in fact range from perfectly liquid to highly liquid. Currency and demand deposits are in spendable form and are therefore perfectly liquid. Bank time deposits are highly liquid because generally they are easily convertible to a spendable form. Savings and loan deposits, deposits at mutual savings banks, and credit union accounts are also highly liquid assets. Furthermore, changes in liquid assets generally produce a more immediate impact on short-run economic activity than changes in less-liquid financial instruments such as long-term bonds or stocks.

---

[2] Holders of time and savings deposits in commercial banks and other financial institutions can be required to wait a specified period of time before receiving their deposit funds; however, in practice this stipulation is usually waived and payment is made immediately on request. In Federal Reserve System publications, the term *savings account* refers to such deposits as passbook savings and Christmas club accounts, while *time deposits* include certificates of deposit (CDs). When it is not necessary to distinguish between savings and time deposits, we shall use the term *time deposits* inclusively as the total of savings and time deposits.

In the remainder of this text, both the functional and the policy definitions of money are used. Ordinarily we shall use the term *money* to mean those things that are commonly used for transactions purposes. However, when the focus is on policy, it may be preferable to use the policy approach to defining money. Of course there is the possibility that the functionally defined money stock will also produce the best policy results, and if this is the case, the functional and policy monetary measures will be one and the same.

WHAT CONSTITUTES THE MONEY STOCK
OF THE UNITED STATES?

In 1980 the Federal Reserve System was reporting data for five measures of money—M-1A, M-1B, M-2, M-3, and L—often referred to as monetary aggregates. Table 2–1 lists data for each of these measures. The M-1A and M-1B aggregates are nearest to the functional concept of money discussed in the previous section. M-1A consists of currency and commercial bank demand deposits and therefore includes items that are commonly used as a means of payment.

M-1B also includes certain other checkable deposits such as Negotiable Order of Withdrawal (NOW) accounts. NOW accounts were initially offered in 1972 by state-chartered mutual savings banks in Massachusetts, and savings and loans in Massachusetts and New Hampshire were authorized to follow suit in 1974.[3] NOW accounts are interest-bearing deposits on which an order to pay a third party can be written, and they differ from bank checking deposits since they are interest bearing while the payment of interest on demand deposits is currently prohibited. As indicated previously, credit unions began issuing share draft accounts in 1974; these accounts, which are also included in M-1B, are the credit unions' equivalent of NOW accounts. Finally, Automatic Transfer Service (ATS) accounts in banks and thrift institutions are included in M-1B; ATS funds can be shifted automatically from saving to checking when a check is written.

The M-2, M-3, and L monetary aggregates contain large proportions of nontransactions balances and can be thought of as policy measures of money. The reader can see in Table 2–1 that M-2 is obtained by summing M-1B, savings, and small-denomination time deposits at all depository institutions, money market mutual funds, and various minor items. Money market mutual funds sell stock to

---

[3] We shall refer to savings and loans, mutual savings banks, and credit unions as *thrift institutions* to distinguish them from the other major financial intermediary, commercial banks.

TABLE 2–1
Monetary aggregates, January 1980 (seasonally adjusted data, $ billions)

Monetary aggregates	Amount ($)	Percent
M-1A		
Currency in circulation	$ 107.3	29%
Commercial bank demand deposits*	265.3	71
Total M-1A	$ 372.6	100%
M-1B		
M-1A	$ 372.6	96%
Other checkable deposits at banks, savings and loans, mutual savings banks, and credit unions	16.5	4
Total M-1B	$ 389.1	100%
M-2		
M-1B	$ 389.1	25%
Savings and small-denomination time deposits at all depository institutions, money market mutual funds, and various minor items	1,143.7	75
Total M-2	$1,532.8	100%
M-3		
M-2	$1,532.8	86%
Large-denomination time deposits at all depository institutions and various minor items	252.5	14
Total M-3	$1,785.3	100%
L		
M-3	$1,785.3	83%
Other liquid assets such as banker's acceptances, commercial paper, and Treasury bills	371.2	17
Total L	$2,156.5	100%

*Excludes interbank and U.S. government demand deposits.
Source: *Federal Reserve Bulletin,* April 1980.

obtain funds that are used to purchase high-quality, short-term se-curities; since the shareholders are permitted to write an order to pay third parties out of their share accounts, money market mutual funds can be classified as a "near money." The aggregate M-3 is the sum of M-2, large-denomination time deposits at all depository institutions, and various minor items. L is M-3 plus other liquid assets such as banker's acceptances, commercial paper, and Treasury bills.

In 1970 the Federal Reserve reported data for only one monetary aggregate, which was similar to the present M-1A. The expansion of the number of money stock measures to five reflects two major de-velopments. The first is the impact on the payments mechanism of such innovations as NOW accounts, share draft deposits, and ATS; in particular, the M-1B aggregate reflects these developments. Second, the Federal Reserve introduced new monetary aggregates to try to sharpen its ability to use monetary policy to help manage the level of economic activity. As noted in the previous paragraph, M-2, M-3, and L must be classified as policy measures since they consist to a large extent of deposits that are not money, functionally defined.

WHAT ARE THE FUNCTIONS OF MONEY?

Authors of money and banking textbooks ordinarily list three, four, or occasionally five functions of money. There are those functions that characterize a monetary economy—medium of exchange, standard of value, standard of deferred payment, and store of value. These functions are always present in a fully developed monetary economy. The policy definition of money also suggests the additional monetary function of serving as a device for controlling the level of economic activity. This function will be referred to as the control (of economic activity) function. Each of these five functions of money will in turn be discussed briefly.

The functional definition of money stresses the role of money as a medium of exchange. As we have seen, exchange is facilitated when there is one or more commonly used means of payment. A medium of exchange can be used to purchase goods and services, to pay wages and other expenses, and in numerous other transactions. By permitting and encouraging increased specialization and higher levels of production, the efficiency of the economy is enhanced once money is used to lubricate the process of exchange.

Recall from Chapter 1 that in a monetary economy a common denominator is used to express value, and the standard-of-value function is being performed when there is a commonly used basis for expressing exchange value. Moreover, the standard-of-deferred-payment function arises out of debt contracts in which the amount of the debt is stated in terms of the standard of value. For example, assume that Martin acquires wheat from Simon in return for a promise to make a payment at a future date. If that promised payment is set forth in terms of the monetary unit, then money is performing as a standard of deferred payment.

Money may also serve as a store of value in that it can be held in order to be used as a means of payment in the future. Since money is liquid, it is readily available for transactions purposes while other, less-liquid assets may not be so easily convertible to a spendable form. Normally, the more liquid the asset, the smaller its yield; consequently, there is an opportunity cost of holding money. Furthermore, since inflation diminishes the value of money, it is a poor store of value during inflationary times; therefore, if prices are rising rapidly, money holders reduce their money balances, holding instead commodities that appreciate along with the general price level.

The final function of money listed above is its use as a macroeconomic control device. In this context, money functions as a means of managing economic activity. The rate of growth of the money stock can be increased when economic activity is sluggish, while a reduction of money growth may be appropriate when the economy is plagued by inflation.

HOW HAS THE NATURE OF MONEY EVOLVED?

Through time the nature of money has undergone considerable evolution. Until fairly recent times, most money was commodity or commodity-backed money; that is, money consisted of or was backed by some material that had substantial nonmonetary or intrinsic value.[4] For instance, gold and silver have many industrial and decorative uses, and it is well known that numerous societies have also used gold and silver for money. Other commodities that have at one time or another served as money include oxen, seashells, glass, iron, and cigarettes.

When a commodity serves as money, its nonmonetary use value is sacrificed, and most nations have therefore abandoned commodity money systems in favor of money with little or no use value. However, it was not until fairly recently in the United States that the link between gold and the domestic money supply was for all practical purposes eliminated. For decades gold was mined at considerable expense in California, Alaska, Nevada, and elsewhere, then refined, converted to bullion, and transported cross-country to Fort Knox, Kentucky, only to be reburied in a vault to serve as backing for our currency. Such a process obviously entails a considerable use of society's resources as well as a sacrifice of the commodity's use value, but the desire to use commodity or commodity-backed money is rooted in the idea that such a system is safe from governmental mismanagement.

Today, money in the United States is almost all credit money— that is, money with little or no value otherwise.[5] Credit money is cheap to produce, convenient to use, and, in the case of demand deposits, generally safe from theft or loss. Credit money has value

---

[4] When a commodity itself does not circulate but backs the circulating medium according to a specified ratio, the money is called *representative full-bodied money*.

[5] Some old coins with high silver content have considerable nonmonetary value. These coins have virtually disappeared from circulation, having been melted down for nonmonetary uses or gathered by collectors. Coins minted recently have less nonmonetary value than monetary value and therefore are referred to as *token* coins.

because it can be used as a store of value or a medium of exchange; however, it will be accepted as payment only as long as confidence exists that it can be used as a means of payment. There is always the danger that monetary managers will overissue credit money, thereby undermining public confidence in it.[6]

The credit money system itself is currently in evolution. Present arrangements must be improved, or the system will be buried beneath the avalanche of the billions of checks that are now cleared in the United States each year. In the not-so-distant future, instead of writing a check at the grocery store, a customer's bank card will be inserted into a computer terminal, resulting in an instantaneous transfer of funds from the customer's bank account to the store's account. (A flashing red light at the terminal indicating insufficient funds could be quite embarrassing.) The initial appearance of these devices has already occurred, and further applications are inevitable.

HOW IS THE VALUE OF MONEY MEASURED?

The value of money can be measured in terms of what can be purchased with a given number of units of money, say, $100. If over time $100 purchases a smaller and smaller "basket" of goods and services, then the value of money is declining. A declining value of the monetary unit is the equivalent to a rising general level of prices (inflation). Therefore, rising prices and a declining value of the dollar are different sides of the same coin.

Now consider the measurement of price-level changes. The discussion of prices in this section centers on the most-used measure of the general level of prices, the Consumer Price Index (CPI), which is reported monthly by the Bureau of Labor Statistics (BLS) within the U.S. Department of Labor. The BLS publishes Producer Price Indexes covering primary markets, and the Department of Commerce also computes a measure of prices known as the GNP deflator which covers the goods and services in Gross National Product. More will be said about the Producer Price Indexes and the GNP deflator in Chapter 12.

The CPI is based on the cost of a fixed "basket" of goods and services including food, fuel, clothing, medical services, housing, interest rates, and many other items.[7] Obviously some are much

---

[6] Chapter 3 deals in more detail with the issue of the advantages of credit money compared to commodity money.

[7] Adjustments are made to try to correct the CPI for changes in the quality of goods; otherwise, the CPI would be biased upward during periods when quality is improving.

more important elements of consumer spending than others, and the BLS must therefore assign weights to the items contained in the market basket. These weights are determined by surveying households to determine the percent of their budget used for each item in the market basket. Presently the weights used to compute the CPI are based on the buying habits of two groups. There is an index for "all urban consumers" representing about 80 percent of the noninstitutional population, and a less-inclusive survey for "urban wage earners and clerical workers." While the two groups are not the same, the two CPI indexes follow a quite similar pattern. The last surveys covered spending habits in 1972–73, and the weights established by that survey are still in use.

The CPI for January 1980 stood at 233.2 for all urban consumers, indicating that the 1972–73 market basket of goods and services which would have cost $100 in the base year (1967) sold for $233.20 in January 1980. A more pertinent comparison would seem to be the cost of a present-day basket of goods and services relative to what the same collection of products would have cost in prior years. Such a comparison is more difficult, however, because a new survey of spending patterns would be necessary every year, and the expense of undertaking an annual survey of consumer spending patterns precludes the use of a price index using current-period rather than fixed-period weights.

Once a price index has been derived, it can be used to calculate the value of the monetary unit. The following formula shows the value of the monetary unit as a function of the price level:

$$(2\text{–}1) \qquad \text{Value of a unit of money} = \frac{100}{\text{CPI}}.$$

Substituting the January 1980 CPI figure of 233.2 into Equation (2–1), the value of the monetary unit is 0.43 market baskets; that is, a dollar would buy only 43 percent as much of the market basket as it would have purchased in the base year (1967).

Rising prices indicate that the monetary unit's ability to purchase goods and services is diminishing. However, other variables must be considered before a conclusion can be reached concerning what is happening to living standards during a period of inflation. The CPI for January 1980 shows that prices more than doubled between 1967 and the first of 1980. Can we therefore conclude that there was a decline in the standard of living? No such conclusion is possible without further information such as data on wages between 1967 and 1980. If wages tripled during the same period, then *real wages* increased despite the substantial price rise.[8] Thus while price level

---

[8] The term *real* is used when the effects of price level changes have been removed; thus *real wages* are money wages adjusted for inflation.

changes are an important determinant of the standard of living, there are other factors that must be considered as well.

WHAT IS THE VELOCITY OF MONEY?

When monetary authorities use money to help control economic activity, their task is complicated by the fact that money may circulate (turn over) at rates that differ from one time period to another; this circulation rate is referred to as the *velocity of money*. The relationship between the velocity of money *(V)*, the stock of money *(M)*, and monetary value of goods and services produced *(Y)* is illustrated in Equation (2–2)

$$(2\text{--}2) \qquad\qquad MV = Y.$$

Equation (2–2), which is also known as the equation of exchange, states that the money stock *(M)* times its rate of turnover *(V)* is equal to the money value of new goods and services *(Y)*, which is Gross National Product (GNP).[9] Equation (2–2) can alternatively be expressed as Equation (2–3),

$$(2\text{--}3) \qquad\qquad M = kY,$$

where k is defined as $1/V$. In Equation (2–3) k represents the average proportion of Y that is held as money balances during the time period being considered. Since V and k are reciprocals, they vary in inverse proportion. At various times, it may be more useful to focus on either V or k depending on whether we are more interested in the rate at which money is circulating (velocity) or the public's desire for money balances *(k)*.

Table 2–2 lists data on V and k for selected years. The M-1A aggregate is used to derive values of V and k. V increased (k declined) substantially over the period covered in the table. In order to better understand the relation between V and k, observe columns (4) and (5) of Table 2–2 for 1979. V was 6.6, and k was 15.3 percent, indicating that on the average each dollar of M-1A turned over 6.6 times in the purchase of new goods and services and that holdings of M-1A amounted to 15.3 percent of GNP. Another expression of the relation between V and k is as follows: For each dollar of 1979 GNP, there were money balances of 15.3 cents which turned over 6.6 times in 1979. Note that in 1960 for each dollar of GNP, money balances were 27.9 cents which turned over only 3.6 times.

It should be fairly obvious why monetary authorities must carefully monitor and if possible anticipate changes in V (k). If more

---

[9] When money is related to the level of current production and to the income earned in the current production process, V is often referred to as income velocity.

TABLE 2–2
**Money velocity and cash balance percents—selected years,
1960–1979 ($ billions)**

(1)	(2)	(3)	(4)	(5)
	Money Gross National Product		M-1A velocity	M-1A cash balance percents
Year	(GNP)	M-1A*	(V)	(k)
1960	$ 506.0	$141.1	3.6	27.9
1965	688.1	164.9	4.2	24.0
1970	982.4	209.9	4.7	21.4
1975	1,528.8	281.6	5.4	18.4
1976	1,702.2	296.4	5.7	17.4
1977	1,899.5	316.7	6.0	16.7
1978	2,127.6	340.0	6.3	16.0
1979	2,369.4	361.5	6.6	15.3

* Money stock figures are the average of the December money stocks of the year listed in column (1) and the previous year.

Sources: *Survey of Current Business, Federal Reserve Bulletin,* and Board of Governors of the Federal Reserve System.

money is injected to stimulate the economy, but V falls (k rises) unexpectedly, the level of economic activity will not change as anticipated. Movements in GNP may reflect changes in M and/or V (k). The Federal Reserve System can exercise fairly firm control over the money supply, but the actions of the public determine V (k). If V (k) is unstable (fluctuates unpredictably), there will be considerable difficulty administering monetary policy effectively. Part IV deals with the problems of using money to influence the economy.

SUMMARY

In this chapter on money, we have introduced and discussed two ways of defining money. The functional definition states that money consists of anything commonly used as a means of payment. The policy definition defines money as those liquid assets that can be controlled by the monetary authorities and are closely related to the level of economic activity.

In the United States, the Federal Reserve System monitors five monetary aggregates—M-1A, M-1B, M-2, M-3, and L. The M-1A definition includes currency and demand deposits. The M-1B measure encompasses most transactions balances, including such recent innovations as NOW accounts and share draft deposits. The other monetary aggregates—M-2, M-3, and L—include more than transactions balances and conform more to the policy definition of money than to the functional concept.

The functions of money discussed in this chapter include those that are familiar—medium of exchange, standard of value, standard of deferred payment, and store of value—as well as an economic control function. The control function follows from the notion that, if money and economic activity are related, then the money supply might be managed in a way that will promote economic stability.

Money has evolved from commodity money—which has use value as well as value as a medium of exchange—to credit money—which has little or no use value. Credit money is cheap to produce and use, while commodity money involves a high opportunity cost because when a commodity serves as a medium of exchange, its nonmonetary value is sacrificed. Since credit money is so easy to produce, there is always a danger that it will be overproduced. From time to time we hear the argument that we should return to a commodity money standard, but as is explained in the following chapter, commodity money standards are expensive and by no means trouble free.

The value of a unit of money is a function of how much money it takes to purchase a given amount of goods and services, and this value varies inversely with the general level of prices. In the United States the best-known measure of the level of consumer prices is the Consumer Price Index (CPI) reported by the Bureau of Labor Statistics (BLS).

The rate of turnover of money to purchase goods and services is known as the velocity of money. The more often each unit of money is used in a given time period, the less the money balances that are necessary to accomplish a given level of transactions. In 1960, for each dollar of GNP, money balances were 29.7 cents which turned over 3.6 times during the year; by 1979, money was turning over at a much more rapid rate of 6.6 times each year, indicating that people held on average only 15.3 cents of money balances for each dollar of GNP.

REVIEW QUESTIONS

1. Distinguish between the functional and the policy definitions of money. Might the two ever be the same?
2. In February 1980 the Federal Reserve System began publishing data on a new monetary aggregate, M-1B. How did the introduction of this new money supply measure reflect the changing nature of the financial system?
3. Distinguish between commodity and credit money. Discuss the advantages of one compared to the other.
4. What is the Consumer Price Index (CPI), and how can it be used to indicate the value of money?

5. Explain the relationship between cash balance percents and the velocity of money. Why is the velocity of money an important consideration in the management of monetary policy?

SUGGESTIONS FOR ADDITIONAL READING

Galbraith, John Kenneth. *Money: Whence It Came, Where It Went.* Boston: Houghton Mifflin, 1975.

Karnosky, Denis. "A Primer on the Consumer Price Index." *Review of the Federal Reserve Bank of St. Louis,* vol. 56, no. 7 (July 1974), p. 207.

Robertson, D. H. *Money.* 2d ed. Chicago: University of Chicago Press, 1964, chap. 1.

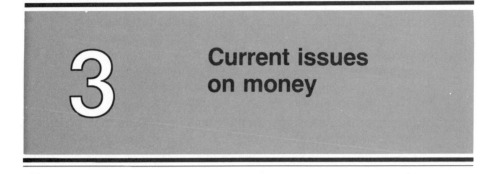

Current issues on money

WARM-UP: *Outline and questions to consider as you read*

What should be included in the monetary aggregates?

Is gold money better than paper money?
  The link between gold and money.
  The argument for paper money.
  The argument against paper money.

Should monetary growth be governed by strict rules?
  The case for rules.
  The case against rules.

NEW TERMS

Debasement: a process whereby the gold or other precious metal content of coin is reduced so that the number of coins can be increased.

Discretionary monetary policy: monetary policy determined by monetary authorities who operate with few or no restrictions on their policy decisions.

Gold certificates: receipts that represent the value of the government-owned gold stock and are issued by the U.S. Treasury to the Federal Reserve System.

Gold money standard: the use of gold coin or gold-backed money as the medium of exchange.

Gold Reserve Act: legislation removing gold coins from circulation as money in the United States and prohibiting the private holding of gold.

Monetary rule: monetary policy conducted according to some rule—for example, increasing the money stock 3 to 5 percent annually.

Paper (credit) money standard: a monetary system in which the items used as money have little or no value except as money.

Transactions balances: money held in order to purchase goods and services.

In this chapter we introduce three current issues related to the composition, nature, and control of the money stock of the United States. The issues can be represented by the following questions: (1) What should be included in the monetary aggregates? (2) Is gold money better than paper money? and (3) Should monetary growth be governed by strict rules, or should the monetary authorities have broad discretion to carry out whatever actions they feel are appropriate? The answers to these questions are complex and have implications that cannot fully be appreciated at this point; however, as more tools and information are presented in the chapters that follow, the reader will acquire additional insights that will bring these issues into sharper focus.

WHAT SHOULD BE INCLUDED IN THE MONETARY AGGREGATES?

In Chapter 2 we discussed the alternative measures of money—the monetary aggregates—currently published and used by the Federal Reserve. The Board of Governors of the Federal Reserve System announced in February 1980 that the monetary aggregates had been redefined. In this section we consider the problem of defining and measuring the stock of money in the United States and discuss whether or not the current measures are suitable.

In recent years more and more attention has been focused on the money stock because most economists now view money as an important determinant of the level of economic activity. Consequently, the size and growth of the money supply are used as indicators of the future course of economic activity, and increased attention is given to the use of money as an economic stabilization device. It is no wonder then that great importance is attached to defining the monetary aggregates properly and to measuring them accurately.

In the previous chapter, two definitions of money were introduced—the functional definition and the policy definition. Attempts to define the monetary aggregates can be viewed in the context of these definitions. We noted that the current (as of 1980) M-1A and M-1B measures roughly correspond to the functional definition in that they are primarily composed of transactions balances. The M-1B measure specifically incorporates relatively new financial developments including credit union share draft balances as well as Negotiable Order of Withdrawal (NOW) accounts and Automatic Transfer Service (ATS) deposits at both commercial banks and thrift institutions.

The policy concept of money purports to define money aggregates in a manner that will permit effective monetary policy. Hence, measures of money reflecting a policy definition are not necessarily confined to assets that can perform the medium-of-exchange function; assets that perform the store-of-value function may also be included. To allow for the possibility that a broadly defined measure of money—one that includes assets performing both a store-of-value and a medium-of-exchange function—may be superior for policy purposes, the Federal Reserve computes several monetary aggregates based on definitions that include various combinations of near-money assets. Currently these are the M-2, M-3, and L measures of money as defined in Chapter 2.

Unfortunately, both the M-1A and M-1B definitions of money may be deficient as transactions balances measures, since important transactions balances may be excluded. The most obvious, but not the only, problem with the currently defined monetary aggregates involves balances in money market mutual funds. Recall that money market funds are companies that sell shares to investors and use the proceeds to invest in high-quality, very liquid, short-term assets. The mechanics of the purchase of such shares resemble a deposit transaction much more than a stock purchase. The investor receives no stock certificates, and the company will repurchase the shares on demand; furthermore, owners of shares in these funds are offered the privilege of writing checks on their investment balances (shares) in the fund. Thus money market funds are similar to bank checking accounts yet are also similar to bank savings accounts in terms of liquidity and yield.

The currently defined monetary aggregates include balances in money market funds as part of M-2. Thus such balances are included with other financial assets to derive a measure of money performing both the store-of-value and medium-of-exchange functions. However, the existence of check-writing privileges raises the question of whether or not it would be more appropriate to include money market mutual funds as part of M-1B.

Does including money market fund balances in M-2 instead of M-1B greatly understate the amount of available transactions balances, and is this a serious problem? A serious problem arises if money market funds are essentially transactions balances, if the transactions measure of money is the most appropriate policy definition, and if balances in money market funds are large, rapidly growing, or very volatile. The relative effectiveness of M-1B as a policy definition is still open to question; however, balances in money market funds are large (over $60 billion in early 1980) and rapidly growing. The inclusion or exclusion of these balances in M-1B could affect its size by more than 10 percent.

The Federal Reserve justifies its inclusion of money market funds in M-2 on the grounds that all such balances are not used for transactions despite the check-writing privilege. Most funds impose restrictions on checks in the form of minimum denominations (usually $500) which eliminate their use in many transactions. In addition, studies have shown that balances in money market funds are relatively stable, which indicates that investors are treating them as savings balances and not transactions balances. Presently, therefore, it seems that a good case can be made for including the money market funds in M-2; however, should investors decide to make full use of their check-writing privileges, the M-1B measure would be inaccurate, which could lead to policy errors.

The difficulties involved in defining and measuring the monetary aggregates were neatly summarized in a statement by Edward Shaw:

> The "supply of money" that central banks manipulate, that people hold most of the time and spend once in a while, that economists investigate is not, then, a simple concept. It can be a figure so transformed in the statistical beauty parlor as to be hardly recognized by its closest friends. There is more than meets the eye in any measurement of the supply or quantity of money.[1]

That "there is more than meets the eye in any measurement of the supply or quantity of money" is well illustrated by money-stock data for late 1978 and early 1979. From the third quarter of 1978 through the first quarter of 1979, the M-1A measure of money grew at an annual rate of 2.9 percent, while M-1B grew at over twice that rate (6.3 percent). Furthermore, in the last quarter of 1979, M-1A was essentially constant, but M-1B grew by almost 6 percent, and M-2

[1] Edward S. Shaw, "Money Supply and Stable Economic Growth," in Lawrence Ritter, ed., *Money and Economic Activity*, 3d ed. (New York: Houghton Mifflin, 1967), p. 355.

grew by almost 8 percent. Such divergent movements in the various aggregates obviously may create dilemmas for the monetary authorities.

For years, only one measure of money was used; it was a transactions balance measure consisting of currency and demand deposits at commercial banks. Thus that definition was essentially the same as the current M-1A. In the 1970s, M-2 was added, and the previous definition was referred to as M-1. Later, M-3, M-4, and M-5 were also added. A continuing controversy existed as to which was the most appropriate measure for policy purposes and as to what should be included in or excluded from each measure. The Federal Reserve staff constantly studied these questions. In February 1980, the latest measures were announced. While the current M-1A resembles the old M-1, there are important differences between the current M-2 and M-3 and the old M-2 and M-3. The old M-4 and M-5 have been dropped in favor of the L measure discussed in Chapter 2.[2]

The discussion in this section is indicative of the everpresent nature of the problem of defining the monetary aggregates and choosing an appropriate policy definition of money. Thus the current definitions of the monetary aggregates represent only one stage in an evolutionary process that will surely continue. As long as the monetary economy continues to evolve there will be a recurring need to reconsider how to define the various measures of money. Furthermore, the continued development of monetary theory will likely suggest new aggregates which are more consistent with theoretical constructs and are therefore capable of improving the results of monetary policy.

IS GOLD MONEY BETTER THAN PAPER MONEY?[3]

Of all commodities that have been used as money, none has a longer or more captivating history than gold. For thousands of years people have been attracted to this scarce, shiny, yellow metal, and nothing else has been so revered as a monetary commodity. This utilization of gold as money was severed for all practical purposes in most nations during the Great Depression of the 1930s. Gradually thereafter the long and heated controversy over the merits and demerits of paper or credit money versus gold money began to abate,

---

[2] See "The Redefined Monetary Aggregates," *Federal Reserve Bulletin*, vol. 66, no. 2 (February 1980), pp. 97–114.

[3] In this section the term *paper money* is often used as a euphemism for credit money including demand deposits. The use of demand deposits is not confined to a paper money system; they would also circulate under a gold standard. The key difference is what the demand deposit can be converted into.

and by the 1960s few voices argued that existing monetary systems should be scrapped in favor of a monetary system based on gold.

The commitment to paper money has faded somewhat in the face of the worsening inflation of the late 1960s and 1970s, which served as a reminder of the many historical experiences in which paper money deteriorated in value. With this declining confidence in paper money, there has been a mild revival of the view that gold should again be used as money. This renewed interest in gold is evidenced by the fact that, as inflation has eroded the purchasing power of paper currencies around the world, more and more investors (and speculators) have sought the security of gold. For example, during 1979 and 1980 the dollar price of Krugerrands (a one-ounce, solid gold coin minted by South Africa) more than tripled to over $800 each. In view of these developments, this section is devoted to a review of the debate over paper money versus some form of gold money.

The link between gold and money

The use of gold as a means of payment goes far back in time, and the story of gold money has many strands running to various countries. Hundreds of years before Christ, nations minted coins of gold or other precious metals, and private enterprises also have been known to mint gold coins. Regardless of who minted the coins, the system was basically simple, with each coin supposedly containing a specified amount of gold. However, counterfeiting, clipping, filing, and adulteration often reduced the gold content of coins; a common form of adulteration was *debasement*, a process of melting coins and reminting them with a lower gold content. As monetary standards evolved, gold coins circulated simultaneously with government-issued and/or bank-issued paper money which was convertible into gold. With the passage of time, only paper money circulated. At first its quantity was limited by the fact that specified quantities of gold had to be held for each unit of paper money issued, but recently even this tie has been severed.

The link between gold and money in the United States changed drastically in 1934 with the Gold Reserve Act which, among other things, prohibited the private holding of gold; gold coins no longer circulated, nor could other forms of money be redeemed for any form of gold. The only legal use of gold was for industrial or dental purposes. However, our money supply remained linked to gold in that 25 percent gold backing was required for Federal Reserve notes, the nation's major form of paper currency. Specifically the link was as follows: The government owned all monetary gold and issued gold certificates to the Federal Reserve in amounts equal to actual gold holdings (valued at $35 per ounce);[4] the Federal Reserve could then issue $4 of Federal Reserve notes for each $1 of gold certificates held; since the Federal Reserve notes in circulation were one component of the money supply, the link between gold and money was to some extent maintained.

In 1968 the requirement that Federal Reserve notes be backed by a gold reserve was dropped, and the last official connection between gold and our money supply was severed. The event caused little notice and even less consternation. Thus from early times when gold was the circulating medium to more recently when paper money served as a type of warehouse receipt, there has been a continually evolving connection between gold and money. In the present stage of this evolution, the link between gold and money has been severed for all practical purposes. Why, after thousands of years as the premier monetary commodity, was gold assigned a back seat to paper and bank liabilities as the primary form of money; and was this a mistake?

The argument for paper money

The reasons for choosing a managed paper currency are threefold: (1) convenience, (2) cost, and (3) controllability. The convenience aspect of money has several dimensions. Money should be easy to transport, store, and exchange. It should be easy to recognize and divide into different denominations. Durability, or lack of rapid deterioration, is another desirable attribute. Paper is preferable to gold in all of these respects except for durability, and its inferiority in this respect is offset by its other advantages. The opportunity cost associated with using commodities as money was noted in Chapter 2; that is, using a commodity as money precludes its use in other ways. Hence, it is advantageous not to use any commodity as money that has a high nonmonetary use value, and accordingly, money should be composed of something that can be produced cheaply. While paper is not a free good, its use as money does not significantly reduce the availability of paper for other purposes. The fact that most transactions are handled by check rather than currency makes the durability and cost-of-production considerations somewhat irrelevant.

Despite paper's relative advantage over other items as money in

---

[4] Those gold certificates were in effect a warehouse receipt evidencing a claim to gold held by the U.S. Treasury. In earlier years, the government had issued gold certificates which circulated as part of the money supply.

terms of cost and convenience, it is paper's advantage in terms of controllability that has made it the primary form of modern money. As noted earlier, it is desirable for money to perform the function of a macroeconomic control variable. It is generally believed that, in order to perform this function, the supply of money must vary in the appropriate manner in response to long- and short-run economic conditions: Over the long run the money supply should increase as the economy grows; for the short run, money has the potential to counteract fluctuations in output and employment. While a monetary standard based on gold (or some other commodity) can be (and has been) devised to provide some degree of macroeconomic control, it is virtually impossible to devise a commodity standard which assures that adjustments will occur at the proper time and in the proper magnitude. In short, for money to perform this control function well, it cannot be allowed to fluctuate more-or-less independently of general economic conditions. Paper or credit money lends itself to management better than any other form of money; its supply can easily be increased or decreased, whereas the supply of gold cannot be expanded rapidly, if at all, and could decline (or increase) at an inopportune time so as to disrupt economic activity.

The argument against paper money

An item can serve successfully as money only so long as it is generally acceptable in exchange for goods and services. No monetary item can remain generally acceptable, however, unless holders and potential holders have confidence that they will be able to exchange it easily for goods and services whenever they are inclined to do so. More specifically, potential holders must believe that the monetary item has stability of value—that is, that its purchasing power will not decline excessively over their planned holding periods. It is crucial, therefore, that whatever would serve as money have stability of value, and the necessary condition for stability of value is not the composition of the monetary item but its continued relative scarcity. Thus for something to serve successfully as money, it must either be naturally scarce, or there must be some mechanism for controlling its production so as to ensure that its supply does not become excessive.

The argument against paper or credit money rests upon the difficulty of assuring its continued scarcity. An item such as paper, with a low cost of production and low nonmonetary value, faces no practical limitation in its use as money. The marginal cost of producing a unit of money is far less than that unit's monetary value. Under such conditions it is profitable for the producer of money to increase production continually, and unless an artificial limiting mechanism is present, we can expect increases in the quantity supplied until the price or value of a unit of money is equal to the marginal cost of producing that unit. Before that point is reached, however, money would cease to be scarce, would become virtually worthless, would lose its acceptability, and would therefore cease to function as money. This chain of events is more likely in the case of credit money. The connection between excessive paper money and inflation has been illustrated numerous times throughout history; most notable among currencies that were overissued are the French assignats, the American Continental dollars issued during the Revolution, the Confederate paper money, and the German marks in the 1920s.

Obviously, since there is no practical limit to the amount of paper that can be used as money, paper money requires an artificial mechanism capable of limiting the amount produced. Historically one limiting mechanism has been the monopoly power of the government over production and control of money. However, government monopoly of the production of paper money only assures that money will not be excessively produced by others within the economy. The government must somehow avoid the temptation to take advantage of the differential between the monetary value of the credit money it produces and the marginal cost of producing that money. Faced with a need for funds for various purposes, government must resist running the printing presses as a substitute for unpopular tax increases. According to critics, it is the great weakness of a credit money standard that no mechanism has been devised that prevents governments from engaging in excessive money creation.[5] Constitutional and statutory safeguards are not an absolute guarantee against overissue, and a sound paper money must ultimately rely on the wisdom and good faith of the issuing authorities.

In the United States, the Federal Reserve System, which is to some extent independent of the government, prints all but a minor proportion of our paper money. This provides some protection from the pressure to overissue because the Fed is not profit oriented nor in need of large sums of money to finance costly programs. Thus the Federal Reserve is isolated to a degree from the temptation to take advantage of the profits from money creation. However, protection from overissue is not perfect under the existing setup; to the extent

---

[5] In Chapter 18, which deals with the problem of inflation, we shall examine the consequences of failure to resist the temptation to overissue.

that the Federal Reserve purchases and holds government debt, government deficit spending is equivalent to running the printing presses.[6]

Some protection from this loophole is theoretically provided by a law prohibiting the U.S. Treasury from borrowing more than $5 billion "directly" from the Federal Reserve; that is, the Fed cannot purchase more than $5 billion in newly issued Treasury securities. However, there is no statutory limitation on indirect government borrowing from the Fed. Indirect borrowing occurs when the Treasury sells its securities to the public, and the Fed then purchases the securities from the public. Thus existing restraints are not completely effective in closing the loophole through which the paper money–issuing privilege can be excessively employed by a financially irresponsible government.

In summary, it is ironic that paper money is potentially the best and worst form of money. It has the advantages of convenience and low cost of production. On the other hand, the argument against paper money rests on the assumption that government lacks the discipline to manage a credit standard properly, while the great advantage of a gold money standard is its relative immunity from overissue and inflation, a characteristic that paper money is much less likely to possess. Yet even the relative scarcity of gold is not a certainty. In 16th-century Spain, for example, prices rose drastically due to the influx of gold from the New World. Furthermore, gold suffers from the disadvantage of being more limited than paper in its potential as a discretionary macroeconomic control device. After weighing all the trade-offs, most economists continue to opt in favor of paper (credit) money.

SHOULD MONETARY GROWTH BE GOVERNED BY STRICT RULES?

As noted in the previous section, the major shortcoming of paper money is the ever-present danger of overissuance by the governmental monetary authorities; given this danger, there are those who argue that the monetary authorities should be forced to operate within very narrow bounds. The so-called rules-versus-discretion

---

[6] The effects, but not the actual mechanics, can be seen in a hypothetical example. Suppose the federal government wishes to spend $10 billion more than it expects to receive from taxes. It borrows this sum by issuing bonds and selling them to the central bank. The central bank pays for these by crediting the Treasury's demand deposit account at the Federal Reserve. Then, when the government spends the proceeds of the bond issue, the money supply expands just as if the government had printed the money to finance the deficit.

debate covered in this section can be seen as an outgrowth of a distrust of paper money.

Part III of this book is devoted to explaining the process by which our money supply is controlled by the monetary authorities of the United States, the Board of Governors of the Federal Reserve System. There remains some question about the precision with which these authorities can actually control the money supply, and as the previous sections of this chapter highlight, the composition, measurement, and nature of the money supply are subject to debate. However, the policy actions of the authorities are presently the main determinants of the volume of money in the economy, especially over longer periods of time. Furthermore, though there is still some disagreement as to its degree of importance, there is a general consensus that money matters. If the supply of money grows too fast or is too great, problems arise; likewise, if the money supply is inadequate or grows too slowly, the economy performs unsatisfactorily. If we grant that the size and growth of the money stock are important, should the monetary authorities be given freedom to control the money supply in accordance with their best judgment, or should their actions be tightly controlled by laws so that there is little room for discretionary action? Note that the issue is not whether to control money; rather, it concerns the degree of discretionary power that the monetary authorities should be granted.

With the formation of the Federal Reserve in 1913, the United States initiated a course of action that permitted considerable discretion on the part of the Fed's Board of Governors. Not everyone agrees that the Federal Reserve should have been granted such vast authority over monetary policymaking, but the majority of economists remain committed to the belief that discretion is necessary for effective money supply management. Prior to 1913 when the Federal Reserve Act was passed, there was no central bank to implement monetary policy. Does this mean that there were no restraints on the money supply? In the sense that there was no conscious control, it does. However, it does not mean that the growth of the money stock was unchecked; market forces operating through the gold standard limited the money supply. Therefore, the issue of rules versus authorities is not one of control versus aimless movement but rather of how much latitude the central bank should have in controlling the money supply.

The case for rules

Proponents for the rules side rest their case primarily on two propositions:

1. Attempts at discretionary monetary policy have led (and presumably will continue to lead) to erratic swings in the money supply which have proven to be more destabilizing than stabilizing.
2. A discretionary approach to monetary policy bestows too much centralized power in the hands of a few people and is, therefore, a hazard to freedom in a democratic society and a free-enterprise economy.[7]

Most of the controversy in the rules-versus-authority issue is over the first proposition; hence, the following discussion focuses only on it.

Critics of a system granting discretion to the authorities argue that a study of central banks' performances in the United States and other countries does not justify the degree of discretionary power that monetary authorities now enjoy. According to these interpretations of the historical record, discretionary management of the money supply has resulted in abrupt "stop-go-reverse" patterns of money-supply changes that have had a destabilizing effect on national economic activity. This record of perverse performance could be improved, critics argue, if the central bank were forced to follow a rule that limits the discretion of the authorities.

The most striking example of perverse discretionary policy cited by critics is the performance of the Federal Reserve during the Great Depression; between 1929 and 1932 the Fed caused—or at best allowed—the nation's money supply to fall by about 33 percent. This policy, critics argue, greatly aggravated deteriorating economic conditions, causing the Great Depression to be much worse than it would have been otherwise. The critics do not contend that every instance of economic instability has been caused by the monetary authorities. Some were; still others were only aggravated; and in some instances, discretionary policy was actually helpful. However, they argue that, on the whole, discretionary actions have intensified the instability of the economy relative to what it would have been if the monetary authorities had acted in a more neutral manner.

Proponents of a rules approach argue further that the factors that have led to a poor record of performance under discretionary policy in the past are inevitably present and are likely to result in continued poor performance under a discretionary approach to monetary policy. The main source of the problem, they say, is the long and variable lag between the time that money supply changes are initiated by

---

[7] Henry C. Simons, "Rules versus Authorities in Monetary Policy," *Journal of Political Economy*, vol. 44 (February 1936), pp. 1–30; and Milton Friedman, *A Program for Monetary Stability* (New York: Fordham University Press, 1960).

the authorities and the time that the primary effect of those changes is felt in the economy. For example, restrictive actions undertaken by the monetary authorities in January may not have a major effect on the economy until midyear or later, and at that time, a restrictive effect may not be appropriate; in fact, it is possible that a restrictive policy could worsen an otherwise minor downturn.

Successful discretionary monetary policy requires that the monetary authorities know the approximate timing of the effects of policy actions on the economy and the condition of the economy when the effects will be felt. Critics of a discretionary approach argue that long and variable lags prevent the authorities from knowing the former while inability to forecast accurately makes the latter knowledge impossible. Therefore, while discretionary policy actions may occasionally be helpful, they are as likely to be harmful.

The case against rules

Opponents of a fixed-rule approach to monetary policy are quick to point out that the evidence cited by fixed-rule advocates is far from conclusive, and they raise strong practical and theoretical objections to the rules approach. Opponents of a rules approach question the interpretation of the historical record cited by rules proponents as evidence that discretionary policy has worked poorly.[8] The claim that monetary policymakers must contend with long and variable lags is also contested on the basis that the statistical methods used to estimate the lags are invalid. Furthermore, the authorities do not have complete control over the money supply since it is possible for cause and effect to run from economic activity to the money supply; therefore, it is invalid for fixed-rule proponents to cite specific episodes of money-supply change as the cause of poor economic performance.

Another argument raised in opposition to the fixed-rule position is the practical problem of what the proper rule should be. Opponents of rules argue that the real world is so complex that no simple rule can be devised that would give better results than well-informed, discretionary action by the authorities. In fact, if an "optimal" rule could be discovered, any sensible authority would follow the course of action prescribed by that rule, and there would be no distinction between the results under a rules approach and the results under a discretionary approach.

Other reasons can be offered for rejecting a rules approach to

---

[8] John H. Karaken and Robert M. Solow in the Commission on Money and Credit, *Stabilization Policies* (Englewood Cliffs, N.J.: Prentice-Hall, Inc., 1963), pp. 15–18.

monetary policy. For example, it is argued that a poor record of discretionary money management in the past is no reason to disallow discretion in the future. In recent years we have learned much about the forces that control our economy, and our monetary authorities should be able to do a better job in the future than their predecessors did in the past. (In the minds of some, however, the record of the 1970s casts doubt on the validity of this argument.) Opponents of rules also pose the problem of inflexibility. A rule may produce optimum results when adopted but may later prove to be inappropriate as economic conditions change. Thus a rule that generates good results in the 1980s may not work as well in the 1990s because of changes in the nature of the economy. To formulate new rules as economic conditions change is a modified version of discretion.

The rules-versus-authority debate cannot be separated from the related issue of what the rule should be. There is no lack of potential candidates, but there is a lack of consensus among rules advocates. Some simple rules have been proposed, as have some very complex ones. In particular two proposed rules have received much attention: (1) the price level stabilization rule and (2) the constant growth rate rule.

The price level stabilization rule was first proposed in 1936 by the late Henry C. Simons of the University of Chicago.[9] Under it, the central bank would be charged with managing the money supply and credit conditions so as to achieve a stable level of prices. In short, the price level would be not only the ranking goal of the monetary authorities but in fact the exclusive goal. Other major economic policy goals such as full employment, the level and rate of growth of production, and the country's balance of payments position would not affect the authorities' decisions as to how much money to create. The proponents of the stable price rule do not mean to imply that employment and production objectives are necessarily less important than stable prices; rather they see stable prices as the best means of achieving employment and production goals.

Milton Friedman is a leading advocate of the constant growth rate approach to monetary policy; Friedman proposed that the Fed follow a simple rule of letting the money supply grow at a constant rate regardless of the status of the economy. The rate at which the money supply should be increased is less important, he argues, than keeping the rate of increase constant. However, a rate of increase of from 3 to 5 percent probably would lead to stable prices since the potential growth of real output is of a similar order of magnitude.

Other rules have been proposed which are somewhat more com-

---

[9] Simons, "Rules versus Authorities," pp. 1–30.

plex. For example, William Poole advocated a version of the constant growth rate rule that would provide a less-than-average growth rate of money during slack periods of economic activity and a higher-than-average rate during periods of accelerated economic activity.[10] Martin Bronfenbrenner proposed a rule with a variable rate of growth of money based on changes in productivity, the size of the labor force, and the velocity of money in the previous quarter.[11]

As our knowledge of the monetary economy increases, other, more complex rules are likely to emerge, and it is possible that a rule will be proposed that will promise such improved results that a consensus would form in favor of its adoption. At the present time, however, the rules-versus-authority question seems likely to remain an unsettled issue with the discretion of the authorities continuing as the foundation of monetary policy.

SUMMARY

In order to understand the monetary economy, it is necessary to have measures of the money supply. This, as it turns out, is no easy task, and one of the issues continuously facing monetary policymakers is the determination of appropriate measures of money. As the financial system evolves, new assets are created, and old assets are modified. Since some of these assets perform one or more functions of money, an appropriate measure of money in one time period may be inappropriate in another. Indeed, recent developments in the financial system have caused the measures of money to be revised, and new definitions of the monetary aggregates were formulated in February 1980. However, the currently defined monetary aggregates are unlikely to be the final word, and the question of what is the most appropriate policy definition of money will continue to be an issue.

Most people living today are accustomed to using paper money, but there are those who believe that paper money is inferior to gold money. Paper is an ideal monetary substance in most respects: it is portable, easily divisible, and has a low opportunity cost, while the major shortcoming of paper money is its susceptibility to overissue and inflation. A good paper money requires maturity and discipline on the part of the monetary authorities. Gold money, on the other hand, is much more difficult to overissue than paper. Though this may be an advantage, it does present an obstacle to the use of money

---

[10] William Poole, "Optimal Choice of Monetary Policy Instruments in as Simple Stochastic Macro Model," *Quarterly Journal of Economics*, vol. 74 (May 1970), pp. 177–216.

[11] Martin Bronfenbrenner, "Statistical Tests of Rival Monetary Rules," *Journal of Political Economy*, vol. 69 (February 1961), pp. 1–14.

as a macroeconomic control variable, and few nations are willing to omit this tool from their kit of economic policy weapons.

The final issue discussed in this chapter concerns the appropriate degree of discretion to be given to the monetary authorities. Should they be forced to operate within very confining rules or be given the freedom to operate as their wisdom dictates? Proponents of strict rules argue that long and variable monetary policy lags create the strong likelihood of harmful monetary policy results. A better outcome can be achieved, they say, by taking discretionary power away from the authorities and forcing them to act in a "neutral" manner. So far, however, no one has been able to propose a rule that a consensus favors over the discretionary approach.

REVIEW QUESTIONS

1. Discuss the relative merits of the M-1A, M-1B, and M-2 aggregates, first as they relate to the functional definition of money and second as they relate to the policy definition.

2. From a recent issue of the *Federal Reserve Bulletin*, obtain data on the money supply (M-1A and M-2 only) and Gross National Product. Plot the behavior of each for the past ten years. What conclusions can you draw?

3. What are money market mutual funds? Should balances in such funds be included in M-1B or M-2? Discuss.

4. Comment on the statement "Gold is too scarce to be used as money."

5. Under what circumstances would the use of gold either as circulating money or as backing for paper money serve to prevent inflation?

6. In the absence of major gold discoveries, would the use of gold as money guarantee that the money supply could not be increased excessively so as to result in inflation?

7. Discuss the advantages and problems of discretionary money supply management.

SUGGESTIONS FOR ADDITIONAL READING

Davenport, John A. "A Testing Time for Monetarism." *Fortune*, vol. 102, no. 7 (October 6, 1980), pp. 42–48.

Friedman, Milton. "Commodity Reserve Currency." *Journal of Political Economy*, vol. 59 (June 1951), pp. 203–32.

Hayek, F. A. *Denationalization of Money*. London: Institute of Economic Affairs, 1976.

Samuelson, Paul. "Reflections on Central Banking." *The National Banking Review*, vol. 1 (September 1963), pp. 15–28.

Simons, Henry C. "Rules versus Authorities in Monetary Policy." *Journal of Political Economy,* vol. 44, no. 1 (February 1936), pp. 1–30.

Staff of the Board of Governors of the Federal Reserve System. "A Proposal for Redefining the Monetary Aggregates." *Federal Reserve Bulletin,* vol. 65, no. 1 (January 1979), pp. 13–42.

Staff of the Board of Governors of the Federal Reserve System. "The Redefined Monetary Aggregates." *Federal Reserve Bulletin,* vol. 66, no. 2 (February 1980), pp. 97–114.

II

THE FINANCIAL SYSTEM OF THE MONETARY ECONOMY

4

The U.S. financial system: An overview

WARM-UP: *Outline and questions to consider as you read*

What is the nature and role of a financial system in a monetary economy?

What are the major financial intermediaries in our financial system?

    Commercial banks.

    Mutual savings banks.

    Savings and loan associations.

    Credit unions.

    Investment companies.

    Pension funds.

    Insurance companies.

    REITs.

    Finance companies.

    Federally sponsored intermediaries.

How are commercial banks different from other financial institutions?

What are the characteristics of the major financial instruments?

    Money market instruments.

    Capital market instruments.

What are the functions of interest rates in our financial system?

NEW TERMS

Broker: a middleman who brings buyer and seller together.

Budget deficit unit (BDU): an economic unit whose purchases of goods and services exceed current-period income.

Budget surplus unit (BSU): an economic unit with current-period income in excess of purchases of goods and services.

Capital market: the financial market dealing with claims that have maturities longer than one year.

Capital market instruments: long-term financial claims, including debt instruments such as bonds issued by corporations and governments and also including equity-type securities such as common and preferred stocks.

Dealer: a middleman who purchases goods or securities with the intention of reselling them to an ultimate buyer.

Financial claim: documentary evidence held by an economic unit of an amount of money owed to it by some other economic unit.

Financial intermediary: a financial institution that expedites the flow of funds between BDUs and BSUs by obtaining funds from BSUs and then supplying the funds to BDUs.

Financial transaction: the exchange of money for financial assets such as stocks or bonds.

Loanable funds: funds exchanged in credit markets by suppliers and demanders of credit (BSUs and BDUs).

Money market: the facilities and procedures through which short-term, high-quality financial claims are bought and sold.

Money market instruments: short-term financial claims such as Treasury bills, commercial paper, and negotiable certificates of deposit.

Nominal rate of interest: the observed market rate of interest on a particular financial claim.

Primary market: the "new securities" market through which newly issued financial claims are bought and sold.

Real estate investment trust (REIT): a business that pools funds to invest in a portfolio of real estate ventures.

Real rate of interest: the nominal rate of interest minus the anticipated rate of inflation.

Real transaction: the exchange of money (or a good or service) for goods and services.

Secondary market: the "used securities" market through which outstanding securities are bought and sold.

In this chapter we explore the basic elements of the United States financial system. We start with its nature and functions and then proceed to introduce the major types of financial institutions and their primary roles in the system. Particular attention is paid to commercial banks and how they differ from other major financial institutions. Since various financial instruments or financial claims are necessary in a functioning financial system, those that play important roles in our economy are presented and their special features noted. The essence of a modern financial system is credit, and where there is credit, there is interest. The last section in this chapter introduces the nature and role of interest rates.

WHAT IS THE NATURE AND ROLE OF A FINANCIAL SYSTEM IN A MONETARY ECONOMY?

An economic system comprises the mechanisms and institutions used by society to determine what to produce, how to produce, and for whom to produce. In a market economy, resource-use decisions are based upon signals generated by the relative prices of the different goods and resources. A price is simply the ratio at which two things are exchanged. In a monetary economy, prices, or values of different items, are quoted in terms of the society's monetary unit or, as economists call it, the numéraire. In the United States that unit is the dollar.

In a monetary economy, economic units—households, governments, and businesses—may be divided into two groups. One group, which we shall call Budget Deficit Units or BDUs, consists of those units who, in the current time period, wish to purchase more goods and services than their current incomes will allow. The other group, which we shall call Budget Surplus Units or BSUs, consists of those units whose current income exceeds the amount needed to execute their current planned purchases of goods and services. As noted in Chapter 2, money serves not only as a medium of exchange but also as a store of value that allows budget surplus units to maintain claims on goods and services through saving part of their current-period income.

At this point, it is useful to distinguish between two different types of transactions that occur in the monetary economy.[1] One type involves the exchange of goods and services for money. This type of

---

[1] Actually, transactions involving goods and services may be further categorized on the basis of purpose such as consumption or capital formation. Such distinctions are not necessary at this stage of analysis.

FIGURE 4–1
Illustration of a real transaction in a monetary economy

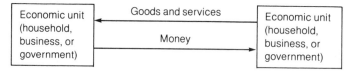

exchange is illustrated in Figure 4–1, and we shall refer to such exchanges as real transactions. The other type of transaction in which we are interested at this point is labeled a financial transaction, and it differs from a real transaction in that money is exchanged for financial assets rather than for goods and services.[2] The transfers involved in a financial transaction are illustrated in Figure 4–2.

Money represents a claim on goods; financial assets represent a claim to money and hence are indirect claims on goods. For this reason, we shall refer to financial assets as financial claims. In reality, the term financial asset is only one side of the coin. It is not only an asset to the economic unit that holds it but also a liability of the economic unit that issues it. In cases where the claim is evidenced by something physical, as in the case of a bond or a stock, the claim is sometimes referred to as a financial instrument. We shall look at various financial claims in more detail later in the chapter.

The existence of a financial sector gives BSUs a wider range of options with respect to how to utilize their money balances. In addition to holding money balances or acquiring goods, BSUs may choose to acquire financial assets that are not direct entitlements to goods but are direct entitlements to money and hence indirect claims on goods. Financial assets are usually superior to money in one important respect—the holder expects to receive a monetary return or yield that would not be obtained if money were held.[3]

As a financial system grows and matures, it becomes more complex, and a variety of different financial claims are issued by budget deficit units. In addition, businesses are formed whose primary function is to facilitate the credit process. These businesses are generally referred to as financial institutions and can be classified into two general categories:

---

[2] Of course in a mature economy the financial system is likely to utilize more than one form of money. Hence, financial transactions may involve switching from one form of money (demand deposits) to another form (currency, NOW accounts, or share drafts).

[3] This statement must be qualified if the general level of prices is declining or if money is being held in the form of NOW accounts or share drafts.

FIGURE 4–2
Illustration of a financial transaction in the monetary economy

1. Brokers and dealers in financial claims who facilitate financial transactions by expediting direct transfers between BDUs and BSUs.
2. Financial intermediaries who facilitate the credit process indirectly.

Brokers expedite the process by helping BDUs and BSUs come together. Rather than each BDU and each BSU searching out an appropriate trading partner, the broker specializes in this search function and thus performs it more efficiently. For these efforts, the broker is paid a commission by the BSU, the BDU, or both. Brokers do not take title to financial claims nor transfer any of their own money; they only perform a search function. A dealer, on the other hand, will buy and temporarily own financial claims until they can be sold to an interested BSU. The dealer's compensation is the spread between the purchase and sales prices. The involvement of brokers and dealers in financial transactions is illustrated in Figure 4–3.

Financial intermediaries expedite financial exchanges by performing functions similar to those of BSUs and BDUs. Like BDUs, intermediaries obtain funds from BSUs by issuing financial claims;

FIGURE 4–3
Financial transactions involving brokers and dealers

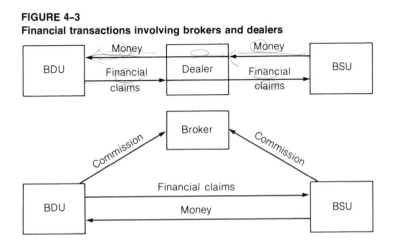

like BSUs, intermediaries transfer funds to BDUs in return for claims issued by the BDU. The end result of the intermediation process is a transfer of funds from BSUs to BDUs, but in the process, the BSU acquires the secondary claims of the intermediary rather than primary claims on the BDU. The latter claims are held by the intermediary.

Brokers, dealers, and intermediaries are all middlemen, and there is a distinct similarity in their activities. However, unlike intermediaries, brokers and dealers do not issue secondary financial claims on themselves. They merely transfer the primary claims on the BDUs to the BSUs. Figure 4–4 illustrates the distinction between intermediaries and other financial middlemen. The figure shows that the flow of funds between BDUs and BSUs can be direct or indirect. If the flow is indirect, it goes through a financial intermediary. Since this book focuses on the role of banks in our financial system, we have divided financial intermediaries in Figure 4–4 into two categories—commercial banks and nonbank financial intermediaries.

The process of financial intermediation increases the efficiency of the financial sector. This greater efficiency results from the fact that intermediaries are less restrictive than individual BDUs and BSUs with respect to the maturities and sizes of financial claims that they are willing to issue or hold. Thus going through an intermediary allows the small BSU to exchange a small amount of money for a correspondingly small financial claim, and by pooling the funds of

FIGURE 4–4
Financial sector flows in the monetary economy

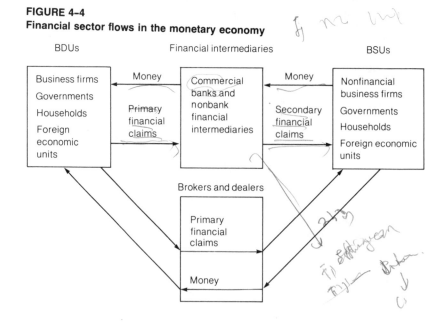

many small BSUs and issuing financial claims on itself, the intermediary is not forced to match the size and timing desires of individual BSUs and BDUs. Therefore, the process of intermediation
reduces search costs.

Not only do intermediaries increase the efficiency of the financial
sector, but they also reduce the risk involved in financial transactions. They can become specialists while at the same time diver-
sifying their holdings of financial claims to a much greater extent
than would be possible for most individual BSUs. Unlike most
BSUs, an intermediary's sole function is dealing in financial claims.
Because of this specialization in acquiring and issuing financial
claims, intermediaries are much better at assessing risk than most
BSUs can ever hope to be. Furthermore, by pooling the funds of
many BSUs, intermediaries are able to have much larger and much
more diversified portfolios of financial claims. This ability to recognize and reject extreme risks and to reduce risk through diversification enables the intermediary to reduce overall losses and the costs
of financial transactions.

The transactions involving BDUs and BSUs take place in financial
markets. Here the term *market* does not refer to a location but denotes the set of institutions and arrangements through which the
forces of supply and demand for financial claims operate. Financial
markets are usually classified into different categories, the custom-
ary classification being capital markets and money markets. The
distinction between capital and money markets is based on the term
to maturity of the financial claims and the liquidity and quality of
the claims traded. Although the dividing line is somewhat arbitrary,
highly liquid financial claims maturing in one year or less are usually referred to as *money market instruments*. Those with maturities
greater than one year are referred to as *capital market instruments*.
Among the former are such liquid financial claims as Treasury bills,
commercial paper, and negotiable certificates of deposit. Capital
market instruments include bonds issued by corporations, state and
local governments, the U.S. Treasury, and various federal government agencies. Also traded on the capital market are financial claims
in the form of equity-type securities such as common and preferred
stocks.

Another common classification of financial markets is primary
markets and secondary markets. The *primary market* is the market
for newly issued securities, while the *secondary market* handles
previously issued or "used" securities. A security or financial claim
can only be traded once on the primary market, but it may be traded
many times on the secondary market. Secondary market transactions
occur because economic units who have previously acted in a BSU

capacity wish to convert their claim back into money earlier than the scheduled maturity of the claim. Without the ability to do this in the secondary market, few BSUs would supply long-term credit and whatever long-term funds were available would be quite expensive to BDUs, with the result that economic efficiency would be greatly impaired.

WHAT ARE THE MAJOR FINANCIAL INTERMEDIARIES IN OUR FINANCIAL SYSTEM?

A partial listing of the major financial intermediaries in the United States financial system is shown in Table 4–1, and the remainder of this section presents a brief description of each intermediary in terms of its importance, the financial function in which it specializes, and its primary sources and uses of funds. The first four intermediaries listed in Table 4–1 are sometimes referred to as savings or depository intermediaries. These intermediaries collect the savings and other deposits of the public. In contrast are the borrowing intermediaries whose funds come from borrowing from other institutions and the public.

Commercial banks

Commercial banks have been and are the most important of the country's financial intermediaries. In terms of assets they are more than twice the size of the second-largest intermediary. Historically the development of commercial banks preceeds that of the other institutions listed in Table 4–1. The importance of banks can be

TABLE 4–1
Major financial intermediaries in the United States, by size, January 1, 1980

Intermediary	Total assets ($ billions)
Commercial banks	$1,351
Mutual savings banks	163
Savings and loan associations	582
Credit unions	65
Life insurance companies	428
Investment companies*	44†
Money market funds	50
Finance companies	141

* Excludes money market funds and closed-end investment companies.

† Market value of assets less current liabilities.

Source: *Federal Reserve Bulletin*, March 1980.

explained primarily in terms of the more diversified nature of their activities and the fact that, up until recently, they were the only intermediary offering deposit accounts upon which checks could be written. Therefore, banks have had more to offer in terms of both loan and deposit services. The unique and essential nature of bank services accounts for the fact that only the smallest of communities is without the services of a banking office. Because of the importance of commercial banking in our economy, an entire chapter (Chapter 5) is devoted to the business of banking.

Mutual savings banks

A mutual savings bank is a state-chartered financial institution operated by a board of trustees for the mutual benefit of its depositors or savers and thus is a form of financial cooperative. Mutual savings banks are confined primarily to the northeastern United States and particularly the states of New York and Massachusetts. Historically mutual savings banks acquired funds by issuing passbook savings accounts and savings certificates. In recent years some mutual savings banks have begun to offer negotiable order of withdrawal (NOW) accounts. Mutual savings banks have channeled most of their funds into the home mortgage market, although they do invest in government securities and high-grade corporate bonds and can now make business loans on a limited basis. On a nationwide basis the number of these institutions is small when compared to commercial banks or savings and loan associations, but they are considered as major financial intermediaries in those parts of the country in which they are concentrated. At the beginning of 1979, there were 465 mutual savings banks in the United States as compared to over 14,500 commercial banks; in Massachusetts, however, the number of mutual savings banks exceeded the number of commercial banks. New York, Connecticut, New Jersey, and Maine all have substantial numbers of these institutions operating within their boundaries.

Savings and loan associations

In terms of size and number, savings and loan associations are second in importance only to commercial banks among the nation's financial intermediaries. S&Ls, as they are commonly called, are also known as building, savings, or homestead associations. Savings and loan associations are organized as either stock companies or as non-profit mutual associations (cooperatives). The S&Ls are very similar to mutual savings banks in terms of their sources and uses of funds; most of their assets consist of residential mortgages, and most of their funds are derived from passbook-type savings accounts and from the issuance of savings certificates. These savings accounts or deposits are also referred to as *shares* or *savings capital* and may be insured by the Federal Savings and Loan Insurance Corporation (FSLIC). Traditionally S&Ls have been a very specialized form of institution existing primarily for the purpose of making housing loans, and today they are the most important lender in this field. Savings and loan associations, like banks, may be either state chartered or federally chartered and are subject to regulation by the various states and by the Federal Home Loan Bank Board.

Credit unions

Credit unions are another type of financial association owned and run for the benefit of their users. A credit union is composed of individuals with some common interest—place of employment, fraternal order, church, or well-defined residential location—who form the credit union for the purpose of pooling their savings and making loans to each other. These individuals are known as *members* of the credit union, and their savings accounts or deposits are known as ownership *shares*. To be a member, one must be eligible and must acquire ownership shares by making a deposit in the institution; only members may borrow from the credit union.

The income of each institution is derived primarily from interest on loans made to members (most of these loans are consumer loans with repayment on an installment basis) although the institution may also have some earnings from other investments. Income earned by the credit union is distributed to the members in the form of dividends. The source of most credit union funds is member ownership shares. In recent years credit unions have been allowed to offer *share-draft* accounts much like NOW accounts and similar to demand deposit accounts of commercial banks.

While credit unions are not as important within our financial system as commercial banks, S&Ls, or even mutual savings banks, they have been increasing in size and number at a rapid pace in recent years and are considered an important supplier of consumer credit. In early 1980 credit unions supplied over 15 percent of consumer installment credit funds. In 1979 there were over 22,000 credit unions in this country with a membership in excess of 36 million. In 1945 there were fewer than 3 million credit union members.

Investment companies

Investment companies are devices that allow budget surplus units to pool their funds and purchase interest in a diversified portfolio of financial claims by way of an ownership interest in the investment company. There are two types of investment companies—*open-end* investment companies and *closed-end* investment companies. Open-end companies are often referred to as mutual funds. These companies stand ready at all times to issue new shares or to repurchase their own outstanding shares from investors. Closed-end investment companies issue a fixed amount of shares, and investors who want to purchase shares in these companies must do so from other investors. Likewise, the owners of shares of closed-end investment company stock must sell their shares on the open market. Both types of companies acquire funds by selling shares of stock in the investment company. When an investor purchases shares in a closed-end company in the over-the-counter market or on the organized exchanges, a regular commission is paid. If shares are purchased from an open-end or mutual company, the investor may or may not have to pay a sales charge. Some funds, called *no-load* funds, do not assess a commission and sell their shares at net asset values; the net asset value of the share is determined by dividing the difference between the value of the company's assets and its liabilities by the number of shares outstanding.

Historically, investment companies have channeled most of their funds into the purchase of common stocks. Investment companies may specialize: some emphasize growth; others emphasize income or stability; still others specialize in the stock of companies in a particular industry. In recent years companies have been organized that use their funds to purchase bonds, and they are referred to as bond funds. Even within bond funds there is specialization: some emphasize income; others specialize in tax-free or municipal issues; while still other funds, the *money market* funds or *liquid asset* funds, specialize in high-grade, short-term securities. As noted earlier, the money market funds are becoming increasingly important.

One of the primary advantages that investment companies offer to BSUs is the ability to take small amounts of savings, pool these funds, and invest them in a diversified portfolio. As noted earlier, diversification reduces the risk associated with financial investments. Another advantage claimed by investment companies is the ability to provide expert management of the investment portfolio.

Investment companies grew rapidly in size and number after World War II and particularly in the 1960s; however, the stock market performance of the 70s dulled the image of investment companies, and their growth pace was not maintained. The recent expansion of money market funds is an exception, however.

Pension funds

Pension funds result from employee and employer contributions out of earnings which are set aside and invested to provide benefits for workers when they retire. Pension funds may be divided into three categories: private pension funds, state and local government funds, and the various federal government funds which include social security (Federal Old Age and Survivors Insurance Trust Fund), the Civil Service Retirement Fund, and the Railroad Retirement Account.

Pension funds have grown rapidly in recent years as more and more firms have established retirement plans as part of their total fringe benefit packages. Other factors contributing to this growth have been an expanding labor force and increased emphasis by unions on nontaxable fringe benefits as opposed to taxable wages. Pension funds are classified as either insured or noninsured: under an insured plan, the proceeds of employee and employer contributions are used to purchase retirement benefits in the form of annuities from life insurance companies; under noninsured plans, the funds generated from contributions are managed by a trustee—a commercial bank trust department, the employer, or some entity other than a life insurance company. The funds are invested so as to provide a stream of benefits when the employees retire. Pension funds tend to invest heavily in long-term financial claims. The noninsured funds have emphasized common stock investments while the insured funds have invested heavily in corporate bonds.

Insurance companies

Insurance companies are by far the largest of the nondepository financial intermediaries. Insurance companies generate pools of funds from the premium payments of policyholders. Rather than hold these funds as cash until claims are filed, the funds are invested. The primary financial claims purchased vary among the different types of insurance companies, but holdings are concentrated in corporate bonds, state and local government bonds, mortgages, and corporate equities. Insurance companies are usually classified as life insurance companies or property and casualty companies. Also, they may be classified as stock companies or mutual companies. Stock companies are operated for the benefit of the owners or shareholders; mutual companies are operated for the benefit of their policyholders. In terms of numbers, most life insurance companies are stock companies, but the mutuals are much larger in size and hold a majority of the industry's assets.

It may seem strange to classify insurance companies as intermediaries. However, a portion of the premiums generated by life insurance companies in any time period represents saving. Companies sell several types of life insurance policies including whole or ordinary life policies and term policies. The premium for a term policy is payment for risk protection only, but the premiums for other policies contain a relatively large savings element which may be returned to the policyholder before his death. Even in the case of policies issued by property and casualty companies, the premiums paid for risk protection are received in advance of the insured losses and the subsequent disbursements. This lag creates a pool of investable funds which is used to purchase financial claims.

Because the companies' disbursements arising out of property and casualty contracts are much less predictable in terms of amounts and timing than payments required under life insurance contracts, property and casualty companies tend to invest their funds in very liquid assets while life insurance companies commonly hold less-liquid assets such as corporate equities, corporate bonds, mortgages, and longer-term government securities.

REITs

Real Estate Investment Trusts or REITs (pronounced "reets") are similar to closed-end investment companies except that the REIT invests in a portfolio of real estate ventures rather than in a portfolio of securities. Real estate investment trusts are a device to allow real estate investors with limited funds to achieve diversification and liquidity. Rather than owning a share of common stock, the investor in a REIT owns a *certificate of beneficial interest*. REITs often adopt the role of BDUs and supplement their equity funds with borrowings from banks and insurance companies. The practice of using at least some borrowed funds to finance operations is referred to as leverage. In the past, some of the more debt-heavy REITs experienced difficulties when their investment income proved insufficient to cover carrying costs associated with these debts. Real estate investment trusts are sometimes categorized as *mortgage REITs* or *equity REITs* depending upon whether the trust takes a credit or an equity position with respect to most of its investment activities. REITs began to generate a lot of attention in the mid-1960s and grew rapidly until 1973, when economic conditions weakened the real estate market and depressed the income of the trusts.

Finance companies

Finance companies traditionally have been divided into two categories—consumer finance companies and sales finance companies. This classification was based on the types of lending in which the company specialized. In recent years, this tendency to specialize has become less pronounced as each type of finance company has invaded the domain of the other. Businesses borrow from sales finance companies in order to finance accounts receivable and inventories. Often sales finance companies are established as subsidiaries of parent companies to finance the credit sales of the parent companies. Consumer finance companies, or small loan companies, typically make personal loans to individuals purchasing automobiles or other consumer durables, usually on an installment basis. Both types of finance companies obtain most of their funds by borrowing. Most of this borrowing is, in turn, by way of long-term debt, although the larger companies raise substantial amounts of funds through issuing short-term debt.

Federally sponsored intermediaries

The financial intermediaries discussed above (with the exception of government pension funds) are sometimes collectively referred to as private financial intermediaries. They are responsible for most of the intermediation that occurs in the economy. However, Congress has at times felt that certain sectors of the economy were not being adequately served by the private intermediaries, and, as a result, several agencies operated or sponsored by the federal government have been created to fill these voids. Chief among these are the following agencies:

1. Federal Land Banks which issue long-term bonds on themselves and use the proceeds to acquire farm mortgages.
2. Federal National Mortgage Association (FNMA) or "Fannie Mae" which issues debt on itself in the form of certificates of participation and uses the funds acquired to support the market for home mortgages.
3. Federal Home Loan Banks (FHLB) which regulate and advance money to the nation's savings and loan associations in an effort to aid them directly and thus indirectly aid the housing markets. The FHLB obtains funds by selling stock to and accepting deposits of member S&Ls and by issuing financial claims on themselves.
4. Government National Mortgage Association (GNMA) or "Ginnie Mae" which acquires funds from the Treasury and raises money

in the financial markets by issuing claims on itself. The proceeds are used to buy residential mortgages.

5. Banks for Cooperatives which issue short- and intermediate-term claims on themselves to raise funds which are then loaned to various types of agricultural cooperatives.

6. Federal Intermediate Credit Banks which raise funds by issuing claims on themselves and use the proceeds to make loans to institutions making intermediate-term loans to farmers.

7. Farmers Home Administration (FMHA), an agency within the Department of Agriculture that extends loans in rural areas to finance farms, homes, businesses, and community facilities. The FMHA raises the necessary funds by selling obligations on itself.

8. Export-Import Bank which is owned by the government and operated to promote the financing of foreign trade by making loans to importers and exporters and guaranteeing their obligations. It raises funds by selling certificates of participation in the loans.

9. Federal Financing Bank which coordinates the financing activities of federally owned agencies by purchasing new or outstanding debt of the agencies as well as some of the loans of the agencies. The funds to make these acquisitions are obtained by issuing its own debt or (more commonly) by borrowing from the Treasury.

The government agencies discussed above are often divided into two categories—government-sponsored agencies, and federally operated agencies. The major federally operated agencies are the Federal Financing Bank, the Export-Import Bank, the Farmer's Home Administration, and the Government National Mortgage Association. The remainder of the agencies discussed above are government sponsored. In the case of the sponsored agencies, ownership is by member organizations and the general public. While principal and interest on the securities of the federally operated agencies are guaranteed by the government, this is not the case with respect to securities issued by federally sponsored agencies.

HOW ARE COMMERCIAL BANKS DIFFERENT FROM OTHER FINANCIAL INSTITUTIONS?

The various financial intermediaries in our economy are distinguishable from each other because of differences in their sources and uses of funds. In short, the different intermediaries have tended to specialize in performing certain functions or in performing these functions in a unique manner. The chief distinguishing characteristic of commercial banks has been their ability to create a portion of

the economy's means of payment; that is, at least some of the financial claims issued by commercial banks have served as part of the
country's money supply. In earlier times, bank notes issued by the
commercial banks made up a large portion of our money supply.
After the 1860s, banks began to issue claims against themselves in
the form of demand deposits rather than bank notes.[4] Bank notes
were transferable written promises issued by a bank promising to
pay to the bearer on demand an amount of government-issued coin
or currency equal to the amount denominated on the bank note.

The fact that some bank liabilities can perform all of the functions
of money has been the key distinguishing characteristic of commercial banks. The liabilities of other intermediaries can perform some
of the functions of money, particularly the store-of-value function,
but among intermediaries, only banks have been able to issue financial claims that perform the medium-of-exchange function of money.
Recent developments, however, have diminished the uniqueness of
commercial banks in that other financial intermediaries that are
major competitors of commercial banks are now issuing financial
claims that perform the medium-of-exchange function. As noted in
Chapter 2, both NOW accounts at savings and loan associations and
share drafts at credit unions have been introduced in recent years
and are spreading in use. The general consensus in that it is only a
matter of time until NOW accounts or something similar spread to
banks and thrift institutions throughout the country since the Depository Institutions Deregulation and Monetary Control Act of 1980
allows all banks and thrifts to offer NOW accounts. These developments mean that banks have lost their most distinguishing characteristic—they are no longer the only private financial institutions
whose liabilities perform the medium-of-exchange function.

Because a sizable portion of their liabilities serve as a means of
payment, commercial banks are heavily involved in the process of
transferring money balances between economic units. The check-
clearing activities of commercial banks are an important part of this
process and will be discussed in Chapter 5 as one of the functions of
commercial banks.

WHAT ARE THE CHARACTERISTICS
OF THE MAJOR FINANCIAL INSTRUMENTS?

Financial instruments and claims handled within the financial
markets are varied in nature. Probably the most important distin-

---

[4] The National Banking Act of 1863 was instrumental in bringing about this
change (see Chapter 8).

guishing characteristic of different financial instruments is the degree of liquidity they possess. Liquidity is a multifaceted concept which has to do with the "moneyness" of an asset. Liquidity implies marketability; little cost and effort are necessary to convert liquid assets into money. The more quickly and easily an asset can be sold, the more liquid it is, other things being equal. Liquidity also implies that the price at which the asset can be sold is known with a great deal of certainty. Thus when a highly liquid asset is sold, there is a very low probability that the seller will suffer substantial loss. Financial instruments can be ranked according to the degree of liquidity they possess; the range extends from demand deposits to the common stocks of small, tightly held corporations. Table 4-2 lists the major financial claims in approximate order of liquidity. The table reflects the widely used classification of some financial instruments as money market instruments or capital market instruments, and we shall use this categorization in the following sections.

Money market instruments

As indicated earlier, money market instruments are highly liquid, short-term financial claims. The major money market instruments are Treasury bills, negotiable certificates of deposit, commercial paper, bankers' acceptances, and federal funds. The first three,

TABLE 4-2
Major financial instruments ranked in approximate order of liquidity

Demand deposits
NOW accounts at savings and loan associations and mutual savings banks
Share drafts at credit unions
Time deposits at commercial banks, mutual savings banks, and savings and loan asso-
    ciations
Credit union ownership shares
U.S. savings bonds
Money market instruments:
  U.S. Treasury bills
  Federal funds
  Commercial paper
  Negotiable certificates of deposit
  Bankers' acceptances
Capital market instruments:
  U.S. Treasury notes
  U.S. Treasury bonds
  U.S. agency securities
  Municipal bonds
  Corporate bonds
  Mortgages
  Corporate equities
    Preferred stock
    Common stock

which are largest in terms of volume, are discussed in this chapter; the others are covered in Chapter 6.

Commercial paper. Commercial paper is the unsecured promissory notes of the largest and most credit-worthy business firms. Those notes are short-term securities with maturities varying from a few days up to 270 days. Because they are unsecured, only large, well-known firms with very strong credit ratings are able to sell their paper. Commercial paper is usually sold to a dealer who in turn sells it to BSUs.

Commercial paper is purchased by all types of businesses; manufacturing firms, public utilities, insurance companies, pension funds, and other institutional investors with a temporary excess of cash are all potential buyers of commercial paper. Interest rates on commercial paper are usually slightly lower than the prime rate— the interest rate charged by banks to their best customers. Commercial paper is issued by all types of firms, but finance companies are the largest issuers. In recent years, however, more and more nonfinancial business concerns have begun to utilize commercial paper as a source of short-term financing. This trend is the result of several periods of tight money when bank loans were hard to obtain. The normally favorable rate differential between commercial paper and the prime rate has also contributed to this trend. At the same time the demand for commercial paper has increased because of a growing desire to minimize idle cash holdings.[5]

Treasury bills. Treasury bills are short-term obligations of the U.S. government and are the single most important money market instrument. Treasury bills, or "T bills," are issued in denominations of $10,000, $50,000, $100,000, $500,000, and $1 million for maturities of 91 days, 182 days, or 52 weeks. Treasury bills do not pay interest but are sold at a discount at weekly auctions. Buyers may submit either a competitive bid or a noncompetitive bid through any Federal Reserve bank or branch. Those would-be purchasers who submit the highest competitive bids earn the difference between their bid and the face value of the bills purchased. Those who enter noncompetitive bids are assured of receiving their full order of bills (up to $200,000) at a price equal to the average price of competitive bids accepted on that auction day.

In addition to the 91-day, 182-day, and 52-week bills, the Treasury occasionally offers special issues of other maturities. These are *tax anticipation bills* and *reopenings*. Tax anticipation bills are issued to mature around the times when quarterly tax payments are

---

[5] The commercial paper market was temporarily disrupted in 1970 by the bankruptcy of Penn Central which had large amounts of commercial paper outstanding.

due and thus help the Treasury obtain needed funds prior to collection of tax receipts. At the same time, firms with excess cash that will eventually be needed to pay taxes are able to earn a return until the taxes are actually due. Reopenings represent the sale of additional securities of an issue of Treasury bills currently outstanding. These reopened issues are sometimes known as *cash management bills;* maturities on these bills have been as short as nine days.

Because of their short maturity and because of a large and active secondary market, Treasury bills are regarded as perhaps the safest and most liquid of all investments. Among the major holders of Treasury bills are commercial banks, the Federal Reserve System, nonfinancial corporations, U.S. government investment accounts, state and local governments, mutual savings banks, insurance companies, and savings and loan associations.

Negotiable certificates of deposit. Negotiable Certificates of Deposit (CDs) were first issued in 1961 and since have become a major money market instrument. The primary issuers of negotiable CDs are the very large banks, and the primary purchasers are business corporations. The issuing bank receives a deposit and in return issues a certificate that is negotiable and entitles the owner to receive the deposit and any accumulated interest at the time of maturity. These CDs are usually issued in denominations of $100,000 and up, although some are issued for $25,000. An active secondary market has contributed to the growth of this instrument. Negotiable CDs vary in maturity, but most are issued to mature in from one to four months. The rates paid on CDs depend on conditions in the money market at the time they are issued. Until 1974 the rates that banks could pay for these CDs were limited by the Federal Reserve System. This limitation was suspended in 1973, and now rates are determined by market forces. While the primary purchasers of CDs are corporate treasurers who want to maximize the returns on temporarily idle funds, other purchasers include states and political subdivisions, foreign governments, individuals, and institutional investors.

Capital market instruments

Less-liquid, longer-term financial instruments are generally classified as capital market instruments. There are three major types of capital market instruments in the U.S. financial system. These major types can be further subclassified, but our emphasis here will be on the main features of common stocks, preferred stocks, and debt instruments.

Common stocks. Common stocks are different from the financial claims previously discussed in that they represent evidence of ownership rather than of creditor interest. Common stocks are issued by every business corporation, and shares of stock of the larger corporations are actively traded on an organized stock exchange or in the over-the-counter market. In general, common stocks are the most risky of financial instruments; however, the shares of some companies are relatively safe investments in that they can easily and quickly be sold at prices that are relatively stable. Although common stocks sometimes possess a par value, they do not have set denominations as debt instruments do. Also unlike debt instruments, common stocks do not have a fixed maturity date. The yields on common stocks vary greatly between issues and over time. The major holders of common stocks are individuals, investment companies, nonfinancial corporations, and life insurance companies. Because of the risk generally associated with common stocks, legal restrictions normally prohibit banks from holding them. Banks may occasionally acquire common stock that was pledged as collateral on defaulted loans. These acquisitions are not typical, however, and stock so acquired is usually disposed of quickly.

Preferred stocks.   These hybrid securities possess some features of debt instruments and some features of common stocks. Like common stocks, preferred stocks pay dividends rather than interest; these dividends are not a legal obligation of the issuing company, and failure to pay them does not constitute default. Nevertheless, companies view preferred dividends as a fixed obligation since common stockholders cannot receive any dividends until the preferred stockholders receive theirs (including, in the case of cumulative preferred stock, all unpaid past dividends). Like common stock, preferred stock does not carry a stated maturity date. The major types of investors who purchase preferred stock include individuals, insurance companies, investment companies, nonfinancial corporations, and pension funds. As with common stock, banks generally are prohibited from owning preferred stock due to the risk involved.

Preferred stocks are not a widely used form of financing under ordinary circumstances because for most companies preferred dividend payments, unlike the interest on bonds, are not a tax-deductible expense. Thus bonds have a lower after-tax cost which gives them a strong competitive edge over preferred stocks. Most new issues of preferred stock are by public utility firms or by financially troubled firms undergoing reorganization. The disadvantages of preferred stock are evidenced by the fact that in 1976 corporations raised over $42 billion by issuing bonds and less than $4 billion by issuing preferred stock.

Debt instruments.   Capital market debt instruments may be classified by type or by issuer. Corporations issue several types of debt claims on themselves. Corporate bonds are the primary long-term debt instrument issued by corporations, and these instruments may be further classified according to collateral as secured or unsecured. Secured bonds are referred to as mortgage bonds if they are secured by real estate, collateral trust bonds if they are secured by marketable securities held in trust, or equipment trust certificates if the ultimate security is some form of easily transferable equipment such as railroad rolling stock or aircraft. Unsecured bonds are called *debentures*. Corporate bonds are usually issued in $1,000 denominations with different issues having different maturities. In recent years bonds have been much more important than stock as a means of raising funds for corporations. Corporate bonds vary greatly in risk; some are very safe, but as a class, they are generally regarded as much less safe than the securities issued by the federal government and its agencies. Because of this risk, legal and traditional restraints have caused banks to avoid holding these securities.

The federal government is the largest participant in U.S. financial markets. Not only does the Treasury raise large amounts of funds in the money market by issuing Treasury bills, it also raises large amounts of funds in the capital market by issuing Treasury bonds and Treasury notes. U.S. Treasury bonds are long-term debt obligations with maturities as long as 40 years. Treasury obligations with maturities in the range of 1 to 7 years are called *Treasury notes* to distinguish them from the longer-term issues. In common usage, the term bond is often applied to both types.

State and local governments raise large amounts of funds in the capital markets. The securities issued by these governments are referred to as *municipals* and have one feature that distinguishes them from the securities of other issuers. This distinguishing feature is that interest earned by holders of these securities is exempt from the federal income tax. (In some cases, municipals are also exempt from state income tax in the state of issue.) U.S. Treasury securities are exempt only from state income taxes. Banks hold large amounts of municipals in their portfolios because of these tax advantages.

Included in the category of municipal securities are the issues of various semigovernmental units such as port authorities, airport authorities, industrial development authorities, separate school districts, and water and sewer associations. These units are the creation of some state or local government which seldom assumes responsibility for the securities issued by these authorities. Securities that are dependent for servicing upon revenues generated by some particular activity or activities and cannot draw upon general tax collections are known as revenue bonds. On the other hand, bonds that may draw upon the full taxing power of the issuer are known as General

Obligation (GO) or full faith and credit bonds. In short, in the use of general obligation bonds, the issuer's promise to pay principal and interest is not qualified or limited in any way.

In addition to those capital market securities discussed above, the issues of federally operated or sponsored government agencies are becoming increasingly important in the capital markets. The most important of these agencies were discussed in the previous section; collectively they had outstanding securities totaling over $160 billion at the end of November 1979. These securities are regarded almost as highly as Treasury securities, and many banks hold significant amounts of them in their investment portfolios.

WHAT ARE THE FUNCTIONS OF INTEREST RATES IN OUR FINANCIAL SYSTEM?

Interest rates perform a vital function in the monetary economy; they act much like a thermostat by regulating the flows of funds and financial claims between budget deficit units and budget surplus units. In this section we introduce some of the general features of interest rates: interest is defined; a distinction is made between observed market rates of interest on particular financial claims and the pure rental payment for the use of funds; the forces that determine interest rates are introduced; and the pricing function of interest rates in a monetary economy is discussed.

From the standpoint of the BDU, interest is the price paid for credit or the price paid for the use of money; hence, interest can be considered as a rental payment for the services of money over some time period. On the other hand, the price of money is the amount of goods or services that must be given up to obtain a unit of money. Thus interest should not be thought of as the price of money but as a rental payment for the use of money. We can most meaningfully take into account the characteristics of interest by expressing it as a rate—the amount of money paid per dollar of credit used per period of time.

The amount of interest on different types of financial claims varies greatly because of risk and other differences. The interest rate paid by a BDU is obviously the rate received by the BSU. Thus just as interest can be viewed as the payment by the BDU for the use of money, it may also be viewed as the return to the BSU for holding financial claims in lieu of money. In the analysis that follows the student will find it useful to keep in mind that the suppliers of financial claims (BDUs) are the demanders of loanable funds (credit), and the demanders of financial claims (BSUs) are suppliers of loanable funds (credit).

Consider for a moment the interest rate on a particular type of financial claim—commercial paper. Recall that commercial paper is a very short-term debt instrument issued by the largest and most credit-worthy business firms. What rate of interest will these firms have to pay in order to induce BSUs to hold commercial paper? The exact rate will depend on the supply and demand conditions for commercial paper at the time of issue. At any given time, BSUs are willing to supply various amounts of loanable funds to the commercial paper market depending upon such factors as their income levels, expectations, rates of return that can be earned on other financial assets, the perceived risk associated with commercial paper and other financial claims, and the current interest rate or yield that they can earn on the commercial paper. The effects of these factors on the funds that BSUs are willing to invest in commercial paper can be captured in the concept of the supply function for loanable funds available in the commercial paper market. A loanable funds supply function can be presented as an equation, a schedule, or a graph; in Figure 4–5 it is presented as the S curve. Likewise, we can construct a demand schedule for loanable funds for BDUs who issue commercial paper. This function is represented by the D curve in Figure 4–5. The demand function will reflect all the influences on BDUs that cause them to consider issuing various amounts of commercial paper. Expectations regarding future profit opportunities, current

FIGURE 4–5
Illustration of interest rate determination in the commercial paper market

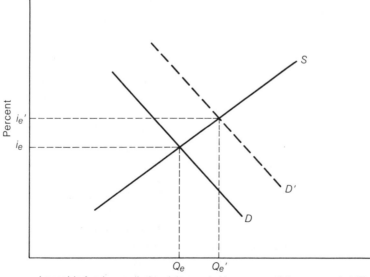

Loanable funds supplied and demanded in commercial paper market ($)

income and expenditure plans, rates on alternative financial claims, the commercial paper rate, and other factors all play a role.

We are particularly interested in the effect of interest rates on commercial paper. Conventional demand-supply analysis would lead us to expect that the higher (lower) the commercial paper rate, the less (more) the amount of loanable funds demanded by BDUs, other things being equal; similarly the higher (lower) the commercial paper rate, the more (less) loanable funds supplied by BSUs. All of the forces affecting both the demand for and supply of loanable funds in the commercial paper market interact to determine the locations of the supply and demand curves and the rate of interest on commercial paper.

The relationships between the interest rate and quantities of loanable funds supplied and demanded in the commercial paper market (given constant levels of the other variables that affect the supply and demand functions) are illustrated in Figure 4-5. If other factors such as income levels change, the curves would shift. The interest rate, i_e, at which the amount of loanable funds demanded is equal to the amount supplied will be established as the equilibrium rate; at this rate the amount of loanable funds and the value of commercial paper traded will be equal to Q_e.

Since other financial claims are different from commercial paper in certain respects—length to maturity, risk of default, degree of liquidity, etc.—their supply and demand functions will differ from those of commercial paper, and their interest rates will also be different from the rate on commercial paper to the extent necessary to adjust for the different characteristics of the other claims that may be considered more or less desirable from the standpoint of the BSUs and BDUs. While rates on different financial claims may vary, they are not independent. The presence of arbitrage in the financial markets causes the yields on particular financial assets to enter into the supply and demand functions for other financial assets. Arbitrage is the process of purchasing a good in one market and selling it in another market in order to profit by a price differential in the two markets. The good is purchased in the market with the lower price, adding to demand pressure in that market and eventually causing an upward movement in the price. The good is then sold in the market with the higher price thereby increasing supply and exerting downward pressure on prices in that market. Thus arbitrage assures that the price of a given item must be the same in all markets except for a differential reflecting the cost of arbitrage.

It is sometimes useful to view the current market interest rate on a particular financial claim as being made up of several components. This is illustrated in Figure 4-6 where the rate of interest is decomposed into a pure rental payment for the use of money plus various

FIGURE 4–6
**Composition of the interest rate
on a particular financial claim**

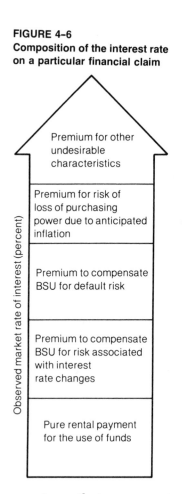

premiums that compensate the BSU for risks associated with that claim. The pure rental payment for money is the same for all claims, but the risk premiums will vary with the characteristics of the claim. For instance, the greater the possibility that the issuer will be unable to pay principle and interest, the greater the default risk and the larger the required annual yield. Thus municipal revenue bonds will have higher yields than U.S. Treasury bills because of the existence of a premium for default risk.

If investors expect inflation, interest rates will contain an inflation premium as compensation for the expected loss of purchasing power. In recognition of the effects of inflation on interest rates, economists distinguish between *real* rates of interest and *nominal* rates of interest. Nominal rates are the observed market rates with no adjustment for the effects of inflation, while real rates are the nominal rates minus the rate of inflation. Obviously, inflation causes real rates to be less than nominal rates.

Other undesirable characteristics may lead to higher interest rates in the form of various premiums. The possibility of fluctuations in the market value of a financial claim due to interest rate changes (interest rate risk), the lack of liquidity, and excessive administrative costs are some of the other factors that affect interest rates.

The above analysis implies that interest rates determine the actual quantities of loanable funds and the amounts of various types of financial claims that will be traded in the financial markets. Thus the primary function of interest rates is to assure that the quantities of loanable funds supplied match the quantities demanded. Such an adjustment mechanism is necessary if the financial sector of the economy is to operate smoothly. Interest rates are therefore like all prices in that they perform a rationing function which serves to allocate a limited supply of credit among the many competing demands for it throughout the economy.

For example, suppose that optimism about profit opportunities causes BDUs in the form of business firms to increase the demand for loanable funds (shift the demand curve to D' in Figure 4–5). Following this increase in demand, a shortage of loanable funds will exist as long as interest rates remain the same (at i_e in Figure 4–5). But the shortfall of quantity supplied relative to quantity demanded will begin to generate higher interest rates as suppliers take advantage of the increased demand for funds. As interest rates rise, some BDUs will no longer find it profitable to borrow and will be forced from the market, while at the same time, lenders (BSUs) will be induced to offer more funds to take advantage of the higher rates. When interest rates have risen (to i_e'), the shortage of loanable funds will disappear, and a greater quantity of funds will be exchanged.

SUMMARY

In this chapter we have looked at the nature and role of the financial sector of the monetary economy. The financial sector allows budget surplus units to convert their temporarily idle nonearning funds into interest-earning financial claims issued by budget deficit units or financial intermediaries. As a result the economy achieves a more efficient utilization of its resources. The process of intermediation greatly enhances the efficiency of the financial system by reducing risk and search costs.

The financial system of the United States is characterized by a variety of financial claims. To some extent this variety reflects specialization by different financial intermediaries. A summary of the major financial claims used and held by different intermediaries is presented in Table 4–3.

TABLE 4-3
Primary sources and uses of funds for major financial intermediaries in the United States

Financial claim	Commercial banks	Savings and loan associations	Credit unions	Investment companies	Finance companies	Mutual savings banks	Insurance companies	Pension funds
Demand deposits	Major source							
NOW accounts	Source	Source						
Share draft accounts			Source					
Time and savings deposits*	Major source	Major source	Major source			Major source		
U.S. Treasury securities	Major use	Use	Use			Use	Use	Use
Commercial paper	Use				Major source		Use	
Corporate bonds				Use	Source	Major use	Major use	Major use
Corporate equities				Major source and use			Major use	Major use
Municipal bonds	Major use					Use	Use	
Consumer loans	Major use		Major use		Major use			
Business loans	Major use				Major use		Use	
Mortgage loans	Use	Major use	Use			Major use	Major use	

* Other than NOW accounts and share draft accounts.

Interest rates are the regulating mechanism in the financial system. They act to adjust the flows of new financial claims being issued by BDUs and the amount of loanable funds supplied to the financial markets by BSUs. Financial claims may be of two types: primary claims issued by budget deficit units and secondary claims issued by financial intermediaries. Both types of financial claims vary greatly in maturity, risk, and other features. These differences lead to variations in interest rates paid to holders of the different types of financial claims.

REVIEW QUESTIONS

1. Explain how financial intermediaries act as both a budget surplus unit and a budget deficit unit.
2. Distinguish between capital markets, money markets, primary markets, and secondary markets.
3. Explain how financial intermediaries reduce risk.
4. Using a supply and demand graph for loanable funds, explain what would happen to commercial paper rates given the occurrence of each of the following events:
    a. Incomes rise sharply.
    b. Business borrowing for new investment declines sharply out of fear of a recession.
    c. Due to heavy borrowing by the federal government, interest rates on government securities rise sharply.
    d. Both borrowers and lenders expect a sharp increase in the rate of inflation.
5. From a recent *Wall Street Journal*, compare interest rates on commercial paper, CDs, Treasury bills, 5-year corporate bonds, 30-year U.S. Treasury securities, and a recent issue of municipal securities. Try to account for the differences.
6. Occasionally a writer will refer to "the" interest rate. Since there are many different interest rates, what does reference to "the" interest rate mean?

SUGGESTIONS FOR ADDITIONAL READING

American Council of Life Insurance. *Life Insurance Fact Book.* Washington, D.C.: American Council of Life Insurance, annual.

Chandler, Lester V. *The Monetary-Financial System.* New York: Harper & Row, 1979.

Harless, Doris E. *Nonbank Financial Institutions.* Richmond, Va.: Federal Reserve Bank of Richmond, 1975.

Investment Company Institute. *Mutual Fund Fact Book.* Washington, D.C.: Investment Company Institute, annual.

Monhollon, Jimmie R., and Picou, Glenn. *Instruments of the Money Market.* Richmond, Va.: Federal Reserve Bank of Richmond, 1974.

Smith, Paul F. *Money and Financial Intermediation.* Englewood Cliffs, N.J.: Prentice-Hall, Inc., 1978.

U.S. Savings and Loan League. *Savings and Loan Fact Book.* Chicago: U.S. Savings and Loan League, annual.

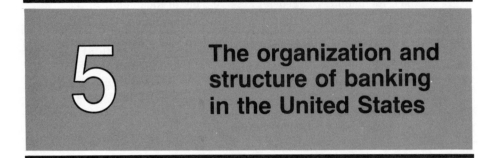

5

The organization and structure of banking in the United States

WARM-UP: *Outline and questions to consider as you read*

What are the requirements for opening a new bank?
    Capital requirements.
    Future earnings prospects.
    Convenience and needs of the community.
    Management of the proposed new bank.
    Opposition to new banks.
What forms of bank organization operate in the
  United States today?
    Branch banking.
    Bank holding companies.
    Chain banking.
Who regulates banks and why?
    The Federal Reserve System.
    The Comptroller of the Currency.
    Federal Deposit Insurance Corporation.
What are the primary categories of bank regulation?
    Control over entry.
    Capital requirements.
    Control over lending and investing activities.
    Reserve requirements.
    Geographic restrictions on operations.
    Limitations on merger and holding company
      activities.
    Limitations on prices paid and charged.

NEW TERMS

Bank holding company: a corporation that owns or controls one or more banks; bank holding companies are generally classified as one-bank holding companies or multibank holding companies depending on whether or not they control one or more than one bank.

Bank Holding Company Act of 1956: the federal law that requires bank holding companies to register with the Federal Reserve and obtain approval of new holding company formations; the act was amended in 1970 to include one-bank holding companies.

Bank Merger Act of 1960: the federal law requiring the regulatory authorities to assess both anticompetitive effects of proposed mergers and banking factors before ruling on merger requests.

Bank run: a situation in which a large proportion of a bank's depositors converge on the bank to withdraw their deposits.

Branch bank: a bank operating more than one office.

Chain banking: indirect linking of banks through common ownership of the stock by one or a few individuals.

Comptroller of the Currency: federal agency with chartering and supervisory authority over national banks.

Dual banking system: term applied to the U.S. banking system in which state-chartered banks and nationally chartered banks operate side by side.

Federal Deposit Insurance Corporation (FDIC): the federal agency that insures bank deposits.

Unit bank: a bank operating only one office.

The organization and structure of the American banking industry reflects the interaction of both economic and legal forces. There has been some dissatisfaction with the results created by unconstrained economic forces, and as a consequence of this dissatisfaction, the power of legal forces has been used to shape and alter the structure of the industry. In this chapter, we shall look first at some of the legal requirements that must be met to enter the banking business and then at the organizational forms that banking firms can and do take. The major bank regulatory authorities and their primary functions are introduced, and the major types of restrictions imposed by these authorities are noted. The structure of the banking industry reflects the organizational form taken by banks, the number and relative size of banks within given markets, and any linkages among banks that might affect competition. Structure is considered important because economic theory leads us to believe that the market structure of an industry affects the performance of firms in that industry.

WHAT ARE THE REQUIREMENTS FOR OPENING A NEW BANK?

Since the founding of the Republic, government has exercised considerable control over entry into the banking industry. In most industries a new firm can be started if the owners have access to adequate financing, managerial talent, and a belief in the economic feasibility of the new venture. The owners will often have to pay a small license fee to some government, but if those owners are competent and willing to risk their capital, government approval is usually a formality. In the case of those who would form a new banking firm, however, government permission is a crucial and formidable barrier that must be overcome.

Most businesses may choose from several organizational forms— single proprietorship, partnership, corporation, or cooperative. Commercial banks, though, must choose the corporate form of organization. Therefore, before a new bank can begin operation, it must have a corporate charter—a formal written approval to operate—issued to it by either the federal government or the government of the state in which it will be located. Thus there are two sources of bank charters—the states and the federal government. The ability of banks to acquire state or federal charters has led the American banking system to be referred to as a dual banking system.[1]

The existence of a dual banking system means that organizers of a new bank must choose the type of charter they will seek, which in turn determines the regulatory authorities to whom they will be responsible. A bank is known as a national bank if it obtains its charter by applying to and being approved by the Comptroller of the Currency—an agency within the U.S. Treasury Department charged with regulatory powers over national banks. On the other hand, a bank obtaining a state charter is referred to as a state bank. The name of the state agency issuing the charter varies from state to state as do the requirements that must be met before the charter is issued. Since the requirements for state charters are not uniform, the emphasis here will be on the requirements for a national bank charter.

National bank charter requirements are generally more stringent than state charter requirements; however, bank organizers have not been able to escape federal chartering regulations simply by obtaining a state charter. Almost all new banks wish to have their deposits insured by the Federal Deposit Insurance Corporation (FDIC)—the federal agency that insures bank deposits. FDIC insurance is necessary if the new bank is to compete effectively with established banks for deposit dollars. However, before the new bank can obtain federal

---

[1] The reader is referred to Chapter 8 for a summary of the history of dual regulation of commercial banking in this country.

deposit insurance, it must satisfy the FDIC that it meets requirements set down by that agency, and these conditions, as set forth in the Banking Act of 1935, parallel those for obtaining a national charter. Thus the requirements for a national bank charter are quite representative of the factors that must be considered in organizing any new bank. *because they wish to have deposit insurance*

The organizers of a new national bank must satisfy the regulatory authorities that certain minimum chartering requirements are met. For their part, the authorities supply the organizers with instructions and forms for filing the charter application. The information supplied when the application is filed, along with findings of the regulatory authority's own investigation, form the basis for the decision that the requisites for a charter are or are not met. The organizers will often seek the aid of a consultant in finance or economics who will conduct a feasibility study. This study will supplement information specifically requested by the application and will help the organizers and the Comptroller assess the need for a new bank. Some of the major requirements that must be met before a new charter will be granted are discussed below.

Capital requirements

The organizers of the new bank must satisfy the regulatory authorities that the bank will be adequately capitalized. As discussed in more detail in the following chapter, capital helps protect the bank's depositors from losses. Adequate capital is considered particularly important for a new bank which may experience losses in the initial years of operation. Minimum capital requirements for national banks vary with the size of the city in which the bank is located. For places with populations 6,000 and under, the minimum capital required by law is $50,000; if the population is from 6,000 to 50,000, the minimum capital required is $100,000; and if the population exceeds 50,000, minimum capital requirements are $200,000. These requirements were set by statute many years ago, and today the Comptroller can, and virtually always does, require substantially larger amounts of capital. The allocation of a minimum proportion of the new bank's capital into paid-in surplus and paid-in undivided profits is also required.

Future earnings prospects

Prior to deposit insurance, the consequence of a bank's failure constituted a considerable hardship on its depositors. Consequently, the need to prevent bank failures has always been listed as one of the factors justifying strict government control over the formation of new banks. Therefore, the regulatory authorities feel that the organizers of a new bank must establish that the future earnings prospects of the bank are favorable. To do this the organizers are required to supply projections of deposits, loans, earnings, and expenses over the first three years of the new bank's life. These projections must be supported by other economic data pertaining to the market area the bank will serve as well as the competition it will face from other banks and from nonbank financial institutions such as savings and loan associations, mutual savings banks, and credit unions. The authorities also require data on the past banking history of the area and particularly on any bank failures that have occurred there. As noted earlier, the organizers usually obtain the services of a consultant to provide them with an economic feasibility study of the proposed new bank.

Convenience and needs of the community

The regulatory authorities are required by law to assess how well the new bank would serve "the convenience and needs of the community." Not only does this phrase relate to how the public would benefit from the new bank, but it has come to encompass how existing banks would be affected by competition from the new bank. If the new bank can succeed only at the expense of established banks, the area may be no better off with the new bank. Thus the authorities try to determine if there is legitimate need for additional banking services in the market the new bank proposes to enter. Authorities also seek answers to such questions as: Are the present offices of existing banks inconvenient to a significant segment of the banking public? Have existing banks failed to offer all of the services that the public normally enjoys from banks? Are the loan rates and service charges of existing banks higher than would exist if more competition were introduced into that banking market? Does the economic growth of the area indicate that additional banking services will be required in the future? The answers to these and similar questions help the authorities determine whether or not the convenience and needs of the community would be served by the proposed new bank.

Management of the proposed new bank

Usually the organizers of a new bank serve as its board of directors. The success of the new bank and how well it serves the community are to a large extent determined by this group. Thus the regulatory authorities are interested in the business ability and the moral character of the organizers. Information covering their business and financial background, their place of residence, and any record of illegal conduct must be submitted as part of the application. If some or most of the organizers reside outside the area the proposed new bank would serve, the authorities may interpret this as indicative of a lack of familiarity with and concern for the community's banking needs. Such a conclusion would greatly jeopardize the organizers' chances of getting a charter. Needless to say, if one or more of the organizers had criminal records or were under indictment, the charter application would almost certainly be rejected. There are also minimum stock ownership requirements for bank directors; hence, the personal financial condition of the organizers should indicate an ability to purchase a substantial number of shares of the new bank's stock. The financial histories of the organizers should reflect a record of success in managing their personal financial affairs.

Opposition to new banks

Even if the organizers of a new bank think they can meet all the formal requirements for a charter, they are still likely to find that receiving a charter is no mere formality. The regulatory authorities must give public notice of the application, and anyone opposed to the granting of the charter has the right, within a limited time period, to protest the granting of the charter and register the reasons for opposing it. Not surprisingly, established banks in the community where the proposed new bank would be located often go to considerable trouble and expense to try to prove that the charter application should be denied. Often a hearing is held in which the established banks present their case that a new bank is not needed and might even be harmful. If the existing banks fail to convince the authorities not to issue the charter, they sometimes go a step further and appeal the decision in the courts. Even when all of the chartering requirements are met, it can be several years before the new bank can actually begin operations.

The fact that new bank charters are often vigorously opposed has led to charges of politics and discrimination with respect to decisions by the regulatory authorities at both the state and national levels. The existence of a dual source of charters has been cited as protection against arbitrary decisions on charter applications, and many observers feel that this protection alone justifies the continued existence of the dual chartering system.

WHAT FORMS OF BANK ORGANIZATION
OPERATE IN THE UNITED STATES TODAY?

At the beginning of 1978, there were over 14,700 commercial banks in the United States. Most of these (10,066, or about two thirds) were state banks. Most were also unit banks—that is, they operated only one office. Virtually all these banks were insured by the FDIC, but only about 39 percent were members of the Federal Reserve System. Figure 5–1 presents a breakdown of the number and status of banks in the United States.

While the number of banks in the country has remained relatively stable in recent years, this has not always been the case. As shown in Table 5–1, the number of banks in the United States reached a peak in 1920; in that year there were over 30,000 banks in operation. A sharp decline in the number of banks began at that time and continued until the mid-1930s. This decline in banks is often attributed completely to the Great Depression, but as Figure 5–2 indicates, a sharp decline was underway prior to 1929. Between 1921 and 1929 the number of banks in operation dropped by over 5,000, and from

FIGURE 5–1
Number of commercial banks in the United States by type and affiliation, January 1, 1978

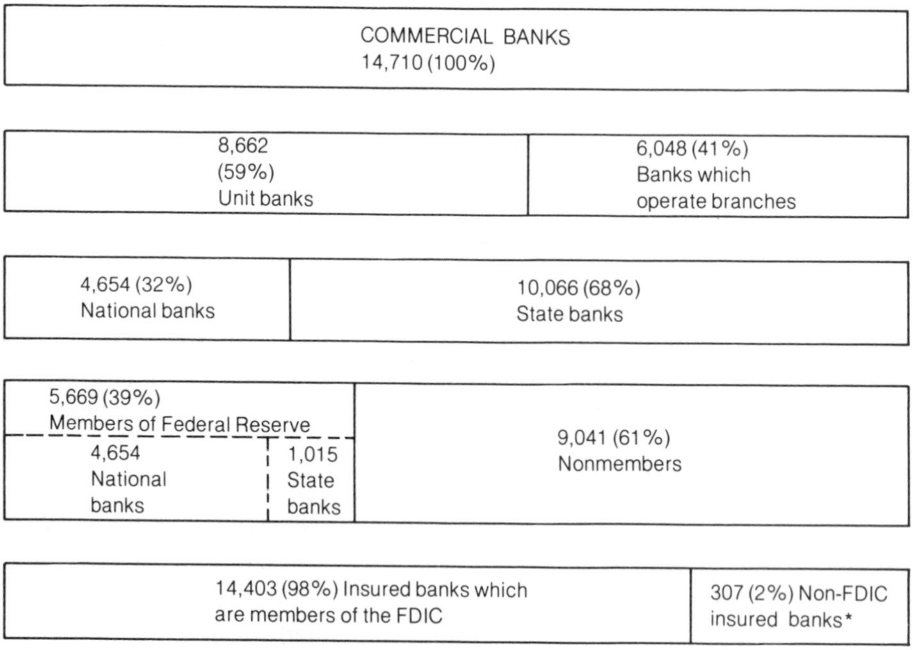

COMMERCIAL BANKS 14,710 (100%)	
8,662 (59%) Unit banks	6,048 (41%) Banks which operate branches
4,654 (32%) National banks	10,066 (68%) State banks
5,669 (39%) Members of Federal Reserve — 4,654 National banks / 1,015 State banks	9,041 (61%) Nonmembers
14,403 (98%) Insured banks which are members of the FDIC	307 (2%) Non-FDIC insured banks*

* Includes 85 nondeposit trust companies.
Source: Federal Deposit Insurance Corporation, *Annual Report*.

TABLE 5-1
Commercial banking offices by type of bank

			Total number		Total banking offices	
Year	Unit banks	Branch banks	Banks	Branches	Number	Percent unit banks
1900	12,340	87	12,427	119	12,546	98.4
1905	17,956	196	18,152	350	18,502	97.0
1910	24,222	292	24,514	548	25,062	96.6
1915	26,993	397	27,390	785	28,175	95.8
1920	26,761	530	30,291	1,281	31,572	94.3
1925	27,722	720	28,442	2,525	30,967	89.5
1930	22,928	751	23,679	3,522	27,201	84.3
1935	14,666	822	15,488	3,156	18,644	78.7
1940	13,575	959	14,534	3,531	18,065	75.1
1945	13,110	1,016	14,126	3,723	17,849	73.4
1950	12,905	1,241	14,146	4,721	18,867	68.4
1955	12,121	1,659	13,780	6,710	20,490	59.2
1960	11,143	2,329	13,472	10,216	23,688	47.0
1965	10,664	3,140	13,804	15,486	29,290	36.4
1970	9,694	3,994	13,688	21,424	35,112	27.6
1975	9,111	5,521	14,632	29,795	44,427	20.5
1977	8,662	6,048	14,710	32,890	47,600	18.2

Sources: Gerald C. Fisher and Carter H. Golembe, "The Branch Banking Provisions of The McFadden Act as Amended: Their Rationale and Rationality," *Compendium of Issues Relating to Branching by Financial Institutions,* Subcommittee on Financial Institutions of the Committee on Banking, Housing, and Urban Affairs of the United States Senate (Washington, D.C.: Government Printing Office, 1976), p. 41; and *Annual Report of The Federal Deposit Insurance Corporation,* 1977, p. 136.

FIGURE 5-2
Commercial banks in the United States, number by class

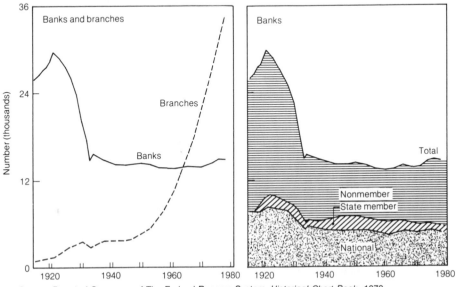

Source: Board of Governors of The Federal Reserve System, *Historical Chart Book,* 1979.

1930 to 1933 the number of banks dropped by 10,763. The earlier decline was largely the result of depressed economic conditions in the agricultural areas of the country; the resulting shift in population from rural to urban areas reduced the number of banks needed. The bank failures of the early 30s were associated with the depressed economic conditions throughout the country. Then as now, banks disappeared for two reasons—failure and absorption by another bank; however, the two reasons were not always independent. During the period 1920–33, some weak banks avoided failure by merging with stronger banks. Hence, the decline in banking facilities was less drastic than the decline in the number of separate banks. Since 1935 there has not been a significant upward or downward trend in the number of banks.

Branch banking

Up until 1920, only a handful of banks operated more than one office—that is, were what is known as branch banks. Interest in the opening of branches began to increase after California allowed statewide branching in 1909. The McFadden Act of 1927, as modified in 1933, permitted national banks to operate branches in accordance with state laws. The act was not the result of probranching sentiment in Congress but represented a desire to strengthen national banks by allowing them to compete equally with state banks in the establishment of branches.

The McFadden Act along with the modifications resulting from the Banking Act of 1933 remains the basis of federal control over branching. These acts give national banks whatever branching rights are granted by the state in which the bank is located. While interest in and controversy over branching increased during the 1930s, the real surge in branching did not come until after World War II. In 1945, the total number of branch offices was 3,723 (see Table 5–1). In the next ten years, the number of branches almost doubled; and, by 1975, the number of branches was approaching 30,000. At the end of 1977, there were almost 32,900 branches operating in the United States. Despite the tremendous growth in branching activity, a number of states still restrict branch banking in various ways: some restrictions are geographic; others are in terms of number of offices; and still others are in terms of functions that can be performed. Geographic restrictions by the various states are given in Table 5–2.

From the 1920s to the present, the debate over branch banking has been heated. Even today branching remains a controversial and unsettled issue, and both the probranching and the antibranching

TABLE 5–2
Geographic restrictions on branching by states

Statewide branching permitted

Alaska		Oregon
Arizona	Maine	Rhode Island
California	Maryland	South Carolina
Connecticut	Nevada	South Dakota
Delaware	New Jersey	Utah
Hawaii	New York	Vermont
Idaho	North Carolina	Virginia
Louisiana		Washington

Branching permitted within limited geographic areas

Alabama	Kentucky	New Mexico
Arkansas	Louisiana	Ohio
Florida	Massachusetts	Pennsylvania
Georgia	Michigan	Tennessee
Indiana	Mississippi	Wisconsin
Iowa	New Hampshire	

Branch banking prohibited*

Colorado	Missouri	Oklahoma
Illinois	Montana	Texas
Kansas	Nebraska	West Virginia
Minnesota	North Dakota	Wyoming

  * Some of these states allow varying degrees of off-premise facilities that perform at least some branching functions.
  Source: American Bankers Association.

forces have marshaled evidence to support their positions. Proponents of removal of branching restrictions argue that branching results in a safer, more stable network of banks. Indeed, branching does permit greater geographic diversification within a bank's loan portfolio which reduces the riskiness of that portfolio. Also, funds may be shifted from branch to branch to meet local withdrawal needs. Furthermore, relative deposit variability may be less in a system of branches than it would for particular unit banks. Finally, proponents of branching argue that it results in a greater range of banking services, more diversified facilities, and lower costs to bank customers.

Opponents of branching argue that unit banks are more sensitive to local community needs and that a branch system would drain loanable funds from small towns and use these funds in other areas. They argue that more permissive branching would allow concentration of economic power in the hands of a few large branch banks. Because of the decrease in competition that would occur, the price of bank services would be higher even if branch systems were more efficient than independent unit banks. Conclusive evidence in support of claims by either side does not exist, but most researchers in this area believe that some degree of branching is beneficial.[2]

Bank holding companies

A bank holding company is a corporation that owns or controls one or more banks. Typically, bank holding companies are classified as either one-bank holding companies or multibank holding companies. As the names imply, multibank holding companies control two or more banks, whereas one-bank holding companies control only one bank. By far the majority of holding companies are of the one-bank variety. Like all holding companies, bank holding companies may be further classified as conglomerates or congenerics. The company would be classified as a conglomerate if its affiliates engaged in several unrelated activities or as a congeneric if its affiliates engaged in the same or very similar activities. Thus a holding company which owned only commercial banks would be a congeneric.

The bank holding company form of organization has become increasingly popular in this country. Initially most bank holding companies were of the multibank variety, but in the 1960s a wave of one-bank holding company formations swept the country. In 1955 there were 117 one-bank holding companies with deposits of $11.6 billion, or less than 2 percent of all bank deposits. In 1975 the number of one-bank holding companies had grown to over 1,400, and they held almost 30 percent of all bank deposits. The turn to one-bank holding companies resulted from restrictions imposed by the Bank Holding Company Act of 1956 which required Federal Reserve Board registration and approval of new multibank holding companies and of acquisitions of additional banks by existing holding companies. The act also limited activities in which registered holding companies could engage. Activities outside the banking business were essentially prohibited, and the act required that the Federal Reserve Board consider the effects of new holding company acquisitions on competition, the soundness of the banking system, and the convenience and needs of the communities involved. It

---

[2] For more detail, consult the following works: Gary C. Gilbert and William A. Longbrake, "The Effects of Branching by Financial Institutions on Competition, Productive Efficiency, and Stability: An Examination of the Evidence," *Journal of Bank Research*, vol. 4, no. 3 (Autumn 1973), and vol. 4, no. 4 (Winter 1974); and Jack M. Guttentag, "Branch Banking: A Summary of the Issues and the Evidence," *Compendium of Issues Relating to Branching by Financial Institutions*, prepared by the Subcommittee on Financial Institutions of the Committee on Banking, Housing, and Urban Affairs, U.S. Senate (Washington, D.C.: U.S. Government Printing Office, October 1976), pp. 99–112.

turned out that the 1956 Holding Company Act had a major loophole—it did not apply to one-bank holding companies. This loophole was a key factor leading to the tremendous growth of one-bank holding companies formed in the 1960s.

A major reason for the formation of the multibank holding companies was a desire to avoid restrictions on bank branching activities. With the holding company device, banks could put together organizations that could escape branching restrictions as well as engage in activities outside the normal realm of banking. Because of their activities in the late 1920s, Congress acted in 1933 to restrict bank holding company formations by forcing the holding company banks to cut their ties with affiliates in the securities industry. The speculative excesses in our securities markets in the 1920s were believed to have been partially caused by these ties. Interest in holding company formation by banks waned for a while but gradually increased again, and by the 1950s there was much concern over the potential concentration of financial power that could result from unchecked holding company activity. The Bank Holding Company Act of 1956 was passed in an effort to prevent this growing concentration of power in the financial sector and to limit existing bank holding company activities to the traditional functions of banking.

With the 1956 Bank Holding Company Act, holding company growth was forced to take on new motives and a new method. The act's loophole—the one-bank holding company—offered banks no chance to escape geographic branching limitations but did provide them an opportunity to expand into many nonbanking activities. The holding company device also offered other advantages. It proved particularly useful as a means of generating funds for banks that were scrambling for dollars during the tight money periods of the latter 1960s. The holding company could issue commercial paper, stocks, or bonds by offering returns above those that banks could pay for deposits, and the funds so acquired could then be channelled into subsidiary banks. These funds were not subject to reserve requirements or deposit insurance premiums and sometimes could be obtained at a lower cost than going rates on bank CDs.

The 1970 amendments to the Bank Holding Company Act of 1956 brought one-bank holding company formations and activities under the control of the Federal Reserve. The amendments, in effect, extended the provisions of the 1956 act to include one-bank holding companies and gave the Fed authority to permit holding companies to engage in certain approved nonbanking activities if those activities were closely related to the traditional functions of banks. A list of currently permitted functions is shown in Table 5–3.

The holding company form of organization has come to dominate

TABLE 5–3
Approved nonbanking activities for bank holding companies

1. Dealer in banker's acceptances
2. Mortgage banking
3. Finance companies
4. Credit card issuance
5. Factoring company
6. Industrial banking
7. Servicing loans
8. Trust company
9. Investment advising
10. General economic information
11. Portfolio investment advice
12. Full payout leasing
13. Community welfare investment
14. Bookkeeping and data processing services
15. Insurance agent or broker—credit extensions
16. Underwriting credit life and credit accident and health insurance
17. Courier service
18. Management consulting to nonaffiliate banks
19. Issuance of travelers checks
20. Bullion broker
21. Land escrow services
22. Issuing money orders and variable denominated payment instruments

Source: Dale S. Drum, "Nonbanking Activities of Bank Holding Companies," *Economic Perspectives*, Federal Reserve Bank of Chicago (March–April 1977), p. 14.

the banking industry despite attempts at restricting its growth. In 1975 there were over 1,800 bank holding companies registered with the Federal Reserve System. These holding companies controlled $528 billion in deposits, or two thirds of all bank deposits. However, the majority of bank holding companies, 78 percent, were one-bank holding companies, and they held 44 percent of bank holding company deposits. Thus approximately 22 percent of bank holding companies were multibank holding companies, and they held about 56 percent of bank holding company deposits. It is the multibank holding companies that create the danger of excessive concentration in the banking industry. However, the real power of the bank holding companies may be outside of banking in those related industries in which bank holding companies can engage. For example, one-bank holding companies control large segments of the finance company industry, the factoring business, and the mortgage lending business.

The holding company movement is a controversial force in our financial system, and whether or not it has been beneficial or detrimental remains an unsettled question. Obviously, many banks believe the holding company form of organization is beneficial from their standpoint, but even if they are correct, it does not necessarily follow that bank holding companies are beneficial to society in general. Claims and counterclaims abound: Advocates argue that the holding company arrangement makes better managerial talent available to small banks, allows them to strengthen their capital structure, stimulates the provision of additional banking services, lowers costs through increased efficiency, and results in a better allocation of credit.

Opponents counter these claims with several arguments. The most important are that the holding company movement destroys competition, creates excessive market power, and increases the possibility of bank failures. While several research studies have analyzed the performance effects of bank holding companies, the results are inconclusive. If holding companies have affected bank performance, the effects are either so small or so complex that available research methodologies cannot detect them.[3] However, several studies have consistently detected differences in the composition of assets of holding company banks and non–holding company banks. Holding company banks have been found to offer a wider range of services and to place more emphasis in their portfolios on loans and municipal security investments and less emphasis on holding cash and federal government securities. This may be interpreted as serving local communities better though some increase in risk occurs in the process. Evidence of the effects of holding company affiliation on bank profits is mixed. The available studies do not support the conclusion that independent banks have been harmed by competition from holding company affiliates or that banking competition has been significantly reduced. The conclusions summarized above relate primarily to multibank holding companies, and less is known about the effects of one-bank holding companies.[4]

---

[3] See Samuel H. Talley, *The Effects of Holding Company Acquisitions on Bank Performance*, Staff Economic Study (Washington, D.C.: Board of Governors of the Federal Reserve System, 1971); Robert Lawrence, *The Performance of Bank Holding Companies* (Washington, D.C.: Board of Governors of the Federal Reserve System, 1967); and Robert F. Ware, "Performance of Banks Acquired by Multi-Bank Holding Companies in Ohio," *Economic Review*, Federal Reserve Bank of Cleveland (March/April 1973).

[4] A good summary of the holding company question is found in Peyton F. Roden, Louis J. James, Gordon A. Saussy, and Douglas A. Nettleton, *Louisiana's Debate over Multibank Holding Companies*, Occasional Paper no. 6, Division of Business and Economic Research, University of New Orleans, 1974. A recent review of holding company studies is found in Norman N. Bowsher, "Have Multi-Bank Holding Companies Affected Commercial Bank Performance?" *Review of the Federal Reserve Bank of St. Louis*, vol. 60, no. 4 (April 1978), pp. 8–15.

Chain banking

Chain banking is not really an organizational form; rather it is an indirect linking of banks through common ownership of the stock of two or more banks by one or a few individuals. Statistics on the extent of chain banking are limited, but chain banking is certainly a minor source of economic concentration in our financial system in comparison to holding company banking. The Bank Control Act of 1978 (Title VI of the Financial Institutions Regulatory and Interest Rate Control Act of 1978) requires the bank regulatory authorities to monitor and regulate chain banking formations more closely than before. The appropriate regulatory authority may disapprove any transaction that conveys control of 25 percent of the voting stock of a bank to another person or persons acting together.

WHO REGULATES BANKS AND WHY?

As noted above, commercial banks are subject to a multitude of regulations. Most of these regulations come from one or more of the following agencies: (1) the Federal Reserve System, (2) the Comptroller of the Currency, (3) the Federal Deposit Insurance Corporation, or (4) the state agencies charged with monitoring and regulating banking activities within the various states. There is considerable overlap in many of the activities of these authorities, and all banks are affected in varying degrees by one or more of these agencies.

The primary regulatory agencies have established a framework for cooperation that eliminates some of the overlap and duplication of their activities. When the different agencies are charged with essentially the same regulatory responsibilities, they often exchange information and accept each other's reports of examination. With respect to common activities, the following division of authority is practiced by the three federal agencies: The Comptroller of the Currency focuses its attention on national banks; the Federal Reserve concerns itself with state banks that are members of the Federal Reserve System; the FDIC assumes responsibility for insured nonmember state banks. The major goals and functions of the primary regulatory authorities are the subject of this section, and while the discussion here is limited to only three federal agencies, the reader should remember that banks are also subject to the regulatory decisions of other state and federal agencies. The agencies discussed here, however, represent the predominant source of government control over banking.

The Federal Reserve System

The Federal Reserve System, which is discussed in detail in Chapters 8 to 11, is charged with regulatory power over those banks that have elected to join the System. In 1979 these included 4,564 federally chartered banks and 1,015 state-chartered banks for a total of 38 percent of all commercial banks. Historically Federal Reserve regulations have been based upon the primary objective of preserving stability within the financial system and the national economy. It has long been recognized that the activities of commercial banks can at times have destabilizing effects. Thus the dominant objective of the Federal Reserve's regulatory actions has been to moderate or prevent these destabilizing activities on the part of commercial banks. How the Fed attempts to do this is the subject of Part III of this book. There we shall see that the Federal Reserve System attempts to stabilize the economy by using its regulatory power to influence the ability and willingness of commercial banks to make loans and investments and to affect the interest rates at which banks undertake these activities.

The Fed engages in other regulatory activities which are somewhat secondary to its major objective. These secondary regulatory functions arise out of its enforcement of federal banking regulations which may not relate directly to national economic stability objectives but which are, nevertheless, applicable to commercial banks. Truth-in-lending regulations, bank merger legislation, and bank holding company legislation are cases in point.

The Comptroller of the Currency

The office of the Comptroller of the Currency was created by the National Bank Act of 1863. This act established a bureau within the Treasury Department charged with administering provisions of the act. The Comptroller was given chartering and supervisory power over those banks that elected to obtain a federal charter. Until the passage of the Federal Reserve Act 50 years later, the Comptroller was the sole federal bank regulatory agency. While it was hoped that the regulatory activities of the Comptroller would prove to have a stabilizing effect on the banking system in particular and the national economy in general, the Comptroller's role in bringing about stability was not viewed as an active one. Rather, any stabilizing effect would be a by-product of the sounder banking and currency system that would result from stricter national laws and the more thorough supervisory examinations carried out by the Comptroller's office. Hence, the role of the Comptroller might be pictured as that of a policeman of national banks.

In 1979 there were 4,564 national banks (31 percent of all banks) subject to control by the Comptroller of the Currency. At least once each year examiners from the Comptroller's office conduct an unannounced examination of each national bank to determine if that bank is in compliance with the national banking regulations. In addition to the on-premise examinations, national banks must file periodic reports and statements with the Comptroller's office.

Federal Deposit Insurance Corporation (FDIC)

In the early 1930s the United States went through the worst banking crisis in its history. Thousands of banks failed, and their depositors lost hundreds of millions of dollars. Largely as a result of that experience, the Federal Deposit Insurance Corporation (FDIC) was created by the Banking Act of 1933. The FDIC's primary objective is to protect bank depositors throughout the country, and the corporation has been very successful in achieving this objective. The FDIC has provided protection through two approaches to the depositor loss problem: First, deposit accounts up to a specified maximum (currently $100,000) are insured against loss; second, the FDIC maintains regulatory standards governing bank activities that are designed to minimize actions that might lead to bank failure and consequent depositor losses. Regular supervisory examinations of insured banks are conducted to make certain that these standards are being met.

All national banks and all state Federal Reserve member banks are required by law to participate in the Federal Deposit Insurance program. Participation, of course, makes the bank subject to the FDIC's regulatory powers. While not required to do so, virtually all state banks presently participate in the FDIC insurance program; only about 2 percent of the more than 14,700 banks in the country remain outside the program. The bulk of these are located in three states— Colorado, Illinois, and New York. Since a state bank electing to obtain FDIC coverage of its deposits comes under the regulatory powers of the FDIC, deposit insurance has been the vehicle by which most federal banking regulations are extended to state-chartered banks. While state banks view the additional regulation with distaste, the competitive necessity of deposit insurance is strong enough to overcome the burden of FDIC regulation.

For a bank to participate in the FDIC insurance program, it must not only agree to subject itself to the regulations of that agency, it must also agree to pay an annual premium assessment of $1/12$ of 1 percent of the bank's assessable deposits. The effective cost of this insurance to the bank has been reduced by the FDIC's practice of using part of the premium as a credit against the next year's assessment. In recent years the net assessment paid by insured banks has been as low as $1/27$ of 1 percent of assessable deposits. This premium income is invested in government securities to provide income to the FDIC in the form of interest. If premium and investment income plus accumulated surplus should prove insufficient to cover payments to depositors for losses, the corporation is authorized to borrow up to $3 billion from the Treasury as supplemental funds. Such supplemental borrowing has never been needed, for ironically, the very existence of deposit insurance has almost eliminated the need for it. Historically, periods of heavy depositor losses have been associated with bank runs—a situation in which a large proportion of a bank's depositors try to withdraw funds. No bank is liquid enough to withstand a heavy run, and if all banks are under pressure, attempts to liquidate assets result in losses that bring about the very condition feared by depositors. FDIC insurance has removed most of the fear element and has made bank runs a very rare occurrence today.

While the FDIC's primary concern is with the safety of depositors' funds and the soundness of the bank's operations, most federal banking legislation passed since the inception of the FDIC charges the corporation with enforcing the laws with respect to insured state banks that are not members of the Federal Reserve System. Thus the FDIC engages in the enforcement of federal legislation governing such areas as consumer protection, mergers, holding company applications, and insider transactions in addition to providing protection to depositors through insurance of their checking and savings accounts.

WHAT ARE THE PRIMARY CATEGORIES OF BANK REGULATION?

Commercial banks are subject to most of the laws to which other business firms are subject, and many actions of banks are controlled by specialized regulations not applied to other firms. Thus many functions that for most business firms are determined by economic forces are prescribed by law in the case of banks. Reference has already been made to some of the key areas of bank regulation. The motivation behind most of these regulations can ultimately be traced to one or more of three major goals:

1. To enhance the soundness and stability of the banking system and the economy.
2. To enhance competition in the banking industry and prevent the formation of concentrations of market power.

3. To prevent discrimination or to ensure fairness by banks in their dealings with customers.

These objectives are not always independent; in fact, they may even be in conflict at times. For example, banking regulations have the effect of making entry into the banking business difficult, a reflection of the soundness and stability objective. At the same time these regulations prevent the competition that would result from more banks, a result that clearly conflicts with the competition goal. The following major forms of bank regulations are discussed below:

1. Control over entry.
2. Capital requirements.
3. Control over lending and investing activities.
4. Reserve requirements.
5. Geographic restrictions on operations.
6. Limitations on merger and holding company activities.
7. Limitations on prices paid and charged.

Control over entry

Entry into a particular banking market occurs in one of two ways: (1) a new bank is formed or (2) an established bank opens a branch in a new market.[5] Both methods of entry are tightly controlled by existing banking regulations. The difficulty of obtaining a new charter has already been noted, and the second method of entry is impossible in the many states that do not allow branch banking. In other states the difficulty of acquiring permission to open new branches varies, but in general the barriers are less formidable than those facing the organizers of a new bank.

The stringency of regulations governing new bank entry has not been uniform over time. Originally, permission to form a new bank or to open a branch was extremely difficult to obtain; usually an act of the state legislature was required. With the advent in the 1830s of what was known as *free banking*, bank charters became much easier to obtain, and hundreds of new banks were organized. However, easy entry did not last. By the 1920s and 1930s, the idea of *overbanking* had become prevalent, with regulatory authorities operating under the presumption that too much bank competition was detrimental to the safety and soundness of the banking system. Today the authorities seem to be taking a pragmatic view; new banks and

---

[5] While holding company acquisitions and mergers allow a particular bank to enter a new market, they do not result in a net gain in competition in that market. Thus that aspect of entry is not considered here.

branches are allowed when it can be shown that the public will benefit, even though the result may be the loss of some business by existing banks. However, if the new bank or branch appears likely to cause the failure of an existing bank, the authorities will almost certainly forbid its formation. In recent years there appears to have been a shift toward greater emphasis on competition and less emphasis on protecting existing banks.

Capital requirements

Bank capital represents the funds invested in the bank by the owners. These funds may have come from the sale of stock or from the retention of earnings. Except for the minimum capital requirements set by statute as a condition for organization, the authorities have no direct control over a bank's capital. Nevertheless, capital requirements are of ongoing importance to the regulatory authorities, and the adequacy of a bank's capital is one of the factors monitored during their periodic examinations. The level of capital that is adequate is a subjective matter that varies from bank to bank and is subject to indirect influence by the authorities. For example, if the authorities feel that a particular bank is undercapitalized and "suggest" that the bank raise additional capital, the bank may choose not to do so. However, the next time the bank files an application to open a new branch, it may find its application repeatedly turned down until the bank's capital position is improved. Bank capital must also be "adequate" as a condition for obtaining FDIC insurance. Thus suggestions by the regulatory authorities that capital is inadequate usually receive serious consideration.

Control over bank capital is primarily a result of the safety objective of bank regulation. Theoretically, a bank's capital is a measure of the amount of losses it could take before it would be unable to repay its creditors—which are for the most part its depositors. As one writer put it, "The primary function of bank capital is to demonstrate to the public and to the supervisory authorities the bank's ability to absorb unanticipated losses."[6] A more detailed discussion about the role of bank capital is contained in Chapter 6.

Control over lending and investing activities

The lending and investing activities of commercial banks are subject to important legal and regulatory constraints. These con-

---

[6] Oliver G. Wood, Jr., *Commercial Banking* (New York: D. Van Nostrand Co., 1978), p. 111.

straints are primarily designed to prevent banks from taking undue risks which might impair their safety and soundness. The more important restrictions are as follows:

1. Limitations exist on the amount a bank may lend to a single borrowing entity, usually 10 percent of the bank's capital and surplus. This rule helps assure diversification within the bank's loan portfolio and thus limits concentration of risk.

2. Banks are restricted as to the types of securities in which they may invest. They may not purchase securities that are relatively high in default risk; common stocks, preferred stocks, corporate bonds, and low-rated state and local government securities are normally off limits.

3. Loans to bank *insiders* (directors or bank officers) are restricted with respect to terms and amounts. Such loans cannot be at preferential rates and usually must be approved by the board of directors. This regulation is to prevent conflicts of interest and possible adverse effects on the safety of the bank. (See Chapter 7 on insider transactions.)

4. Loans made by banks for the purpose of purchasing securities are subject to a regulation referred to as margin requirements. The effect of this regulation is to restrict lending to purchase securities when the purchased securities are to serve as collateral for the loan. This safety-oriented restriction resulted from the excessive use of bank credit to speculate on stocks in the 1920s.

5. With respect to making loans, banks are prohibited from discriminating on the basis of race, color, religion, sex, or national origin.

6. The Flood Disaster Protection Act of 1973 prohibits banks from making certain loans in areas subject to flooding unless the property involved has flood insurance. While this requirement may enhance the safety of the banks, its prime purpose is to force communities to comply with the zoning requirements of the act.

7. The Community Reinvestment Act of 1977 requires that the bank regulatory authorities take steps to see that bank lending activities are not withheld from certain groups or geographic areas within their market. If strictly enforced, this act could put the regulatory authorities in the business of allocating credit.

8. Bank lending to consumers is subject to all the provisions of the Consumer Credit Protection Act which imposes many requirements on bank consumer lending activities. These requirements cover disclosure of charges, advertising practices, discrimination, debt collection practices, credit reporting, and other activities relating to consumer credit.

Reserve requirements

Reserve requirements, which rank among the most important of all bank regulations, are discussed in detail in Chapters 9 and 10. Required reserves are the cash holdings that banks are required to keep either in their vaults or on deposit at a Federal Reserve Bank (or at another commercial bank in the case of nonmember banks). Reserve requirements are important not only because they help ensure the liquidity, safety, and soundness of banks but because, as we shall see later, they give the Federal Reserve powerful leverage in controlling the monetary and credit conditions in the economy.

Geographic restrictions on operations

As discussed earlier, geographic restrictions on bank operations refer to the branching limitations which vary from state to state. Under no circumstances, however, can a bank operate or branch outside of the state in which the head office is located. To some extent a multibank holding company can avoid geographic limitations imposed by banking laws, but geographic expansion of holding companies is subject to restriction by many states and must also be approved by federal bank regulatory authorities. All things considered, geographic restrictions on bank activities remain quite strong, but there are indications that they are weakening.

Limitations on merger and holding company activities

For many years there was practically no effective control over bank merger activities. In each decade since the 1920s, except for the 1940s, there have been in excess of 1,000 mergers—between 1921 and 1975 there were 11,805 mergers. Obviously, the disappearance of so many competitors had a detrimental effect on competition, and this effect did not go unnoticed. The Bank Merger Acts of 1960 and 1966 require both the courts and the regulatory authorities to consider the competitive effects of mergers in the light of antitrust laws (the Sherman Act and the Clayton Act) which had previously not been applied to the activities of banks. In addition to looking at the competitive effects of proposed mergers, the authorities are also required to assess the impact on the "convenience and needs of the community." If the latter impact outweighs any anticompetitive effects, the merger can be approved. As a result of these developments, mergers within the same market area are not likely to be approved unless one of the banks is in danger of failing and no other solution to its problem is evident.

As noted earlier, the formation of both one-bank and multibank holding companies is now subject to regulatory approval under the Bank Holding Company Act of 1956 and the amendments of 1970. Holding companies must register with the Federal Reserve, new acquisitions must be approved, and any nonbanking activities engaged in by the holding company must be consistent with the Federal Reserve Board's list of approved activities. Among other limitations, holding company banks cannot tie the sale of banking services to the bank customer's purchase of other products or services from the holding company's nonbanking affiliates. The Bank Holding Company Act amendments of 1970 appear to have established firm regulatory control over this aspect of banking.

Limitation on prices paid and charged

A major regulation affecting commercial banks is the restriction on the amounts of interest they may pay to depositors in an effort to attract additional deposits. By law banks may not pay interest on demand deposits, and the rates of interest they may pay for most categories of time deposits are subject to upper limits set by the Federal Reserve. The effectiveness and wisdom of these controls have been questioned, with the result that they are in the process of being removed (see Chapter 7). Banks are also subject to the usury laws of the various states and federal government. During most time periods these restrictions are irrelevant since market rates are lower than the maximum rates permitted by the usury laws. However, during occasional periods of high interest rates, usury laws may have a restrictive effect on banks.

SUMMARY

Commercial banks play a crucial role in the financial system and the economy in general. For many years it has been widely believed that the organization and structure of the banking industry affects the ability and willingness of banks to perform many important functions. This belief has been transformed into legislation governing the formation of new banks and the branching, merging, and holding company activities of established banks. Existing legislation reflects many unsettled issues with respect to bank organization and structure. Some states prohibit branching; some allow it on a limited basis; and other states have no limitations. Current laws place rather strict controls over bank mergers and holding company formations; however, prior to the enactment of these laws, mergers and holding company formations resulted in considerable concentration of market power within the banking industry.

Most regulation of the banking industry is the responsibility of three federal government agencies: the Federal Reserve System, the Comptroller of the Currency, and the Federal Deposit Insurance Corporation. In addition, each state has its own legislation affecting bank operations within its borders. The result is a banking industry consisting of thousands of separate firms operating more than 47,000 offices throughout the country. Many of these are linked through holding companies and branching systems. It is quite likely that the structure and organization of the industry will continue to change as new technology and legislation come on the scene. Some of the likely directions of change are explored in Chapter 7.

REVIEW QUESTIONS

1. Speculate as to why the U.S. banking system is characterized by thousands of unit banks while the banking systems of most countries consist of a few large branch banking systems.
2. "It is too difficult to obtain a new bank charter." Comment.
3. Discuss the extent of competition in the U.S. banking industry.
4. Should statewide or perhaps even interstate branching be allowed? Discuss the pros and cons.
5. The holding company movement in the United States was dominated by the formation of one-bank holding companies in the 1960s, whereas prior to then, most bank holding companies were of the multibank variety. What factors accounted for this change?
6. Distinguish between the major bank regulatory agencies with respect to functions and objectives.
7. Do you think that it is appropriate for the banking industry to be regulated to a much greater extent than other industries? Why or why not?

SUGGESTIONS FOR ADDITIONAL READING

Alhadeff, D. A. *Monopoly and Competition in Banking.* Berkeley: University of California Press, 1954.

Benston, George J. "The Optimal Banking Structure: Theory and Evidence." *Journal of Bank Research*, vol. 3, no. 4 (Winter 1973), pp. 220–37.

Brown, William J. *The Dual Banking System in the United States.* New York: Department of Economics and Research, American Bankers Association, 1960.

Fischer, Gerald C. *American Banking Structure.* New York: Columbia University Press, 1968.

Gilbert, Gary A., and Longbrake, William A. "The Effects of Branching by Financial Institutions on Competition, Productive Efficiency, and Stability: An Examination of the Evidence." *Journal of Bank Research,* vol. 4, no. 3 (Autumn 1974), pp. 154–67; also, vol. 4, no. 4 (Winter 1974), pp. 298–307.

U.S. Congress. Senate Subcommittee on Financial Institutions of the Committee on Banking, Housing, and Urban Affairs. *Compendium of Issues Relating to Branching by Financial Institutions.* 94th Congress, 2d session, Washington, D.C.: U.S. Government Printing Office, 1976.

Wood, Oliver G. *Commercial Banking.* New York: D. Van Nostrand Co., 1978.

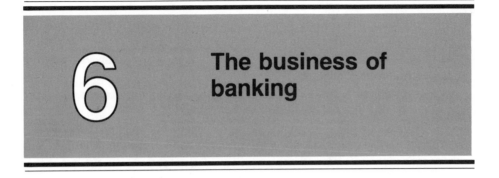

6 The business of banking

WARM-UP: *Outline and questions to consider as you read*

What are the major activities of banking firms?
How do banks obtain funds?
    Demand deposits.
    Time deposits.
    Federal funds purchased.
    Other sources of funds.
    Capital.
How do banks use funds?
    Factors affecting bank lending and investing
      activities.
    Investment activities.
    Lending activities.
    Federal funds sold and other uses of funds.
What are bank reserves?
What is the role of capital in a bank?

NEW TERMS

Banker's acceptance: a draft or written order instructing the bank to pay a specified sum of money and which the bank agrees to honor by writing ''accepted'' on the face.

Clearinghouse: a central location where banks in the same city or area meet for a common clearing of checks.

Commercial paper: the unsecured, short-term promisory notes of large, credit-worthy businesses.

Correspondent bank: a bank which holds a deposit of another bank (the respondent bank).

Credit (default) risk: the possibility that the borrower will not pay some or all of principal due on a loan.

Eurodollars: deposits which are denominated in dollars and held in banks outside the United States.

Federal funds: commercial banks' deposits at Federal Reserve banks which are loaned on a very short-term basis to other banks.

Interest-rate risk: the possibility of fluctuations in the prices of outstanding marketable securities resulting from changes in market interest rates.

Municipals: debt obligations of states and political subdivisions (cities, counties, etc.).

Repurchase agreements (repos or RPs): sales of marketable securities accompanied by a simultaneous contract to repurchase the securities for a higher price at a specified future time.

Reserves: bank assets such as cash, deposits at Federal Reserve banks, or deposits at other commercial banks. Reserves are classified as follows:

  Excess reserves: reserves held over and above the minimum required by law.

  Required reserves: the amount of reserve assets that banks are required by law to hold.

  Secondary reserves: assets that are not reserves in the legal sense but are highly liquid and thereby can be easily converted to legal reserves.

  Total (legal) reserves: the sum of required plus excess reserves.

Subordinated notes and debentures: unsecured intermediate and long-term debt sold by banks to investors.

The primary objective of banking firms is to make profits and thereby increase the wealth of the owners of the bank. They attempt to do this by taking funds entrusted to them by depositors and lending and investing these funds at rates more than sufficient to cover costs. There are several constraints, however, within which every bank must operate as it strives to make profits for its stockholders. The most important constraint, the maintenance of adequate liquidity, is imposed by the market and the nature of the banking business. Other constraints—reserve requirements, branching limits, and so forth—are government imposed. Given these market and government-imposed constraints, banks strive for the profits that are the reward of successful economic performance. The following sections describe typical banking activities, sources and uses of funds, reserves, and bank capital.

WHAT ARE THE MAJOR ACTIVITIES OF BANKING FIRMS?

Banks are first and foremost financial intermediaries. As such, the very essence of their activities is the transfer of funds between savers, or budget surplus units, and borrowers, or budget deficit units. In this respect banks are like all intermediaries; they accept funds from depositors, and in return, they issue claims upon themselves in the form of demand and time deposit liabilities. The funds acquired by the bank from its depositors are then converted into earning assets via the bank's lending and investing activities which channel funds to borrowers in return for direct claims against the borrowers. Despite the introduction of some new activities, the essence of the banking business remains the holding and servicing of deposits and the lending and investing of the funds so acquired.

Banks, by way of holding and servicing demand deposits, are responsible for much of the country's payments mechanism. The day-to-day operation of this mechanism—a process referred to as check clearing—constitutes one of the commercial banking system's most important and expensive operations. Every check is, in effect, an order for the bank to transfer title to funds out of the drawer's account and remit these funds (or titles) to the payee. Of course, the drawer's bank cannot do this until it actually receives the check. The check, however, may have originated as a result of a transaction that occurred thousands of miles away, or it may have been written locally with another customer of the bank as the payee. Millions of checks originating from transactions all over the country are written each day, and these checks must be quickly, safely, and efficiently routed to the banks upon which they are drawn. Unless this occurs, demand deposits could not serve as the major component of our money supply. This transfer of funds is a major task of the banking system.

The process of clearing checks varies depending upon the circumstances. One way of classifying the various check-clearing processes is according to the geographic locations of the banks involved. In order of increasing complexity, the different possibilities are as follows:

1. Checks drawn upon and presented for payment at the same bank.
2. Checks drawn upon one bank and presented for payment at another bank in the same city.
3. Checks drawn upon one bank and presented for payment at another bank which is either in the same Federal Reserve District or uses the same correspondent bank.
4. Checks drawn upon one bank and presented for payment at another bank in another Federal Reserve District.

The simplest case occurs when a check is deposited or presented for payment at the bank upon which it is drawn. In this case, the bank merely deducts the amount of the check from the account of the drawer and either remits cash or credits the payee's account.

The check-clearing process becomes more involved if the check is deposited in a bank other than the one upon which it is drawn. In such cases the check must be physically transported to the drawer's bank. In the days before demand deposits became popular, the regular mail or a special messenger was used for this task, and remittance was usually in currency; today, when checks have become the dominant means of payment, a clearinghouse arrangement is more efficient. Regardless of how the check is transported to the drawer's bank, the latter bank must somehow remit funds to the payee's bank. In any case, the drawer's bank reduces the drawer's demand deposit balances by the amount of the check. The remittance of currency can be cumbersome, inefficient, and unsafe, and so two methods of avoiding these difficulties have evolved; they are interbank deposits and clearinghouses.

Banks keep deposits in other banks in return for the performance of certain services. This type of relationship is referred to as a *correspondent relationship,* with the bank performing the services known as the *correspondent bank* and the depositing bank—the bank receiving the services—known as the *respondent bank.* One of the major services performed by the correspondent is aiding the respondent in clearing checks. If the bank upon which a check is drawn happens to be a correspondent for the bank remitting the check, then the correspondent can simply credit the respondent bank's account and no currency need be transferred. Moreover, if the drawer's bank and the payee's bank happen to use a common correspondent, the transfer of currency can be avoided. For example, if bank C is a correspondent for both bank A and bank B, which are located in different areas, a check drawn on B and deposited in A can be sent to bank C, which credits bank A's account and debits bank B's account. In practice, large numbers of checks are grouped by regions or banks and remitted for clearance through major correspondent banks in that region. Generally, the larger banks in a region serve as correspondents for the small banks in that region. The correspondent banking network has aided in providing an efficient, safe, and convenient method of facilitating the country's check-clearing process. With the advent of the Federal Reserve System in 1914, the regional Federal Reserve banks and their branches began to augment the correspondent network in the clearing of checks.

A *clearinghouse arrangement* occurs when banks in the same city or area arrange for a common clearing of checks. A central meeting place and time is determined, and each bank participating in the clearinghouse association totals the checks drawn on each of the other clearinghouse banks and then pays to (or receives from) the clearinghouse the difference between the total of checks it presents and the total of checks presented to it. For example, if bank A and bank B form a clearinghouse, and on a particular day, bank A holds a total of $10,000 in checks drawn upon bank B which in turn holds a total of $9,500 of checks drawn on bank A, only the difference ($500) need be transferred between the two banks. To facilitate the process even further, all participating banks can maintain small balances at the clearinghouse (assuming the clearinghouse is large enough and has the facilities) for purposes of settling between members, or they may settle through changes in balances kept with their Federal Reserve bank, a common correspondent, or with one another.

The check-clearing process becomes more complicated as the geographic distance between the banks involved becomes greater. While it is not feasible to discuss all possible situations here, a general example is presented that illustrates the basic process involved. Suppose bank A, which is not a member of the Federal Reserve System, receives a check drawn upon bank B, which is a member bank.[1] One of the functions of the Federal Reserve System is to aid banks in clearing checks, and in this example the check clearing could be effected as follows: Bank A sends the check to its correspondent (a Federal Reserve member bank) and receives credit on its account with the correspondent. The correspondent, in turn, sends the check to the district Federal Reserve bank (or its branch) and receives credit on its account at the Federal Reserve bank. Since bank B is a member bank, it has an account at the regional Federal Reserve bank which the latter debits for the amount of the check; the regional bank then forwards the check to bank B. Bank B deducts the amount of the

---

[1] As noted earlier, commercial banks may or may not be members of the Federal Reserve System. The country is divided into 12 Federal Reserve Districts with each district having a separate Federal Reserve bank.

check from the drawer's account, and the check-clearing process is now complete. If bank A and bank B happen to be located in different Federal Reserve districts, then two Federal Reserve banks would be involved through the Fed's Interdistrict Settlement Fund. The latter is used to transfer funds between Federal Reserve Districts.

It should be noted that, despite the efficiency with which such a complicated process is carried out, it may take several days for the check to make its way back to the bank upon which it was drawn. Thus, banks involved in the clearing process usually do not receive immediate credit for checks they present to other banks or the Federal Reserve for collection; rather, credit is given only after the check has cleared or after a prescribed time period has elapsed. Nevertheless, in some cases one bank may receive credit for the check being collected before the payee's bank actually remits funds. When this occurs, double counting of reserves and deposits results. The double-counted reserves, referred to as float, are discussed in more detail in Chapter 9.

The transfer of funds between depositors has been an important and unique function of commercial banks for well over 100 years; this uniqueness is disappearing as thrift institutions offer transactions-related deposits such as NOW accounts and share drafts. The consensus is that it is a matter of time until NOW accounts become widespread enough to effectively destroy the commercial banking system's monopoly over the country's private payments mechanism.

In addition to the transfer of depositors' funds and the financial intermediary role, banks have, via the bank holding company movement, expanded into nonlending and noninvesting activities. At present, the law requires that such activities be related to the traditional functions of banks. Because of legal restraints, bank holding company activities are unlikely to alter the traditional functions of commercial banks as much as was initially expected.

While commercial banking is the primary focus of this chapter, a brief comparison of banks with other financial intermediaries is relevant because they perform many similar functions and because the lines separating banks from other financial institutions are rapidly shifting. Other financial intermediaries have been more specialized than banks: savings and loan associations tend to specialize in loans to home buyers; credit unions have emphasized consumer loans for automobiles and other durable goods; insurance companies invest in mortgages, stocks, and bonds; and similar specializations are found with respect to mutual funds, pension funds, and other financial intermediaries. Banks, on the other hand, make loans to large businesses, to consumers, to farmers, to stockbrokers, to governments, and to others; they make loans for purposes ranging from real estate to stereos; they make short-term loans and, on occasion, long-term loans and are much more flexible in what they can and will do than are other financial intermediaries.

While a more detailed discussion of the range and relative importance of commercial bank activities follows in the next two sections, we can summarize by saying that the major activities of commercial banks are lending, investing, holding deposits, and transferring funds. The fact that all of these activities are major functions of banks distinguishes them from other financial intermediaries. However, it should be emphasized that a definite movement toward decreasing specialization on the part of other financial intermediaries is underway.

Finally, a very important by-product of commercial banks' lending and investing activities is an effect on the nation's money and credit conditions. The nature and consequences of this connection constitute much of the subject matter of the remainder of this book; however, it is sufficient at this stage to note that, when a commercial bank makes a loan or an investment, it may increase the nation's money supply. This effect makes the proper functioning of the banking system crucial to the economic health of the country.

HOW DO BANKS OBTAIN FUNDS?

There is no better way to gain an understanding of the basic activities of commercial banks than by studying their financial statements. Rather than try to select a particular bank's statements as typical, we have presented consolidated financial statements of the entire banking system in Tables 6–1 and 6–2. The asset portion of the balance sheet (report of condition) shows how banks use available funds. The liabilities and capital listings present the sources of funds. The next two sections discuss deposits, which are by far the most important source of funds, accounting for over 80 percent of the total funds acquired.

Demand deposits

There are two basic deposit types—demand deposits and time deposits. Demand deposit accounts, or checking accounts, are deposits upon which checks may be written and withdrawals made upon demand. Historically demand deposits have been the most important single source of funds for banks, but in recent years time deposits have become more important. Demand deposits currently account for approximately 38 percent of the total deposits of com-

TABLE 6–1
Assets and liabilities of all insured commercial banks in the United States, September 30, 1978 ($ billions)

Account		Amount ($ billions)	Percent of total
Assets			
Cash and items in process		$ 158.4	13.2%
Total securities held		262.2	21.9
Federal funds sold		41.3	3.5
Other loans (gross)		675.9	56.4
Real estate loans	$203.4		
Loans to financial institutions	37.1		
Loans to farmers (except real estate)	28.1		
Commercial and industrial loans	213.1		
Loans to individuals	161.6		
All other loans	69.7		
Building, furniture, and real estate		22.4	1.8
Other assets (net)		38.3	3.2
Total		$1,198.5	100.0%
Liabilities			
Total deposits		$ 960.9	80.2
Demand deposits	$369.0		
Time deposits	368.6		
Savings deposits	223.3		
Federal funds purchased		92.0	7.7
Bank acceptances outstanding		16.7	1.4
Other liabilities		37.6	3.1
Total liabilities		$1,107.2	92.4%
Equity capital		85.5	7.1
Preferred stock	0.1		
Common stock	17.9		
Surplus, undivided profits, and other capital resources	67.5		
Subordinated notes and debentures		5.8	.5
Total		$1,198.5	100.0%

Source: Board of Governors of the Federal Reserve System, *Federal Reserve Bulletin,* vol. 65, no. 9 (September 1979), pp. 418–19.

mercial banks and about 31 percent of the total funds acquired by banks. Demand deposits are generally classified according to ownership into four principal categories: (1) business and individual deposits, (2) deposits of domestic banks, (3) deposits of governmental units in the United States, and (4) deposits of foreign governments and banks. The distribution of commercial bank deposits by ownership category is presented in Table 6–3.

Banks are prohibited from paying interest on demand deposits; however, their demand deposit customers often receive implicit payments in the form of services provided at no cost or at fees below the bank's cost. Among the services provided are accounting and safekeeping functions and, as noted earlier, the processing of de-

TABLE 6-2
Income and expenses for all insured commercial banks, 1978

Item	Amount ($ billions)	Percent of operating income
Operating income—total	$113.2	100.0%
Interest on:		
Loans.....................................	75.9	67.0
Balances with other banks	6.7	5.9
Federal funds sold and securities		
purchased under resale agreements.....	3.7	3.3
Securities:		
U.S. Treasury and agency	9.3	8.2
States and political subdivisions	6.0	5.3
Other	1.1	1.0
Trust department income.....................	2.1	1.9
Service charges on deposits.................	2.0	1.8
Other charges, fees, etc.	2.9	2.6
Other operating income	3.5	3.1
Operating expenses—total	98.1	86.7
Salaries, wages, and		
employee benefits......................	18.7	16.5
Interest on:		
Time and savings deposits	50.1	44.3
Federal funds purchased		
and securities sold under		
repurchase agreements	7.2	6.4
Other borrowed money	1.5	1.3
Capital notes and debentures..............	0.4	0.4
Occupancy expense (net)	5.6	5.0
Provision for loan losses	11.2	9.9
Other operating expenses	3.4	3.0
Income before taxes and securities		
gains or losses	15.1	13.3
Applicable income taxes	4.2	3.7
Income before securities gains or losses	10.9	9.6
Net securities gains or losses (−) after taxes	−0.2	−0.2
Net income	10.7	9.5
Cash dividends declared	3.7	3.3

Source: Board of Governors of the Federal Reserve System, *Federal Reserve Bulletin, vol. 65, no. 9 (September 1979), p. 704.*

positors' checks. In recent years the cost of providing these services has increased along with other banking costs, and only a few banks continue to provide these services free. Service charges, which vary greatly among banks, are usually levied against demand deposit accounts. Currently service charges on deposits account for only about 2 percent of the operating income of commercial banks.

While historically banks have been the only financial intermediary to issue demand deposits, this is no longer the case. The NOW accounts discussed earlier appear to be the forerunners of

TABLE 6–3
Demand deposits in all commercial banks by ownership
category, September 30, 1978

Ownership category	Amount ($ billions)	Percent
Business and personal deposits	$279.7	75.8%
Domestic banks*	40.9	11.1
Domestic governmental units	25.0	6.8
Foreign banks and governments	9.1	2.6
Other	14.3	3.9
Total............................	369.0	100.0

* Includes deposits of mutual savings banks.

Source: Board of Governors of the Federal Reserve System, *Federal Reserve Bulletin*, vol. 65, no. 9 (September 1979), p. A-19.

financial changes that will erode the clear distinction between demand deposits as issued by banks and the various types of interest-bearing "savings" accounts issued by banks and other financial intermediaries. NOW accounts are currently offered by some federally insured commercial banks, savings and loan associations, and mutual savings banks.

Time deposits

Time deposits, as the term is generally used, refers to deposit accounts that technically may not be withdrawn upon demand. They are further distinguished by the fact that banks are allowed to (and do) pay interest on them. When the term is used in this second sense it includes deposits that are classified specifically as *savings* or *passbook savings* deposits, *open-account* time deposits, and *time certificates of deposits*.[2]

Passbook savings are deposits that are evidenced by recorded entries in a passbook kept by the depositor. The bank can require at least 30 days' notice before a withdrawal can be made from such an account, but in practice banks seldom invoke this requirement. Hence, the funds can usually be withdrawn upon demand. While such accounts constitute extremely liquid assets, they do not perform the medium-of-exchange function of money. They cannot be used to acquire goods and services without first being converted into currency or demand deposits. For this reason, savings accounts are often referred to as *near-money* assets. Because of the ease of with-

---

[2] For a more thorough discussion of the different types of time deposits, see Federal Deposit Insurance Corporation, *Rules and Regulations*, part 329.1.

drawal associated with these accounts, interest rates earned on them are below those that can be earned on other types of time deposits. An open-account time deposit is defined by the FDIC as follows:

> . . . a deposit, other than a "time certificate of deposit," with respect to which there is in force a written contract with the depositor that neither the whole nor any part of such deposit may be withdrawn . . . prior to the date of maturity, which shall not be less than 30 days after the date of deposit, or prior to the expiration of the period of notice which must be given by the depositor in writing not less than 30 days in advance of withdrawals.[3]

Examples of accounts falling under this category are Christmas Club accounts, Vacation Club accounts, and Golden Savings accounts.

Time certificates of deposit, or CDs, are of two types—negotiable and nonnegotiable; the latter are also referred to as *consumer certificates of deposit* and are issued in designated denominations with fixed maturity dates and specified rates of interest. The negotiable CDs are usually in large denominations ($1 million) and are issued by large banks to large business customers. They compete with other money market instruments for the temporary excess cash of large corporations, and since they are negotiable, there is an active secondary market which makes them highly liquid. Unlike other types of bank time deposits, these types yield interest rates that are not limited but are determined by market forces. This feature, coupled with the fact that banks can tailor the maturity to meet the customer's needs, aids banks in competing for funds in periods of tight money.

Data indicate that time deposits account for 31 percent of total funds raised by banks; savings deposits account for 19 percent. Thus time and savings deposits together account for about 50 percent of the banking system's total funds and about 62 percent of the total deposits of banks. Interest paid on time and savings deposits constitutes the largest expense of banks; during 1978 this item was 51 percent of the operating expenses of all insured commercial banks. In recent years time and savings deposits have constituted an ever-increasing proportion of total bank deposits. As late as 1956, less than one third of banks' deposits were made up of time and savings deposits with over two thirds consisting of demand deposits. Not only has this relationship almost reversed itself since then, but also the interest rates that banks have had to pay on time and savings deposits have increased considerably. Both of these trends have put severe upward pressure on bank costs; consequently, bankers have

---

[3] Ibid., part 329.1 (d).

had to seek ways to boost revenues and cut costs in other areas so as to protect profit margins.

Federal funds purchased

At the end of 1978, banks were obtaining over $92 billion by purchasing federal funds (see Table 6–1). "Federal funds purchased" was the largest nondeposit source of funds for banks and accounted for 7.7 percent of total funds obtained. Federal funds result from excess deposits that some banks maintain at Federal Reserve banks. On any one day, some banks temporarily have more funds on deposit than they wish; other banks will have a temporary shortage of funds in the sense that their reserves are below the levels required by the regulatory authorities. There are several approaches a bank can take in order to increase its reserves, but in cases where the deficiency is only temporary, a common approach is to borrow (usually on a one-day basis) the unneeded reserves of some other bank. Reserves are nonearning assets, and banks holding more reserves than they need are willing to convert them into earning assets by lending them to other banks. When such transactions occur, the bank that borrows reserves is said to have purchased federal funds, and the lending bank is said to have sold federal funds. The rate of interest paid for the federal funds is referred to as the federal funds rate and is determined by supply and demand conditions. This rate is an important barometer of money market conditions, and in the 1970s, it played a vital role in the determination of monetary policy actions.

There are three basic types of federal funds transactions. The most common is a *straight* transaction consisting of the purchase and sale of federal funds on an unsecured overnight basis; secured transactions occur when the buyer of federal funds pledges collateral to secure the loan; and a third type of transaction is known as a repurchase agreement. With repurchase agreements, the borrowing bank sells government securities to the lending bank under an agreement to buy them back the following day at a price differential sufficient to provide for the appropriate interest return. Banks engage in repurchase agreements with other banks, U.S. government security dealers, and other investors.

Other sources of funds

While federal funds purchased constitute the major nondeposit liability of commercial banks, there are several other nondeposit liabilities that may be used to obtain funds. Among these are (1) Eurodollars, (2) bankers' acceptances, (3) loans from Federal Reserve banks ,or other commercial banks, (4) commercial paper, and (5) subordinated notes and debentures. At the end of 1978, the total of nondeposit liabilities (excluding federal funds purchased) accounted for less than 5 percent of the funds acquired by banks.

Eurodollars are deposits that are denominated in dollars and held in banks outside the United States. The banks holding these deposits may be either foreign banks or foreign branches of U.S. banks. The name Eurodollars was applied to these deposits because of their location in banks in major European cities. In recent years, as billions of U.S. dollars found their way overseas, tight money conditions in the United States forced some American banks to borrow significant amounts of these dollars. These borrowings were especially heavy in 1968 and 1970.

A *banker's acceptance* is a particular type of draft or written order to the bank instructing the bank to pay a specified sum of money on or after a specified date. The order is written or drawn by an individual or business firm that is a customer of the bank. If the bank *accepts* the draft, it agrees or guarantees to make the called-for-payment, and the amount specified becomes a liability of the bank. Of course, the bank will not accept the draft unless it feels certain the customer will provide the necessary funds to cover the liability. To offset its liability for the acceptance, the bank simultaneously acquires an asset in the form of a claim on the customer. The asset is generally listed as *customer's liability on acceptances*. In effect a banker's acceptance allows a firm to substitute the bank's credit, which has a higher rating, for its own; the customer is charged a fee for use of the bank's credit. Note that the liability *bank acceptances* does not constitute a discretionary source of funds for the bank since a corresponding use of funds is automatically generated at the same time.

Loans from Federal Reserve banks represent funds obtained by the way of the Federal Reserve's "discount window" and represent another way whereby banks can acquire funds on a temporary basis. The discount procedure is one of the Federal Reserve's instruments of monetary policy and is discussed in more detail in Chapter 10. In addition to federal funds transactions discussed earlier, banks on occasion borrow funds on a temporary basis from other commercial banks. Such transactions are most likely to occur between small banks that are not members of the Federal Reserve System and their correspondents.

Commercial paper comprises the unsecured, short-term promissory notes of large, credit-worthy businesses. Historically, banks have not issued commercial paper in significant amounts even though other business firms raise large sums of money by issuing such notes. The issuance of commercial paper by banks is now under the control of the Federal Reserve in the form of interest rate restrictions and reserve requirements. These controls have almost eliminated any incentive banks might have for raising funds in this manner.

Subordinated notes and debentures represent unsecured intermediate- and long-term debt sold by banks to investors. While such securities are liabilities of the issuing bank, they are often regarded as debt capital and are discussed in more detail later in this chapter.

Capital

Capital represents a source of funds for banks. This source accounts for about 7 percent of the funds obtained by banks if subordinated notes and debentures are excluded. Most bank capital is obtained by way of retained earnings and the sale of common stock.

HOW DO BANKS USE FUNDS?

As discussed earlier, banks acquire funds from several sources, the most important of which is deposits. We have noted that the goal of the banking firm is to make profits for its stockholders, and the way in which banks do so is largely determined by how they use these funds. By lending and investing funds at suitable rates of interest, the successful bank earns enough interest to cover its costs of operation and have some earnings left over for its owners. This section discusses the different types of loans and investments in which banks engage and some of the major considerations affecting bank lending and investing activities.

Factors affecting bank lending and investing activities

Not all funds made available to the bank by depositors are available for lending and investing purposes. Some funds must be held in cash or reserve form to meet liquidity needs and legal requirements; such funds are referred to as reserves. Banks may choose to use available funds to make any combination of several different types of loans and investments. In allocating funds among these different uses, the bank evaluates each potential loan or investment with respect to several factors:

1. The interest rates or returns available from the various alternative lending and investing activities.
2. The risk of loss associated with the various potential lending

and investing activities and the willingness of bank management to take risks.

3. The liquidity of funds tied up in various lending and investing activities.

4. Legal constraints regarding what are acceptable loans and investments.

5. Characteristics of the bank's overall liability structure.

It has been said that the fundamental problem of bank management is achieving the proper balance between return and risk. In their lending and investing activities, banks must remember that the funds being used belong to their depositors, and these depositors have the right to withdraw their funds from the bank; furthermore, a proportion of these funds is subject to withdrawal on demand. Thus prudent banking dictates that banks maintain enough cash or highly liquid loans and investments to be able to meet such withdrawals as could reasonably be expected to occur. If there were the slightest hint or suspicion that a particular bank could not meet its depositors' withdrawal demands, there would be a rush of depositors converging on the bank to obtain their funds before the bank ran short. Such a condition is referred to as a *bank run*. There are many historical examples of bank runs, and such instances often culminated in the downfall of the bank involved. The advent in 1933 of Federal Deposit Insurance covering most bank deposits has greatly reduced the possibility of bank runs. Nevertheless, banks try to maintain adequate liquidity by holding cash or primary reserves and highly liquid investments, sometimes referred to as secondary reserves.

In addition to maintaining adequate liquidity, banks must constantly guard against excessive losses from lending and investing activities. If a bank made too many bad loans, the value of its assets could fall below the amount of its liabilities, a situation known as *insolvency*. Short of contributions of additional capital by the owners, the bank would have no possible way of repaying its depositors and other creditors. Since over 90 percent of the funds invested in assets typically are provided by nonowners—a situation referred to as a *high degree of leverage*—a drop in the value of assets by 10 percent would render most banks insolvent. Thus, should a bank be unfortunate enough to have several large loans go bad within a short period of time, it would be in serious trouble. Banks protect themselves in several ways: (1) by obtaining collateral in connection with most loans, (2) by diversification so that large proportions of the bank's funds are not tied up in any one type of loan or to any one borrower, (3) by carefully selecting and training the bank officials who make loans, and (4) by subjecting many loan decisions to review by other officers, a loan committee, or sometimes by the bank's board of directors.

The risk that a borrower will not be able to repay a bank loan or that the issuer of a bond purchased by the bank will be unable to redeem that bond is an obvious risk to anyone in the lending and investing business. However, there is another major type of risk to banks or anyone who invests in marketable securities; this type of risk is often referred to as *interest-rate risk*. Banks, as purchasers of large amounts of government bonds, must be aware of the potential for loss that can occur due to interest rate changes. Even bonds with no default risk are subject to interest-rate risk.

Interest-rate risk occurs because of the inverse relationship between interest rates and the market prices of marketable securities. The market price of a bond is determined by (1) the face value of the bond, (2) the dollar amount of interest to be received each period by the bondholder, (3) the number of interest periods, and (4) current market interest rates on bonds with similar risk and other characteristics. The basic relationship between current interest rates and current market prices of outstanding bonds is given by

$$P = \sum_{t=1}^{n} \frac{I}{(1 + i)^t} + \frac{F}{(1 + i)^n}$$

where

P = the current market price of the bond;
I = the dollar amount of interest the bondholder receives per period: the product of the face value of the bond and its interest rate (coupon rate);
n = the number of time periods until the bond matures;
i = the current market interest rate on bonds of the same type and risk;
F = the face value of the bond.

For example, suppose that the U.S. Treasury wants to issue a ten-year bond having a face value of $1,000 at a time when market rates on ten-year government securities are 8 percent. The Treasury would have to pay 8 percent interest in order to sell the bond for $1,000 because its yield must be competitive with current market rates. An 8 percent bond with annual interest payments and a face value of $1,000 will yield the owner $80 per year until it matures; at that time the investor will receive the additional sum of $1,000 as the bond is redeemed. Suppose a bank purchases the bond when it is first issued and two years later wishes to sell it. If interest rates have risen, say to 10 percent, the bank will not be able to sell the bond for $1,000; the bond will have a market value of only $893.31. The price of $893.31 returns the current rate, an effective yield of 10 percent, to the buyer.[4] On the other hand, if interest rates had declined, the bond would have increased in value. The reader can verify this by changing the interest rates used in this example.

The longer the maturity of the bond, the greater will be the effect on its price of a given change in interest rates. Thus if the bond in the above example had been a 20-year bond that the bank had held for 2 years, the market value when interest rates rose 10 percent would have been $829.73, or $63.58 less than the price of the 10-year bond cited earlier. Hence, a bank that buys long-term bonds subjects itself to greater interest-rate risk than a bank that buys short-term bonds; however, the short-term bond will usually have a lower yield.

These relationships have an important implication for banks; they cannot avoid some risk in their investments even when they purchase such default-free bonds as U.S. Treasury securities. Also, while marketable securities represent a source of liquidity in that they can be sold quickly, the bank will suffer losses in liquidating the securities if interest rates have risen since the securities were purchased; the losses will be especially large if the securities are long term. For these reasons, long-term investments are not regarded as very liquid.

State and federal banking laws also influence bank loan and investment activities. The following regulations are examples: National banks cannot make a loan to any one borrower in an amount exceeding 10 percent of the bank's capital and surplus; likewise, national banks are limited in the total amount they can invest in various types of securities and must abide by certain regulations concerning loans to officers and directors; insured banks are prohibited from making loans secured by mobile homes that are located in designated special flood hazard areas; and loans made by banks to their affiliates within a holding company are subject to strict regulations. These are only a few of the areas in which bank loan and investment activities are constrained by legal bounds. Most of these regulations are designed to ensure that banks do not take undue risks in the use of their depositors' funds.

The characteristics of a bank's liability structure influence its lending and investing activities. For example, the greater the proportion of a bank's deposits that is made up of demand deposits, the more volatile and uncertain will be the bank's need for cash to meet

---

[4]$$\text{Price} = \sum_{t=1}^{8} \frac{\$80}{(1 + .10)^t} + \frac{\$1,000}{(1 + .10)^8}$$

$$= \$426.80 + \$466.51$$

$$= \$893.31.$$

deposit withdrawals. A bank with a relatively high ratio of demand deposits would have to hold more cash relative to loans and investments than would a bank holding predominantly time deposits; or at least the former's investment portfolio would need to be more liquid. A bank with large seasonal variations in its deposits should take these fluctuations into account as it formulates lending and investment policy. If a large proportion of its time deposit funds consist of relatively low-cost savings deposits rather than more costly CDs, the bank does not have to earn as much on its asset portfolio in order to maintain its profit levels. All of these considerations along with interest rates, other risk factors, and the various legal constraints must be considered by a bank as it allocates funds among the various loan requests and investment alternatives it faces. Within this framework, the following sections discuss the various types of bank loans and investments.

Investment activities

The distinction between an investment and a loan is not always clear. While both result from debtor-creditor transactions, loans are generally not marketable but investments are. Loans arise out of personal negotiation between the bank and a customer while personal contacts are not required with investments, which can be acquired in the open market. As shown in Tables 6-1 and 6-2, investments account for 22 percent of total bank assets but generate less than 15 percent of total bank operating income. Banks make investments for several reasons. Loan demand may be insufficient to absorb all of the bank's available funds. Rather than hold idle funds, banks invest in securities which generate some income and mature or can be sold as needed to meet loan demand. Even in the face of high loan demand, banks purchase some liquid securities as a substitute for holding cash reserves; these investments are often referred to as secondary reserves. Banks invest in highly liquid securities for secondary reserve purposes because doing so allows them to earn some income while remaining in a position to obtain cash quickly to meet sudden deposit withdrawal demands. On the other hand, holding cash to meet unknown but potential withdrawal demands results in the loss of interest earnings, while loans might not be a sufficiently liquid use of the funds.

Due to safety and legal requirements, banks confine the bulk of their investment activities to the securities issued by various governments. These are classified according to issuer as (1) U.S. Treasury obligations, (2) obligations of states and political subdivisions, and (3) U.S. government agency securities. Treasury obligations currently make up 36 percent of the total securities held by banks and consist of three types: (1) Treasury bills or short-term obligations of the U.S. government commonly issued at a discount to mature in either 3 months, 6 months, or 12 months; (2) Treasury notes or coupon securities issued with an initial maturity of from 1 to 7 years; and (3) Treasury bonds which may range in maturity up to 40 years. Treasury bills are a particularly desirable form of investment for banks because their short maturities make them subject to very little interest-rate risk; hence, they qualify as ideal secondary reserves.

Obligations of states and political subdivisions, or *municipals*, encompass all of the securities issued by states and their political subdivisions. The most distinctive characteristic of municipals is that interest on them is not subject to the federal income tax, a feature making them attractive to banks. Municipals are divided into two general categories: (1) general obligation bonds which can draw upon the full taxing power of the issuing government as a source of revenue for servicing the debt; and (2) revenue bonds which are dependent upon the revenue generated by a particular activity (for example, toll bridge fees, sewer and water charges) for repayment of principal and interest. Government agency securities, or *agencies*, are obligations of various government agencies such as (1) the Federal National Mortgage Associations, or "Fannie Mae"; (2) the Government National Mortgage Association, or "Ginnie Mae," (3) the Farmer's Home Administration; (4) the Federal Home Loan Bank; (5) the Federal Land Banks; (6) the Bank for Cooperatives; and others. While these securities are theoretically less safe than the direct obligations of the government, most banks regard them as completely safe from default risk, and agencies are being included in growing proportions in bank investment portfolios.

Lending activities

Loans constitute the single most important use of funds for most banks. As indicated in Tables 6-1 and 6-2, loans account for 56 percent of total bank assets and 67 percent of total bank operating income.[5] Bank lending activities can be categorized according to security, length of maturity, and purpose; the last classification is used in this section.

Commercial and industrial loans. The largest category of bank loans is commercial and industrial loans (see Table 6-1). This category has traditionally been the dominant form of bank loans and accounts for the origin of the term *commercial* bank. In recent years

---

[5] Excluding federal funds sold, which are discussed separately.

such loans have accounted for about one third of total bank loans. The range of commercial and industrial loans made by banks is very diverse and includes loans for virtually every conceivable business purpose and maturity. In the past, most of these loans were for working-capital purposes, but there has been a trend toward longer-term loans for non-working-capital projects. Thus commercial and industrial loans now finance new plant and equipment as well as inventory and accounts receivable. There is little in the nature of these loans that is standardized; collateral, rates, maturity, and payment schedule are all determined by negotiation between the bank and the borrowing firm.

Real estate loans. The second-largest category of bank loans is real estate loans. This category accounts for over 30 percent of total bank loans. Real estate loans have not always been this important in the loan portfolios of banks. American banking history is replete with examples of losses arising out of loans made on real estate. These bad experiences coupled with years of prohibition against such loans by the National Banking Act kept real estate loans out of the portfolios of many banks. However, today many banks readily make real estate loans for such diverse properties as residences, office buildings, retail stores, amusement centers, hotels and motels, and farmland. Many commercial bank real estate loans are in the form of government guaranteed VA and FHA mortgage loans.

Loans to individuals. Loans to individuals or consumer loans have only recently come to occupy a prominent place in bank loan portfolios. Today such loans account for over 24 percent of bank loans. Most of these loans are installment loans that finance such consumer durable goods as automobiles, boats, home appliances, and furniture. Since these loans are usually repaid in installments, their yield is often the highest of any bank asset. This feature, along with rising bank costs, has caused consumer loans to increase greatly in importance since World War II.

Loans to farmers. Agricultural loans (excluding real estate loans to farmers) are no longer a major form of bank lending. At the end of 1978, such loans accounted for less than 5 percent of total commercial bank loans; obviously this proportion is higher for individual banks located in agricultural areas. Much of today's agricultural credit is supplied by specialized institutions such as the Federal Land Banks and the Production Credit Associations which were organized specifically to serve agriculture. The existence of these institutions has reduced the demand for agricultural loans at banks.

Other loans. Banks make a variety of other types of loans. Among the most important are loans to investors and securities brokers and dealers for the purpose of purchasing or carrying securities. Such loans are often referred to as call loans. Banks also make loans to financial institutions including loans to other commercial banks and to foreign banks. Finally, commercial banks make loans to some state and local governments.

Federal funds sold and other uses of funds

As noted above in the discussion of federal funds purchased, banks often lend temporarily unneeded balances at Federal Reserve banks. The lending bank carries such loans on its books as an asset called *Federal funds sold and securities resale agreements*. Banks on the average use slightly less than 5 percent of their funds for this purpose, and less than 4 percent of bank operating income is derived from this source. Other uses of funds are minor. The fixed assets of banks, in contrast to most business firms, constitute a very minor proportion of total assets. Buildings, furniture, and equipment comprised less than 2 percent of bank assets at the end of 1978. Included in other uses of funds are such various and sundry items as customers' liability for bank acceptances outstanding, investments in unconsolidated subsidiaries, and direct lease financing.

WHAT ARE BANK RESERVES?

Bank reserves consist of that part of the bank's assets that are maintained in cash form. These reserves may be in the form of vault cash, deposit balances at a Federal Reserve bank, or, in the case of nonmember banks, deposit balances in other commercial banks. While the public usually thinks of banks as places where large amounts of cash are held, banks typically keep only a small fraction of their assets—less than 2 percent—in the form of vault cash. Most reserves are kept in the form of deposits at other banks including the Federal Reserve banks. The total amount of reserves maintained by all banks is less than 10 percent of their assets.

Banks hold reserves for several reasons, with the two major ones being the day-to-day need for cash to meet check-cashing and deposit withdrawal demands and the legal requirements imposed by federal and state banking laws. These laws or regulations are referred to as reserve requirements. For banks that are members of the Federal Reserve System—and this includes all federally chartered banks and some state-chartered banks—the reserve requirements are set by the Federal Reserve System according to procedures discussed in Chapter 9. The current requirements are listed in the *Federal Reserve Bulletin* and can be changed by the Federal Reserve System within certain ranges established by Congress. State-chartered banks that have elected not to become members of the Federal Reserve System are subject to the reserve requirements imposed by their respective states and the Federal Reserve System. These requirements vary considerably from state to state.[6]

The amount of reserves that banks are legally required to hold constitutes the banks' *required reserves*. Any reserves held by a bank in addition to the amount of its required reserves are referred to as *excess reserves*. Obviously total reserves must equal the sum of required reserves plus excess reserves. The total of the bank's cash reserves is also sometimes referred to as primary reserves while certain of the bank's investments—short-term government securities, banker's acceptances, commercial paper, and other highly liquid assets—are referred to as *secondary reserves*. A bank earns no direct income from its primary or cash reserve holdings, and while it may receive some "free" services in return for balances at other banks, it generally regards primary reserves as unproductive and strives to minimize them.

Even if there were no legal requirements to do so, banks would be forced to hold some cash reserves. This would be necessary in order to be able to meet customers' deposit withdrawal demands and to cash checks. Since banks do not know ahead of time what their need for currency will be, they must always maintain some vault cash even though no income is earned on this idle balance. One of the most difficult tasks for the bank is maintaining adequate cash reserves to meet legal requirements and withdrawal demands while incurring the least possible loss of income from nonearning assets. This job is made even more complicated by seasonal and other variations in business activity and the need for currency.

WHAT IS THE ROLE OF CAPITAL IN A BANK?

The typical business firm raises capital by selling stock and bonds and by retaining earnings. In that respect banks are no different from other business firms in the private sector. However, for the banking firm, capital does not constitute a major source of funds to be used in acquiring assets. In this respect, the capital of a banking firm is less important than the capital of most business firms. The reason that banks are not as dependent upon capital as firms in other industries is the relatively large amount of funds banks raise via deposits. Thus

---

[6] For a summary of state laws governing bank reserves, see R. Alton Gilbert and Jean M. Lovati, "Bank Reserve Requirements and Their Enforcement: A Comparison across States," *Review of the Federal Reserve Bank of St. Louis*, vol. 60, no. 3 (March 1978), pp. 22–32. Recent legislation granted the Fed the authority to set reserve requirements on checkable deposits in nonmember banks and thrifts.

banks possess more leverage than does the typical firm. The depositors of a bank are technically creditors of the bank, and their deposits are liabilities of the bank. These creditor-depositors are at the same time bank customers who utilize the bank as a depository for their money and near-money balances.

As shown in Table 6–4, the bulk of the capital funds of commercial banks consists of equity funds—that is, funds supplied directly (through stock purchases) or indirectly (through retained earnings) by the owners. Equity funds, therefore, represent the owners' claims against the bank. Over 93 percent of bank capital falls in this category, with less than 7 percent arising out of the sale of debt. Debt capital is in the form of subordinated notes and debentures and has increased in importance in recent years. Subordinated notes and debentures place the lender's claim against the bank behind the claims of other creditors, particularly the bank's depositors.

The major function performed by bank capital is to cushion, or protect, depositors from losses the bank may incur. Capital generates this protective cushion directly by providing a source of funds (but not a pool of funds) in addition to those provided by depositors. Capital also generates indirect protection for depositors by creating a vested interest on the part of the owners in the sound operation of the bank. This latter protection becomes more significant when one considers some of the practices and abuses that characterized early American banking history; numerous problems arose for some depositors in the early American banks because investment and lending practices were carried out almost entirely with depositors' funds. Bankers with practically no funds of their own at stake were too often tempted to engage in very risky and speculative activities in

TABLE 6–4
Capital of insured commercial banks

Capital item	Amount ($ billions)	Percent of total capital	Percent of total assets
Preferred and common stock	$17.9	19.6%	1.5%
Surplus	32.3	35.4	2.7
Undivided profits	33.5	36.7	2.8
Reserves for contingencies and other capital reserves	1.8	2.0	0.2
Total equity capital	85.5	93.7	7.2
Subordinated notes and debentures	5.8	6.3	0.5
Total capital	91.3	100.0	7.7

Source: Board of Governors of the Federal Reserve System, *Federal Reserve Bulletin*, vol. 65, no. 9 (September 1979), p. A-19.

the hopes of reaping the higher potential returns that can accompany the greater risks. One of the ways in which public regulation has made itself felt on the banking industry is in the matter of capital requirements, and today chartering statutes for banks at both the state and national levels impose minimum capital requirements. Also, the various bank regulatory agencies in their periodic bank examinations consider the adequacy of the bank's capital.

It follows that, if the major purpose of bank capital is to protect depositors, then the amount of capital a bank needs is a function of the risk to which its depositors' funds are subjected. Thus today's bank-regulatory authorities consider the makeup of a bank's assets—its loans and investments—and the quality of those assets in assessing the adequacy of a particular bank's capital. Banks with sound loans and investments need less capital than banks that have a high proportion of "problem loans" or investments that seem likely to generate losses. This approach to analyzing a bank's capital needs has evolved over time. The earliest approach to capital regulation was to set absolute limits on the minimum amount of capital required; these limits were dependent upon the size of the city in which the bank was located. Later, bank capital requirements came to depend upon the amount of deposits that the bank held. This view was based on the theory that a bank's deposit totals represented the amount of funds that needed to be protected by capital. It was not until the banking disasters of the 1930s that the current approach to bank capital regulation began to develop. Other factors that presently influence a bank's need for capital include (1) the quality and character of the bank's management and ownership, (2) the potential volatility of the bank's deposits, (3) the liquidity of the bank's assets, (4) the past and projected earnings record of the bank, and (5) the state of the economy.

SUMMARY

This chapter explores the bank as a business firm striving to make profits by lending and investing funds on deposit in the bank. Most bank income is derived from lending activities, and the most important types of loans are business loans, consumer loans, and real estate loans. Banks invest primarily in securities issued by the federal government and its agencies or by state and local governments. Banks offer various types of deposits in an effort to attract funds; in recent years, time deposits have replaced demand deposits as the most important source of funds.

Banks are highly constrained in their search for funds and in their lending and investment activities by various government-imposed regulations and by the nature of risks in the banking business. A major constraint is the need to keep reserves. As will be described in later chapters, commercial bank actions and the supply of money and credit are influenced when the Federal Reserve changes bank reserve requirements.

REVIEW QUESTIONS

1. Rank the major sources and uses of bank funds in order of increasing risk.
2. Is the federal funds rate a good barometer of credit conditions? Explain.
3. Distinguish between required reserves, excess reserves, and secondary reserves.
4. Why do the regulatory authorities require banks to keep funds tied up in reserves that are nonearning assets? Is this justifiable?
5. What is interest-rate risk, and how can banks minimize their exposure to it? Should banks try to avoid interest-rate risk?
6. The Bank of Jonesville purchased a 15-year Treasury bond three years ago. The bond has a coupon rate of 10 percent and a face value of $1,000; interest is paid annually. The bank, faced with heavy loan demands, has decided to sell the bond. Current yields on similar bonds are 9 percent. How much will the Bank of Jonesville receive when it sells the bond?
7. Given the functions of bank capital, should the regulatory authorities count subordinated notes and debentures in determining whether or not a bank has adequate capital? Explain.

SUGGESTIONS FOR ADDITIONAL READING

Havrilesky, Thomas M., and Boorman, John T. (eds.). *Current Perspectives in Banking: Operations, Management, and Regulation.* Arlington Heights, Ill.: AHM Publishing Co., 1976.

Mayer, Martin. *The Bankers.* New York: Weybright and Talley, 1974.

Nadler, Paul S. *Commercial Banking in the Economy.* 2d ed., New York: Random House, 1973.

Reed, Edward W.; Cotter, Richard V.; Gill, Edward K.; and Smith, Richard K. *Commercial Banking.* Englewood Cliffs, N.J.: Prentice-Hall, Inc., 1976.

Trescott, Paul B. *Financing American Enterprise: The Story of Commercial Banking.* New York: Harper & Row, 1963.

Wood, Oliver G. *Commercial Banking.* New York: D. Van Nostrand Co., 1978.

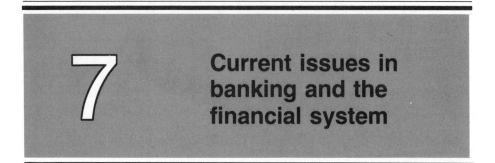

7 Current issues in banking and the financial system

WARM-UP: *Outline and questions to consider as you read*

The evolving financial system: What is its future?
    The growing competition between banks and other thrift institutions.
    The increased mechanization of funds transfer.
Do we need more than one regulatory agency?
    Problems of overlapping regulation.
    Slippage in Federal Reserve control.
Insider transactions: What should be done?
Should interest rates on deposit accounts be limited?

NEW TERMS

Automated clearinghouse (ACH): a system for channeling payments and receipts to and among banks and bank customers by electronic means.

Automatic teller machines (ATMs): machines that are capable of providing many of the services available at the teller's window of a bank or thrift institution.

Customer-bank communication terminals (CBCTs): the name given to remote electronic terminals that allow bank customers to make withdrawals, deposit cash or checks, verify balances, transfer funds, and so forth from locations away from the bank premises, or at the bank after hours.

Depository Institutions Deregulation and Monetary Control Act of 1980: major banking legislation that increased Federal Reserve control over financial institutions and removed certain regulatory barriers to competition between financial institutions.

Disintermediation: the process by which savers withdraw funds on deposit in banks, savings and loans, and other financial intermediaries and invest these funds directly in the money market.

EFTS: electronic funds transfer system.

Insider transactions: transactions between a bank and officers or directors of that bank.

Money market certificates: time certificates of deposit issued for six months with a minimum denomination of $10,000 and paying a rate of interest tied to the six-month Treasury bill rate at the time of issue.

Point of sale (POS) terminals: machines at retail outlets that are linked electronically with banks or thrifts and that can provide a variety of banking services.

Regulation Q: the Federal Reserve System regulation specifying interest rate limitations on time deposits.

Remote service units (RSUs): name given to remote electronic terminals owned by savings and loan associations.

Most students of the American financial system would attest to its dynamic nature. The institutions, their practices, and their relationships with one another have exhibited a continuing process of evolution. While legal restrictions may have slowed this process at times, there have been other times when the imposition of new or changed regulations stimulated change within the system. It appears that the next few years will be a time of rapid and significant changes in our financial system, and many of these changes will be spurred by regulatory developments. Several of the more significant developments are introduced in this chapter.

THE EVOLVING FINANCIAL SYSTEM: WHAT IS ITS FUTURE?

The growing competition between banks and other thrift institutions

One development that is almost certain to occur is an increase in competition between commercial banks and the other major types of thrift institutions in the United States. Chief among these thrift institutions are savings and loan associations, credit unions, and mutual savings banks. Historically, commercial banks have competed on a limited basis with these institutions in terms of both uses and sources of funds. With respect to sources of funds, commercial banks have traditionally relied on demand deposits as their chief source of funds. Thus they faced no competition from the thrift institutions since the latter had neither the experience nor the legal authority to issue checking accounts. The thrift institutions competed among themselves for savings balances but could only concede demand deposit business to commercial banks. Only to the extent that bank customers could be induced to substitute near-money balances for money balances could competition take place. The necessity of maintaining demand deposit balances coupled with low rates on savings accounts isolated bank demand deposit business from significant competition from the thrift institutions.

With respect to time deposits, banks of course competed directly with the thrift institutions. However, until relatively recently, time deposits were a much less important source of funds for commercial banks than they are today. Currently 60 to 70 percent of the deposit funds of many banks come from time and savings deposits, and these are subject to competition from thrift institutions. Less than a generation ago, the situation was just the opposite, with most bank funds coming from demand deposits.

Another factor leading to increased competition among banks and thrift institutions is the move in recent years by the thrifts toward the issuance of demand deposits in the form of NOW accounts and share drafts. The fact that savers can now effectively write checks on such accounts means that commercial banks face competition for transactions-related accounts. These developments have produced a blurring of the lines between checking and time deposits and between banks and thrift institutions that issue NOW accounts or share drafts.

The increased competition for transactions-related balances will be heightened by the growth of EFTS—electronic funds transfer systems. EFTS technology is still in the developing stage, but certain possibilities are already clear. Remote terminals at such locations as shopping centers, airports, and factories will allow customers to transfer funds from their accounts and thus pay bills without writing checks or using cash. These remote transfers of funds will not be limited to commercial bank demand deposits. Some savings and loans have already made remote transfer service available to their depositors; furthermore, mutual savings banks and savings and loans have for some time provided a similar arrangement whereby customers can implement a transfer of funds by telephone out of their accounts to third parties. The trend toward increased competition among banks and thrifts for the depositors' dollars is evident in Table 7–1 which lists recent regulatory and legislative developments having an effect on the evolving competition among the major financial intermediaries.

Banks and other thrift institutions are becoming more competitive with respect to their uses of funds, that is, in the acquisition of earning assets. There is a trend among thrift institutions to become much less specialized in their lending activities than in the past. As this occurs, there is increased competition in lending markets traditionally dominated by commercial banks. Mutual savings banks and savings and loan associations, which have a long history of specialization in home mortgage lending, are beginning to enter the consumer lending field, including the credit card market. Credit unions, which have been competitors of banks in the consumer installment loan business, are now beginning to engage in long-term mortgage lending as well as credit card lending.

While thrift institutions are moving into lending areas traditionally "reserved" for banks, banks are moving more and more into some of the lending areas long dominated by the thrift institutions. Although some banks avoid long-term mortgage lending, both the Federal Reserve Board and the Hunt Commission—a special committee appointed by President Nixon to study the nation's financial system—recommended measures to stimulate real estate lending by commercial banks. This nation in recent years has given a high priority to the construction of new housing, and the constant search for ways to channel new funds into the housing markets is a reflection of that priority. It therefore seems reasonable to expect Congress to encourage even more housing-related lending by commercial banks, and future legislation is likely to stimulate the movement already under way by commercial banks. To the extent that this occurs, it would of course put banks in more direct competition with the mutual savings banks and S&Ls.

TABLE 7-1
Recent legislative and regulatory changes leading to increased deposit competition among banks and other major thrift institutions

September 1970

Savings and loan associations (S&Ls) are permitted to make preauthorized nonnegotiable transfers from savings accounts for household-related expenses.

June 1972

Massachusetts mutual savings banks (MSBs) begin to offer NOW accounts.

New Hampshire MSBs begin to offer NOW accounts.

January 1974

All depository institutions in Massachusetts and New Hampshire (except credit unions) are authorized by congressional action to offer NOW accounts.

January 1974

Nebraska S&L begins point of sale (POS) electronic funds transfer system. First Federal S&L of Lincoln, Nebraska, places an electronic terminal in a supermarket. The terminal allows customers of the S&L to pay for groceries, make deposits to or withdrawals from their savings accounts.

April 1974

State of Washington enacts legislation that allows state-chartered commercial banks, MSBs, and S&Ls to establish automated facilities throughout the state, provided that those operating these facilities share the cost and operations of the terminals when asked to do so by the state authorities. Commercial banks are required to share facilities with other commercial banks and have the option of sharing them with thrift institutions. Thrifts are permitted, but not required, to share facilities.

June 1974

New York State bank regulation permits MSB to offer non-interest-bearing NOW accounts (NINOWs).

August 1974

Administrator of the National Credit Union Administration grants three federal credit unions temporary authority to begin offering share drafts.

September 1974

Pennsylvania attorney general rules MSB may legally offer a form of NOW account.

December 1974

Comptroller of the Currency's interpretive ruling permits national banks to operate customer-bank communication terminals (CBCTs).

Federal Home Loan Bank Board (FHLBB) adopts a regulation that gives depositors traveling more than 50 miles from their homes access to their savings account balances through any other federally insured S&L by means of a travelers convenience withdrawal (wire or telephone access).

TABLE 7–1 *(continued)*

April 1975

FHLBB adopts two regulations:

1. Authorizes federal S&Ls to offer their customers bill-paying service from interest-bearing savings accounts.
2. Allows federal S&L service corporations and companies to make consumer loans.

Commercial banks are authorized to make transfers from a customer's savings account to a demand deposit account upon telephone order from the customer.

June 1975

Oregon governor signs into law legislation that allows the state's only MSB to offer checking accounts.

U.S. district court rules CBCTs authorized for national banks by the Comptroller of the Currency are illegal and must be shut down.

September 1975

Massachusetts MSB introduces variable rate mortgage (VRM) program.

Commercial banks are authorized to make preauthorized nonnegotiable transfers from a customer's savings account for any purpose.

October 1975

State legislation permits state-chartered thrift institutions in Maine to offer personal checking accounts.

December 1975

State legislation permits thrift institutions in Connecticut to offer personal checking accounts.

Additional credit unions began to offer share draft accounts following the end of the six-month pilot program initiated in fall 1974.

February 1976

Congress authorizes all depository institutions in New England to offer interest-paying NOW accounts.

May 1976

New York governor signs legislation permitting checking accounts, including overdraft privileges, at state-chartered MSBs and S&Ls.

October 1976

U.S. Supreme Court lets stand ruling that CBCTs are bank branches.

April 1977

All but 15 of the nation's 470 MSBs have either NOW accounts, traditional checking accounts, or a combination of the two.

Legislation enacted to expand credit union lending authority, including authority to make 30-year mortgage loans.

March 1980

Depository Institutions Deregulation and Monetary Control Act authorizes nationwide NOW accounts beginning December 31, 1980, and makes permanent the existing authority for bank automatic transfer services, savings and loan remote service units, and credit union share draft accounts.

Source: Adapted from Jean M. Lovati, "Growing Similarities among Financial Institutions," *Review of the Federal Reserve Bank of St. Louis,* vol. 59, no. 10 (October 1977), pp. 6–7.

The increased mechanization of funds transfer

There is little doubt that Electronic Funds Transfer (EFT) will come to occupy a more prominent place in this country's payments mechanism. Furthermore, the development of systems of EFT will change not only the mechanics of making payments but also the financial institutions that are involved in the process. As this occurs, certain issues will arise which will have to be decided by the regulatory authorities and by Congress. Among the issues currently emerging are the following: Who should own the physical facilities of the system? Should EFT transactions be regulated? If so, who is to have regulatory authority over such facilities and the transactions carried out through them? What should be the goals of the regulatory authorities? Should these remote facilities be treated as branches? Will EFT systems lead to invasions of privacy with respect to an individual's finances?

Forms of mechanized funds transfer. Mechanization of funds transfers is taking on several general forms; one form is the Automated Clearing House (ACH). An ACH is comparable to the clearing-house for checks discussed in Chapter 6 except that the items processed are not pieces of paper but electronic impulses on magnetic computer tapes. The substitution of magnetic tapes for paper instruments reduces the time and costs associated with the payments process. This is especially true where repetitive transfers are involved as in the case of payroll deposits, mortgage payments, and insurance premiums. For example, an employee (customer) can give a standing authorization for wage (bill) data to be included on a magnetic tape that will be sent by the employer (seller) to the latter's bank. That bank, known as the originating bank, sends a tape of data to the ACH which sorts the data according to other banks involved. The ACH then forwards to each of these banks a taped, printed, or punched record of transactions affecting its customers; each receiving bank notifies its customers via a bank statement of the transactions affecting their accounts.

In 1978 a nationwide linkage between different ACH associations and facilities of the Federal Reserve System was finalized; the network ties together 32 regional ACH associations throughout the United States and uses computers in 34 Federal Reserve offices. Linked to the system are some 9,400 banks, 1,500 thrift institutions, and almost 6,000 customer corporations. Throughout the network, any financial institution that is a member of an ACH association can transport payment transfer instructions nationwide by way of magnetic tape entries. Currently, most transactions carried out through the network involve payments of a recurring nature.

A second form of development of EFT systems involves the use of *electronic terminals*. This term is applied to a variety of machines, facilities, and systems that facilitate financial transactions. One type of electronic terminal is the automatic teller machines or ATMs which have been widely installed since 1970. These machines are capable of providing many of the services normally available at a teller window in a bank or thrift institution and are called various names by different institutions. These names, such as redi-teller, anytime-teller, mini-teller, imply one of the major ATM advantages—an ability to provide customer service on a 24-hour, seven-day basis. Thus a customer may make cash withdrawals, cash deposits, credit card withdrawals, or transfer funds between savings and checking accounts. Since these machines are not always attached to the bank's premises, the question of whether or not they constitute branches has become an issue.

Electronic terminals of another type are known as Point Of Sale (POS) terminals. These are manned machines that may be located at major retail outlets and can provide a variety of services such as accepting deposits, allowing withdrawals, verifying balances, and transferring funds between different accounts. POS terminals operated by commercial banks are known as Customer-Bank Communication Terminals (CBCTs) while savings and loan associations refer to them as Remote Service Units (RSUs). Of all the EFT systems, POS systems seem the most likely to lead to significant changes in our payments system because they can be applied to the millions of daily transactions that make up the bulk of our funds transfers. Since POS terminals would allow payments without either currency or checks, their increasing adoption would indeed herald the advent of the checkless society.

Regulatory and control issues. Thousands of point of sale terminals are being installed in various areas of the country. In many cases it is the S&Ls that are leading the way. The issue of whether or not such facilities should be construed as a form of branching has been raised and remains unsettled. As noted in Table 7–1, the courts have tended to regard them as branches and therefore subject to branching restrictions, a ruling that has undoubtedly retarded the adoption of these facilities. The Supreme Court has ruled that CBCTs constitute branches if deposits and withdrawals are made through them. The ultimate resolution of this issue will lie with Congress; unless Congress frees the banks to develop POS terminals to their full potential, the move toward electronic money will be slowed considerably.

The clearing of checks is the most expensive function performed by our financial system, and the potential for resource savings through continued adoption of EFT systems is obvious. Widespread placement of POS terminals linked to bank computers which in turn are linked to an ACH network would allow us to reduce the physical exchange of currency and checks. If we are correct in assuming that our financial system will continue to adopt these new technologies as they become feasible, to what extent should society impose controls to guide the system in its evolution?

Looking first at the question of who should be allowed to own and operate EFT facilities, several options are possible. Commercial banks, which traditionally have been heavily involved in our payments mechanism, could be granted sole authority to own and operate the ACHs, POS terminals, and automatic teller machines. Alternatively, in order to increase competition, other thrift institutions could be granted authority equal to that of banks. This latter possibility seems to be the direction in which current policy is moving. Still another line of approach would remove all restrictions on the ownership of parts of the EFT systems. Likely entrants from the nonfinancial sector would then include the telephone companies, computer firms, and data-processing organizations.

The approach that is chosen from among the above alternatives is likely to hinge on a tradeoff between two factors—efficiency and competition. Normally it would be desirable on efficiency and consumer welfare grounds to have as much competition as possible; in some circumstances, however, competition reduces efficiency when compared to the alternative of fewer but larger operators. If the operations of an ACH are similar to those of a telephone system or electric utility system, there could be significant economies of scale, and the level of output required to achieve maximum efficiency of operations would be very large. In such situations we have generally foregone competition among firms in favor of one or a few large firms able to operate at a highly efficient (low-cost) level. We have, however, subjected those firms' operations to the regulations of some government body or agency. The early evidence seems to indicate that the available economies of scale, at least with respect to ACH operations, are exhausted rather rapidly and that most markets will thus support several entrants.[1] There does not, therefore, seem to be strong sentiment for severely limiting the formation of ACH systems.

The situation with respect to electronic terminals is less clear. The POS systems require an initial capital investment that is difficult to justify in terms of cost savings unless the system handles a large

---

[1] Charles J. Smaistrla, "Current Issues in Electronic Funds Transfer," *Review of the Federal Reserve Bank of Dallas* (February 1977), pp. 1–2.

volume of transactions.[2] Thus in markets with small volumes, we may be faced with the choice of joint purchase and operation of the machines by different institutions—a situation with potential for collusion and likely to be viewed as counter to the spirit of our antitrust laws—or of foregoing the potential cost savings that such machines could bring.

An alternative solution is for a third party in the form of a large institution to own the machines and allow shared use of them by a number of small institutions on a fee basis. Such an arrangement still leaves some unsolved problems. For example, if a large correspondent bank purchases a POS system, installs it in a small-town shopping center, and licenses the two local banks to use it, what happens if a local S&L also wants to participate? Or, what if a bank in another city demands access? In short, will use of the facility be restricted, and if so, how, and on what grounds? Will the Federal Reserve have the ultimate say since banks are involved? What if the banks are not member banks? If savings and loan associations also use the system, will they be subject to Federal Reserve authority, or will they remain solely under the authority of the Federal Home Loan Bank Board, the traditional regulatory body of the federally chartered S&Ls? The question of whether or not such terminals should be regarded as bank branches has already been noted. A related aspect of the question is whether or not banks or other financial institutions can use electronic terminals to establish "offices" across state lines contrary to current branching restrictions.

Monetary policy issues. The advent of EFT systems may have implications for the effectiveness of monetary policy. The functions performed by EFT systems are similar to the functions currently performed in any payments system, the primary function being the transfer of purchasing power. Under EFT, purchasing power is transferred via electronic impulses rather than by physically exchanging pieces of paper or metal. This change in the manner of transferring purchasing power will affect the ways in which the public holds and manages its money as well as the definitions of money and the Federal Reserve's methods of controlling the supply of money. While there is still much debate about how to administer monetary policy most effectively, the Federal Reserve directs most of its efforts towards the money supply and credit conditions. EFT is likely to affect monetary policy management in that defining, measuring, and therefore controlling money will be more compli-

---

[2] David A. Walker, *An Analysis of EFTS Activity Levels, Costs, and Structure in the U.S.*, Federal Deposit Insurance Corporation, Working Paper no. 76-4 (Washington, D.C.: U.S. Government Printing Office, 1976).

cated. The problem of how the money stock should be defined and measured is a complex issue as was noted in Part I, especially in Chapter 3.

EFT will also make the administration of monetary policy more complicated because of the increased speed and efficiency that will be introduced into the country's payments mechanism. Money will change hands more quickly or, put another way, it will take a smaller volume of money to carry out the total number of desired economic transactions. As noted in Chapter 2, economists refer to the average number of times a unit of money changes hands as the velocity of that monetary unit. The increased use of EFT systems should result in an increase in the velocity of money. There will be smaller idle balances as those balances primarily held for transaction purposes can be used more efficiently; other things being equal, the economy will need a smaller money supply than it would need without EFT. The burden of adjusting the money supply appropriately to counter the effects of EFT on velocity will fall upon the Federal Reserve System. The faster the move toward EFT within the financial system, the more rapidly adjustments will have to be made and the more difficult it will be to regulate the magnitude and timing of these adjustments.

The fact that EFT will facilitate the transfer of funds from one type of account or institution to another will cause all types of deposit balances to be more sensitive to interest rate changes. Hence, balances in accounts that are held primarily for transactions purposes are likely to be more volatile than in the past. This will make monetary management increasingly difficult during short time periods.

As will be explained in Chapter 9, the Federal Reserve cannot control the money supply directly; it must do so indirectly by controlling the monetary base and the reserves of the banking system. If EFT systems shift more and more of our money supply to accounts at thrift institutions, the Fed's control over bank reserves could become a less-effective means of controlling the total money supply. Furthermore, under existing reserve requirements, a given level of reserves can support different levels of the money supply depending on whether the reserves are held by small banks or large banks and on whether or not deposits are held in demand deposit or time deposit form. Thus if the Fed is to have effective control over a broadly defined measure of the money supply (including balances in institutions other than member banks), broad and uniform control over reserve requirements is necessary. This was a major consideration in the passage of the Depository Institutions Deregulation and Monetary Control Act of 1980.

The privacy issue.   Still another issue that arises in connection with the emerging EFT system is that of privacy. There is some apprehension on the part of consumers that a system containing a large mass of data on the financial transactions of individuals may encourage abuse of the rights of personal privacy. To a large extent, this issue may be more apparent than real since the existing paper-based system of payments results in the collection and storage of data on individuals' transactions. Whether they occur by check or through EFT, most transactions generate some kind of record for the consumer to use in verifying amount, dates, parties, etc. These transactions records must be kept for a period of time consistent with the need to verify the accuracy of the transaction involved. By changing to a computer storage system, will records be kept longer than they are now, and will it be easier for unauthorized parties to obtain access to these records? For example, participation by the Federal Reserve, which may be considered an arm of the government, in the EFT system through ACH operations might make it easier for other arms of the government to obtain financial data on private citizens in ways that violate rights to privacy.

The National Commission on Electronic Funds Transfer (NCEFT) devoted a full chapter in its final report to the question of privacy. Likewise, the Privacy Protection Study Commission argued that EFT expands the potential for abuse of personal privacy. The basis for these fears is the fact that EFT would lower the cost and increase the ease of access to personal financial information. It should be stressed, however, that the type of records and the information retained under EFTS would not differ significantly from information currently retained; only the form in which the information is transferred and stored will differ. If the reduced cost of record keeping results in the storage of information over longer time periods, this could increase the risk that the records would be abused. The Bank Secrecy Act calls for collection, storage, and reporting of substantial amounts of information on individual financial transactions, and the Supreme Court has held that there is no constitutional guarantee of the individual's right to privacy with respect to information maintained by his depositor institution.[3] Thus as the EFT systems evolve, the matter of privacy of payments information will be a matter for Congress to determine. The Right to Financial Privacy Act of 1978 moves one step toward resolving these issues; it generally restricts

---

[3] Bank Secrecy Act: 12 U.S.C. Sections 1829b (1951–59) and U.S.C. Sections 1051–1122 (1970); *United States* v. *Miller*: 425 U.S. 436 (1976) and 92 S. Ct. 1619 (1976).

access by federal agencies, other than the bank regulatory agencies, to customer financial records held by banks.

DO WE NEED MORE THAN ONE REGULATORY AGENCY?

The current banking regulatory framework is a labyrinth of laws, agencies, and appendages resulting from 200 years of dual federal and state control of banking. A study of American banking history reveals a policy of reacting to financial crises by adding new regulatory bodies without dismantling the old ones; often, the new bodies were assigned functions that overlapped those of existing agencies. The National Banking Act set up the position of Comptroller of the Currency in 1863 with the power to grant bank charters and supervise the new national banks. Since the states were already in the bank-chartering business, a dual banking system arose in the United States. The Federal Reserve System was formed in 1913 in response to the panic of 1907. This agency was charged with supervising and regulating the national banks, which were already under the jurisdiction of the Comptroller of the Currency, and any state-chartered banks that elected to become members of the Federal Reserve System. In 1933, in response to the bank failures that accompanied the Great Depression, the Federal Deposit Insurance Corporation was organized and given regulatory power over all banks applying for federal deposit insurance. Since insured banks may be either federally or state chartered and may or may not belong to the Federal Reserve System, another layer of regulatory framework was imposed on the banking system. The complex and overlapping nature of bank regulation is illustrated in Figure 7–1.

Problems of overlapping regulation

Our network of bank regulatory agencies creates several problems. Many banks are subject to regulation by different agencies, and these agencies sometimes have different rules and standards for the banks under their jurisdiction. Hence, not all banks operate under the same rules, and charges of unfair and discriminatory regulation arise. Consider, for example, the case of state-chartered banks that elect not to join the Federal Reserve System. Prior to enactment of the Depository Institutions Deregulation and Monetary Control Act, nonmember bank reserve requirements were set entirely by the states. In some states, reserve requirements on demand deposits were as low as 7 percent, of which one fourth could be short-term U.S. government securities. On the other hand, Federal Reserve

FIGURE 7–1
Regulatory structure of the commercial banking system

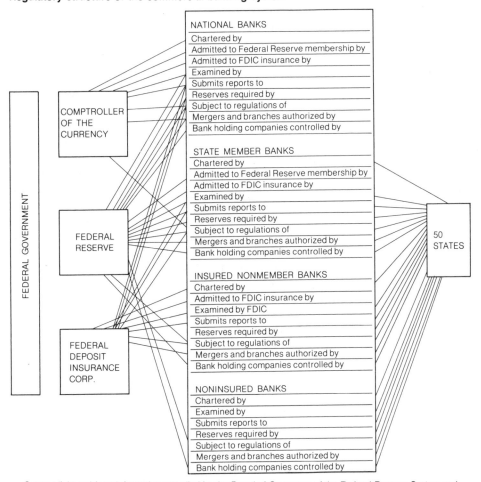

Source: Adapted from information compiled by the Board of Governors of the Federal Reserve System and reprinted in *Financial Institutions: Reform and the Public Interest,* Staff Report, 1973, 93d Congress, 1st Sess. (Washington, D.C.: U.S. Government Printing Office, 1973), p. 7.

member banks in the same state had to meet reserve requirements set by the Federal Reserve, and these requirements were as much as 16.25 percent; this differential put member banks at a disadvantage in competing with state nonmember banks. Member banks were often at a further disadvantage because their reserves had to be held in the form of vault cash or deposits at Federal Reserve banks; either form of reserves was a nonearning asset. Such a situation, it was argued, discriminated against the stockholders, and, perhaps, the customers of the national banks.[4]

Other problems arise because a bank may be regulated by more than one agency. In some cases the various agencies have conflicting rules, and a decision must be made as to which agency's rules shall be binding. For example, the 50 states have different laws with respect to branching: some prohibit it; others allow it on a limited basis; still others permit it virtually without limits.[5] Furthermore, should federally chartered banks be subject to state branching laws, or should they be subject to federal laws? If the latter, which federal agency or agencies should have the authority over branching regulations? Initially the state and federal authorities went their separate ways; national banks were not allowed to branch regardless of state law, while some states allowed their state-chartered banks to do so. Congress eventually passed legislation subjecting national banks to branching laws of the states in which they operate. In the case of the regulation of stock market credit, Congress took a different approach. In this matter Congress gave the Federal Reserve effective control over all banks including state-chartered nonmember banks.

Another illustration of conflicting regulations coming out of different regulatory agencies concerns the inclusion of capital notes and debentures as capital in calculating a bank's legal lending limit. In 1961 the Comptroller of the Currency ruled that subordinated notes and debentures could be considered as a portion of the unimpaired capital of national banks when calculating legal lending limits. The Board of Governors, on the other hand, ruled that state member banks may not include capital notes and debentures as a part of capital in arriving at legal lending limits. State laws in this matter are mixed, with about 50 percent of them allowing this inclusion.

There have been other cases of conflicts among rulings of the three federal agencies; a 1973 staff report of the House Committee on Banking and Currency cites the following examples:

1. Member banks "buying" reserves from other member banks:
    Comptroller—such purchases and sales do not constitute borrowing for purposes of statutory limitations on loans and borrowings.
    Board of Governors—such transactions constitute loans and borrowing under statutory provisions.

---

[4] Because of the higher reserve requirements, the bank might raise fees and loan rates to maintain its profit position. This would shift some of the cost of higher reserves to the bank's customers.

[5] Refer back to Table 5-2.

2. Purchase of stock of foreign banks:

    Comptroller—national banks may directly purchase stock of foreign banks.

    Board of Governors—direct acquisition and holding by member banks of foreign bank stocks is not permissible.

3. Purchase of stock of banks:

    Board of Governors—state member banks cannot lawfully purchase the stock of another domestic bank.

    Comptroller—national banks may lawfully acquire such stock.[6]

Obviously such situations create confusion and result in inefficiencies in the regulatory process.

Slippage in Federal Reserve control[7]

Another frequent complaint against the multiagency regulatory framework is that it weakens Federal Reserve control over the banking and monetary system. With the exception of some reserve requirements, most Fed controls extend only to member banks, the number of which has declined by more than 300 between 1970 and 1978. While member banks still do the bulk of the nation's banking business and hold a substantial majority of the banking system's deposits (about 70 percent in 1980), many observers see shortcomings in the present arrangements. Many banks escape important regulations imposed by the Fed on member banks. Not only does this result in unfair, or at least uneven, regulation, but it also may impair the Fed's ability to transmit monetary policy actions efficiently and completely throughout the system. The problem is potentially even more serious because banks have the option of remaining national banks (and member banks) or becoming state banks (and possibly nonmembers), and vice versa. Thus in times when Federal Reserve regulatory policy is more stringent than state regulations, banks may avoid the more restrictive regulations by dropping their Federal Reserve membership and becoming state banks. This puts the Fed in a dilemma: Should it adopt policies that are less restrictive than it considers desirable, or should it impose the more restrictive policies and risk driving more banks out from under Fed control? If the latter alternative is chosen, both present and future policies may have less

---

[6]U.S. Congress, House Committee on Banking and Currency, *Financial Institutions: Reform and the Public Interest*, Staff Report, 1973, 93d Congress, 1st Sess. (Washington, D.C.: U.S. Government Printing Office, 1973), pp. 58–59.

[7] This topic is treated in detail in Chapter 11.

impact because they would be applicable to a smaller number of banks.

The recent introduction of transactions balances at S&Ls, credit unions, and mutual savings banks has further complicated this issue. These institutions are subject to their own respective regulatory bodies—the Federal Home Loan Bank Board regulates the federally chartered S&Ls, and the National Credit Union Administration oversees the credit unions. A coordinated approach to regulating the monetary activities of these thrift institutions must be worked out by their respective regulating authorities on the one hand and the Federal Reserve on the other. Present evidence, based on the Depository Institutions Deregulation and Monetary Control Act, indicates that Congress will move in the direction of granting more power to the Fed.

INSIDER TRANSACTIONS: WHAT SHOULD BE DONE?

The issue of bank insider transactions came into prominence in the case of former director of the Office of Management and Budget, Bert Lance. Lance, a banker before coming to Washington as a member of the Carter administration, was alleged to have used his position of power within a bank he controlled to engage in transactions that would have been impossible or illegal for outsiders. The subsequent investigation into Lance's financial dealings raised questions regarding what constitutes acceptable bank behavior in cases where a bank official's personal business becomes intertwined with the bank's business as carried out by the official. The final repercussions of the Lance affair are not yet known, but one effect has been more restrictive legislation with respect to insider transactions.

The problem of insider transactions can best be illustrated by several examples. Consider the following hypothetical situation: Noel Jones is president of Hometown Bank and Trust Co. which utilizes Big City National Bank as a correspondent bank. Following a long-established practice within the banking industry, Hometown Bank and Trust maintains a $200,000 deposit balance with Big City National as compensation for services performed. These services would include assistance in clearing checks, supplying currency and coins, participating in large loans, handling foreign exchange requests, and providing market information. One day Jones requests a $50,000 loan from Big City National to purchase additional stock in Hometown Bank. Furthermore, Jones makes it very clear to Big City National that a preferential rate is expected. Let us suppose that Jones's personal financial condition and reputation are very strong, and Big City National has every reason to believe that the loan would be a safe one. Should Big City National grant the loan? Should it do so at a preferential rate? Should it risk losing a profitable correspondent balance account by refusing to make Jones a loan on terms better than are available to other good customers? If Hometown Bank and Trust did not use Big City National as its correspondent, should the latter bank make the loan in an effort to secure a profitable correspondent balance?

In October 1973, the U.S. National Bank in San Diego became insolvent and was absorbed by the Crocker National Bank of San Francisco. U.S. National, with $1.3 billion in assets, 64 offices, and 350,000 depositors, was at that time the largest U.S. bank ever to fail. Its failure resulted from insider transactions on a massive scale. The bank had made large loans to companies in which the bank president, C. Arnholt Smith, had financial interests. When these loans turned bad, the bank was doomed. It is generally conceded that these insider transactions were the major factor contributing to the bank's demise.[8]

What should U.S. National Bank have done with the loan applications of firms in which the bank's president had an interest? Should these companies have been forced to carry their banking business elsewhere? Should bank officials be barred from owning stock in firms that do business with the bank? In the aftermath of the failure of U.S. National, the Board of Governors of the Federal Reserve System requested that Congress pass legislation that would allow the board to exercise more effective control over such insider transactions by imposing limitations on the amount of the combined borrowings of an insider and related business interests. Thus if A. B. Ivy were a bank director and had an interest in business X and business Y, the bank would be required to combine Ivy's personal loan at the bank with the loans to the business firms. The combined total would be treated as outstanding to a single borrower and would be subject to existing state and federal lending limitations. In 1978, Congress passed the Financial Institutions Regulatory and Interest Rate Control Act granting the Federal Reserve additional powers to regulate insider transactions. In addition to limiting the amount of insider loans, the act also contains limitations on other types of insider transactions. For example, loans by a bank to insiders of another bank cannot be made at preferential rates. Thus in the hypothetical case presented earlier, Big City National would be in violation of the new law if it granted Jones' request.

---

[8] Robert Heller and Norris Willatt, *Can You Trust Your Bank?* (New York: Charles Scribner's Sons, 1977), pp. 136–42.

Another example of a common type of insider transaction involves loans by a bank to its own officials and directors at preferential rates—that is, rates not normally available to outsiders. For example, Brown, a local merchant, sits on the board of directors of First State Bank and is a successful entrepreneur who has a large personal net worth and possesses an excellent reputation in the community. Brown's personal and business accounts are very valuable to the bank, which is one reason Brown was elected to the board. When Brown applies for either a personal or business loan at the bank, should the bank be allowed to grant the loan at a preferential rate?

The problem posed by the foregoing example is made even more complex by the fact that the bank's cost of doing business with insiders is likely to be lower than the cost of dealing with other customers since the bank's knowledge of the creditworthiness of insiders is likely to be better or at least less costly to obtain. Also, banks have traditionally recognized that the business of some customers is more profitable than the business of others. Regardless of whether they are dealing with outsiders or insiders, banks have shown a willingness to make loans at lower rates to customers who maintain large deposit balances with the bank. This willingness reflects competition for profitable accounts, but it may also be construed as a form of preferential treatment.

Another complicating consideration with respect to the question of insider transactions involves the "ownership rights" that may be involved. If, in our above example, Brown were a large stockholder—and therefore part owner—of the local clothing store, very little thought would be given to whether or not the owner should have the right to purchase shoes at a lower price than other customers. However, as a bank stockholder and director, the right to loans at preferential rates is seriously questioned. Do bank stockholders possess fewer ownership rights than the owners of other businesses? This is one of the issues involved in the regulation of insider transactions.

One may argue that there is an important consideration that strengthens the case for limiting ownership rights where banks are concerned. The public, in the form of the bank's depositors, has the potential of being affected by insider transactions to a greater extent than in the case of most nonbank insider transactions. Take the case of U.S. National Bank of San Diego and C. Arnholt Smith; when Smith's insider transactions at U.S. National resulted in losses for the bank, this put the bank's creditors (depositors) in greater jeopardy than would be normal for most nonbank enterprises. If other businesses in which Smith had an ownership interest wish to sell to him on credit at preferential prices so that lower profits or even bankruptcy occurs, it is primarily Smith and the other owners who will be harmed. On the other hand, opponents of regulation of insider transactions may argue that, in the case of nonbank insider transactions, the firm's creditors also stand to be harmed, and thus the situation is really no different than with respect to banks. However, the potential harm is usually much greater for banks since few business firms operate with debt-equity ratios as high as banks. Ultimately, then, we can say that the relatively high debt-equity ratios of banks make them very sensitive to losses.

There are other reasons why the potential for losses becomes great in cases of insider transactions. Too often insider transactions may short-circuit an otherwise sound decision-making process and result in riskier loans which lead to losses that are materially harmful to the bank's depositors. In fact, there are many cases in American banking history where this has occurred. These instances and the above line of reasoning are largely responsible for existing regulations concerning bank insider transactions. These regulations are discussed below, but first we note additional arguments by opponents of these regulations.

There appear to be three primary defenses raised by opponents of regulations governing bank insider transactions. One of these, the ownership rights issue, has been dealt with to some extent above and will not be repeated here. Another defense is based on the argument that a bank must offer its officers and directors adequate compensation if it is to secure competent management. Since loans at preferential rates, overdraft privileges, and other benefits to insiders are a form of indirect compensation, such transactions help banks attract and hold qualified directors and officers. To prohibit such transactions would force the bank to increase direct compensation which, because of tax effects, may be more expensive. Proponents of regulations may reply by asking what is wrong with legitimate direct compensation.

A more theoretical, but perhaps stronger, case against additional regulations governing insider transactions can be made by arguing that the bank's costs are lower when dealing with insiders, and it can, therefore, "rebate" some of this cost savings to the customer in the form of preferential rates. Lower costs may arise because of greater knowledge of the customer and less need for time-consuming and expensive credit analysis.

In conclusion, it should be observed that whether or not to regulate bank insider transactions is not the issue; the issue is how much regulation and in what form. The principle of regulation of insider transactions is well established by the presence of several laws that have been on the books for many years. Going back to 1913, the

Federal Reserve Act prohibits a member bank from buying or selling property in a transaction with a director on terms that are preferential to the director; member banks are prohibited from paying preferential interest rates on the deposits of insiders; a person engaged in the business of underwriting may not serve as a director, an officer, or an employee of a member bank; extension of credit by a member bank to its own executive officers or to a partnership involving one of the bank's executive officers is limited with respect to amounts, conditions, and required reports, and such extensions of credit may not be on terms more favorable than those available to other borrowers.[9]

SHOULD INTEREST RATES ON DEPOSIT ACCOUNTS BE LIMITED?

Banks have been limited in the rates of interest they can offer depositers in order to attract additional deposits. These interest limitations take two forms: (1) federal banking laws impose an absolute prohibition against the payment of interest on demand deposit accounts, and (2) the maximum rates that can be paid for various types of time and savings deposits have been controlled by the Federal Reserve System through what is known as Regulation Q. Both forms of interest controls were implemented during the Depression. Prior to the passage of the Banking Act of 1933, commercial banks engaged in the practice of paying interest on demand deposits. That act and the Banking Act of 1935 authorized the Federal Reserve Board and the Federal Deposit Insurance Corporation to regulate the rates of interest paid on bank time deposits. In 1966, Congress gave the Federal Home Loan Bank Board (FHLBB) authority to regulate interest payments on funds held in the nation's savings and loan associations. Thus three federal regulatory bodies have shared control of interest rates paid to depositors.

The rationale behind the initial introduction of controls over deposit interest rates resulted from three propositions:

1. The payment of "too much" interest on deposits would induce banks to acquire risky assets in an attempt to offset the resulting high cost of funds.
2. Larger city banks would outbid smaller country banks for deposits and thus initiate a drain of funds from rural areas and small towns to large cities.
3. Lowering the return to depositors would reduce bank costs and result in lower interest costs to borrowers.

---

[9] Comptroller of the Currency, *Comptroller's Manual for National Banks*, 1977 Supplement, sect. 1, pp. 14, 38, and 39.

The extension of controls to savings and loan associations was motivated by several objectives. Chief among these was the desire to assure a steady and inexpensive flow of funds into the residential construction market: during periods of high interest rates, thrift institutions would not be forced to pay high rates for funds; hence their lending rates would remain lower, and prospective homeowners would not be driven out of the housing market because of high financing costs. As we shall see, interest rate ceilings have not always worked in this manner.

Several problems arise in connection with deposit interest limitations. There is a distributional problem in that deposit interest limitations subsidize borrowers at the expense of savers. Financial institutions are only intermediaries that channel the funds of savers to borrowers. Do we want public policy to encourage borrowing? If so, what kinds of borrowing? The sentiment in the United States has been that borrowing to finance the purchase of a home is worthy of encouragement by public policy. What about other borrowing? Is it worthwhile public policy to encourage the purchase of a new automobile by promoting low-cost bank loans? More important, are the benefits of subsidizing borrowers sufficient to offset the costs such policies impose upon savers? Such costs may not be limited to the private effects on savers, since economic inefficiencies may be created that impose an opportunity cost on society as a whole.

A related issue involves the distribution of the cost burden among savers. It is generally agreed that small savers are hurt most by interest rate ceilings; large savers avoid the effects of rate ceilings by investing directly in primary financial claims. For example, Smith, a wealthy investor, might obtain 10 percent or better by investing in Treasury bills which are virtually free of risk. Jones, an average saver with $2,000 in a savings account, has no recourse but to accept a lower interest return because the minimum investment in Treasury bills is $10,000. Furthermore, interest rates paid by commercial banks on negotiable CDs of $100,000 or more are not regulated, while the small saver can only receive up to whatever the rate ceiling allows. In recent years, when the rate of inflation has run between 6 and 14 percent, small savers have had no alternative but to keep funds in accounts yielding less than the rate of inflation. Large savers have been able to shift funds away from the financial intermediaries or purchase large CDs and obtain higher market rates. In view of these considerations, there were many observers who questioned the fairness of a system of interest rate ceilings.

Still another problem connected with interest rate regulations is the process of disintermediation—a situation in which savers withdraw funds from financial intermediaries and invest them directly in primary financial claims. This process occurs when market interest rates exceed the legal limits that banks and thrift institutions can pay to attract deposits. By causing disintermediation in times of tight money, interest rate ceilings have proved to be harmful rather than protective of the nation's financial intermediaries. In fact, the only protection provided intermediaries by rate ceilings is protection from competition among themselves.

Still another consideration is the effect on economic efficiency and productivity within the financial sector of our economy. The process of financial intermediation increases the efficiency of the financial sector; it lowers the costs associated with savings, reduces risk through diversification, and lowers the cost of borrowing. Disintermediation, a direct result of interest rate ceilings, destroys some of these gains. Also, since interest rate ceilings result in a lower return to savers, the amount of savings within the economy is lower, with the likely effect of a reduced economic growth rate. Finally, interest rates are signals that serve to channel savings where they are most needed, and when these rates are not free, resources may be allocated inefficiently.

Recent developments have greatly affected the future of interest ceilings and prohibitions. These trends include the introduction of NOW accounts, share drafts, and automatic transfer plans which are eliminating the distinction between time and demand deposits. Thus, for all practical purposes, the prohibition of interest on demand deposits is becoming a moot question. Another development weakening the impact of interest rate ceilings is the introduction of money market certificates by banks and thrift institutions. In 1978, banks and S&Ls were given the authority to issue time certificates of deposit with the rate paid being tied to the going rate on U.S. Treasury bills. This device was designed to circumvent interest rate limitations. Given the above considerations, in 1980 Congress reevaluated the desirability of interest rate controls, and the Depository Institutions Deregulation and Monetary Control Act provides for the eventual phasing out of Regulation Q.

SUMMARY

The American financial system is a constantly evolving set of institutions and practices. Historically, it has undergone its most significant changes in response to periods of crisis. However, the system is currently undergoing a period of rather rapid modification brought about primarily by new technology rather than by crisis.

Change always causes controversy, and change in our banking and financial system is no exception. This chapter introduces some of the changing directions within the system and some of the issues that have arisen as a result.

Most of our financial institutions operate in a highly regulated environment that has traditionally resulted in separate and rather distinct "domains" for the different types of financial intermediaries. Currently the boundaries separating these domains are breaking down, causing greater similarity and competition between banks and other intermediaries. This breakdown is the result of efforts to introduce more competition into the financial system and of the advances in electronic funds transfer.

The advent of EFT systems has not only been a contributor to the breakdown of the lines separating traditional roles of banks and other intermediaries but has also created some separate issues. Among these are its effects on monetary policy and citizens' rights to privacy with respect to information on their financial transactions.

Because of the evolutionary nature of our financial system, we currently have a multiagency regulatory framework which has produced overlapping and conflicting regulations. Thus there are those who advocate simplifying our regulatory system by bringing all banks under control of a single regulatory agency.

The final issue examined in this chapter dealt with efforts to remove limitations on rates that financial intermediaries can pay for funds; however, recent legislation and such developments as automatic transfer plans and money market certificates are rapidly eroding the effects of interest rate limitations.

REVIEW QUESTIONS

1. How are current regulatory trends intensifying competition between banks and other financial intermediaries? Do you see this as desirable or undesirable? Explain.

2. How will EFT blur the distinction between banks and thrift institutions?

3. Discuss the advantages and disadvantages of a multiagency bank-regulatory framework.

4. Should banks be allowed to offer banking services to directors and officers at preferential rates? Justify your position.

5. From a recent issue of the *Federal Reserve Bulletin*, obtain the Regulation Q ceilings on various categories of time deposits. How do these ceiling rates compare with current interest rates on Treasury bills, corporate bonds, and money market certificates? What conclusions can you draw?

SUGGESTIONS FOR ADDITIONAL READING

Bowsher, Norman N. "Usury Laws: Harmful When Effective." *Review of the Federal Reserve Bank of St. Louis,* vol. 56, no. 8 (August 1974), pp. 16–23.

Federal Reserve Bank of Boston. *The Economics of a National Electronic Funds Transfer System. Proceedings* of a conference held in October 1974, Boston, Mass.

Lovati, Jean M. "The Growing Similarity among Financial Institutions." *Review of the Federal Reserve Bank of St. Louis,* vol. 59, no. 10 (October 1977), pp. 2–11.

Report of the President's Commission on Financial Structure and Regulation. Washington, D.C.: U.S. Government Printing Office, 1971.

Smaistrla, Charles J. "Current Issues in Electronic Funds Transfers." *Review of the Federal Reserve Bank of Dallas* (February 1977), pp. 1–7.

Smaistrla, Charles J. "Electronic Funds Transfer and Monetary Policy." *Review of the Federal Reserve Bank of Dallas* (August 1977), pp. 6–12.

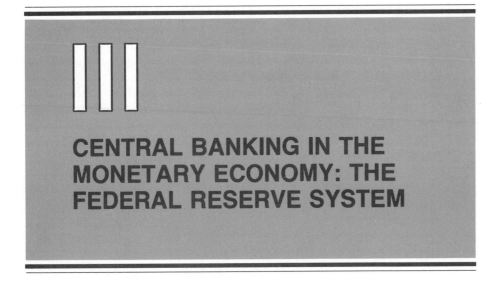

CENTRAL BANKING IN THE MONETARY ECONOMY: THE FEDERAL RESERVE SYSTEM

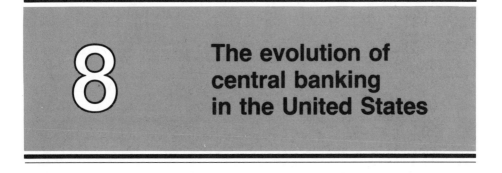

8 The evolution of central banking in the United States

WARM-UP: *Outline and questions to consider as you read*

Who managed the monetary system in the pre–Federal Reserve era?
   The First Bank of the United States.
   The Second Bank of the United States.
   The central banking hiatus, 1837–1914.
Why was the Federal Reserve System formed?
What are the Federal Reserve's major functions?
What is the organizational structure of the Fed?
   The Board of Governors.
   The Federal Open Market Committee.
   The 12 Federal Reserve banks and their 25 branches.
   The member banks.
Who controls the Federal Reserve System?

NEW TERMS

Bank note: a type of currency once issued by commercial banks in the form of a printed promise to pay specie (gold or silver) or government currency on demand.

Banking Act of 1933: an act creating the Federal Deposit Insurance Corporation (FDIC) and establishing an open market committee to supervise the Fed's purchase and sale of U.S. government securities.

155

Banking Act of 1935: an act which strengthened the Federal Reserve by giving new responsibilities to the Board of Governors including authority to set reserve requirements.

Board of Governors of the Federal Reserve System: the seven-member policymaking body of the Federal Reserve.

Federal Open Market Committee (FOMC): a 12-person group which controls the Fed's purchases and sales of U.S. government securities.

Federal Reserve Act of 1913: an act establishing a central bank designated as the Federal Reserve System.

First Bank of the United States: a nationally chartered bank, partially owned by the federal government, which performed many central banking functions from 1791 to 1811.

Free banking: a system in which bank charters are granted by banking agencies applying legislated guidelines rather than by special legislative acts.

Lender of last resort: a function performed by a central bank when it makes loans to banks in emergency situations.

National Bank Act of 1863: legislation passed in 1863 which enacted regulations for chartering and operating national banks.

Second Bank of the United States: similar to the First Bank but in operation from 1816 to 1836.

The monetary history of the United States is a fascinating panorama of changing institutional and legal arrangements. From the early days of the Republic until today, there have been intense conflicts concerning the nature and scope of the nation's monetary framework, and these struggles are reflected in the great diversity of past and present U.S. monetary arrangements. In the first section of this chapter, we discuss some of the more important institutions and events that comprise our early monetary history; this background is essential in order to understand why the Federal Reserve was created in 1913 and why its structure is unique.

WHO MANAGED THE MONETARY SYSTEM IN THE PRE-FEDERAL RESERVE ERA?

This nation's financial system is a product of several conflicting political and economic viewpoints. Most, if not all, of the major pieces of legislation relating to the monetary sector have been compromises reflecting divergent economic interests and opposing philosophies concerning the role that government should play in controlling money and the banking structure.

The early debates usually pitted Jeffersonians, who favored a limited role for the federal government in monetary as well as other affairs, against Alexander Hamilton and his Federalist party followers who believed that the central government should take an active part in regulating money, banking, and credit. Besides the debates that took place along political and philosophical lines, there were those where economic self-interest was the divisive factor: southern and western agrarian interests were in conflict with northern and eastern industrial and commercial interests; frequently the interests of debtor groups clashed with the positions taken by bankers and other segments of the financial community; and export industries commonly were at odds with industries facing stiff foreign competition.

The First Bank of the United States

The monetary affairs of the new nation during the first years of its existence were greatly influenced by Alexander Hamilton. In three reports—one on public credit, one on a national bank, and one on coin and currency—Hamilton advocated a monetary framework that he believed would help the new nation prosper. Hamilton felt that the central government should play an active role in the financial system. In his 1790 *Report on a National Bank,* Hamilton argued that a national bank would help the government manage its fiscal affairs and would also encourage a stronger economy by increasing the nation's productive capital through the bank's issuance of a sound paper currency. After a heated debate over the constitutionality of the proposed bank, Congress passed a bill granting a charter, and President Washington signed it in February 1791.

The First Bank of the United States was chartered for 20 years, and the federal government subscribed to one fifth of the bank's original $10 million in capital, with private subscriptions constituting the other four fifths; the $10 million was raised by issuing and selling 25,000 shares at $400 each. The bank had 25 directors, with the government selecting 5 and private shareholders the remaining 20. The First Bank was therefore a mixture of public and private interests as was the Second Bank of the United States, which was chartered in 1816. The First and Second banks were operated to make a profit for the private shareholders, but at the same time they supplied certain public services that central banks are called upon to provide. The private-public format was adopted again in 1913 when the Federal Reserve System was established.

The First Bank in its capacity as a central bank made a positive contribution to the nation's economy during its 20-year existence. Its bank notes were readily accepted and gave the economy a much-needed supply of currency. The bank also provided valuable assistance to the national government by receiving tax payments, disbursing governmental funds, making loans to the government, and otherwise helping with fiscal operations. Finally, the First Bank was to some extent able to regulate and add stability to the banking system.

To understand how the First Bank (and later the Second Bank) could exercise some control over state banks, it is important to understand how a commercial bank typically made loans to its customers. Until the mid-1800s when checking accounts began to become popular, it was common for a borrower to receive the proceeds of a loan in currency. The lending bank usually made the loan by issuing its own currency, otherwise known as *bank notes*; consequently, there were at least as many types of currency as there were banks. Banks were supposed to redeem their notes in specie (gold or silver) on demand but were frequently unable to do so, especially during times of local or national financial crisis. Since many of the operations of the First Bank resulted in receipt of state-bank notes, the central bank could help restrain overissuance of these notes by demanding specie from any bank on which it had notes.

Regulation of the banking system by the First Bank was inadequate to prevent many abuses, especially in those states where a sound banking tradition had not had time to develop. However, most students of the period credit the First Bank with having helped the budding economic system during its early years of development. Nonetheless, the bank's opponents were able to block attempts to recharter it. Opposition came from several sources:

1. Some bankers did not like the regulatory aspects of the First Bank—in particular, bankers and easy-money advocates generally believed that the First Bank was excessively restrictive in regulating issuance of state-bank notes.
2. On the other hand, hard-money advocates opposed the First Bank's issuance of paper money (in the form of bank notes).
3. Others were hostile because they believed that the federal government's participation was unconstitutional.
4. Some were antagonistic to foreign ownership of part of the bank's stock.

The Second Bank of the United States

After the demise of the First Bank in 1811, the War of 1812 created conditions that caused the relatively stable prewar financial system to fall into considerable disarray. In particular, state banks suspended redemption of their notes in specie. Consequently, support grew to charter a new national bank, and in 1816 Congress voted to charter the Second Bank of the United States, which was similar in most respects to the First Bank.

The early years of the Second Bank were not successful; the first president, William Jones, mismanaged the bank and by the time that he resigned in 1819, the reputation of the Second Bank had been badly tarnished. Branches of the Second Bank were located throughout the country, and those in the South and West overissued bank notes by lending excessively on land and other real estate. The notes issued in the West often ended up in the East to pay for goods purchased from eastern merchants. These notes were then presented to eastern branches of the Second Bank for redemption, thereby causing a drain of specie from the Second Bank. The bank was thus forced to issue bonds to obtain funds for importation of specie from Europe to keep up with redemptions of its notes. The bank's problems became glaringly apparent when its Baltimore branch collapsed.

Jones was succeeded by Langdon Cheves who put the bank on a more solid footing. However, Cheves's actions severely reduced the loans and discounts of the Second Bank and caused great difficulties among the debtor classes in the South and West. The reduction of the bank's investments caused profits to fall, and stockholder discontent forced Cheves to resign in 1823. Cheves was replaced with a man who still stands as the nation's most famous and controversial central banker, Nicholas Biddle.

Biddle astutely reestablished the reputation of the Second Bank by reviving many of the policies of the First Bank: state-bank notes were regulated; the government's fiscal transactions were supervised efficiently; and the notes of the Second Bank became a readily accepted component of the nation's money stock. Unfortunately, Biddle's flair for bank management was not matched by political acumen. By 1829 the bank was entering a period of turmoil that ultimately led to its dissolution.

The demise of the Second bank (and of central banking in the United States until 1914) was the culmination of Biddle's feud with Andrew Jackson. Soon after his election in 1828, Jackson made it clear that he distrusted the bank, arguing that it was unconstitutional. Jackson began his campaign against the Second bank by pressuring Biddle to employ men loyal to the administration. Jackson's opposition intensified, and during the presidential campaign of 1832, the Second bank became a major issue. Henry Clay, Jackson's opponent, was a strong advocate of the bank, and Clay convinced Biddle to press for renewal of the charter in 1832 though the charter was not due to expire until 1836. The rechartering bill passed Congress but was vetoed by Jackson. The bank's allies failed to override the veto, and Jackson's reelection spelled the end of the bank's chances for survival. From 1836 until 1914 a central banking hiatus existed in the United States, a rather startling situation for a country that was by 1914 an industrial power with a complex financial system.

The central banking hiatus, 1837–1914

The demise of the Second Bank did not end the need for central bank functions to be performed. While such needs sometimes went unmet, alternatives were developed so that various central bank activities came to be dispersed among several agencies. For instance, the government no longer had a centralized fiscal agent, and funds were for a time placed in state banks. But a desire to divorce the federal government from the banking system prompted the establishment in 1840 of the Independent Treasury System which except for a brief period served as the fiscal agent for the federal government until 1921. The expectation that the Independent Treasury System would isolate the government from the banking system was naive, however, because when taxes were collected, funds flowed from the banking system to the Treasury, and when the government expended funds, money flowed back into banks.

After 1836 there was no federal authority to restrain unsound banking practices. Consequently, many problems developed, and the period from 1837 to 1863 represents perhaps the most troubled time in this nation's banking history. Prior to 1838, a bank charter was granted by a special act of a state legislature, a practice that severely limited the number of banks in existence. Most bank charters were granted as political favors, and pressure mounted to reform the process. Beginning in 1838 states began to pass so-called free banking laws, and charters were granted by state banking agencies according to specified guidelines. Free banking resulted in a rapid growth in bank numbers—from 1836 to 1860 the number of banks grew from 788 to 1,562. Many of the institutions were established in frontier areas where there was little capital or managerial know-how. The unlikely locations of banks in backwoods areas during this time prompted the labeling of the 1837–62 period as the Era of Wildcat Banking.

As one would expect, the quality of banking varied greatly from state to state and from region to region, but in general the better banking systems were in the East. At the turn of the 19th century, Massachusetts had already passed and was vigorously enforcing laws regulating note issuance and redemption as well as capital requirements. In 1838 New York passed the first successful free banking act, a law that later became the model for the National Bank Act of 1863. Outside the East, Louisiana had one of the nation's best pre–Civil War systems with one large, dominant parent bank in New Orleans serving the entire state with branches.

Unfortunately the banking systems in many other states did not fare as well as those just mentioned. Numerous inadequacies existed, the more common being (1) insufficient capitalization, (2) lax enforcement of banking regulations, (3) inefficient bank management, and (4) overissuance of bank notes. The last problem was the most serious; by 1860 there were over 1,500 banks issuing their own currencies, and, as might be expected, the monetary system was in chaos—counterfeiting was rampant, and bank notes often continued to circulate after banks had become insolvent. Guides were published listing insolvent banks and giving information to help identify counterfeit bills.

Finally, in 1863 Congress passed the National Bank Act to try to remedy the deficiencies of the banking and monetary structure. The improvements brought about by the National Bank Act were significant, yet Congress waited another five decades to create a much-needed central bank. There were several important provisions of the National Bank Act (as amended in 1864):

1. In essence the act established free banking at the national level by creating a federal bank-chartering agency (the Comptroller of the Currency) which received applications and made chartering decisions based on legislated guidelines. A bank granted a charter was required to include the word *National* in its name.
2. Capital requirements were established; for example, the minimum capital for a bank located in a city with a population of 50,000 or more was $200,000.
3. The act provided for issuance of a new currency to be known as national bank notes, which had to be backed by U.S. government securities.
4. Reserve requirements for deposits in national banks were stipulated; the requirements ranged from 15 percent for banks in small towns to 25 percent for banks in large cities. A portion of a bank's reserves could be held in other banks except in the case of banks located in larger cities which were designated as *reserve cities*.
5. Size and type limitations were placed on bank loans and investments. Banks were prohibited from speculating in real estate and could not make a loan larger than 10 percent of their capital.

The National Bank Act established a dual banking system in the United States with charters being issued by the national and the various state governments. In fact, one of the original purposes of the act was to eliminate state banks by inducing them to convert to national banks. However, when there was no rush to join the national system, Congress in 1865 levied a 10 percent tax on the issuance of state-bank notes. The purpose of the tax was to drive state banks into the national system by making it unprofitable to issue state-bank notes, and the number of state banks did actually decline from 1,064 in 1864 to 325 in 1870. But demand deposits were growing in popularity at this time, and while state banks could not profitably issue state-bank notes, they could issue demand deposits and did so in growing volume. The decline in state-chartered banks was reversed, and by 1875 the number of state banks had climbed to 1,260.

WHY WAS THE FEDERAL RESERVE SYSTEM FORMED?

Congress rectified some of the worst abuses of the monetary system with the National Bank Act. However, many money-related problems continued to plague the economy, and the need for a central bank to coordinate monetary and banking policies became more and more apparent as the economy grew and became more complex. By 1900 a host of weaknesses in the monetary framework had become apparent.

First, the supply of currency was not closely linked to the needs of the economy. National-bank notes were a major component of the currency supply, and they had to be backed, dollar for dollar, with U.S. government bonds. Thus the issuance of national-bank notes was dependent on the amount of government securities held by banks which in turn was largely dependent on the amount of bonds outstanding. The volume of bonds reflected the financing needs of the government, not the currency requirements of the nation; consequently, under this system, as economic activity waxed and waned, there was no mechanism to assure that a proper amount of currency would be in circulation. As a matter of fact, when tax revenues would rise during periods of prosperity, the government typically redeemed some of its outstanding bonds, thereby reducing the base for national bank notes. Also, during boom periods, a strong demand for loans generated high interest rates, and banks would substitute loans for government securities in their investment portfolios. Thus at the very time that the economy needed more currency, the banking system's ability to create it was reduced; the currency supply was therefore *inelastic,* meaning that it did not expand and contract in tune with the needs of the economy.

Second, small banks could hold a portion of their reserves in larger banks which often paid interest on the funds. Consequently, reserves were often pyramided, with large, reserve-city banks holding reserves for several smaller banks. As seasonal changes in economic activity occurred or as a financial crisis developed, the smaller banks would withdraw reserves from the larger banks, putting pressure on the latter to reduce loans and investments. During a panic, large withdrawals of currency from the banking system often occurred, and the pyramiding of reserves tended to magnify the problem by transmitting the effects of the withdrawals from smaller to larger banks.

In the third place, the absence of a central bank meant that certain "banker's bank" functions were not performed adequately. Check clearing was not centrally coordinated and was thus cumbersome and inefficient. No "lender of last resort" stood ready to loan money to banks in temporary difficulty; during the panic situations alluded to above, there was no central bank to prevent a minor problem from getting out of hand. Often, well-managed banks found themselves caught up in a regional or national panic with nowhere to turn for temporary funds. The banking system was in dire need of a banker's bank that could provide temporary funds and offer service functions such as a centralized system of check clearing.

Fourth and finally, no agency existed to coordinate the fiscal activities of the federal government with the banking system. The First and Second banks had acted as a fiscal agent for the government, but Congress later had tried to separate the government and the banking system by establishing the Independent Treasury System. However, as we have seen, this separation was not possible, and better coordination of banking with the fiscal activities of the government was needed.

The problems caused by the absence of a central bank produced a great amount of discussion about establishing one, but no consensus could be reached until the tide was finally turned by the Panic of 1907. When problems in the securities market precipitated a financial panic in October, the Knickerbocker Trust Company, a bank in New York City, was forced to close, and subsequently all the New York City banks began to experience deposit withdrawals. The crisis spread to other parts of the country, and as other banks were affected, they began to withdraw their reserves from larger banks including those in New York City. These withdrawals further aggravated the situation and forced numerous banks into bankruptcy.

In May 1908 Congress at last acted to remedy the country's monetary weaknesses. A National Monetary Commission composed of nine senators and nine congressmen was established to recommend changes in the money and banking system. The committee was chaired by Sen. Nelson Aldrich, and in 1912 he introduced a bill that came to be known as the Aldrich Plan. The legislation soon ran into trouble, however, with opponents arguing that the system was too centralized and gave too much control to bankers. Thus the Aldrich Bill failed, but a House bill drafted by Congressman Carter Glass and a staff expert, Dr. H. Parker Willis, was offered as a compromise plan. Another Senate bill was introduced by Robert Owen of Oklahoma, and after each bill passed its respective chamber, House-Senate conferees worked out a compromise known as the Federal Reserve Act. The bill was signed by President Wilson on December 23, 1913, and the Federal Reserve System began operations in August 1914.

WHAT ARE THE FEDERAL RESERVE'S MAJOR FUNCTIONS?

After the expiration of the charter of the Second Bank of the United States in 1836, there was no longer a single entity capable of performing a variety of central banking functions. Therefore, the passage of the Federal Reserve Act in 1913 was a milestone in United States banking history in that the Federal Reserve was empowered to perform numerous central banking activities. Initially though, the Fed was not endowed with all of the important powers of today's typical central bank. In 1913 there was widespread public distrust of the "money trust," supposedly comprised of the large eastern banks and other big financial interests, and many people feared that a strong central bank would lead to too much government intervention in the banking industry and in the economy in general.

Consequently, the Federal Reserve Act reflected many compromises. Advocates of a strong central bank were unable to create an agency with far-reaching power over the nation's monetary system; instead a "decentralized" central banking system was instituted with power dispersed among 12 regional Federal Reserve banks and various committees and boards. However, as the system has evolved, additional power has either been granted to the Board of Governors (originally the Federal Reserve Board) through passage of various pieces of legislation, or the board has interpreted the original act in a manner that expanded board responsibilities.

A central bank's functions can be divided into three broad categories as follows: (1) banker's bank activities, (2) bank for the central government, and (3) manager of the nation's monetary policies. The founders of the Federal Reserve saw the banker's bank function as the main reason for establishing the Fed. Banker's bank activities include regional and national clearing of checks, dispersal of coin and currency to the banking system, lending to banks in emergency situations, and in general regulating and supervising banks.

During the 1920s the scope of Federal Reserve activity began to expand. In 1922 the Independent Treasury System ceased operating, and the Federal Reserve assumed responsibility for many governmental fiscal operations. Government checking accounts were maintained at Federal Reserve banks, and the Federal Reserve began to take a more active role in all phases of the government's fiscal activities. Today the Federal Reserve handles a major portion of the paperwork associated with the federal debt: securities are redeemed as they mature; interest coupons are paid; different denominations of securities are exchanged; and other functions necessary to service the federal debt are performed. Also, in the 1920s the Federal Reserve began to engage in certain activities that influenced the supply of money and credit and therefore affected the level of economic activity.

In the 1930s, in the wake of the collapse of the economy and the closing of thousands of commercial banks, several pieces of legislation were passed that gave the Federal Reserve more authority and otherwise strengthened the financial system. The Banking Act of 1933 established the Federal Deposit Insurance Corporation (FDIC), and today the FDIC insures over 98 percent of all bank deposits in the United States, giving great stability to the banking system. Furthermore, the act prohibited payment of interest on demand deposits, extended the Fed's bank-regulatory powers, and formally sanctioned the System's use of open market operations.

The Banking Act of 1935 further extended the powers of the Federal Reserve. This act was largely a product of then-governor (chairman) of the Federal Reserve Board, Marriner Eccles, and its primary provisions were as follows:

1. The seven-person Federal Reserve Board was renamed the Board of Governors, requirements for membership on the Board were revised, and the term of appointment was increased from 12 to 14 years.
2. A Federal Open Market Committee (FOMC) was established in its present form to supervise the system's purchases and sales of U.S. government securities.
3. The Board of Governors was given authority to set reserve requirements on deposits in member banks within prescribed limits.

The Banking Act of 1935 was one of the most decisive steps ever taken by Congress to vest power in the country's central bank.

The Depository Institutions Deregulation and Monetary Control

Act of 1980 (hereafter referred to as the Monetary Control Act) also promises to have a tremendous impact on the Federal Reserve and on the entire financial sector. The legislation affects the operations of the Federal Reserve in numerous ways. First, the Fed's power to set reserve requirements was extended to include certain types of deposits at nonmember banks and thrift institutions. Second, the Federal Reserve's authority to make emergency loans through its "discount window" was broadened with respect to nonmember banks and thrifts. Third, the Fed's services (clearing checks, electronic transfer of funds, disbursal of coin and currency, and so forth) were made available to all depository institutions, and those services are to be provided on an explicit-fee basis. Formerly, the services were free to member banks while some were available on a fee basis to nonmember institutions.

WHAT IS THE ORGANIZATIONAL STRUCTURE OF THE FED?

The Federal Reserve System is an interesting blend of private and public elements. On paper it is a corporation with stock held almost entirely by member banks of the system. (Recall that fewer than 40 percent of the banks in the United States are Reserve System members, but that these banks hold the majority of total bank assets.) The Federal Reserve is not an ordinary corporation, however, since Congress, not the stockholding banks, oversees the operations of the Federal Reserve. Congress established the Federal Reserve, set up its organizational structure, and can reshape the System at its discretion. Presently the primary responsibility of the Federal Reserve is to the public at large. As we have seen, the System also assists the nation's banks and the federal government in numerous ways, but its chief purpose is to pursue policies that will foster monetary conditions conducive to economic growth, a low unemployment rate, and price stability.

The organizational structure of the Federal Reserve consists of four major elements.[1] They are as follows:

1. The Board of Governors.
2. The Federal Open Market Committee.
3. The 12 Federal Reserve banks and their 25 branches.
4. The member banks of the Federal Reserve.

The first two groups listed above are primarily the policymaking and supervisory bodies while the other two are the operating elements of the System.

---

[1] The Federal Advisory Council and the Consumer Advisory Council can be considered fifth and sixth elements of the System. Since both play a relatively minor and purely advisory role in Federal Reserve policymaking, they are not discussed.

The Board of Governors

The Board of Governors is the managing agency of the Federal Reserve System; the board makes or participates in all important policy decisions, is involved in the operation of the Federal Reserve banks, and regulates many member bank activities. The board consists of seven members appointed by the president with the advice and consent of the Senate. The members serve 14-year terms with appointments staggered at 2-year intervals, and they may serve only one full term. These provisions are intended to isolate board members from political pressures as much as possible. Besides appointing members to the board, the president designates one of the members as chairman for a 4-year term. The chairman is the main representative of the System at congressional hearings and executive branch economic policy discussions and is the chief public spokesman for the Federal Reserve.

While the extent of Board of Governors authority is great, only a few of its more important powers will be listed here. The governors approve the discount rate (the rate of interest charged on loans to member banks) and supervise lending to member banks; they also set reserve requirements within limits established by Congress and serve on the Federal Open Market Committee. In addition to the activities that relate to management of the supply of money and credit, the board appoints three directors—designated the class C directors—to the nine-member board of directors of each Federal Reserve bank.[2] These directors nominate a president and first vice president for each Federal Reserve bank, but the Board of Governors must approve their nominees. Finally, the Board of Governors admits and can expel member banks and establishes many other regulatory requirements for bank operations.

The Federal Open Market Committee

The 12-member Federal Open Market Committee (FOMC) consists of the Board of Governors plus the president of the New York Federal Reserve Bank (because securities trading for the entire system is conducted through the New York Federal Reserve Bank) and 4 of the other 11 Federal Reserve bank presidents on a rotating basis. The FOMC determines Federal Reserve policy for buying and selling U.S. government securities, a process that is known as open market

---

[2] The remaining six directors, three class A and three class B, are elected by the member banks in the district. The class A directors must be bankers. Class B and class C directors may not be officers, directors, or employees of any banks; they are to represent the public and are to be chosen with due, but not exclusive, consideration to the interests of agriculture, commerce, industry, services, labor, and consumers.

operations and constitutes the most important monetary policy instrument.

The 12 Federal Reserve banks and their 25 branches

Presently the operating activities of the Federal Reserve are decentralized. The nation is divided into 12 regions with a Federal Reserve bank in each region. For example, much of the southeastern part of the United States is in the Sixth Federal Reserve District with a Federal Reserve bank in Atlanta. Each district also has at least one Federal Reserve branch bank. Figure 8–1 shows the districts, the 12 Reserve banks, and the 25 branches.

The Federal Reserve banks supervise check clearing, perform

FIGURE 8–1
The Federal Reserve System

Source: *Federal Reserve Bulletin.*

other banker's bank functions, and act as fiscal agents for the federal government. The Federal Reserve banks' operations earn a sizable surplus each year which is generated primarily by the holdings of U.S. government securities. The surplus is turned over to the Treasury after stockholders (the member banks) are paid 6 percent return on their investment. The fact that much of the surplus of the Federal Reserve goes to the Treasury instead of being paid to the stockholders demonstrates the public nature of the Federal Reserve—the procedure hardly typifies a private corporation.

The member banks

The member banks of the Federal Reserve presently buy stock in the system equal to 3 percent of the individual member bank's capital account. The proportion of the nation's banks that belong to the Federal Reserve System declined throughout the 1970s, and the Board of Governors argued that this trend was diluting the System's ability to achieve monetary policy objectives. Therefore, the Board sought legislation that would extend control to nonmember banks and thrifts; as mentioned previously, the Monetary Control Act of 1980 granted the Fed additional controls over the financial system.

WHO CONTROLS THE FEDERAL RESERVE SYSTEM?

Control of the Federal Reserve System, and therefore control of monetary policy, is profoundly important to the citizens of the United States. Following the creation of the Federal Reserve in 1913, there have been numerous legislative revisions of the Federal Reserve Act including the Banking Acts of 1933 and 1935. Thus Congress can modify or even eliminate the system if it desires to do so. In addition, the president can influence the Fed through appointments to the Board of Governors and by designating a chairman.

On the other hand, there has been a conscious effort to endow the Fed with a degree of independence: members of the Board of Governors are appointed for 14-year terms; the Fed has its own sources of revenue and does not depend on congressional appropriations; and the Federal Reserve is not subject to the normal auditing procedures applied to other government agencies. The rationale for the special treatment afforded the Fed is that a central bank must be isolated from political pressure if it is to conduct monetary policy judiciously. The merits of this argument are discussed in Chapter 11.

Control within the Fed itself is dispersed among several groups. A former Board of Governors member, Sherman Maisel, argues that internal control of the system is distributed as follows: "Chairman of the Board of Governors, 45 percent; staff of the Board of Governors, 25 percent; other Board of Governors members, 20 percent; the Federal Reserve banks, 10 percent."[3] Obviously these percentages will vary according to who occupies the various positions listed above, but it is interesting that Maisel believes that the chairman plays such a dominant role in operations of the Federal Reserve.

As of 1980, 12 men—including the present chairman—have headed the Federal Reserve, and their backgrounds are surprisingly diverse: 4 were businessmen; 3 were bankers; 3 were attorneys; 1 was an economist; and the chairman at the time of this writing, Paul A. Volcker, was the president of the New York Federal Reserve Bank prior to his appointment in 1979. Of the 48 others who have served as board members, 9 had backgrounds in business, 14 were bankers, 2 were attorneys, 13 were economists, 7 were engaged in agriculture, and 3 were in government service. In the System's early years, bankers were prevalent on the board, but recently economists have been predominant. As a matter of fact, in recent years as many as five of the seven members were economists; these figures reflect the evolution of the Federal Reserve from primarily a banker's bank to a full-scale central bank responsible for managing the nation's supply of money.

President Carter's appointment in early 1978 of G. William Miller to replace Arthur Burns as chairman was at least mildly controversial. Burns was a highly regarded economist who at one time or the other had chaired the Council of Economic Advisors, had served as a personal advisor to the president on national economic affairs, and had been president of the prestigious National Bureau of Economic Research (NBER). Before Burns, William McChesney Martin had occupied the chairman's seat from 1950 to 1970, the longest term as chairman in the history of the Fed.[4] Martin had previously served as assistant secretary of the Treasury and president of the Export-Import Bank.

Thus the appointment of Miller, a corporate executive, was a break with the recent past in that he was not intimately acquainted with central banking and monetary policy. Managing Federal Reserve policy has become a highly technical process, and some have questioned the wisdom of appointing someone with little or no knowledge of central banking. Miller's tenure as a Fed chairman was brief, however. In summer 1979 he resigned in order to become the

---

[3] Sherman J. Maisel, *Managing the Dollar* (New York: W. W. Norton and Company, 1973), p. 110.

[4] Martin had originally been appointed to serve out an unexpired term of office, then was reappointed for another full 14-year term.

secretary of the Treasury in the Carter administration. Miller was replaced by Paul Volcker, a highly respected central banker.

As was pointed out previously, the Fed is subject to outside influences and pressures from, among others, the Congress and the president. Maisel estimates the relative importance of these influences; he says that of the total outside effects on the system, the administration accounts for 35 percent, Congress for 25 percent and a host of others for 40 percent.[5] Of course, these proportions will vary somewhat according to who is president, the leaders in Congress, and other factors.

As a final consideration, it is debatable whether it is proper to give the Fed the independence that it presently enjoys. The power of the Federal Reserve has prompted some to refer to it as a fourth branch of government. Is it appropriate in a democracy that unelected officials be given so much authority? Many argue that this arrangement is inconsistent with democratic principles, and from time to time there are efforts to lessen the power of the Fed.

With the passage of the Federal Reserve Reform Act of 1977, Congress required that the Federal Reserve consult with Senate and House banking committees on a regular basis; the consultation process includes a report on the estimated growth of monetary and credit aggregates for the next year. In the opinion of some, still stronger measures to reduce Fed independence are warranted. In a modern monetary economy there must be a central bank to manage the technical aspects of the monetary system, but the responsibility of monetary policymaking may be more appropriately assigned to the president, who bears a major responsibility for designing and implementing economic policy. The debate over Fed independence will continue to wage. Some are convinced that independence must be preserved if the ravages of politically inspired policies are to be avoided; others feel that the present arrangement should be abolished because it is undemocratic; and still others favor independence but at the same time call for an overhaul of the system because they believe that the present structure produces poor monetary policy. Short of a severe economic crisis, however, the Fed is unlikely to be modified greatly, at least in the foreseeable future.

SUMMARY

This chapter has surveyed the evolution of central banking in the United States. The more important landmarks in the development of the nation's monetary framework include the First Bank of the United States, which operated from 1791 to 1811, and the Second

---

[5] Maisel, *Managing the Dollar,* p. 110.

Bank of the United States, whose charter ran from 1816 to 1836. After attempts to recharter the Second Bank failed, central banking functions were not again unified until Congress passed the Federal Reserve Act in 1913. For the period from 1837–1913, the National Bank Act stands as the single most important attempt to strengthen the nation's financial structure.

When the Federal Reserve System began operations in 1914, its activities were limited primarily to banker's bank functions, but Congress has given the Fed many other powers during the intervening years. Presently the Fed is a full-scale central bank acting as the federal government's fiscal agent and managing the nation's supply of money and credit in addition to serving as a banker's bank. Many believe that the power and independence now enjoyed by the Fed should be reduced, but others contend that monetary policy is best conducted in an atmosphere free, as far as possible, from political pressure.

REVIEW QUESTIONS

1. What contributions did the First and Second Banks of the United States make to the nation's economy?
2. What were the major problems experienced during the "free-banking" era?
3. What effects did the National Bank Act have on U.S. banking and the monetary structure? What weaknesses in the monetary framework still existed after the act?
4. What are the functions of a central bank?
5. What changes in the banking system were legislated in the Banking Acts of 1933 and 1935?
6. What are the major responsibilities of the Board of Governors?
7. The Federal Reserve is sometimes referred to as a quasi-governmental agency. In what sense is this statement true?

SUGGESTIONS FOR ADDITIONAL READING

Burns, Arthur F.   "The Independence of the Federal Reserve System." *Federal Reserve Bulletin*, vol. 62, no. 6 (June 1976), pp. 493–96.

Friedman, Milton, and Schwartz, Anna Jacobson.   *A Monetary History of the United States, 1867–1960*. Princeton, N.J.: Princeton University Press, 1963.

Maisel, Sherman J.   *Managing the Dollar*. New York: W. W. Norton & Co., 1973.

Studenski, Paul, and Krooss, Herman E.   *Financial History of the United States*. New York: McGraw-Hill Book Company, 1952.

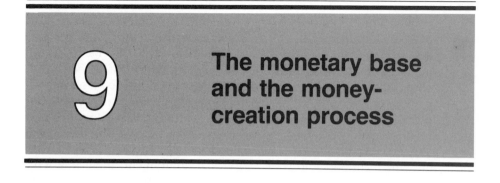

9 The monetary base and the money-creation process

WARM-UP: *Outline and questions to consider as you read*

What are the major elements in the money-creation process?
What are the various reserve categories?
What factors determine the monetary base?
How do changes in the monetary base lead to changes in the money supply?
  A simple example of deposit expansion.
  A more realistic example of money creation.
  Other considerations.

NEW TERMS

Float: the double-counted reserves resulting from the Federal Reserve's check-clearing procedures which often involve crediting the receiving bank's reserve account prior to the time when the check is deducted from the paying bank's account.

Monetary base (B): total bank reserves plus currency in the hands of the nonbank public.

Money multiplier (M): the ratio of the final change in the money supply [Δ(M-1A)] to a change in the monetary base (ΔB).

Tax and loan accounts: U.S. Treasury accounts at commercial banks.

173

The previous chapter surveyed the history of central banking in the United States concluding with a discussion of the nature and structure of the Federal Reserve System. This chapter is the first of two concerned with the process of money and credit expansion and contraction.[1] The present discussion sets forth the key facets of the monetary framework, and the following chapter deals specifically with monetary policy instruments. Much of the explanation of money and credit management is a description of seemingly mechanistic relationships, and understanding the monetary process requires fitting together several pieces of a puzzle. There are two dangers associated with putting the puzzle together: First, as we attempt to understand each individual component, there is a tendency to lose sight of the more important entirety, and second, the formal model indicates a degree of precision that is not borne out in actual practice. Our response to the first danger is to begin with an overview of money and credit control and to refer to this framework frequently so that the various individual components are kept in perspective. Regarding the second danger, care is taken to point out certain forces that have not been internalized in the formal model but that may in fact affect actual events.

WHAT ARE THE MAJOR ELEMENTS IN THE MONEY-CREATION PROCESS?

An overview of the monetary structure of the United States is presented in Figure 9–1. The large block on the right side represents bank demand deposits. Since banks are required to back their deposits with specified assets which have been designated as reserves, a rectangle representing total bank reserves has been placed in the center of the figure to the left of bank deposits. The reserve block is smaller than the deposit block because reserve requirements are a fraction of deposits. The rectangle on the left side of the figure denotes the monetary base which is composed of (1) deposits of banks at Federal Reserve banks, (2) Federal Reserve notes outstanding, and (3) U.S. Treasury currency.[2] The monetary base minus Federal Reserve notes and U.S. Treasury currency in the hands of the public is equal to total bank reserves. Thus the base and bank reserves differ by the amount of the public's holdings of currency.

The Fed controls the size of the monetary base mainly through use

---

[1] Since, over the long run, growth of the economy requires an expanding supply of money and credit, most of the examples of this chapter deal with the process of expansion.

[2] The designation *U.S. Treasury currency* includes paper money (U.S. notes) and coin issued by the Treasury.

FIGURE 9–1
Major elements in the money creation process

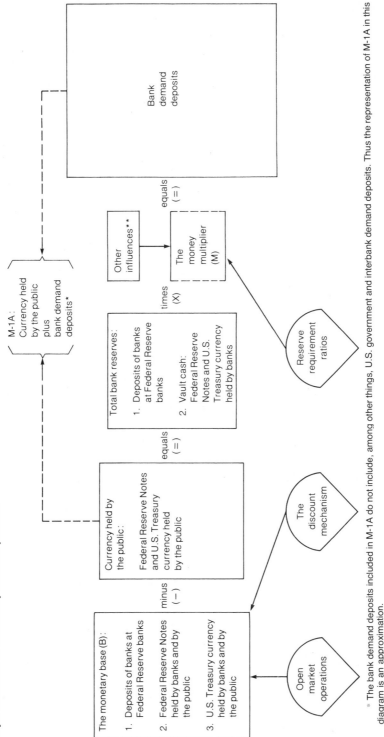

* The bank demand deposits included in M-1A do not include, among other things, U.S. government and interbank demand deposits. Thus the representation of M-1A in this diagram is an approximation.
** The other influences include the public's deposit-to-currency ratios and the banking system's propensity to hold excess reserves.

of open market operations (see Figure 9–1). If we concede at this point that the Federal Reserve can manipulate the size of the monetary base, then it is easy to envision how changes in the base lead to concurrent changes in bank reserves. There may be some slippage between the base and reserves due to changes in the demand for currency by the public, but a close relation does exist between changes in the base and changes in reserves.

If the Fed acts to enlarge the monetary base and thus reserves, forces are set in motion that will generate larger deposits. Remember that reserves are a fraction of deposits, and consequently a dollar of new reserves will support more than a dollar of new deposits. Figure 9–1 shows that reserve requirements along with certain other influences determine the size of the money multiplier which, when multiplied by bank reserves, gives the total amount of demand deposits. Furthermore, it is noted that the total of currency held by the public and bank demand deposits (with minor adjustments) is equivalent to the Fed's M-1A measure of money. Though the process is not evident in Figure 9–1, an increase in deposit liabilities generated via a bigger monetary base (and more reserves) also results in the creation of new bank loans and investments. Fix firmly in mind the relations portrayed in Figure 9–1: Open-market operations can be used to control the monetary base; changes in the base in turn lead to changes in reserves, which set the stage for a multiple change in bank deposits (and bank loans and investments); the ultimate outcome depends on reserve requirement ratios and certain other influences which are discussed below.

WHAT ARE THE VARIOUS RESERVE CATEGORIES?

Minimum and maximum reserve requirements are established by Congress. The Federal Reserve sets reserve ratios within these limits and designates those bank assets that qualify as reserves—presently deposits at the Federal Reserve and vault cash. Required reserve ratios for demand and some time deposits are set on a graduated basis. For instance, in early 1980 reserves on demand deposits could be no less than 7 percent of the first $2 million of deposits, and for the next $8 million of deposits (the $2–10 million category), reserves could be no less than 9.50 percent. A similar arrangement is also used for time deposits, which means that on average large banks are required to hold more reserves than small banks.[3] The Monetary Control Act of 1980 provided for the phasing in of a significant

---

[3] Computation of required reserves and use of reserve requirements to control the supply of money is discussed in Chapter 10.

change in reserve requirements for Federal Reserve member banks and extended the Fed's authority to set reserve requirements to nonmember institutions. The student may consult a recent *Federal Reserve Bulletin* for current reserve requirements. For simplicity, all examples in this chapter will assume a constant 15 percent reserve requirement for demand deposits and a 4 percent reserve against time deposits.

Required reserves are the minimum level of bank reserves required for a bank's deposit liabilities; *total* or *legal reserves* are the actual holdings of reserve assets; and the difference of total minus required reserves is *excess reserves*. Another, less-used reserve definition is *net free reserves*: net free reserves are positive when excess reserves exceed Federal Reserve loans to member banks; on the other hand, if excess reserves are smaller than loans from the Fed, then net free reserves are negative and are sometimes referred to as net borrowed reserves.

WHAT FACTORS DETERMINE THE MONETARY BASE?[4]

The Federal Reserve's efforts at controlling the money supply generally focus on managing the monetary base. Thus our discussion begins with an analysis of the forces that increase or decrease the base. Two of the three components of the monetary base—deposits of member banks at the Federal Reserve, and Federal Reserve notes—are liabilities of the Federal Reserve System. The other component, U.S. Treasury currency, is not a Federal Reserve liability, but it constitutes less than 10 percent of the total base. Since the major elements of the base are liabilities of the Fed, we begin the analysis of the factors supplying and absorbing the base with a discussion of the Federal Reserve balance sheet.

Table 9–1 is the Federal Reserve's balance sheet as of February 27, 1980. Item 1 is the gold certificate account and includes Special Drawing Rights (SDRs).[5] The gold certificate account is related to the U.S. Treasury's gold stock holdings; as the Treasury increases or reduces its holdings of gold, the changes are ordinarily reflected in the gold certificate account of the Federal Reserve. Changes in the gold certificate account reflect Treasury operations, and the role of

---

[4] The presentation in this section is based on Anatol B. Balbach and Albert E. Burger, "Derivation of the Monetary Base," *Review of the Federal Reserve Bank of St. Louis*, vol. 58, no. 11 (November 1976), pp. 2–8. Also, see Dwayne Wrightsman, *An Introduction to Monetary Theory and Policy*, 2d ed. (New York: The Free Press, 1976), chap. 3.

[5] Special drawing rights (SDRs) are sometimes referred to as paper gold; they are a form of money used by central banks and are discussed in Chapter 21.

TABLE 9-1
Consolidated balance sheet of 12 Federal Reserve banks, February 27, 1980
($billions)

Assets		Liabilities and capital account	
1. Gold certificates (includes SDR certificate account) .....$ 14.2		6. Federal Reserve notes $109.6	
2. Federal Reserve holdings of U.S. government securities* 120.5		7. Member bank deposits 29.1	
3. Federal Reserve loans to member banks 4.3		8. U.S. Treasury deposits 4.5	
4. Cash items in the process of collection 11.1		9. Deferred availability cash items 6.4	
5. Other Federal Reserve assets 4.9		10. Other Federal Reserve liabilities 2.9	
		11. Capital account 2.5	
Total $155.0		Total $155.0	

* Includes holdings of federal agency obligations.
Source: *Federal Reserve Bulletin*, March 1980.

the Federal Reserve is simply to hold title to the gold (the certificates represent title). Although the account is outside Federal Reserve control, we shall see later that unwanted fluctuations in the certificate account, or for that matter any other account not under direct Federal Reserve control, can be offset through use of certain policy instruments.

The Federal Reserve's most important policy instrument, open-market operations, involves buying and selling U.S. government securities. The securities account (item 2) contains $120.5 billion of securities. In Chapter 8 we noted that the Fed annually pays its member banks a return on their investment in the Federal Reserve System and that, after the stockholding banks are paid, a sizable surplus remains and is turned over to the U.S. Treasury. The source of most of the Fed's earnings is the interest earned on the System's holdings of U.S. government securities. Another policy-related item is account 3, Federal Reserve loans to member banks. Banks may borrow from the Federal Reserve in order to meet a temporary deficiency of reserves, and these loans, which are administered through the Fed's "discount window," are reflected in account 3. Management of the discount mechanism and open-market operations are discussed in the following chapter.

Federal Reserve check clearing is reflected by accounts 4 and 9, and an example will demonstrate the relationship between the two items. Let's assume that Williams has a checking account at New Orleans National Bank and has traveled to Atlanta and paid for a new coat in an Atlanta clothing store with a $300 check drawn on a

New Orleans checking account. The clothier will deposit the check in its checking account at Atlanta National Bank, thus initiating the check-clearing process. Atlanta National will of course wish to collect the proceeds of the check from New Orleans National Bank and will send the check, say on day 1, to the Atlanta Federal Reserve Bank, which handles the check clearing.

The following T-account, dated day 1, shows the effect of Atlanta National's deposit on the balance sheet of the Atlanta Federal Reserve Bank. The Federal Reserve T-account shows initial increases of $300 in cash items in the process of collection and in deferred availability cash items.[6] Notice that the Federal Reserve does not immediately pay Atlanta National, nor is the check immediately deducted from New Orleans National's account. The delay exists because it will take some time to route the check to New Orleans.

Federal Reserve Bank of Atlanta,
Day 1

Δ Assets		Δ Liabilities	
4. Cash items in the process of collection	+$300	9. Deferred availability cash items	+$300

The Federal Reserve pays and collects checks according to a prescribed schedule. Assume that on day 2 Atlanta National is paid; however, the check will not be deducted from the account of New Orleans National until the check reaches New Orleans, say on day 3. The day-2 T-account changes are as follows:

Federal Reserve Bank of Atlanta,
Day 2

Δ Assets		Δ Liabilities	
		7. Atlanta National Bank reserve account	+ $300
		9. Deferred availability cash items	− $300

The member bank reserve account (item 7) is increased $300 when Atlanta National is paid, and the deferred availability account is simultaneously decreased.

When New Orleans National receives the check on day 3, the amount of the check is deducted from its reserve account, and since the check has now been cleared, cash items in the process of collection are reduced by $300.

---

[6] The numbering of the accounts corresponds to the balance sheet items in Table 9–1.

Federal Reserve Bank of Atlanta,
Day 3

Δ Assets		Δ Liabilities	
4. Cash items in the process of collection	− $300	7. New Orleans National reserve account	− $300

The check-clearing procedure described above creates what is known as *float*, which is the difference between cash items in the process of collection (item 4 in Table 9–1) and deferred availability cash items (item 9). In our example, $300 of float is created on day 2 because some reserves are being double counted—Atlanta National's reserve account has been increased, but New Orleans National's reserve account has not yet been reduced. The double counting of reserves and, hence, float arises on those occasions when one bank receives credit for a check before it is deducted from the account of the bank on which it is drawn. In our illustration, float is eliminated on day 3 when the $300 check is deducted from New Orleans National's reserve account. Float rises and falls with the volume of check-clearing activity and is not, therefore, a Federal Reserve policy instrument. In Table 9–1, Federal Reserve float is $4.7 billion ($11.1 − 6.4).

Turning to the liabilities side of the Federal Reserve balance sheet in Table 9–1, account 6 is Federal Reserve notes outstanding; most of these are in the hands of the public with banks holding the remainder as a reserve asset. Account 7 is deposits which member banks are required to maintain with the Fed as a part of the reserves on time and demand deposits. Item 8 is the U.S. Treasury's checking account. We have already discussed account 9, and accounts 10 and 11 are of relatively minor importance, as is account 5 on the asset side.[7]

Our main purpose in this section is to derive a general formula for the monetary base. The Federal Reserve balance sheet as rewritten in Table 9–2 is the first step in deriving such an equation. In this table, accounts 4 and 9 have been netted into a float account, and three of the less-important accounts—5, 10, and 11—have been combined and listed as other Federal Reserve accounts netted. Finally, U.S. Treasury currency has been added as item 12 since it is a component of the monetary base. In order that the right- and left-hand sides of Table 9–2 will be equal and hence constitute an equation, U.S. Treasury currency must be added to both sides.

Table 9-3 contains the monetary base equation and is obtained by

---

[7] Account 5, Other Federal Reserve assets, includes the bank's premises and holdings of coin; account 10 includes deposits of foreign central banks; account 11 consists of capital paid in, surplus, and other capital accounts.

TABLE 9–2
Derivation of the monetary base—an intermediate step

1. Gold certificates (includes SDR certificate account)	6. Federal Reserve notes (held by banks and by the public)
+	+
2. Federal Reserve holdings of U.S. government securities	7. Member bank deposits
+	+
3. Federal Reserve loans to member banks =	8. U.S. Treasury deposits
+	+
4.– 9. Float (account 4 minus account 9)	10. Other Federal Reserve
+11. accounts netted (account 10
– 5. plus account 11 minus account 5)
+	+
12. U.S. Treasury currency (held by banks and by the public)	12. U.S. Treasury currency (held by banks and by the public)

isolating the items in Table 9–2 that constitute the base—6, 7, and 12. To do this, item 8 and other Federal Reserve accounts netted (items 5, 10, and 11) are subtracted from both sides of the equation. The result is the monetary base formula of Table 9–3 where the base is expressed as the difference between what is labeled as factors supplying the base and factors absorbing the base.

TABLE 9–3
The monetary base

The monetary base	Equals (=)	Factors supplying the base	Minus (–)	Factors absorbing the base
6. Federal Reserve notes (held by banks and by the public)		1. Gold certificates (includes SDR certificate account)		8. U.S. Treasury deposits
+		+		+
7. Member bank deposits		2. Federal Reserve holdings of U.S. government securities		10. Other Federal
+11. Reserve accounts
– 5. netted
+		+		
12. U.S. Treasury currency (held by banks and by the public)		3. Federal Reserve loans to member banks		
		+		
		4.– 9. Float		
		+		
		12. U.S. Treasury currency (held by banks and by the public)		

The supply column contains five items. An increase in a supply item will produce an equal increase in the monetary base, assuming that no offsetting changes occur in the factors absorbing the base. For instance, when float rises, the monetary base also rises by an equal amount; this result could be anticipated from our earlier discussion which identified float as double-counted reserves. The concurrent changes in float and member bank deposits typify the impact of a change in a supply item on the monetary base.

On the other hand, an increase in U.S. Treasury deposits in the other column reduces the base since the items in this column are factors absorbing the base. An increase in U.S. Treasury deposits occurs when the Treasury transfers funds from its tax and loan accounts in commercial banks to its Federal Reserve checking account (item 8).[8] The transfer of funds from banks to the U.S. Treasury is accomplished by deducting funds from member bank deposits (item 7) and simultaneously adding the funds to the Treasury's Federal Reserve account (item 8). From this example it should be apparent that an increase in a factor absorbing the base will cause the monetary base to decline.

The utilization of policy items to change the size of the monetary base is explored in detail in the following chapter. However, the formula indicates that, when the Fed buys and sells U.S. government securities (account 2), the base will be affected. Fluctuations in member bank borrowing (account 3) also will cause the base to change. Thus the monetary base formula contains two items that can be manipulated to control the base, and though all items in the equation are not under the direct control of the Fed, unwanted changes can be offset through management of items 2 and 3.

The base contains currency held by banks and by the public plus deposits at the Fed. On the other hand, total bank reserves are smaller than the base since currency held by the public is not a component of reserves. Therefore, any policy that has an impact on the base is unlikely to have an identical effect on bank reserves. For instance, if the Federal Reserve issues more Federal Reserve notes, the base will increase by the amount of the new issue, but reserves will increase by a smaller amount since some of the currency will end up in the hands of the public. While changes in the base and

---

[8] When taxes are paid to the U.S. Treasury, the funds are usually deposited into "tax and loan" accounts in commercial banks; then, when the Treasury needs funds for expenditures, money is transferred from the tax and loan accounts to the Treasury's Federal Reserve account. The procedure prevents a massive flow of reserves from the banking system at tax payment time. By transferring funds only as they are needed, Treasury expenditures are injecting funds into the banking system at about the same rate that they are being withdrawn.

changes in bank reserves may not be the same, the Federal Reserve nevertheless is able to control bank reserves within acceptable limits by managing the monetary base.

HOW DO CHANGES IN THE MONETARY BASE LEAD TO CHANGES IN THE MONEY SUPPLY?

A simple example of deposit expansion

It is now possible to show the relation between changes in the monetary base and changes in deposits. Remember the sequence outlined earlier in Figure 9–1: Manipulation of the monetary base produces changes in the total reserves of the banking system, which in turn sets the stage for a multiple change in the money supply. Our first money-creation example is a simple one. It is assumed that there are no time deposits and no desire by the public to increase its currency holdings during the expansion process. Finally, all banks wish to keep zero excess reserves, and the required reserve ratio is assumed to be 15 percent on all demand deposits.

The expansion is initiated with a $100,000 open-market purchase of U.S. government securities by the Federal Reserve. The purchase could be from a New York bank that deals in the securities market or from one of the 25 or so nonbank securities dealers who operate in New York City. We assume that the purchase is from a bank (bank A), and the T-account below shows how bank A's balance sheet is affected when it sells $100,000 of U.S. government securities to the New York Federal Reserve Bank and as payment receives an increase in its reserve account of $100,000. Of primary importance is the fact that there has been a $100,000 increase in the monetary base (and bank reserves). We assumed initially that banks will not permanently hold excess reserves; thus bank A will utilize the reserves to make a loan or to purchase some other interest-bearing investment.

	Bank A	
Δ *Assets*		Δ *Liabilities*
U.S. government securities	− $100,000	
Deposit at the Federal Reserve Bank of New York	+ $100,000	

The first phase of the process of deposit creation is shown in the following T-account where bank A has utilized its excess reserves by making a $100,000 loan to X Corporation, which receives the pro-

ceeds of the loan in its demand deposit account. The increase in
demand deposits of $100,000 necessitates a $15,000 increase in required reserves which bank A meets by utilizing a portion of its
excess reserves.[9]

Bank A,
Phase 1

Δ Assets		Δ Liabilities	
Loan to X Corporation	+ $100,000	Demand deposit of X Corporation	+ $100,000

At this juncture bank A still has $85,000 ($100,000 − $15,000) of
excess reserves. However, an individual bank would normally expect to lose at least a part of these reserves when X Corporation
begins to write checks on its demand deposit. If these checks are
deposited in other banks, bank A will pay the checks by drawing
down its excess reserves. Of course, some required reserves also will
be freed as the demand deposit accounts diminish. In practice, bank
A can estimate its potential loss of reserves according to loan type(s),
the nature of the loan recipient(s), and other factors.

Concerning the expansion process as a whole, it does not matter
exactly what happens to bank A as long as the excess reserves are
utilized somewhere in the banking system. It may be assumed that
bank A loses all $100,000 of its new demand deposits to other banks.
(The exact amount of bank A's loss will not affect the final totals for
the banking system as a whole; the $100,000 figure is used to
simplify the explanation.) The remaining phase 1 T-accounts show
the loss of demand deposits from bank A and the gain by other banks
which now have excess reserves of $85,000.

Bank A,
Phase 1 (continued)

Δ Assets		Δ Liabilities	
Deposit at Federal Reserve Bank of New York	− $100,000	Demand deposits	− $100,000

Other Banks,
Phase 1 (continued)

Δ Assets		Δ Liabilities	
Deposits at Federal Reserve banks	+ $100,000	Demand deposits	+ $100,000

---

[9] The 15 percent reserve requirement times the $100,000 X Corporation demand
deposit equals $15,000.

TABLE 9–4
Money creation—a simple example

(1) Expansion phase	(2) New demand deposits	(3) New banks loans and investments	(4) New required reserves
1st phase	$100,000	$100,000	$ 15,000
2d phase	85,000	85,000	12,750
3d phase	72,250	72,250	10,837
.	.	.	.
.	.	.	.
.	.	.	.
.	.	.	.
.	.	.	.
nth phase	0	0	0
Final outcome	$667,000	$667,000	$100,000

Phase 2 of the expansion process involves other banks' utilizing their excess reserves to make loans; the transactions are similar to the changes that occurred with bank A. Again, required reserves will increase, this time by 15 percent of $85,000, or $12,750. It should be obvious that the expansion process is still in its early stages since only $27,750 ($15,000 + $12,750) of the original injection of reserves has been utilized at this point. Therefore, the expansion process will continue through many phases before playing out; Table 9–4 summarizes the steps involved. Observe in Table 9–4 that the final expansion of deposits is $667,000; new bank loans and investments also total $667,000; and at the completion of the expansion, all of the $100,000 of originally injected reserves is serving as required reserves for the $667,000 of demand deposits created in the expansion process (15 percent required reserves times $667,000 of newly created demand deposits equals $100,000).

Other Banks,
Phase 2

Δ Assets		Δ Liabilities	
Loans	+ $85,000	Demand deposits	+ $85,000

The final results in Table 9–4 are easily obtainable with the aid of a simple formula. If the original change in the monetary base (ΔB) is multiplied by a money multiplier, the product is the final change in deposits. The simple money multiplier is $1/RR_d$ where RR_d is the reserve requirement on demand deposits. Therefore,

$$
\text{(9-1)} \quad \begin{array}{l} \text{Final change in} \\ \text{bank demand} \\ \text{deposits} \end{array} = \text{Money multiplier} \times \begin{array}{l} \text{Change in the} \\ \text{monetary base} \end{array}
$$

$$
= \frac{1}{RR_d} \times \$100,000
$$

$$
= \frac{1}{0.15} \times \$100,000
$$

$$
= \$667,000.
$$

Use of this formula allows one to see the final results without having to trace each phase of the process.[10]

A more realistic example of money creation

At this point, we make the simple example in the preceding section more realistic by including time deposits and allowing the public to vary desired currency holdings. Also, it is now assumed that banks desire to hold a cushion of excess reserves in order to avoid a penalty for a reserve deficiency due to unexpected deposit withdrawals. The reserve requirement for demand deposits is held at 15 percent, while a 4 percent requirement is assumed for time deposits. Furthermore, assume that the public wishes to divide its money and near-money asset holdings into demand deposits, time deposits, and currency in the proportions $P_d = 0.30$, $P_t = 0.60$, and $P_c = 0.10$, respectively. In other words, the public's desired ratio of time deposits to demand deposits (t) equals 2.0, and the desired ratio of currency to demand deposits (c) equals one third. Finally, banks are assumed to hold excess reserves equal to 0.03 percent of demand deposits. These assumptions are reflected in Table 9-5.

The transaction that initiates the expansion process is assumed to be the same as in the simple example; that is, the Federal Reserve

---

[10] According to the assumptions of the model, a bank is in equilibrium when excess reserves are zero, that is, when total reserves are equal to required reserves. Since there are no time deposits in this example, it follows that, for the system as a whole to be in equilibrium,

$$
\Delta \text{Total reserves} = \Delta \text{Required reserves} = (RR_d)\,(\Delta \text{Demand deposits}),
$$

or

$$
\Delta \text{Demand deposits} = \frac{1}{RR_d}(\Delta \text{Total reserves}).
$$

There is no currency leakage in this example; so the change in total reserves must be equal to the change in the monetary base (ΔB); therefore,

$$
\Delta \text{Demand deposits} = \left(\frac{1}{RR_d}\right)(\Delta B).
$$

TABLE 9–5
Assumed reserve and desired asset ratios

Reserve requirements and desired excess reserve proportion		Public's desired asset proportions
Demand deposits	$RR_d = 0.15$	$P_d = 0.30$
Time deposits	$RR_t = 0.04$	$P_t = 0.60$
Desired excess		$P_c = 0.10$
reserves	$x = 0.0003$	$t = P_t/P_d = 0.60/0.30$
		$= 2.00$
		$c = P_c/P_d = 0.10/0.30$
		$= 0.33333$

purchases $100,000 of U.S. government securities from bank A. However, the steps that follow are more involved; when bank A makes a $100,000 loan (to X Corporation), part of the proceeds is assumed to be taken as demand deposits ($30,000), part as time deposits ($60,000), and part as currency ($10,000). (Refer to Table 9–5 for the values of P_d, P_t, and P_c.) The phase 1 T-account shows

Bank A,
Phase 1

Δ Assets		Δ Liabilities	
Portion of proceeds of loan to X Corporation taken in *currency*	$-$ $ 10,000	Portion of proceeds of loan to X Corporation placed in *demand deposits*	+ $30,000
Loan to X Corporation	+ $100,000	Portion of proceeds of loan to X Corporation placed in *time deposits*	+ $60,000

these changes. On the liabilities side, the portions of the loan taken as demand and time deposits have been entered. On the asset side there are the following changes:

1. There is a currency withdrawal of $10,000. Since the currency withdrawal reduces vault cash, it represents a reduction of bank A's (excess) reserves.
2. The $100,000 loan to X Corporation is entered.
3. While this fact is not reflected in the T-account shown above, additional required reserves are needed because of the new demand and time deposits. Required reserves on the new demand and time deposits are 0.15 × $30,000, or $4,500, and 0.04 × $60,000, or $2,400, respectively.

Since further steps require several entries for each additional phase, no further T-accounts are included. To derive the final outcome, we shall use a money multiplier (M) that incorporates time deposits, currency, and excess reserves.[11] Equation (9–2) is an M-1A multiplier that, when multiplied by the change in the monetary base (ΔB) gives the potential expansion of new demand deposits plus currency:

(9–2)
$$M = \frac{1 + c}{c + RR_d + (RR_t)\,(t) + x}.$$

Using the values in Table 9–5 to derive M,

$$M = \frac{1 + 0.33333}{0.33333 + 0.15 + (0.04)\,(2.00) + 0.0003}$$

$$= 2.3656.$$

The results of the example are shown in Table 9–6. The final change in M-1A is $236,560 (see column 2c) which was obtained by

---

[11] The M-1A money multiplier is derived as follows:

(a) ΔMonetary base = ΔCurrency + ΔBank reserves;

or

(b) $\Delta B = \Delta C + \Delta$Required reserves + ΔExcess reserves;

thus in equilibrium,

(c) $\Delta B = \Delta C + (RR_d)\,(\Delta DD) + (RR_t)\,(\Delta TD) + x(\Delta DD)$.

Since the change in time deposits must be equal to t times the change in demand deposits in order for the public's asset preferences to be satisfied, ΔTD is equal to $(t)(\Delta DD)$. Furthermore, ΔC must be equal to $(c)\,(\Delta DD)$. Hence, Equation (c) can be rewritten as

(d) $\Delta B = (c)(\Delta DD) + (RR_d)\,(\Delta DD) + (RR_t)\,(t)(\Delta DD) + (x)\,(\Delta DD)$.

Solving for ΔDD, the result is

(e) $$\Delta DD = \frac{\Delta B}{c + RR_d + (RR_t)\,(t) + x}$$

or

$$\Delta DD = (\Delta B)\left(\frac{1}{c + RR_d + (RR_t)\,(t) + x}\right).$$

The change in M-1A is equal to the change in currency plus the change in demand deposits;

therefore,

(f) $\Delta(\text{M-1A}) = \Delta DD + \Delta C$

or

(g) $\Delta(\text{M-1A}) = \Delta DD + (c)\,(\Delta DD)$.

Substituting Equation (e) for ΔDD and simplifying, the formula for ΔM-1A is

(h) $$\Delta(\text{M-1A}) = (\Delta B)\left(\frac{1 + c}{c + RR_d + (RR_t)\,(t) + x}\right).$$

TABLE 9-6
Money creation—a more realistic example

(1)	(2)			(3)	(4)	(5)	(6)
	(a) New currency usage	+ (b) New demand deposits	= (c) M-1A	New time deposits	New loans and investments*	New required reserves	New desired excess reserves
Phase							
1st phase	$10,000	$ 30,000	$ 40,000	$ 60,000	$100,000	$ 6,900	$ 9
2d phase	8,309	24,927	33,236	49,855	83,091	5,733	7
.							
.							
.							
.							
.							
.							
.							
nth phase	0	0	0	0	0	0	0
Final outcome	$59,140	$177,420	$236,560	$354,840	$591,400	$40,807	$53

* The final change in new loans and investments can be obtained by summing new currency usage, new demand deposits, and new time deposits or by multiplying the increase in the monetary base (ΔB) by a loan/investment multiplier,

$$\frac{1 + t + c}{RR_d + (RR_t)\, t + c + x},$$

which for our illustration is 5.9140. Therefore, if $\Delta B = \$100,000$, the final increase in new loans and investments is $591,400 ($5.914 \times \$100,000$).

multiplying 2.3656 (M) times $100,000 (the change in the monetary base, or ΔB). Note that the increase in money consists of an increase in demand deposits (column 2b) plus an increase in currency held by the public (column 2a). New time deposits in column (3) are twice new demand deposits. New loans and investments (see column 4) are equal to the sum of new currency, new demand deposits, and new time deposits (or the change in new loans and investments can be derived using the multiplier formula given in Table 9–6). New required reserves (column 5) are 15 percent of new demand deposits ($26,613) plus 4 percent of new time deposits ($14,194), or a total of $40,807. The $40,807 plus the new currency demand of $59,140 plus the $53 of new excess reserves (see column 6) accounts for the original injection of $100,000 of new monetary base into the system by the initial open-market purchase.

Other considerations

At the outset of this chapter we said that the formal model of the expansion process would indicate a degree of precision that is not borne out in actual practice. Our explanation of the monetary change process suggests that the Fed can control the monetary base primarily through use of open-market operations, or the Federal Reserve can also raise or lower reserve requirements to change the value of the money multiplier (M). Therefore, it may seem as if monetary control is a simple, mechanistic process.

Monetary management is complicated by the fact that other influences that affect the money creation process may not be reflected by the formal model. Among these complicating factors are the following items:

1. The public's preference for time deposits, demand deposits, and currency may, and often does vary, and consequently the money multiplier will fluctuate.
2. The banking system's desire to hold excess reserves may change, thereby influencing the expansion or contraction process.
3. Since reserve requirements are on a graduated basis, a shift in deposits between large and small banks would influence the money multiplier.

Consequently, the money multiplier fluctuates over time, often unpredictably. Figure 9–2 plots the M-1A multiplier for several months during 1979 and early 1980.

Monetary management is therefore not as simple and straightforward as our formal model implies. In some cases the complications listed above are of minor importance and for practical purposes can

FIGURE 9–2
M-1A money multiplier (February 20–March 26, 1980)

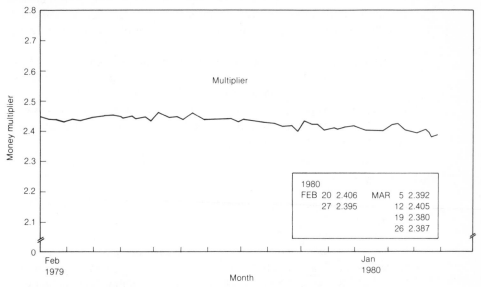

Source: Federal Reserve Bank of St. Louis, *U.S. Financial Data,* week ending April 2, 1980.

be ignored, or the model can be made more realistic, but more complex, by internalizing some of these forces. Even though there are a
number of ways that the monetary management process can be
short-circuited, most economists still feel that it is possible to control the money supply within reasonably narrow limits. Adequacy of
control increases as the time range involved is lengthened; that is,
errors in hitting a target rate of growth of the money stock may be
large for a week or a month, but precision is greatly increased when
the time span is lengthened to six months or a year.[12]

SUMMARY

In this chapter we have analyzed the various components of the
monetary process. The major elements of the discussion are summarized in Figure 9–1, which should provide a meaningful overview
of the monetary management framework. The figure indicates that
open-market operations and the discount mechanism can be used to

---

[12] For a discussion of the control of monetary aggregates, see Leonall C. Andersen
and Denis S. Karnosky, "Some Considerations in the Use of Monetary Aggregates for
the Implementation of Monetary Policy," *Review of the Federal Reserve Bank of St.
Louis,* vol. 59, no. 9 (September 1977), pp. 2–7.

manipulate the monetary base (and reserves), thereby initiating a process that ultimately affects the supply of money. Once the base is changed, bank reserves will be affected, and the impact on bank deposits will subsequently be magnified through the money multiplier (M).

The three general instruments of monetary control include open-market operations, the discount mechanism, and reserve requirements. Each of these can be used by the Federal Reserve to manage the supply of money and credit. The following chapter is devoted to providing details about how the Federal Reserve administers the monetary policy instruments.

REVIEW QUESTIONS

1. What is the monetary base, and how does it differ from total bank reserves?

2. What are the three general instruments of monetary control? How is each instrument related to the money supply process?

3. Define float. Assume that Cooper, who has an account in Denver National Bank, gives a $100 check to Star Corporation, which maintains an account in City National Bank of Colorado Springs. Show how float could arise if the Federal Reserve Bank of Denver handles the clearing of the check.

4. Assume that reserve requirements for demand deposits and time deposits are 0.10 and 0.06 respectively, that the public's desired asset proportions are 0.20, 0.60, and 0.20 for demand deposits, time deposits, and currency, and that all banks belong to the Federal Reserve System and hold zero excess reserves. Further, assume that the Federal Reserve purchases $200,000 in securities from a bank. Derive final outcomes for each of the columns in Table 9–6.

5. Consider how the initial part of the money expansion process would be affected if the purchase of U.S. government securities were from a nonbank securities dealer instead of a bank.

SUGGESTIONS FOR ADDITIONAL READING

Burger, Albert E. "Alternative Measures of the Monetary Base." Review of the Federal Reserve Bank of St. Louis, vol. 61, no. 6 (June 1970), pp. 3–8.

Duesenberry, James. Money and Credit: Impact and Control. Englewood Cliffs, N.J.: Prentice-Hall, Inc., 1972.

Federal Reserve Bank of Chicago. Modern Money Mechanics: A Workbook. Chicago: 1971.

Jordan, Jerry L. "Elements of Money Stock Determination." Review of the Federal Reserve Bank of St. Louis, vol. 51, no. 10, October 1979, pp. 10–19.

10 Federal Reserve monetary policy instruments

WARM-UP: *Outline and questions to consider as you read*

How are reserve requirements administered, and what is the impact of changing them?
   Administration of reserve requirements.
   Impact of a change in reserve requirements.
What is the role of the discount window in Federal Reserve policymaking?
How are open-market operations used to control the monetary base?
What is selective credit allocation, and what is its purpose?
   Usury laws.
   Regulation Q.
   Margin requirements.
   Other selective credit controls.

NEW TERMS

Discount mechanism: the Federal Reserve procedure for making loans to banks and thrift institutions.

General instruments: the monetary management tools that the Federal Reserve uses to control overall monetary and credit conditions and which include reserve requirements, the discount mechanism, and open-market operations.

Margin requirements: a selective credit control that sets the minimum proportion of one's own cash that must accompany any borrowed funds used to purchase stocks and bonds.

Open market operations: a Federal Reserve System general instrument that involves purchases and sales of U.S. government securities.

Regulation A: the Federal Reserve regulation governing administration of loans through the "discount window."

Reserve requirements: a Federal Reserve System general instrument used to control the required reserves of member banks.

Selective credit control: any technique designed to alter market-determined credit allocation.

Usury laws: a type of selective credit control that places legal maximums on interest rates, usually according to the nature and maturity of the loan involved.

The analysis of the mechanics of money creation begun in the previous chapter indicated that, by managing the monetary base, the Federal Reserve can exercise reasonably firm control over the money supply. The link between the monetary base and the money stock was specified in the form of the money multiplier which indicates the potential amount of new currency and demand deposits (M-1A) that can be supported by each extra dollar of monetary base. The present chapter describes how the Federal Reserve System can use the general monetary instruments to manipulate the value of the money multiplier as well as change the monetary base. Finally, in the concluding section we discuss selective credit allocation techniques which attempt to alter the results of unregulated demand and supply forces operating in credit markets.

The term *general instrument* derives from the notion that use of these tools will have a broad impact on financial markets and economic activity. *General* does not necessarily mean that the impact is the same throughout the economy. As a matter of fact, there is considerable debate about the evenness of monetary policy. In this chapter, however, we will not concern ourselves with this issue but will instead focus on how the general instruments are used to control the supply of money and credit.

The Federal Reserve has three general instruments that it can use to manage the money supply—reserve requirement ratios, the discount mechanism, and open-market operations. *Reserve requirement policy* involves raising or lowering the level of reserves required for deposits; the *discount mechanism* refers to Federal Reserve loans to banks and thrift institutions; and *open market oper-*

ations are the Fed's purchases and sales of U.S. government securities. In the previous chapter, Figure 9–1 indicated that the channel of influence of reserve requirements is different from those of
open-market operations and the discount mechanism. Reserve requirements are depicted as operating through the money multiplier
(M), while the other general instruments act on the monetary base.
We explain in the following sections how each instrument influences the money-supply process.

HOW ARE RESERVE REQUIREMENTS ADMINISTERED, AND WHAT IS THE IMPACT OF CHANGING THEM?

Administration of reserve requirements

In the previous chapter, we briefly discussed the Federal Reserve's authority to set reserve requirements. Requirements are based
on deposit type—demand and time—and the percentages are on a
graduated basis. In early 1980 reserve requirements ranged from 7 to
16.25 percent for demand deposits, and from 1 to 6 percent on various categories of time deposits, with a 3 percent minimum average
required on total time deposits in a given bank. The percentages set
by the Federal Reserve must fall within the limits established by
Congress. These limits were originally prescribed in the Banking Act
of 1935 which also gave the Federal Reserve authority to set reserve
requirements. The Monetary Control Act of 1980 provides for a new
structure of reserve requirement ratios for Federal Reserve member
banks and also empowers the Fed to set reserve requirements for
transaction balances and for nonpersonal time deposits at all depository institutions. The new requirements will be phased in for
member banks over a four-year period and over an eight-year period
for nonmember institutions. At the end of the phasein, required reserve ratios are scheduled to be 3 percent on transactions balances
up to $25 million and 12 percent on transactions balances over $25
million; the ratio for nonpersonal time deposits is 3 percent. Also,
the Fed may alter the requirements on transactions balances over $25
million within a range of 8 to 14 percent and on nonpersonal time
deposits within a range of 0 to 9 percent.

Reserve requirements are calculated for each settlement week,
which begins on Thursday and ends the following Wednesday. Required reserves for the settlement week are based on average
end-of-day demand and time deposit balances for the seven-day
period starting two weeks prior to the first day of the settlement
week. We shall refer to this prior period as the base week (the relationship of the base week to the settlement week is shown in Fig-

FIGURE 10–1
Calculating required bank reserves

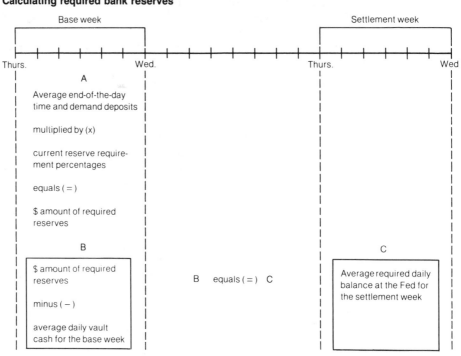

ure 10–1). To calculate the level of required reserves, average daily time and demand deposits for the base week are first determined, and the average deposits are then multiplied by current reserve requirement percents to obtain reserve requirements in dollar terms (see part A of Figure 10–1). Next, average daily vault cash for the base week is deducted from reserve requirements (part B of Figure 10–1). Finally, the bank's average daily deposits at the Fed for the settlement week are compared to the difference between required reserves and base week vault cash (part C of Figure 10–1). If balances at the Fed are insufficient to cover this difference, a charge is assessed. The charge is equal to the amount of the reserve deficiency times a penalty rate.[1]

The discussion of reserve requirements thus far has dealt primar-

---

[1] The penalty rate is the current discount rate plus 2 percent. For a more detailed discussion of how banks determine required reserve levels, see Edward J. McCarthy, *Reserve Position: Methods of Adjustment* (Boston: Federal Reserve Bank of Boston, 1971).

ily with regulations covering members of the Federal Reserve System. Nonmember state banks' reserve requirements have traditionally been set by the individual states, but as mentioned previously, the Monetary Control Act transferred some control over nonmember reserve requirements to the Federal Reserve. A study by R. Alton Gilbert and Jean M. Lovati indicates that reserve requirements for nonmember banks have generally been lower than the requirements imposed by the Fed on member banks. Furthermore, nonmember banks were often permitted to use earning assets to satisfy at least part of their reserve requirement.[2] The generally more lenient state requirements were largely responsible for the relative decline of membership in the Federal Reserve from 47 percent of all banks in 1947 to less than 39 percent in 1980. The shrinking membership in the Fed was to a large extent responsible for legislation granting the Federal Reserve control over reserve requirements of at least some deposits of nonmember institutions.

The Fed makes infrequent use of the reserve requirement instrument because frequent changes in required reserve percents would make bank management more difficult. Bank reserves are kept very close to required levels since banks generally do not earn a return on reserve assets. In early 1980 member bank deposits subject to reserve requirements were $644 billion, while excess reserves totaled only $35 million. If reserve requirement changes were commonplace, then the task of maintaining reserves at or slightly above legal levels would be greatly complicated. Consequently, during the five-year period 1974–79, demand deposit reserve ratios were changed only three times.

Reserve requirement changes are also avoided because even small changes necessitate rather large adjustments in the absolute size of reserves, and in turn, deposits. For example, in early 1980, an across-the-board, 0.5 percent increase in reserve requirements would have necessitated a reserve adjustment of over $3 billion, an adjustment that at the time would have amounted to 7 percent of existing reserve holdings of member banks. The large absolute changes that result from relatively small percentage adjustments are why economists call reserve requirements a "blunt instrument." Thus, recent reserve requirement changes, when they have been made, were in small increments ranging from 0.25 percent to 1 percent, with the most common change being 0.5 percent.

---

[2] R. Alton Gilbert and Jean M. Lovati, "Bank Reserve Requirements and Their Enforcement: A Comparison across States," *Review of the Federal Reserve Bank of St. Louis*, vol. 60, no. 3 (March 1978), pp. 22–32.

Impact of a change in reserve requirements

To show the effects of a change in reserve requirements, we begin with the money multiplier derived in Chapter 9:

$$(10-1) \qquad M = \frac{1+c}{c + RR_d + (RR_t)\,(t) + x}.$$

Reserve requirements on demand deposits (RR_d) were assumed to be 0.15 and on time deposits (RR_t) 0.04. The public's preferred ratios of currency to demand deposits (c) and of time deposits to demand deposits (t) were 0.33333 and 2.00, respectively, and the desired excess reserve ratio is 0.0003. Substituting those values in the money multiplier formula, we obtained 2.3656 as the value of M.

Suppose that the reserve requirement on demand deposits is lowered from 0.15 to 0.14. Changing only the "RR_d" term in the formula to 0.14, the new value of M is 2.4083. Note that a reduction in reserve requirements does not cause the monetary base to change; however, the same monetary base will support a larger money supply. For example, with a demand deposit reserve requirement of 15 percent and a $200 billion monetary base, the potential amount of M-1A is $473.12 billion ($200 × 2.3646). When the reserve requirement is lowered to 14 percent, the potential amount of M-1A is $481.66 billion ($200 × 2.4083) which is an increase of $8.54 billion. Thus, lower reserve requirements will normally produce an increase in the money supply; moreover, future changes in the monetary base will have a greater impact since the money multiplier is now larger.

It should be apparent from this illustration that the amount of M-1A depends on reserve requirements as well as the size of the monetary base. In an effort to reflect this relationship, the Saint Louis Federal Reserve Bank publishes two monetary base series, one unadjusted and one adjusted. The latter series incorporates an adjustment for the effect of reserve requirement changes. For example, the unadjusted base may be constant, but lowering reserve requirements would cause the adjusted base to grow. Such growth in the adjusted base suggests that expansion of the money supply is likely, a result consistent with our example above. Therefore, the adjusted monetary base reflects changes in the base caused not only by open-market operations and loans through the discount window but also by reserve requirement changes.

WHAT IS THE ROLE OF THE DISCOUNT WINDOW IN FEDERAL RESERVE POLICYMAKING?

The discount mechanism was the only general instrument incorporated in the original Federal Reserve Act of 1913. The discount mechanism is administered under the Fed's Regulation A which specifies the conditions under which a bank can borrow from the Federal Reserve. The discount window makes the Federal Reserve a lender of last resort for banks needing temporary funds. Until 1980 only member banks could borrow from the Federal Reserve, except that, under "unusual and exigent" circumstances, the Board of Governors could permit a nonmember bank access to the discount window. However, the Monetary Control Act extended access to the discount window to all depository institutions holding transactions balances or nonpersonal time deposits. At the time of this writing, the Fed was in the process of formulating regulations governing loans to nonmember institutions.

According to Regulation A, borrowing from the Federal Reserve is a privilege, not a right, since loans are at the discretion of the Federal Reserve, not the borrowing banks. Furthermore, according to Regulation A,

> Federal Reserve credit is generally extended on a short-term basis to a member bank in order to enable it to adjust its asset position when necessary because of developments such as a sudden withdrawal of deposits or seasonal requirements for credit beyond those which can reasonably be met by use of the bank's own resources.

Thus loans are generally short-term loans having a maturity of 15 or fewer days; only under unusual circumstances will loans of longer duration be granted.[3] The Federal Reserve therefore expects banks to eliminate reserve deficiencies by means other than continuously relying on Federal Reserve credit. Finally, banks are not to use the discount window to obtain funds for speculation or profitmaking. Such borrowing is improper, and Federal Reserve credit may be withheld in such cases.

During the Federal Reserve's early years, a bank would borrow by presenting a customer loan at the discount window; if the loan were acceptable or eligible for discounting, the Fed would credit the bank's account for the face value of the loan less the discount (sometimes called the *rediscount*) rate. In general, to be eligible for discounting, the loan must have been made for the purpose of financing the short-term working capital needs of business and agriculture. Since it is cumbersome and time consuming (1) to qualify a loan for rediscounting, (2) to transfer it first to the Federal Reserve bank then back for collection, and (3) to accomplish the attendant bookkeep-

---

[3] Regulation A states that loans of longer duration may be made "when necessary to assist member banks in meeting unusual situations, such as may result from national, regional, or local difficulties or from exceptional circumstances involving only particular member banks."

ing, rediscounting eligible customer paper is rarely done today. Instead the Fed more commonly makes an "advance" to a bank in return for the bank's own note to the Federal Reserve secured by U.S. government securities or some other form of eligible collateral. The Federal Reserve often holds bank-owned government securities for safekeeping as a service for banks, and advances therefore require a minimum of paperwork. Assets other than U.S. government securities may be used, but the Fed levies a 0.5 percent penalty when certain types of collateral are pledged.

We have emphasized that the discount mechanism was created for lender-of-last-resort purposes. Nevertheless, increases or decreases in borrowing through the discount window do affect the monetary base and therefore the volume of total bank reserves. The discussion of the monetary base in Chapter 9 indicated that an increase in Federal Reserve loans produces an increase in the monetary base since these loans appear in the factors supplying the base column. This relation can be seen in the following monetary base equation:

			Factors supplying the base		*Factors absorbing the base*
	Monetary base	*Equals (=)*		*Minus (−)*	
			Gold certificates (includes SDR certificate account)		
			+		
	Federal Reserve notes		Federal Reserve holdings of U.S. government securities		U.S. Treasury deposits
	+				+
(10–2)	Member bank deposits		+		Other Federal Reserve accounts netted
	+		Federal Reserve loans to member banks		
	U.S. Treasury currency		+		
			Float		
			+		
			U.S. Treasury currency		

A Fed loan to a member bank will simultaneously increase member bank deposits and Federal Reserve loans to member banks since the proceeds of the loan are added to the borrowing bank's reserve account. The Federal Reserve presently uses the discount mechanism to aid member banks in temporary need of funds, and the impact on the base and on reserves is of secondary importance. Open-market operations can always be used to offset any unwanted reserve changes occasioned by changes in loans to banks through the discount window.

The Fed usually changes the discount rate in order to keep it in line with other interest rates rather than for the express purpose of injecting or withdrawing reserves. However, a change in the discount rate may have an important "announcement" effect. An increase may be interpreted as a sign that the Federal Reserve believes that higher interest rates and tighter money are in order, or a reduction in the discount rate may be viewed as an indication that the Fed desires to pursue an easier monetary policy. Thus financial observers often see discount rate changes as an index of the Federal Reserve's present stance with respect to monetary policy or perhaps as an indicator of future policy.

The discount window is a source of short-term funds for borrowing institutions, and it is therefore appropriate to conclude this section by mentioning another, and actually more important, source of borrowed funds—the federal funds market. This market is a component of the money market, a nationwide network for lending and borrowing large sums of money over short periods. The market for short-term U.S. government securities, for instance, is part of the money market, and so is the market for commercial paper.

Commercial banks are participants in the federal funds market in which banks with excess reserves lend to banks with reserve deficiencies, usually on an overnight basis. This market developed rapidly in the late 1950s and early 1960s and has become an important part of the money market. Federal funds are an attractive alternative to the discount window since borrowing federal funds generally involves less paperwork than discounting. Also, the Fed's administration of the discount window has discouraged the development of discounting: the Federal Reserve stresses that discounting is a privilege, not a right; continuous use of the discount window is discouraged; and loans from the Federal Reserve are not to be used for profitmaking purposes but instead are a source of funds to cover temporary reserve deficiencies. Thus, while the federal funds rate is typically higher than the discount rate, the volume of federal funds loans greatly exceeds borrowing from the Fed.

HOW ARE OPEN-MARKET OPERATIONS USED
TO CONTROL THE MONETARY BASE?

Of the three general instruments used by the Federal Reserve to manage reserves, open-market operations are the most important. As previously noted, the discount mechanism is used primarily as a lender-of-last-resort tool, while reserve requirement changes are so powerful that they are seldom used as a method of monetary control. Thus open-market operations are the day-to-day method for controlling the monetary base and ultimately the nation's supply of money and credit.

Open-market operations involve Federal Reserve purchases and sales of U.S. government securities in the open market. The market for U.S. government securities is one of the most active in the financial sector; several billion dollars worth of trading takes place daily. As a rule, open-market operations are in U.S. government securities, mostly short-term, though other instruments may be traded.

Federal Reserve involvement in the government securities market began soon after the Federal Reserve started operating in 1914. Originally, Federal Reserve participation merely reflected a desire to use excess Reserve System funds to obtain interest-earning assets. However, by the late 1920s, Federal Reserve officials were buying and selling government securities with the specific aim of managing bank reserves. Though open-market operations were already being used to control reserves, Congress formally sanctioned the practice in the Banking Acts of 1933 and 1935, the latter act providing for the Federal Open Market Committee (FOMC) in its current form.

The composition of the 12-person Federal Open Market Committee was discussed in Chapter 8. The FOMC meets approximately once each month to chart the course of monetary policy. Each meeting consists of a discussion of the economy and the current financial situation. Based on staff forecasts and the committee's own assessment of what has been happening and the problems that need to be dealt with, the FOMC formulates the general thrust of open-market policy for the next several weeks. If the economy is sluggish, the FOMC may decide that a faster injection of reserves is warranted; on the other hand, if inflation seems to be a serious threat, reserves may be injected at a slower rate or even withdrawn from the banking system.

Once action has been agreed upon by the committee, a directive is issued to the manager of the System's open-market account. Since the bulk of government securities transactions occur in New York City, the New York Federal Reserve Bank acts as agent for the entire system, and the manager of the open market account is a senior officer of the New York Fed.

The manager of the open-market account must implement the directive issued by the FOMC. The directive is stated in terms of hitting a stated target such as a specific federal funds rate range and/or a growth rate of certain monetary aggregates—for example, M-1A and M-1B. During the 1970s the Fed used the federal funds rate as its primary target, supplying reserves to lower the federal funds rate and withdrawing reserves to raise it. In addition, long- and short-run target rates of growth for the monetary aggregates were set. The manager must rely on his experience and judgment to carry out the committee's orders; frequent consultation with the FOMC members helps the open-market account manager determine whether his actions are in line with the desires of the committee.[4]

Federal Reserve buying and selling of U.S. government securities is on an auction basis. If the System is selling securities, bids are taken and the securities go to the highest bidder(s). On the other hand, purchases are made at the lowest possible price; therefore, securities are bought at the best yield available for the particular type and maturity being purchased. The buying and selling goes on each weekday and involves the Federal Reserve and approximately 25 New York securities dealers.

The discussion of the impact of open-market operations on reserves can best proceed by distinguishing two types of transactors—banks and nonbank dealers; that is, out of the 25 or so securities dealers, some are banks and some are nonbank dealers.[5] Two cases will be considered here, a Federal Reserve purchase from a bank and a purchase from a nonbank dealer. After these cases have been presented, the student should try to analyze sales by the Federal Reserve to the two types of transactors.

The simplest case involves a Federal Reserve purchase of securities from a bank. Table 10–1 shows T-accounts for the Federal Reserve System and for the bank selling the securities. The Federal Reserve bank T-account reflects the acquisition of $10 million of U.S. government securities on the asset side and a $10 million payment for the securities on the liabilities side. The Federal Reserve pays the bank by increasing the bank's reserve account. The bank's T-account shows the sale of the securities and the receipt of the $10 million Federal Reserve payment.

If the student will again refer to the monetary base equation (Equation [10–2]), the impact of the foregoing illustration on the base

---

[4] The problems of selecting a monetary target and using indicators to gauge the thrust of monetary policy are discussed in the next chapter. Table 11–1 compares the target growth rates of the monetary aggregates with the rates actually attained.

[5] The Federal Reserve also deals directly with the U.S. Treasury from time to time, but because such transactions are infrequent and severely limited by law, they will not be considered here.

TABLE 10-1
Illustration of the impact of an open-market purchase from a commercial bank
($millions)

Federal Reserve System

U.S. government securities	+ $10	Member bank deposit	+ $10

Bank A

U.S. government securities	− $10		
Deposit at Federal Reserve bank	+ $10		

is easy to see. The account, Federal Reserve holdings of U.S. government securities, will increase $10 million as a result of the securities purchase, and the member bank deposits account will increase by an identical amount. Open-market purchases thus increase the monetary base and inject reserves into the banking system. Of course open-market sales have the opposite impact; that is, sales withdraw reserves.

When the securities purchase is from a nonbank securities dealer, the result is similar, but the process is a bit more involved. Table 10-2 shows how T-accounts of the Federal Reserve System, bank A, and the nonbank securities dealer are affected by a $10 million purchase. The transactions are broken into three steps. Step 1 reflects the acquisition of the securities by the Federal Reserve and Federal Reserve payment to the dealer; step 2 is the dealer deposit of the Federal Reserve check in the dealer's bank A deposit account; and step 3 shows the clearing of the check which involves an increase in bank A's reserve account.

Once again the open-market purchase has injected reserves into the banking system just as in the previous example. However, when the securities dealer was a bank (Table 10-1), all the new reserves were excess reserves, but when the transaction involves a nonbank dealer, part of the new reserves must be used as required reserves for the dealer deposit reflected in step 2 of Table 10-2. While the injection of total reserves is the same in both cases, a purchase from a bank generates more excess reserves than does a purchase from a nonbank dealer.

Table 10-3 summarizes the salient features of the general instruments of monetary policy. The table indicates the primary purpose of each instrument, its frequency of utilization, how each instrument is applied for restrictive or expansionary purposes, and certain other important characteristics.

TABLE 10–2

Illustration of the impact of an open-market purchase from a nonbank securities dealer ($millions)

Federal Reserve System

S t e p 1	U.S. government securities	+ $10	Outstanding Federal Reserve check	+ $10

S t e p 3		Outstanding Federal Reserve check − $10 Member bank deposit + $10

Nonbank securities dealer

S t e p 1	U.S. government securities − $10 Federal Reserve check + $10	

S t e p 2	Federal Reserve check − $10 Deposit at Bank A + $10	

Bank A

S t e p 2	Federal Reserve check	+ $10	Dealer deposit	+ $10

S t e p 3	Federal Reserve check − $10 Deposit at Federal Reserve bank + $10	

TABLE 10–3
Summary of the important characteristics of the general monetary instruments

General instrument characteristics	Open-market operations	Reserve requirement changes	The discount mechanism
1. Primary purpose	To manage the monetary base and thus control the nation's supply of money and credit	To alter the relation between bank reserves and bank deposits so as to control the nation's supply of money and credit	Allows the Fed to serve as a lender of last resort
2. Frequency of utilization	Daily	Infrequently	Daily
3. Restrictive policy*	Net sale of U.S. government securities	Raise reserve requirement percents	Raise the discount rate to discourage borrowing
4. Expansionary policy	Net purchase of U.S. government securities	Lower reserve requirement percents	Lower the discount rate to encourage borrowing
5. Other characteristics	The most important general instrument	Because of its large impact, often referred to as a blunt instrument	Discount rate changes may have an "announcement" effect and signal future Federal Reserve policy intentions; initiative lies with banks

* Restrictive monetary policy generally involves a slower growth of the money stock rather than an absolute reduction.

WHAT IS SELECTIVE CREDIT ALLOCATION, AND WHAT IS ITS PURPOSE?

Reserve requirements, the discount mechanism, and open-market operations have been identified as general instruments because they have a broad or pervasive effect on economic activity. However, the intensity of the impact may vary considerably from one sector to another; for example, the housing market may bear the brunt of a tight money, high interest rate policy. Thus when general instruments are used to slow money growth, market forces operate to allocate available credit, and the results are sometimes considered to be economically or socially undesirable.

Dissatisfaction with the consequences of market-determined allocation of credit is the reason for selective controls. Selective controls are applied to try to override what the market would do if left to itself to generate what is perceived as an inequitable distribution of credit. As with all attempts to override the market, however, there are attendant costs associated with imposing and enforcing the selective instruments. The nature of these selective credit controls and some of their attendant costs are the subjects of this section.

Usury laws

Selective monetary and credit controls have taken on many forms. Usury laws are a commonplace example of selective credit controls, their intent being to prevent "exorbitant" interest rates on loans. However, interest rate ceilings in the form of usury laws have the same consequences as any other price-fixing scheme. Figure 10–2 depicts the supply and demand for loanable mortgage funds; the market equilibrium is represented by interest rate i_0 and the quantity of mortgage credit extended per time period by L_0. As long as usurious rates are defined as i_0 or above, usury laws will have no impact in this particular market. But if i_2 (or any other rate below i_0) were the maximum rate permissible, then a shortage of funds equal to $L_3 - L_2$ would develop. Lenders would be willing to make loans of only L_2 each time period while borrowers would desire to borrow L_3.

The scarce supply of credit must now be rationed by some means other than the price (interest rate) mechanism. People or groups with personal or political connections of one kind or the other receive preferential treatment while others are unable to obtain a loan. Who is "protected" when a potential home buyer cannot obtain a mortgage because usury laws have forced lenders to reduce the funds they are willing to lend? Certainly not the buyer who would be willing to finance the house at a rate exceeding the legal maximum.

FIGURE 10–2
Supply and demand for loanable mortgage funds

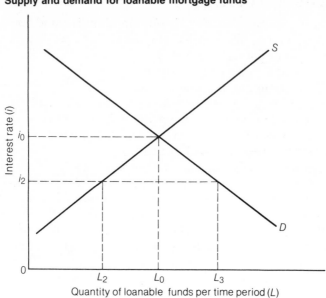

Quantity of loanable funds per time period (L)

Surely not the lender who would make more loans were it not for the artificially low ceiling imposed by law.[6]

Furthermore, as with all price controls, usury laws present enforcement problems. Some agency must see that rates do not exceed the legal maximum, and such enforcement efforts are costly. Writing in the *Journal of Money, Credit, and Banking*, Edward J. Kane notes, "Prototypically bureaucratic controls and market adaptation chase each other round and round, generating additional problems, confrontations, and costs for society at large."[7] Thus the benefits reaped by those who obtain loans at lower-than-market rates are offset by the losses of lenders who must reduce their lending and by those who are unable to borrow. In addition, society must expend resources to enforce such laws.

Therefore, proponents of usury laws as well as other selective credit controls should be aware of the unpleasant side effects of attempts to override the market. Fortunately some of the objectives of selective credit controls can sometimes be accomplished in less

---

[6] There would in fact be some gainers including those preferred customers who were able in our illustration to obtain a loan at a rate below i_0.

[7] Edward J. Kane, "Good Intentions and Unintended Evil: The Case against Selective Credit Allocation," *Journal of Money, Credit, and Banking*, vol. 19, no. 1 (February 1977), pp. 56–69.

onerous ways. For instance, if there is a need to protect borrowers from unscrupulous lenders, then truth-in-lending laws are an alternative. Truth in lending requires that lenders furnish borrowers with all the relevant facts pertaining to a loan such as the true interest rate, precise terms of repayment, and prepayment provisions. It would seem reasonable to arm the consumer, the borrower in this case, with pertinent information and then permit a free and informed choice.

Regulation Q

Regulation Q, discussed in Chapter 7, permits the Board of Governors to set maximum interest rates payable on various categories of time deposits held by Federal Reserve member banks. Coverage of Regulation Q has also been extended to insured banks outside of the Federal Reserve System and to savings and loan associations through the FDIC and the Federal Home Loan Bank Board. As noted in Chapter 7, the effects of Regulation Q include the process of disintermediation which in the past has occurred during periods of rising interest rates when maximum permissible rates were held below market rates on other investments such as Treasury securities. Under those circumstances, funds flow from financial intermediaries, where rates are relatively low, to other financial markets where rates are higher.

Because of the problem of disintermediation and other difficulties, the coverage of Regulation Q has been declining in recent years. For instance, in 1973 interest rates on time deposits of $100,000 or more were eliminated, and in 1978 banks were allowed to offer six-month nonnegotiable certificates of deposit in $10,000 or larger denominations paying a rate of interest equal to the rate on the most recently issued six-month Treasury bills.[8] Continued pressure to eliminate Regulation Q resulted in legislation in 1980 that calls for the complete phasing out of interest rate ceilings on time deposits. This phaseout is to be accomplished over a six-year period by the Depository Institutions Deregulation Committee.

Margin requirements

Regulations T, U, and G are selective credit controls that set margin requirements on credit purchases of stocks and convertible bonds. The margin requirement is the proportion of the stock pur-

---

[8] Maximum interest rates payable on time and savings deposits at federally insured institutions are listed in the *Federal Reserve Bulletin*.

chase price that must come from the buyer's own funds; the remainder (100 percent minus the margin requirement) is the maximum that can be borrowed. Therefore, when the margin requirement is 60 percent, $400 can be borrowed to make a $1,000 stock purchase, and the other $600 (60 percent of $1,000) must be furnished by the stock purchaser.

Federal Reserve authority to set margin requirements followed in the wake of the Great Crash of 1929. By 1929 it was inevitable that a major decline in stock prices would occur. Speculation was rampant, banks required as little as 10 percent margin, and borrowers were paying as much as 20 percent interest on loans used for stock purchases. After the initial break in stock prices in the fall of 1929, the following decline was momentous. The Standard & Poor's index of common stock prices, which stood at 238 in September 1929, plummeted to 36 by June 1932. In order to prevent reoccurrence of the speculative excesses of the late 1920s, Congress, in the Securities Exchange Act of 1934, gave the Federal Reserve authority to set minimum margin requirements in order to control speculation.

Other selective credit controls

In addition to the selective controls discussed in the previous sections, techniques to allocate credit can take on many other forms. For instance, the Defense Production Act passed during the Korean War enabled the Federal Reserve to regulate consumer credit and real estate credit under Regulations W and X. These controls were intended to free resources that normally would have been used to produce houses and consumer durables (automobiles in particular) for use in making war materials.

Regulation W restricted automobile purchases from 1950 to 1952 by setting a minimum down payment of one third the purchase price and a maximum repayment period of 21 months. By requiring a large minimum down payment and shortening the repayment period, monthly payments were increased, causing some potential auto buyers to abandon their plans. The Credit Control Act of 1969 gives the president power to invoke similar controls, which President Carter did for part of 1980.

SUMMARY

The Federal Reserve controls the nation's supply of money and credit by managing the monetary base and bank reserves. The Federal Reserve has three general instruments available for reserve management—reserve requirements, the discount mechanism, and open market operations. The most powerful and least used general instrument is reserve requirement changes. Lowering reserve requirement ratios tends to expand the nation's money supply while raising them has the opposite effect. Present use of this tool by the Federal Reserve causes large reserve changes, and the term *blunt instrument* is consequently applied to reserve requirement changes.

The discount mechanism involves Federal Reserve loans to member banks. The rate of interest charged on these loans is the discount rate. Though the discount mechanism can be used to manage reserves, the present application of the tool is to provide emergency, short-term loans to banks and thrift institutions. Providing emergency credit makes the Federal Reserve a lender of last resort.

The most important general instrument from a reserve-control perspective is open-market operations. The Fed's Federal Open Market Committee directs open-market operations, which comprise the buying and selling of U.S. government securities. Reserves are injected when securities are purchased and withdrawn when they are sold.

Selective monetary controls have a more narrow impact than general instruments. Regulation Q, under which the Federal Reserve sets maximum interest rates on bank time deposits, and Regulations T, U, and G, which relate to stock and convertible bond transactions, are examples of selective controls.

REVIEW QUESTIONS

1. What is the difference between a selective and a general instrument? Do general instruments have an equal impact throughout the economy?

2. How are reserve requirements for member banks set? Explain how member banks calculate the level of required reserves.

3. Who sets reserve requirements for nonmember banks? Generally, how do these requirements differ from those of member banks?

4. How does a change in reserve requirement ratios ultimately produce changes in economic activity? Why does the Fed use this instrument so infrequently?

5. Describe how the Federal Reserve administers the discount window.

6. Assume that reserve requirements on demand and time deposits are initially 20 and 10 percent respectively and that the public's desired asset proportions are 20 percent currency, 40 percent demand deposits, and 40 percent time deposits. Assume that total time deposits are $100

billion. If the Federal Reserve lowers the time deposit reserve ratio to 5 percent, calculate the original and the new money multipliers and determine the potential expansion in M-1A that may result from the lower reserve requirement.

7. What is the federal funds market, and why do most banks prefer to borrow in that market rather than from the Federal Reserve?

8. How did Federal Reserve participation in the U.S. government securities market evolve?

9. Is the impact on bank reserves different if the Federal Reserve purchases U.S. government securities from a nonbank securities dealer as opposed to a commercial bank? Why?

10. What are some of the problems associated with usury laws?

11. Define Regulation Q and discuss its advantages and disadvantages.

SUGGESTIONS FOR ADDITIONAL READING

Board of Governors of the Federal Reserve System. *The Federal Reserve System: Purposes and Functions.* 6th ed. Washington, D.C.: Board of Governors of the Federal Reserve System, 1974.

Kane, Edward J. "Good Intentions and Unintended Evil: The Case against Selective Credit Allocation." *Journal of Money, Credit, and Banking,* vol. 9, no. 1 (February 1977), pp. 56–69.

McCarthy, Edward J. *Reserve Position, Methods of Adjustment.* Boston: Federal Reserve Bank of Boston, 1971.

Smith, Warren L. "The Instruments of General Monetary Control." *The National Banking Review,* vol. 1 (September 1963), pp. 47–76.

Current issues on the Federal Reserve System

WARM-UP: *Outline and questions to consider as you read*

How independent should the Federal Reserve be?
Should membership in the Federal Reserve System
  be required of all banks?
What operating strategy should the Federal Reserve
  follow?

NEW TERMS

The Accord: an agreement in 1951 between the Federal Reserve and the U.S. Treasury which freed the Federal Reserve from the World War II–imposed pressure to support Treasury debt financing.

Economic goals: the desired state of certain economic variables such as full employment, a high level of output, and stable prices.

Monetary indicator: a variable that measures the direction and intensity of monetary policy.

Monetary target: a monetary variable under the influence of the Federal Reserve which is managed in an attempt to achieve the goals of monetary policy.

Net free (borrowed) reserves: the amount by which excess reserves exceed (are less than) member bank borrowing from the Fed.

In this chapter we present three controversies related to the structure and operations of the Federal Reserve System. The first issue deals with whether the Fed should retain its present level of independence or whether it should be made more accountable for its actions. Second, Federal Reserve membership declined during the 1970s, and some analysts have contended that the Fed's ability to manage the nation's monetary structure has been seriously eroded. Thus the issue of compulsory Federal Reserve membership for banks, and perhaps thrifts as well, is explored. Last, because the operating techniques used by the Federal Reserve to conduct monetary policy have often been criticized, the mechanics of monetary management are examined.

HOW INDEPENDENT SHOULD THE FEDERAL RESERVE BE?

The Federal Reserve has gone through considerable evolution since its inception in 1913. The preamble to the Federal Reserve Act stated that the new central bank was ". . . to furnish an elastic currency, to afford means of rediscounting commercial paper, to establish a more effective supervision of banking in the United States, and for other purposes."

It is clear from the foregoing statement and from the debate leading up to the formation of the Federal Reserve that the new system was to be primarily a banker's bank possessing very restricted powers. While the act did contain the provision about an elastic currency, this did not imply that monetary policy should be used as it is currently to help manage economic activity, but rather that the supply of currency should expand and contract automatically in tune with the cyclical movements of the economy. Prior to 1913, national-bank notes constituted the bulk of currency in the United States, and they had a tendency to expand when the economy was contracting and to contract when the economy was expanding. This inelasticity resulted from the requirement that national-bank notes be backed with federal government debt instruments which tended to decline in periods of prosperity and to rise during economic downturns. The issuance of Federal Reserve notes was supposed to correct the problem of an inelastic money stock since the amount of currency that could be issued was based on the amount of customer notes rediscounted at the Fed, which amount was expected to expand and contract with the business cycle.[1] As a banker's bank, the Fed was empowered to provide emergency funds to member banks

---

[1] Federal Reserve notes presently must have as collateral gold certificates, government securities, or high-grade, short-term commercial paper.

through the discount window and to help regulate banking practices. The Fed was also envisioned as a bank for the federal government, though this function was clearly secondary to its primary role as a banker's bank.

As we pointed out in Chapter 10, the only general instrument provided for in the Federal Reserve Act was the discount window. Furthermore, the discount window was the Fed's lender-of-last-resort mechanism and was not originally intended as a monetary policy instrument. Also, the Federal Reserve could purchase U.S. government securities as an investment, but it was not until 1933 that Congress formally recognized open-market operations as a policy instrument. Finally, power to set reserve requirements was not granted the Fed until 1935. Therefore, prior to the 1930s the scope of Federal Reserve authority was greatly limited compared to the agency's present-day powers.

The founders of the Federal Reserve System clearly intended to grant the new central bank a considerable amount of independence. The original Federal Reserve Board included five persons appointed by the president and confirmed by the Senate for ten-year terms.[2] Then, as now, the president also designated a chairman and vice chairman for four-year terms which to this day do not coincide with the president's term of office except by accident. The long terms of office and the fact that appointments were staggered (to try to minimize the number of appointments made by a particular president) indicate that Congress intended to grant the Federal Reserve a great deal of autonomy. Furthermore, the Fed was exempted from the normal budget process by allowing the System to fund its operations out of operating revenues.

Nevertheless, there were some links to the other branches of government. Prior to 1935, in addition to the Federal Reserve Board members who were appointed by the president, the secretary of the Treasury and the Comptroller of the Currency served as ex officio members of the board, thereby providing a tie with the executive branch. Also, Congress has always been able to modify the system through legislative changes, and this possibility provides a channel for congressional influence on the Federal Reserve.

Following the Fed's early years came the Great Depression, when the powers of the Federal Reserve were greatly expanded and the System was granted even greater independence: the Banking Act of 1933 provided formally for open-market operations, allowed the

---

[2] The number of presidentially appointed members was increased to six in 1922, and the terms of office were raised to 12 years in 1933. Further changes which led to the board's present structure are discussed later.

Federal Reserve Board to suspend banks making excessive loans for speculative purposes, and expanded the board's regulatory power over member banks' operations; the Securities Exchange Act of 1934 empowered the board to set margin requirements on stock purchases; the Banking Act of 1935 changed the Federal Reserve Board to a Board of Governors consisting of seven persons serving 14-year terms—the secretary of the Treasury and the Comptroller of the Currency were removed as ex officio members; moreover, the act set up the Federal Open Market Committee in its present form and gave the Board of Governors power to approve appointments of the Federal Reserve bank presidents and set reserve requirements on deposits of member banks.

Following the strengthening of the Federal Reserve in the 1930s, its independence and power were greatly circumscribed as a result of circumstances created by World War II. The Fed assumed the role of assisting the U.S. Treasury in its issuance of the large amount of new federal debt required to finance wartime government expenditures. To suppress the rise in interest rates that would normally have accompanied the massive Treasury borrowing, the Fed used open-market operations to purchase some of the securities. These purchases in turn generated money-stock increases that normally would have caused sizable price rises had it not been for wartime price controls.

Once the war ended and price controls were removed, the Fed saw the need to reassume its independent status rather than, in effect, continue as an arm of the Treasury. There ensued a period of considerable friction between the Federal Reserve and the Treasury until March 4, 1951, when the two agencies reached a so-called Accord which reestablished Fed independence; in the ensuing decades the Fed has exercised its authority by becoming increasingly active in its administration of monetary policy.

In recent years there have been signs that Congress now wishes to reduce the power and independence of the Federal Reserve. As the operation of monetary policy has come to be more clearly understood, it is apparent that inept policymaking can create serious economic problems.[3] Consequently, Congress seems intent on monitoring the Fed's actions more carefully, a move that would reduce the Fed's autonomy. The desire of Congress to have a greater influence on monetary policy is evident in three pieces of recent legislation—House Concurrent Resolution 133, The Federal Reserve Reform Act of 1977, and the Full Employment and Balanced Growth Act of 1978 (the Humphrey-Hawkins Bill).

---

[3] Chapter 3 covered the issue of whether the Federal Reserve should have the authority to control the money stock or whether monetary growth should be fixed by rules.

House Concurrent Resolution 133 required the Federal Reserve to report to Congress concerning its monetary aggregate targets for the following 12 months. The Federal Reserve Reform Act strengthened this reporting procedure by requiring the board "to appear quarterly, alternately before the House and the Senate banking committees, to testify concerning the ranges of monetary and credit aggregates for the upcoming twelve months." Moreover, the act requires, for the first time, Senate confirmation of the chairman and vice chairman of the Board of Governors. Finally, the Humphrey-Hawkins Act requires the Federal Reserve to transmit to Congress, twice each year, written reports on the Fed's conclusions about economic trends, monetary policy objectives, plans of the Board of Governors for the next 12 months, and how these plans relate to the goals set forth in the most recent Economic Report of the President. Each of these acts makes the Federal Reserve more accountable to Congress, and increased accountability reduces autonomy.

There are many who believe that further attempts to bring the Fed under greater congressional or executive branch control would be a mistake since independence supposedly shields the critical process of money creation from political pressure. Given that modern monetary systems are comprised primarily of low-cost-of-production money, the temptation always exists for governments to overissue money, and there are numerous cases in the 20th century where this has happened. Arthur Burns, a former chairman of the Board of Governors, alluded to this danger in a speech on Federal Reserve independence:

> Under our scheme of governmental organization, the Federal Reserve can make the hard decisions that might be avoided by decision-makers subject to the day-to-day pressures of political life.[4]

Furthermore, Burns went on to argue,

> I doubt that the American people would want to see the power to create money lodged in its presidency—which may mean that it would in fact be exercised by political aides in the White House.[5]

The counterarguments advocating more stringent limitations on Federal Reserve power and independence take several forms. There is the legal question of whether it is constitutional for Congress to have created what is often referred to as a fourth branch of government. The analogy has been drawn that it would be unconstitutional to create a Department of War that decided independently of the

---

[4] Speech by Arthur Burns in 1976 at commencement exercises at Bryant College, Smithfield, Rhode Island. The text of the speech is in the *Federal Reserve Bulletin*, vol. 62, no. 6 (June 1976), pp. 493–96.

[5] Ibid.

legislative and executive branches whether to declare or not declare wars and then how to conduct them; some opponents of the Fed contend that the same logic can be applied to the Federal Reserve System.

Furthermore, there are those who argue that effective policy coordination can occur only if the Fed is subjected to closer executive branch control. Thus there is a proposal to make the chairman and vice chairman's term of office coterminous with the president's; this change would assure the president an opportunity of having a chairman with compatible policy views. Moreover, there have been a multitude of proposals that would give either the Congress or the executive branch a greater hand in the Fed's activities.

There is the even stronger contention that the executive branch should control monetary policy completely so that there will be better fiscal-monetary policy coordination. However, opponents of this plan argue that fiscal policymaking is not the sole responsibility of the president; Congress also plays a role, and giving the president the power to manage monetary policy would not necessarily ensure fiscal-monetary policy coordination. According to those who favor a large amount of Federal Reserve independence, the current reporting system, along with other controls and pressures that can be brought to bear on the Federal Reserve, are sufficient to ensure adequate policy coordination.

To some extent the debate over Federal Reserve independence is exaggerated. As we have suggested, if the Fed is too out of step with the sentiments of Congress and the president, pressure can be brought to bear on the Board of Governors by either threatening legislative action or actually enacting changes. The performance of the Federal Reserve in recent years strongly implies that, to a great degree, independence is illusory. In the next part of the book, evidence is cited showing that money-supply growth has been erratic on a year-to-year basis and on average was more rapid in the 1970s than in the two previous decades. There has also been a tendency for the Fed to increase the growth rate of the money stock during presidential election years. As we shall see, the faster growth of the money stock is linked to the propensity of the federal government to run budget deficits. In any event, the high rates of inflation of recent years are closely associated with the higher growth rates of money.

The chairman and members of the Board of Governors have made frequent pronouncements indicating that they realize the role that monetary policy has played in the inflationary process. However, as we shall show in the last section of this chapter, a gap has often existed between these pronouncements and actual practice. The most likely reason for this discrepancy is that the Fed has succumbed to congressional and executive branch pressure on numerous occasions. If this is true, then the argument that the Fed must remain independent in order to assure a sound economy may be of little consequence. In other words, the present "independent" status of the system may not make much difference.

The debate over Federal Reserve independence will probably continue. Recently Congress has been inclined to circumscribe the Fed's authority and independence somewhat, and there are currently a number of proposals that would move further in that direction. On the other hand, the Monetary Control Act grants the Fed greater authority. Presently, it seems unlikely that there will be any far-reaching reshaping of the Federal Reserve in the near future.

SHOULD MEMBERSHIP IN THE FEDERAL RESERVE SYSTEM BE REQUIRED OF ALL BANKS?

In 1947 the Federal Reserve System included 47 percent of all banks; by 1961 the figure had declined to 43 percent. This trend continued through the 1970s as membership shrank to under 37 percent in late 1979. (The number of member banks dropped from over 5,800 in 1970 to approximately 5,450 in 1979; in the first six months of 1979, Federal Reserve membership declined by 83 banks.) The decline in numbers was also accompanied by a reduction in the proportion of total bank assets held by member banks, from over 80 percent in the early 1970s to around 70 percent at the end of the decade.

Banks left the Federal Reserve, or initially sought a state charter, because they believed that the cost of Federal Reserve membership exceeded the benefits derived from belonging to the Fed. The perception of excessive cost resulted primarily from two factors: (1) reserve requirements that were in general stricter than the requirements imposed by the various states, and (2) the requirement that member banks must purchase stock in the Federal Reserve.

The Gilbert and Lovati study cited in Chapter 10 concluded that nonmember reserve requirements were generally lower than those imposed on Federal Reserve member banks; furthermore, earning assets, such as U.S. Treasury securities, frequently could be used to satisfy at least part of state reserve requirements.[6] However, this situation began to change considerably in 1980 when the Federal Reserve started exercising its new authority to set reserve require-

---

[6] R. Alton Gilbert and Jean M. Lovati, "Bank Reserve Requirements and Their Enforcement: A Comparison across States," *Review of the Federal Reserve Bank of St. Louis*, vol. 60, no. 3 (March 1978), pp. 22–32.

ments on transactions balances and nonpersonal time deposits at all depository institutions. As for the second cost factor listed above, recall that member banks must purchase stock in the Federal Reserve amounting to approximately 3 percent of the bank's capital account. The Fed pays each member bank a 6 percent annual return on its investment; however, with market rates of interest now considerably greater than 6 percent, funds used for Federal Reserve stock could be used much more profitably in alternative investments.

Until 1980 only Federal Reserve members were entitled to certain services offered by the Fed. The most important of these benefits included check clearing, coin and currency service, wire transfers, and access to the Fed's discount window. Large banks have tended to utilize these services to a greater extent than smaller banks and thus have derived greater benefits from Federal Reserve membership. However, large banks as well as small have left the Federal Reserve; as a matter of fact, the size distribution (by deposit class) of banks that withdrew from the Federal Reserve during the 1970s was about the same as the size distribution of all member banks.[7]

When the decline in Federal Reserve System membership seemed likely to continue, those in favor of compulsory membership or some lesser extension of Federal Reserve control over the financial system argued that the Fed's ability to control the nation's supply of money and credit was being eroded by the exodus of banks from the system. However, since open-market operations were and still remain the major instrument of Federal Reserve policy, declining membership may not have posed as great a threat to Fed control of money and credit as some contended. Nonetheless, representatives of the Federal Reserve wanted increased authority over nonmember banks and even over thrifts on the basis that thrift institutions were responsible for a growing volume of transactions balances.

Proposals regarding Federal Reserve membership have ranged from membership on a completely voluntary basis (even for national banks) to compulsory membership for all banks (and even thrift institutions).[8] Adoption of either of these extremes has never seemed

---

[7] R. Alton Gilbert, "Utilization of Federal Reserve Bank Services by Member Banks: Implications for the Costs and Benefits of Membership," *Review of the Federal Reserve Bank of St. Louis*, vol. 59, no. 8 (August 1977), pp. 2–15. For more information on the cost and benefits of Federal Reserve membership, see Robert E. Knight, "Comparative Burdens of Federal Reserve Member and Nonmember Banks," *Monthly Review of the Federal Reserve Bank of Kansas City* (March 1977), pp. 13–28. Also, see Peter Rose, "Exodus: Why Banks Are Leaving the Fed," *The Bankers Magazine*, vol. 159, no. 1 (Winter 1976), pp. 43–49.

[8] The argument for voluntary membership can be found in Dean Carson, "Is the Federal Reserve Really Necessary?" *Journal of Finance*, vol. 19, no. 4 (December 1964), pp. 652–61. Also, see William Poole, "The Making of Monetary Policy: Description and Analysis," *New England Economic Review*, Federal Reserve Bank of Boston (March/April 1975), pp. 21–30.

imminent, but the legislation passed in 1980 moved financial institutions closer to compulsory than to voluntary membership. The Federal Reserve was able to convince Congress to give the System authority to set universal reserve requirements on transactions balances and nonpersonal time deposits at all depository institutions. In addition, all institutions subject to the Fed's reserve requirements were given access to the discount window. Moreover, the Fed's other services, including check clearing, were made available to all institutions subject to Fed reserve requirements; however, where previously these services had been free to all member banks, they were put on an explicit-fee basis for all institutions using them.

These changes have extended Federal Reserve control over the financial system and simultaneously have reduced the relative burden of Fed membership. Given the pace of withdrawal from the Federal Reserve in the late 1970s, Congress believed that action was necessary in order to reverse the erosion of Fed control over the financial sector. Though the Monetary Control Act did not require all financial institutions to join the Federal Reserve, it did strengthen the Fed's powers. Thus the act can be viewed as a partial victory for those favoring compulsory membership. While stopping short of that requirement, nonmember institutions were subjected to the major controls over member banks, and the uniqueness of those belonging to the Federal Reserve System has therefore been greatly diminished.

WHAT OPERATING STRATEGY SHOULD THE FEDERAL RESERVE FOLLOW?

Suppose that it is Tuesday morning and time for the monthly meeting of the Federal Open Market Committee (FOMC).[9] Those attending the session include the voting FOMC members—the Board of Governors and 5 of the 12 Federal Reserve bank presidents—as well as the other 7 reserve bank presidents and numerous members of the Federal Reserve staff. The first order of business is for the manager of the system open-market account to report on open-market operations and financial developments since the last meeting. Next, staff members review current domestic economic conditions, the credit and monetary situation, and international trade and financial circumstances.

Let us assume that, among other things, it is reported that unemployment is currently 6.1 percent, real GNP is growing at an annual

---

[9] For a detailed description of a Federal Open Market Committee meeting see the Federal Reserve Bank of New York's, *Open Market Operations* (New York: Federal Reserve Bank of New York), 1964.

rate of 3.3 percent, and the annual rate of inflation is 9.7 percent. Part of the system's responsibility is to use monetary policy to achieve full employment, output growth, and price stability. Given the very limited statistics on the economy cited above, it would seem that the most pressing need would be to reduce the inflation rate—the unemployment rate is not ideal but is within a tolerable range, and GNP growth, while not vigorous, is acceptable.

Thus the FOMC must decide on a course of action aimed at improving the rate of inflation. The strategy to be used will be specified in a directive on open-market operations to the Federal Reserve Bank of New York, which buys and sells government securities for the entire system.[10] Reducing the rate of inflation requires tighter monetary policy, and the directive must therefore spell out the method and extent to which tightening is to occur. In the final phase of the FOMC meeting, the chairman summarizes the salient points of the session and then formulates a consensus statement regarding monetary policy strategy. The FOMC members are given an opportunity to dissent, and the chairman may decide on the basis of these remarks to amend the consensus statement. Finally, a formal vote is taken on the policy directive that will guide Fed open-market actions until the next meeting.

The process of policymaking is complicated by the fact that a considerable lag exists between the time when the policy instruments are applied and when their ultimate economic effect is felt. That is, a tightening of policy today will not effect the inflation rate until several months from now. Given the existence of this time lag, the Fed must adopt operating procedures that permit a more immediate assessment of the degree of stimulus or restraint resulting from its actions.

Most economists now agree that the rate of growth of the monetary aggregates is an important determinant of the level of economic activity: rapid monetary growth is expansionary; slow monetary growth is restrictive. Thus sustained high growth rates of the money stock are inflationary, while an excessively tight rein on money expansion may generate sluggish economic performance. This view is reflected in the current Federal Reserve emphasis on controlling the money stock as a means of influencing economic activity. However, there are a number of economists who think that such emphasis is misplaced and that better results would result from focusing on interest rates rather than money-supply growth.

---

[10] Of course, the Board of Governors may change reserve requirements or the way that it administers discount policy; however, our example deals only with the major tool of policy control—open-market operations.

Even if it is granted that money growth is an important influence on the economy, time lags are still a problem. For example, there is a lag between when the instruments are applied and when money growth is affected, then another lag between the change in the money growth rate and its impact on inflation, unemployment, and growth. Thus the Fed must find some indirect method of judging the ease or tightness of its policy actions, since time lags preclude instantaneous feedback running from instruments to goals and back to instruments.

Faced with the need for continuous monitoring of the thrust of economic policy, the Fed must select and use a monetary indicator. According to Thomas Mayer, a monetary policy indicator should possess the following characteristics:

1. It should be controllable by the Federal Reserve and not determined by endogenous forces.
2. Data on the indicator should be available without delay and should be highly correlated with the target variable.[11]

During the past 15 years or so, the Fed has used different indicators with varying degrees of success. A review of Fed directives shows that different operating strategies have been tried and abandoned. The selection of an effective method of formulating efficient FOMC directives has not been an easy task.

The Fed's problems in implementing monetary policy were apparent in 1966 when the Fed was faced with trying to control a buildup of inflationary pressure. At this time the Fed was using net free reserves as the indicator of the thrust of monetary policy. Net free reserves are positive when excess reserves are greater than outstanding member bank borrowing obtained through the discount window; on the other hand, when borrowing exceeds excess reserves, net free reserves are negative, a situation referred to as net borrowed reserves. The Fed interpreted a rise in net free reserves to mean that credit was easier, while a decline meant tighter credit. This interpretation followed from the assumption that, during a period when credit conditions were easing, excess reserves would rise and/or the level of borrowed reserves would fall, thereby generating a rise in net free reserves; tighter credit conditions, on the other hand, would result in lower excess reserves and/or more borrowing, thereby lowering net free reserves or causing a shift to a net borrowed reserves position.

---

[11] Thomas Mayer, "The Structure of Monetarism (II)," in *The Structure of Monetarism* (New York: W. W. Norton & Co., 1978), p. 26.

However, the following events might easily occur. The Fed in pursuit of tighter credit conditions reduces its target for net free reserves from, say, $300 million to $200 million. Yet if credit demand were very strong, there would be, in any event, a tendency for excess reserves to be reduced and for borrowing to rise, and the resulting decrease in net free reserves might falsely indicate to the Fed that its desired tighter money conditions had been achieved. This interpretation might then prompt an easing of policy and an enlargement of the monetary base. Therefore, a lower net free reserve figure, which supposedly reflected tightened credit conditions, could be accompanied by an increase in the monetary base and, in fact, easier credit conditions. Having come to recognize the deficiencies of net free (borrowed) reserves as a monetary indicator, the Fed began using total reserves as a supplemental indicator in 1966. Then, by the late 1960s, the Fed had changed its primary indicator from net free reserves to the federal funds rate.

The use of the federal funds rate as an indicator throughout the 1970s also resulted in some problems. To illustrate, assume that the Fed's policy directive has been stated in terms of a particular federal funds rate objective, which has just been raised from, say, 9.5 to 10.5 percent; also assume that the Fed has made the change in order to raise the cost of borrowing, slow spending, and thereby reduce inflationary pressures. Normally, one might expect that reserves would have to be withdrawn or at least their rate of injection slowed to produce tightening and thereby generate the desired increase in the federal funds rate. But the following sequence of events is possible, maybe even likely, in an inflationary environment.

A typical consequence of inflation is to push interest rates up as lenders add an inflation premium to their "normal" required rates of return; they add this premium because borrowers will be paying them back with dollars that have less purchasing power. So inflation pushes up interest rates including the federal funds rate, and this process is not easily detectable by policymakers who are trying to control the federal funds rate. Why? Because the Fed will observe that the federal funds rate is rising and may possibly attribute the increase to tighter monetary policy while in fact inflation is the cause. In our example, the effects of inflation may require an injection of reserves to keep the federal funds rate from rising above 10.5 percent. Therefore, though tightening may be the objective, injecting reserves to resist the rise in rates generated by inflation may well generate high rates of monetary growth. This result produces a further feedback in the form of inflation which makes it even more difficult to hold the federal funds rate down. Even if the rate objective is raised again, the Fed may continue to misinterpret the signals it receives by

TABLE 11-1
Target rates of growth of M-1 and M-2 compared to actual rates, 1975-1979

(1)	(2)	(3)	(4)	(5)
	Target growth rates of		Actual growth rates of	
Time period	M-1	M-2	M-1	M-2
IVQ/75–IVQ/76	4½–7½%	7½–10½%	5.4%	10.5%
IQ/76–IQ/77	4½–7	7½–10	6.0	10.9
IIQ/76–IIQ/77	4½–7	7½– 9½	6.0	10.7
IIIQ/76–IIIQ/77	4½–6	7½–10	8.0	11.1
IVQ/76–IVQ/77	4½–6½	7 –10	8.3	9.9
IQ/77–IQ/78	4½–6½	7 – 9½	8.8	9.1
IIQ/77–IIQ/78	4 –6½	7 – 9½	9.2	8.9
IIIQ/77–IIIQ/78	4 –6½	6½– 9	8.0	8.5
IVQ/77–IVQ/78	4 –6½	6½– 9	7.2	8.4
IQ/78–IQ/79	4 –6½	6½– 9	5.0	7.1
IIQ/78–IIQ/79	4 –6½	6½– 9	4.4	7.1
IIIQ/78–IIIQ/79	2 –6	6½– 9	4.9	7.7

Source: *Federal Reserve Bulletin* and *Review of the Federal Reserve Bank of St. Louis,* various issues, 1976–79.

using the federal funds rate as an indicator of the thrust of its policies.

Table 11–1 reflects the problem generated by using the federal funds rate as an indicator. Columns (2) and (3) show Federal Reserve target rates of growth for M-1 and M-2 for 1975–79.[12] The Fed's target for M-1 over the four-quarter period ending in the 4th quarter 1976 was a range of 4.5 to 7.5 percent; the target range for M-2 was 7.5 to 10.5 percent. Columns (4) and (5) of Table 11–1 indicate the actual rate of growth of M-1 and M-2 for each time period. Note that it was common for the actual growth rate to exceed the target range; in fact, for the 12 periods included in the table, the actual growth rate exceeded the target range six times for M-1 and four times for M-2. Also, nine times the M-1 and M-2 growth rates exceeded the midpoints of the ranges. The actual growth of M-1 and M-2 was never below the lower value of the target range.

Why was the actual growth of M-1 and M-2 so frequently outside the target range? The cause lies mainly in the use of the federal funds rate as the primary monetary policy indicator. When the federal funds rate is the focus of Federal Reserve policy, then, for reasons discussed above, it is often impossible to achieve the federal funds rate target and the targeted growth of the aggregates simultaneously.

Earlier it was noted that a monetary indicator should be controllable by the Federal Reserve, that data on the indicator should be

---

[12] M-1 and M-2 are pre-1980 measures of money. M-1 is similar to M-1A while M-2 was M-1 plus most commercial bank time deposits.

available without delay, and that the data should be highly correlated with the target variable. The monetary base or one of its derivatives (total bank reserves, for example) is controllable within tolerable limits, and while the base is affected by endogenous forces (float for one), open-market operations can be used to offset any such effects. Evidence seems to support the conclusion that, if the target variable is one or more of the monetary aggregates (for example, M-1A or M-1B), the monetary base and the monetary aggregates are reasonably well correlated over a 12-month period.[13] Finally, the criterion that data be available without delay holds for the base.

Pressure mounted from Fed critics during the 1970s to adopt a new operating strategy employing the monetary base as its indicator. On October 6, 1979, the Federal Reserve announced that it intended to place greater emphasis on controlling the supply of bank reserves and less emphasis on limiting short-term fluctuations in the federal funds rate. This change is seen by most analysts as a move in the direction of better monetary policy. Using reserves—actually a "family" of "reserve" items that includes the monetary base—as the monetary indicator and using the aggregates (M-1A, M-1B, and so forth) as targets seem likely to improve monetary policy results. Only time will tell if the Fed has in fact altered its operating procedures and if the expected benefits will materialize.

Figure 11–1 summarizes the main elements of the analysis presented in this section. The analogy depicted by the figure is that fuel input is controlled by a fuel-control lever (the instrument) and is simultaneously monitored by the fuel gauge (the indicator); fuel is used to produce BTUs of heat (the target) so that the room can be heated (the goal). In the monetary policy framework, input is controlled through the use of the policy instruments, and policy thrust is monitored with indicators; monetary targets are used in order to achieve certain economic goals.

SUMMARY

The Federal Reserve presently enjoys a considerable amount of independence. While the Congress and the president can monitor and to some extent influence monetary policymaking, the Fed presently is free to choose the course of action that it deems best. The founders of the Federal Reserve System clearly intended to protect the Fed from excessive political pressure, but not until the 1930s did

---

[13] Albert E. Burger, "The Relationship between the Monetary Base and Money: How Close?" *Review of the Federal Reserve Bank of St. Louis*, vol. 57, no. 10 (October 1975), pp. 3–8.

FIGURE 11–1
Monetary instruments, indicators, targets, and goals

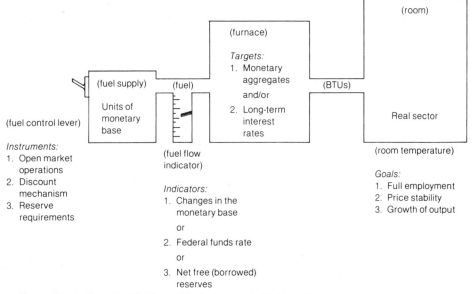

Source: Adapted from Albert E. Burger, "The Implementation Problem of Monetary Policy," *Review of the Federal Reserve Bank of St. Louis,* vol. 53, no. 3 (March 1971), p. 24.

Congress endow the Fed with the broad power and independence that it currently enjoys. Recently, however, some legislative action has sought to make the system more accountable and in the process may have diminished the Fed's independence. There are those who argue that further steps to bring the Federal Reserve under tighter congressional or executive branch control are appropriate. Others, however, contend that the interests of the nation are best served by an independent, powerful central bank, and this view seems to have prevailed in the passage of the Monetary Control Act.

Since shortly after World War II the percent of all banks that were members of the Federal Reserve had been declining, and the pace of the decline had quickened in the late 1970s. Consequently, the Federal Reserve felt that its ability to manage monetary policy was slipping and strongly argued for action to increase its control over the financial sector. While there was little sentiment for requiring Federal Reserve membership of all banks, in 1980 all banks and even thrift institutions were made subject to reserve requirements set by the Federal Reserve; other changes were also enacted that broadened the Fed's authority over the financial sector.

Monetary policy administration runs from instruments to indicators to targets to goals. Indicators measure the thrust of monetary policy, while targets are a variable under Federal Reserve control that are closely related to the goals of monetary policy. The most promising indicator-target combination seems to be the monetary base (indicator) and monetary aggregates (target). Until 1979, though, the Fed used the federal funds rate as its primary indicator. The results were not completely successful, as Table 11–1 indicates. It is hoped that operating procedure changes initiated in October 1979 will produce better monetary policy.

REVIEW QUESTIONS

1. Discuss the following proposal: The Board of Governors should be abolished and the policy functions of the board transferred to a new cabinet-level department in the executive branch.

2. Would it be a good idea for the Federal Reserve to be required to have its money supply targets approved by a vote of Congress?

3. How is the effectiveness of monetary policy linked to the issue of Federal Reserve membership?

4. Comment on why Federal Reserve membership declined in the 1970s.

5. Since open-market operations are the Fed's major policy instrument and affect nonmember banks as well as member banks, why is Federal Reserve control of all banks necessary for monetary policy to be effective?

6. Read the "Record of Policy Actions of the Federal Open Market Committee" in a recent *Federal Reserve Bulletin.* Is the Federal Reserve attaching greater importance to interest rates or monetary aggregates? Justify your conclusion.

7. Prepare a table similar to 11–1 for the period since October 1979. Compare the Fed's recent success in achieving its targets with its results during the time covered in Table 11–1.

SUGGESTIONS FOR ADDITIONAL READING

Board of Governors of the Federal Reserve System. *Annual Report.* Washington, D.C.: U.S. Government Printing Office, recent editions. (Note particularly the sections entitled "Legislative Recommendations" and "Legislation Enacted.")

Burns, Arthur. "The Independence of the Federal Reserve." *Federal Reserve Bulletin,* vol. 62, no. 6 (June 1976), pp. 493–96.

Carson, Deane. "Is the Federal Reserve System Really Necessary?" *Journal of Finance,* vol. 19, no. 4 (December 1964), pp. 652–61.

Gilbert, R. Alton. "Utilization of Federal Reserve Bank Service by Member Banks: Implications for the Costs and Benefits of Membership." *Review* of the Federal Reserve Bank of St. Louis, vol. 59, no. 8 (August 1977), pp. 2–15.

Mayer, Thomas. The Structure of Monetarism. New York: W. W. Norton & Co., 1978. See especially pp. 26–37.

Saving, Thomas R. "Monetary-Policy Targets and Indicators." Journal of Political Economy, vol. 75, no. 4, pt. 2, supplement (August 1967), pp. 445–65.

IV

THEORY AND POLICY IN THE MONETARY ECONOMY

12

Policy objectives in the monetary economy: A brief review

WARM-UP: *Outline and questions to consider as you read?*

How is macroeconomic performance measured?
  Aggregate output.
  Employment and unemployment.
  The general level of prices.
  Flows, stocks, percents, and ratios in economic
    analysis.
What are reasonable macroeconomic objectives?
Macroeconomic performance: Has the United States
  achieved its objectives?
  Gross National Product: Actual versus
    potential.
  Growth of Gross National Product.
  Employment and unemployment.
  The general level of prices.
What is the role of monetary and fiscal policy in
  achieving macroeconomic objectives?

NEW TERMS

Civilian labor force: the total of people who are (1) employed or (2) 16 years of age or older, not working, but currently seeking employment.

Cyclical unemployment: unemployment caused by a downturn in economic activity.

Employment Act of 1946:   legislation that requires the federal government to pursue the goals of maximum employment, production, and purchasing power.

Flow variable: a quantity that is expressed as an amount per unit of time.

GNP deflator: a price index covering the goods and services that comprise GNP.

Humphrey-Hawkins Act of 1978:   also known as the Full Employment and Balanced Growth Act, this bill sets specific unemployment rate and inflation targets and requires that the president submit federal budgets appropriate to fulfilling the goals of the legislation.

Potential GNP: the level of GNP that would be forthcoming if resources were fully utilized.

Productivity (of labor):   output per man-hour worked or the ratio of output to total hours worked.

Real GNP: Gross National Product measured in constant prices:

$$\text{real GNP} = \frac{\text{nominal GNP}}{\text{GNP deflator}} \times 100.$$

Recession: a phase of the business cycle characterized by declining real GNP and rising unemployment.

Rule of 72:   an approximation of the number of years required for a magnitude to double as calculated by dividing the annual rate of growth into 72.

Stock variable: a quantity that is measured as of a given moment in time.

Total labor force: the civilian labor force plus members of the armed services.

Transitional or frictional unemployment: unemployment that is temporary—for example, the unemployment of workers who are changing jobs or entering the work force for the first time.

Unemployment rate: the percent of the civilian labor force not currently working but actively seeking employment.

The preceding chapters have described the major elements of the financial sector of the monetary economy of the United States. The chapters in Part I were concerned primarily with what we call money. Among other things, we defined money, listed its functions, discussed the evolution of money from commodity to credit types, noted the efficiency of a monetary economy relative to a barter economy, and introduced the concepts of the value and the velocity of money.

Part II dealt with our financial system. We discussed the day-to-day operations of banks and other financial intermediaries. Most importantly, these chapters pointed out the rapid evolution, or perhaps we should say revolution, taking place in the financial sector of this nation as the traditional boundaries differentiating banks, savings and loans, mutual savings banks, credit unions, and other financial institutions are rapidly being erased.

Then in Part III we analyzed the role of the Federal Reserve System in the monetary economy; Chapters 8 through 11 described why the Federal Reserve was established and showed how the Fed can use its monetary policy instruments to control the monetary base and ultimately the supply of money and credit.

The present section provides a framework designed to foster understanding of how the total economy functions and how economic policy, particularly monetary policy, can be applied to help the economy better achieve economic objectives. This chapter is a review of some basic concepts related to the objectives of policymaking, and much of the material will be familiar to many readers. While the chapter is therefore basically intended as a refresher, it does set the stage for the material that follows.

HOW IS MACROECONOMIC PERFORMANCE MEASURED?

Macroeconomic performance can be measured in a number of ways. The most important indicator of the strength and vitality of the economy is aggregate output. If one knows the level and rate of growth of total and potential output and can determine the portion of growth that is real versus that which is due to rising prices, then a reasonably clear picture of the macroeconomy emerges. Moreover, the status of some other important macroeconomic performance indicators—unemployment and inflation—are closely related to aggregate output. For example, if actual and potential output are equal, the unemployment rate must be at its target level, but if actual output is below potential, there are idle workers. And when all or most of the increase in dollar-valued production is real, then inflation is not a problem.

However, even if the level and rate of growth of output, the un-employment rate, and the rate of inflation are known, other information may still be needed to complete the picture of the macroeconomy. For instance, though actual output may presently be equal to potential output, inventories may be rising much more rapidly than sales, thus signaling a future problem; a seemingly healthy growth of total output may be a result of new entrants into the work force rather than gains in productivity; or underlying inflationary pressures may be offset temporarily by a seasonal decline in food prices. Thus a considerable amount of information is necessary to discern fully the strength and future movement of the economy.

Aggregate output

In the United States the U.S. Department of Commerce is the agency responsible for measuring and reporting data on aggregate output. The Commerce Department compiles aggregate output data on an annual and a quarterly basis (the quarterly figures are reported at an annual rate). Gross National Product (GNP) is a measure of aggregate output and can be defined as the *final market* value of new goods and services *produced* during a given *period* of time. Note particularly the key words, which are italicized—*final, market, produced,* and *period.* The word *final* indicates that the market value of a new good or service is its exchange value when sold to an ultimate user. Thus the value of a new automobile is what the car purchaser pays the automobile dealer for the car. Or the value of a blast furnace for steel production is the price the steel producer pays the furnace manufacturer for the furnace. On the other hand, if a product is purchased by an intermediate user rather than by the final or ultimate user, its purchase price is not included in GNP, for to do so would involve double counting. For example, the final market value of a candy bar is included in Gross National Product, but the price of the sugar purchased by the candy maker from a sugar refiner is not. Since the value of the candy bar includes the value of the sugar, to count the value of the sugar and the value of the candy bar separately would obviously involve double counting.

In general, GNP includes only the value of those products that are exchanged in the marketplace—that is, through *market* activity.[1] Thus the value of homeowners' services when they mow their lawns

---

[1] There are exceptions where important nonmarket activities are given an imputed value and are included in GNP. For example, the value of food grown and consumed by farm families is given an imputed value and counted in GNP, as is the rental value of owner-occupied houses and the value of certain bank services.

is not counted in GNP, and in fact there is a considerable amount of household production that is not included in the aggregate value of new goods and services. Nonmarket activity is generally excluded because measuring its value is difficult and often involves considerable guesswork.

Produced is the third of the key words appearing in the definition of GNP and denotes that GNP is a measure of production. How many new cars were produced in 1980? How many new television sets? How many service repair calls were made? These activities are included in GNP according to their final market value. We shall demonstrate in the following chapter that, although GNP is a measure of production, valuable information can also be obtained by classifying the purchasers of the production by type, that is, as households, businesses, governments, or foreigners.

The final key word is *period*. Gross National Product is produced during a specified period of time—annually, quarterly, monthly; therefore, GNP is what economists refer to as a flow, that is, an amount per unit of time. One can think of a GNP "meter" being set at zero on January 1, and then as each new good or service is produced over the next 12 months, its value registers on the meter. The cumulative dollar total on December 31 represents the value of the flow of production that has occurred during the year.

When using GNP figures to indicate changes in living standards, it is important to remove the impact of price-level changes. In periods of inflation, unadjusted GNP data will give a misleading impression of what has happened to living standards. The solution to this problem is to convert *nominal* or *money* GNP to *real* or *constant-dollar* GNP. The conversion can be accomplished using the formula,

$$(12\text{-}1) \qquad \text{Real GNP} = \frac{\text{Nominal GNP}}{\text{GNP deflator}} \times 100.$$

The GNP deflator in Equation (12-1) is a price index of the new goods and services that are included in Gross National Product and is the most inclusive measure of the general level of prices available in the United States.

If total output (real GNP) rises, the increase can be attributed to two factors—an increase in the number of hours worked and/or an increase in productivity. The former may occur during the expansion phase of the business cycle as unemployed workers find jobs and as those who have jobs work longer hours. Over the long run, the number of hours worked increases as the population grows and the labor force expands. Thus total output may rise due to increases in hours worked, but gains in output per man-hour (better productivity) are the key to the improvement of economic well-being.

Productivity data are estimated by the Bureau of Labor Statistics (BLS) of the U.S. Department of Labor and are available in the Bureau's *Monthly Labor Review*. The BLS calculates several productivity indexes, the most comprehensive being one for the private business sector. To obtain output per hour of all persons employed in the private business sector, the following formula is used:

$$(12\text{-}2) \quad \text{Productivity} = \begin{matrix} \text{Output per hour of all} \\ \text{persons in the private} \\ \text{business sector} \end{matrix} = \frac{\begin{matrix} \text{Real GNP produced} \\ \text{in the private} \\ \text{business sector} \end{matrix}}{\begin{matrix} \text{Total hours worked by} \\ \text{persons employed in the} \\ \text{private business sector} \end{matrix}}.$$

Employment and unemployment

Labor is our most important resource, and if the labor force is less than fully utilized, the status of the macroeconomy cannot be deemed satisfactory. Labor force data are collected and compiled by the BLS which classifies individuals in one of the following four categories:

1. Employed.
    a. Worked for pay during the survey week.
    b. Worked without pay in a family business at least 15 hours per week.
    c. Has a job but is temporarily idle because of bad weather, a strike, or a vacation.
2. Unemployed: all persons 16 years of age or older who did not work during the survey week, who made a specific effort to find a job, and who were available for work that week.
3. Members of the armed services.
4. Not in the labor force.

The total labor force includes the first three categories while the first two constitute the civilian labor force. When unemployment rates are quoted, the percents are usually derived from the civilian labor force.

Each month the BLS surveys approximately fifty thousand households and, on the basis of the results of the sample, estimates an employment and an unemployment rate. Those persons surveyed are classified according to the criteria for employed and unemployed listed above. Based on the February 1980 survey, the BLS estimated the unemployment rate to be 6.0 percent and the employment rate as 94.0 percent.

The unemployed are of course the focus of concern about the labor market. There are a variety of reasons why a person may be unemployed, and some types of unemployment are not serious, while other kinds are quite difficult to deal with. *Transitional* or *frictional unemployment* is not a serious problem since it is temporary. As a matter of fact, even in efficient labor markets there is some transitional unemployment as people move to jobs where they are more productive or enter the work force for the first time. Some transitional unemployment will always exist, but better coordination between job seekers and employment opportunities can reduce transitional unemployment and create greater labor market efficiency.

It is now generally agreed that transitional unemployment alone will generate an unemployment rate in the neighborhood of 5.0 to 6.0 percent. Once unemployment climbs beyond this range, general economic conditions are to blame. An unemployment rate of, say, 7.0 percent is a reflection of a sluggish economy, and *cyclical unemployment* exists when people are out of work due to insufficient aggregate demand for new goods and services.

The general level of prices

We have previously had a good deal to say about the measurement of prices. In Chapter 2 we discussed the Consumer Price Index (CPI) and related the CPI to the concept of the value of money; the reader might now wish to review the section of Chapter 2 dealing with the price level. Changes in the CPI are a measure of inflation, which is the process of rising prices. If the CPI increases 10 percent during a year, then at year's end, the price of the basket of goods and services that comprise the CPI has risen 10 percent above what it was at the beginning of the year.

As noted earlier, the GNP deflator is a more comprehensive price index than the CPI, but the deflator is published quarterly while the CPI is available monthly. Furthermore, since the CPI relates directly to what consumers pay for the items they purchase, it is more popular than the GNP deflator. At any rate, the two indexes tend to move in tandem: From 1969 to 1979, the largest difference in the annual rate of increase of the two indexes was 2.7 percentage points in 1979; over the entire decade, the CPI rose 98.3 percent compared to a 90.8 percent increase in the GNP deflator.

Price indexes for various components of the CPI and GNP deflator are also available. For example, categories of the CPI include food and beverages, housing, apparel, transportation, and medical care;

durable goods, nondurable goods, and services are among the categories for which GNP deflator data are available.[2] The price index components help pinpoint any extraordinary price movements that may be largely responsible for changes in the general price level indexes.

Finally, the BLS calculates Producer Price Indexes for a wide variety of products. Formerly known as Wholesale Price Indexes (WPI), the Producer Price Indexes (PPI) "measure average changes in prices received in primary markets of the United States by producers of commodities in all stages of processing."[3] Producer Price Indexes are available by stages of production and by commodity groupings. Price increases that show up first in the PPI frequently signal a higher future inflation rate at the consumer level.

Flows, stocks, percents, and ratios in economic analysis

The various measures of macroeconomic performance discussed in the previous sections are of several different types. Gross National Product was identified earlier as a flow; it is the final market value of new goods and services produced during a given period of time, that is, between two points in time. Income earned by individuals and businesses, government spending, and imports of goods and services are also examples of economic-flow variables. Care must always be taken to specify the period over which the flow occurred— per day, per month, per year, and so forth. Also, the relation of one flow to another is often important as with the current level of GNP relative to potential GNP, aggregate spending relative to aggregate production, and inventory change relative to sales change.

Stocks are measured at a given point in time: the civilian labor force was 104.3 million persons as of a particular day in February 1980; the money stock (M-1A) was $376.3 billion in February 1980; companies' balance sheets indicate their asset, liability, and capital account positions on a particular day. A stock may increase or decrease between two points in time as a result of additions to or subtractions from the original quantity. For example, a business firm may own plant and equipment worth $100,000 as of January 1, 1981, then as new fixed assets are purchased and the existing facilities wear out or become obsolete, the book value of the firm's fixed assets changes. Assuming that the firm purchased new machines worth

---

[2] Data on the GNP Deflator are available in the Department of Commerce's *Survey of Current Business* and *Business Conditions Digest* which are excellent sources for current economic statistics.

[3] *Monthly Labor Review*, vol. 103, no. 4 (April 1980), p. 88.

$50,000 during 1981 and depreciation was $25,000, then the value of the plant and equipment would have increased from $100,000 on January 1 to $125,000 on December 31, 1981. Obviously stocks and flows, while different concepts, are related to one another in that flows generate changes in stocks. For example, investment and depreciation, both flows, generate changes in the stock of capital.

Economic variables are often expressed as a percent. For instance, the unemployment rate averaged 5.8 percent in the United States in 1979, and consumer prices were 133.3 percent greater in January 1980 than they were in 1967. Of course, index numbers can be readily converted to show proportional or percentage changes, as is the case when annual changes in the Consumer Price Index are calculated from the CPI at two separate points in time; that is, if the CPI = 150 at the beginning of a period and 225 at the end of the period, there was a price rise of 50 percent.[4]

Finally, some economic measurements are ratios involving stocks, flows, or stocks and flows. Productivity is a ratio of two flows—real output to total hours worked. Another often-used ratio is the velocity of money, which is the ratio of a flow to a stock—GNP to the money supply. Therefore, it is important when dealing with economic measurements to pause and consider whether the magnitude is a flow, a stock, a ratio, or a percent; careful attention to the nature of economic measurements often will help avoid confusion.

WHAT ARE REASONABLE MACROECONOMIC OBJECTIVES?

Now that we have discussed the measurement of aggregate output (GNP), productivity, employment, and the general level of prices, it is time to discuss objectives for each of these variables. In very general terms, macroeconomic goals include the short-run objectives that actual GNP be equal to potential GNP and that the general level of prices be stable. It is redundant to add full employment to the list of goals, since if potential and actual GNP are equal, then by definition unemployment is at its target level. However, because employment is such a highly visible indicator of economic performance, full employment is generally included as a separate objective. For the

---

[4] Thus,

$$\frac{\text{End of period CPI}}{\text{Start of period CPI}} - 1.00 = \frac{\text{Proportional}}{\text{change in CPI}};$$

in the example,

$$\frac{225}{150} - 1.00 = 0.50 \text{ or } 50\%.$$

long run, growth of productivity and therefore GNP are important goals.

Macroeconomics is an analysis of the total economy over a relatively short time period, and short-term objectives are therefore the focus of macro-policy. However, it is impossible for macroeconomics to ignore productivity and growth completely. If improper monetary and fiscal policies generate high rates of inflation which periodically push the economy into recession, then it is almost certain that the long-run growth of productivity, and consequently GNP, will be reduced. Thus while our analysis emphasizes the short-run macro objectives, the longer-period implications of policy and other macroeconomic forces are not ignored completely.

The Employment Act of 1946 committed the federal government to the maintenance of maximum employment, production, and purchasing power. More recently, another bill was extensively debated and finally passed that committed the government to pursue policies to achieve a specific unemployment objective. The Full Employment and Balanced Growth Bill, more commonly referred to as the Humphrey-Hawkins Bill after its Senate-House sponsors, was signed into law in late 1978. The original version committed the government to achieving a 3 percent unemployment rate, but the final bill modified the unemployment target to 3 percent for individuals aged 20 and over and 4 percent for teenagers 16 and over. The bill also called for reducing the inflation rate to not more than 3 percent. Both the inflation and unemployment rate targets are for 1983. The president of the United States is charged with the responsibility of submitting a federal budget appropriate to fulfilling the goals of the act, and the Federal Reserve must formulate monetary policy in a manner consistent with the act's objectives.

This section heading asks, "What are reasonable macroeconomic objectives?" and it is pertinent to ask whether the unemployment-rate targets contained in the Humphrey-Hawkins Act are reasonable. For several years in the late 1960s the unemployment rate averaged less than 4 percent, but throughout the 1970s, it remained above that level. A major reason for the rise was the changing structure of the labor force; that is, the proportion of very young workers and of women in the work force increased.[5] Since unemployment rates for young workers and women are higher than the average rate for the remainder of the work force, the overall unemployment rate has increased. Also, unemployment benefits and welfare payments have

---

[5] The flood of new workers in the 1970s was precipitated by the post–World War II baby boom and by the increasing inclination of women to enter the work force.

become more generous, and this tends to add to the unemployment rate by cushioning the impact of being out of work and reducing the incentive to find employment. Consequently, most economists view the unemployment-rate targets contained in the Humphrey-Hawkins Bill as unreasonably low, with 5 to 6 percent being a more reasonable objective under present conditions.

The GNP objective can be expressed in terms of actual GNP relative to potential or "high-employment" Gross National Product. Potential GNP is an estimate of what GNP would be if labor and other resources were fully utilized. If actual GNP is less than potential GNP, there are idle resources and a recessionary gap exists. The larger the gap, the further the economy is from its GNP goal.[6]

As for inflation, "reasonable" price stability is the goal. It is interesting to note that during the 1960s this meant no increase in prices (0 percent inflation). While that objective was rarely attained, the annual inflation rate was consistently below 3 percent until the final years of the decade. During the 1970s, however, inflation became a persistent and unyielding plague, and it is not uncommon to hear that the "underlying" inflation rate is 5 or 6 percent or more.

Sustained growth of real GNP of 3.5 percent or more would be considered acceptable by most economists, and economic growth of this magnitude yields startling results. There is a simple formula known as the *Rule of 72* which translates a growth rate into the approximate number of years required for a magnitude to double at the specified rate of growth. Equation (12–3) expresses the Rule of 72:

$$(12\text{–}3) \quad \frac{\text{Approximate number of years for}}{\text{a given magnitude to double}} = \frac{72}{\text{annual percentage rate of change}}.$$

Therefore, if the GNP growth rate is 3.5 percent, GNP will double approximately every 20.6 years.

Table 12–1 summarizes the goals discussed in this section. It should be noted that a number of other objectives could be listed that are closely related to those appearing in Table 12–1. For instance, external stability (the existence of conditions conducive to orderly international trade) is an important goal and one that is related to the

---

[6] Conceptually, the notion of potential GNP seems fairly straightforward; in practice, however, the concept is somewhat nebulous. Among other things, calculation of potential GNP requires that a "reasonable" unemployment rate be selected which, as has been noted, is not an easy task. For a good discussion of the pitfalls of estimating potential GNP, see William Fellner, "Structural Problems behind Our Measured Unemployment Rates," *Contemporary Economic Problems* (Washington, D.C.: American Enterprise Institute for Public Policy Research, 1978), pp. 83–112.

TABLE 12–1
Reasonable macroeconomic objectives

Macroeconomic variable	Objective
Short run	
1. Real GNP	Actual real GNP equal to potential GNP
2. Unemployment	An unemployment rate of approximately 5.0 to 6.0 percent
3. Price level	Price stability
Long run	
4. Growth rate of real GNP	Sustained annual growth of approximately 3.5 percent

performance of the macroeconomy. Also, a cleaner environment might be listed as an objective, one whose pursuance certainly affects the growth of GNP in that investment dollars spent on pollution abatement devices cannot be used for investment in new output-producing equipment. Therefore, there are other important economic objectives that are not macroeconomic objectives but are closely related to the performance of the macroeconomy.

MACROECONOMIC PERFORMANCE: HAS THE UNITED STATES ACHIEVED ITS OBJECTIVES?

Macroeconomic performance is discussed here and also in the following chapters. At this point our aim is to give an overview of recent macroeconomic performance in the United States. Later chapters will be more specific about the performance of the economy and about the policies that have been used to try to move the economy nearer to the objectives listed in the previous section.

Gross National Product: Actual versus potential

Figure 12–1 shows actual and potential GNP from 1968 to 1978. The line representing potential GNP is based on the assumption that resources are fully utilized; the other line depicts the course of actual GNP. When actual GNP is below potential GNP, unemployment is above its target, and the larger the gap the more serious the labor market problem.

Note the large decline in GNP beginning in 1973 and ending in 1975. The 1973–75 recession was the most serious since the depres-

FIGURE 12-1
Actual and potential Gross National Product, 1968-1978

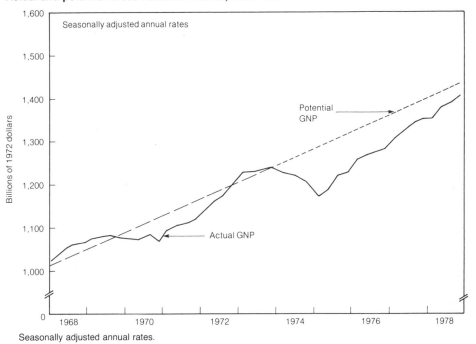

Seasonally adjusted annual rates.

Source: *Economic Report of the President* (Washington, D.C.: U.S. Government Printing Office, 1979), p. 75.

sion of the 1930s.[7] The unemployment rate had soared to 9.2 percent by May 1975, and the shortfall of actual GNP relative to potential GNP was running at an annual rate in excess of $100 billion at the bottom of the downturn. From Figure 12-1 it is apparent that, in the 1970s, the United States did not consistently meet the GNP objective stated in the preceding section.

Growth of Gross National Product

Table 12-2 shows the growth of GNP from 1950 to 1979. Data are given for three subperiods—1950-60, 1960-70, and 1970-79—and for 1950-79. For each period, initial-year and terminal-year real GNP and population figures are given, in columns (2) and (3). Next, average annual growth rates of real GNP and population are shown in

---

[7] A widely used definition of a recession is two successive quarters of declining real GNP.

column (4). Of the three subperiods listed in Table 12-2, the highest growth of real GNP, 3.9 percent, occurred from 1960 to 1970, and the lowest, 3.2 percent, from 1970 to 1979. Column (5) gives a comparison of per capita GNP growth for each period. Again the greatest growth occurred during the 1960s, with the 1970s second, and the 1950s third.

The last row of the table covers the entire period. From a long-run perspective, the record of economic performance depicted in Table 12-2 is impressive. It is true that the economy has not consistently performed at peak levels; nevertheless, the overall growth record is still good. Real GNP increased at an average annual rate of 3.5 percent from 1950 to 1979, and per capita real GNP grew at a 2.2 percent annual rate. However, a disconcerting aspect of Table 12-2 is the growth record for the 1970s, which fell short of the performance in the previous decade.

Employment and unemployment

Table 12-3 summarizes employment and unemployment performance for the years 1950 to 1979 and the three subperiods 1950-60, 1960-70, and 1970-79. The employment statistics in Table 12-3 indicate that the average annual increase in employment was larger for each successive subperiod, reaching 2.4 percent for 1970-79. On the other hand, the unemployment data point to a deterioration of labor market performance in the 1970s compared to the two previous decades. Not only was the unemployment rate in the 1970s the highest (6.2 percent), but an 8.5 percent rate in 1975 also marked the peak of the entire 1950-79 period.[8]

Thus the employment and unemployment data are somewhat contradictory for the 1970s: on the one hand, large numbers of new workers were absorbed into the work force; yet, the average unemployment rate for all of the 1970s was greater than for either of the two previous decades. However, the total employment and unemployment rate trends can be reconciled with a few pieces of pertinent information. First, employment increased rapidly in the 1970s because the labor market was absorbing a flood of new entrants: members of the post-World War II baby boom, now grown up, and the increasing percentage of women seeking paying jobs. While most of these new workers found employmemt, the higher unemployment rate reflected the problem created by the influx of workers. Also, the

---

[8] Though the unemployment rate during the 1970s averaged more than the rate for the previous decades, the problem was mild compared to the experience of the Great Depression. The annual unemployment rate averaged 18.2 percent in the 1930s with an average rate of 24.9 percent in 1933.

TABLE 12-2
Growth of real GNP and population in the United States, 1950–1979
(billions of 1972 dollars; population in millions)

(1)	(2) Initial year		(3) Terminal year		(4) Average annual growth rate		(5) Average annual growth rate of real per capita GNP
Period	Real GNP	Population	Real GNP	Population	Real GNP	Population	
1950–60	$ 533.5	152.3	$ 736.8	180.7	3.3%	1.7%	1.5%
1960–70	736.8	180.7	1,075.3	204.9	3.9	1.3	2.6
1970–79	1,075.3	204.9	1,431.6	220.6	3.2	0.8	2.4
1950–79	533.5	152.3	1,431.6	220.6	3.5	1.3	2.2

Sources: *Economic Report of the President and Federal Reserve Bulletin.*

TABLE 12-3
Employment and unemployment in the United States, 1950–1979

	Employment			Unemployment		
Period	Initial year (millions)	Terminal year (millions)	Average annual growth rate (percent)	Lowest annual rate	Highest annual rate	Average annual rate
1950–60	58.9 (1950)	65.8 (1960)	1.1%	2.9% (1953)	6.8% (1958)	4.5%
1960–70	65.8 (1960)	78.6 (1970)	1.8%	3.5% (1969)	6.7% (1961)	4.8%
1970–79	78.6 (1970)	96.9 (1979)	2.4%	4.9% (1970, 1973)	8.5% (1975)	6.2%
1950–79	58.9 (1950)	96.9 (1979)	1.7%	2.9% (1953)	8.5% (1975)	5.2%

Source: *Economic Report of the President.*

higher unemployment rate in recent years is due to more generous unemployment benefits and welfare payments. As the rate of labor market growth diminishes in the 1980s, there is reason to expect that the unemployment record will improve.

The general level of prices

Table 12–4 lists price-level data for the United States from 1950 to 1979; again the records for the 1950s and 1960s are quite similar, with annual price-level increases averaging under 3.0 percent for both periods. It is startling to those of us accustomed to living with inflation to observe that the general price level actually declined in 1954 by 0.5 percent. The price-level record deteriorated greatly during the 1970s when price increases averaged 7.2 percent per year. Notice that both unemployment rates and inflation rates were higher in the 1970s than in previous decades. Tables 12–3 and 12–4 cast suspicion on the proposition that higher inflation rates can be "traded" for lower unemployment. We will have more to say in later chapters about the possibility of an inflation-unemployment trade-off.

WHAT IS THE ROLE OF MONETARY AND FISCAL POLICY IN ACHIEVING MACROECONOMIC OBJECTIVES?

In the following seven chapters we explore the role of monetary and fiscal policy in achieving the macro objectives listed in this chapter. Since this book focuses on the monetary processes at work in the economy, we are more concerned with monetary than with fiscal policy. However, it has become clear in recent years that monetary and fiscal policy are closely related. Therefore, fiscal policy cannot be ignored if the role of monetary policy is to be assessed properly.

TABLE 12–4
Price level changes in the United States, 1950–1979

Prices	Lowest annual rate of price change*	Highest annual rate of price change*	Average annual rate of increase in prices
1950–60	−0.5% (1954)	5.9% (1951)	2.1%
1960–70	0.7% (1961)	6.1% (1969)	2.7%
1970–79	3.4% (1971, 1972)	13.3% (1979)	7.2%
1950–79	−0.5% (1954)	13.3% (1979)	3.9%

* December to December.
Source: *Economic Report of the President* and *Monthly Labor Review*.

Both monetary and fiscal policy are aimed at controlling purchases of new goods and services. However, there is considerable disagreement over the emphasis that should be given to monetary as compared to fiscal policy and over the proper techniques to use in the conduct of both types of policy. One group of economists, known as Keynesians or fiscalists, have traditionally emphasized fiscal policy; their policy prescriptions are drawn from an interpretation of John Maynard Keynes's *The General Theory of Employment, Interest, and Money* which was published in 1936. Keynes constructed a framework to deal with the depressed economic conditions of the 1930s, and the policy actions that he seemed to be recommending favored fiscal policy and placed monetary policy in a clearly secondary role. Until recently, Keynesian analysis has dominated macroeconomic policymaking, but there is now considerable disenchantment with the Keynesian model because it seems to provide inadequate solutions for coping with simultaneous unemployment and inflation.

Dissatisfaction with the ramifications of the Keynesian system has generated alternative approaches. Milton Friedman, a Nobel laureate in economics, is largely responsible for developing what has come to be known as the monetarist model of macroeconomic activity. Several aspects of the monetarist and Keynesian models are different, and these differences frequently result in disagreements between economists of monetarist and Keynesian persuasion over the appropriate course for economic policy. However, the gap separating the two camps has narrowed in recent years as research has provided answers to several once-unresolved issues.

Many economists find themselves on a middle ground; that is, they feel that elements of both Keynesian and monetarist analysis are useful. At the policy level, there are presently few economists who take the extreme Keynesian position that "money doesn't matter," nor are there many monetarists who argue that "money alone matters." Consequently, an eclectic approach has developed which draws from both the monetarist and the Keynesian models.

In the following chapters we attempt to present a balanced view of monetary and fiscal policymaking. Chapter 13 contains a simple Keynesian-type model without a monetary sector. Chapter 14 analyzes the role of money on economic activity from the perspective of the Keynesian and monetarist systems. Chapter 15 builds a formal model with money, and there is considerable discussion of monetary and fiscal policy differences between monetarists and Keynesians. Chapter 16 analyzes fiscal policy but emphasizes the interrelationships that link monetary and fiscal policy. Chapters 17 and 18 are on inflation, and the final chapter of this section discusses some current policy issues related to the conduct of monetary and fiscal policy.

The question posed at the beginning of this section concerning the proper role of monetary and fiscal policy in achieving macroeconomic objectives has not been answered; we have merely raised the question in order to point out some key issues related to policymaking which are addressed in the chapters that follow. As the discussion proceeds the student should come to appreciate the complexities of formulating economic policies so as to achieve the objectives set forth in this chapter.

SUMMARY

Consideration of macroeconomic performance involves measuring aggregate output (GNP), employment, and the general level of prices. Gross National Product is the final market value of goods and services produced during a given period of time and is the best available indicator of macroeconomic performance. Employment and the general level of prices are among the other important macro variables. Employment and unemployment rates indicate the proportions of those working and those seeking a job; and inflation is the process of a rising general price level. Some macroeconomic variables such as GNP are flows occurring between two points in time, while others are stocks measured at a given point in time.

The information presented in this chapter suggests that the U.S. economy has performed rather well during the post–World War II era. The 1960s were a gold era for the economy: growth of GNP was rapid; unemployment declined and was near or below 4 percent for the last part of the decade; and prices were relatively stable until the end of the period. Performance from 1970–79 was less satisfactory: the inflation that had begun as the previous decade waned became more deeply engrained in the economy, and the 1973–75 recession was the worst since the Great Depression. The 1970s ended with double-digit inflation, sluggish growth of GNP, and prospects for rising unemployment.

In this chapter we have reviewed the more important goals of the macroeconomy of the United States. These are the primary goals of both monetary and fiscal policy. This material, along with the information in the previous chapters, provides the facts and information needed to develop and understand models of the macroeconomy. The remaining chapters of this section build those models and show how they can be used for policymaking purposes.

REVIEW QUESTIONS

1. Distinguish between real and nominal GNP. Why are adjustments for price-level changes necessary for accurate interpretation of GNP data?

2. How is the unemployment rate derived? What criteria are used to classify an individual as employed or unemployed?

3. Explain why "full" employment may be said to exist even though the unemployment rate may be as high as 5 or 6 percent.

4. Obtain recent quarterly and annual data on GNP. How does the recent rate of growth of real GNP compare with the figures in Table 12–2? Has there been or is there currently a recession? What is the basis for your answer?

5. Compare recent inflation and unemployment rates with the rates in Tables 12–3 and 12–4.

SUGGESTIONS FOR ADDITIONAL READING

The Brookings Institution. *Setting National Priorities.* Washington, D.C.: The Brookings Institution, most recent issue.

The Council of Economic Advisers. "The Annual Report of the Council of Economic Advisers." *Economic Report of the President.* Washington, D.C.: U.S. Government Printing Office, most recent issue.

Dittenhafer, Brian D. "A Primer on Productivity." *Monthly Review of the Federal Reserve Bank of Atlanta,* vol. 59, no. 10, October 1974, pp. 150–54.

Fellner, William, ed. *Contemporary Economic Problems.* Washington, D.C.: American Enterprise Institute for Public Policy Research, 1978.

13

Aggregate economic activity:
A simple model without money

WARM-UP: *Outline and questions to consider as you read*

How is aggregate production measured?
    The income approach.
    The expenditures approach.
What is aggregate demand, and why is it
    important?
    Consumption.
    Investment.
    Government spending.
What is meant by equilibrium in aggregate
    production?
What is the multiplier process?
What are the uses and limitations of the
    $C + I + G$ model?

NEW TERMS

Aggregate demand ($C + I_d + G$):   the total spending on new goods and services per time period, including consumption, desired investment, and government spending.

Aggregate production (GNP):   the total output of new goods and services per time period.

Average propensity to consume (APC):   the proportion of total income that is used for consumption.

Closed economy: an economy that does not engage in foreign trade.

Consumption *(C):* the flow of household spending on new goods and services.

Disposable (personal) income: the aftertax, spendable income available to households for either consumption or saving.

Endogenous variable: the effect variable in a cause-and-effect relationship.

Exogenous variable: an economic magnitude whose impact is assumed to be constant for purposes of analysis.

Government spending *(G):* the flow of government purchases of new goods and services.

Income-consumption function: the relationship specifying how consumption is influenced by income.

Investment: purchases of new plant and equipment, residential construction, and inventory change.

Macroeconomic equilibrium: a condition in which aggregate production is equal to aggregate demand so that both will be maintained at existing levels.

Marginal propensity to consume (MPC): the proportion of any change in total income that is used for consumption spending.

Multiplier process: the process by which a change in an exogenous spending variable such as government expenditures generates a larger change in equilibrium GNP.

Proportional income tax: a tax structure whereby the tax rate remains constant regardless of the level of income.

Value-added approach: a method of measuring GNP that involves summing the value added at each stage of the production process.

In the previous chapter we set the stage for this and the following chapters of this section by introducing certain key macroeconomic variables including aggregate production (Gross National Product), total employment, and the general level of prices; then we presented the more important macroeconomic objectives; finally, we offered a brief review of the performance of the United States economy during the post–World War II era and speculated on the role of policy in achieving macroeconomic objectives. With this background, it is now appropriate to begin an analysis of the forces that determine the level of aggregate economic activity.

Our model of the macroeconomy in this chapter focuses on real aggregate production levels, while employment and the price level are relegated to the background. However, one should remember that aggregate production and employment are quite closely related so that, if aggregate output is rising (falling), aggregate employment normally will be moving in the same direction. Furthermore, while ignored here, inflation is treated in detail in the chapters that follow. Since the concept of aggregate production plays such a central role in the analysis of a monetary economy, this chapter begins by expanding the discussion of Gross National Product measurement that was begun in the preceding chapter.

HOW IS AGGREGATE PRODUCTION MEASURED?

Previously we defined Gross National Product (GNP) as the final market value of the new goods and services produced during a given time period. The earlier discussion pointed out certain words in the definition of Gross National Product—*final, market, produced,* and *period*—as keys to its nature. Also, recall that an accurate portrayal of aggregate output during periods of changing prices requires that nominal or money GNP be adjusted by removing the effect of price-level changes. For the most part, in this and in following chapters we have used real data for GNP and its various components since prices have been rising significantly in recent years.

While GNP is a measure of aggregate production, it is useful to know the portion of the new goods and services that were actually purchased during the same time period and, furthermore, to know who purchased them. Figure 13-1 is a simple circular flow diagram showing two parts of the economic process—production and spending.[1] The figure indicates (upper loops) that producers make new goods and services and that purchasers buy them. The lower loops denote that purchasers earn income to purchase goods and services by selling their productive resources—labor, for instance—to producers. Therefore, Figure 13-1 suggests two approaches to measuring GNP: (1) the income approach, which focuses on producers and the income generated in the production process and (2) the expenditures approach, which concentrates on purchasers.

One particular shortcoming of Figure 13-1 is the implication that in any particular time period the dollar value of intended purchases is always equal to the flow of production. Such an equality is quite unlikely for a large economy such as ours which turns out over $2 trillion worth of new output each year. When the rate of intended

---

[1] Of course, a large proportion of the population engages in both activities; that is, they are both producers and purchasers.

FIGURE 13-1
The circular flow of spending, income, production, and resources

aggregate spending is not the same as the flow of production, the difference will be reflected by inventories which are being unintentionally depleted or accumulated. As our discussion proceeds, more will be said about total intended spending relative to total production and the role of inventory change in the equation.

The income approach

Calculating GNP using the income approach involves use of the value-added method. To illustrate this technique, consider the production of an automobile that reaches its final point of sale after going through three stages of production—(1) production of raw materials used to make the car, (2) fabrication and assembly of the auto's components, and (3) dealer preparation and sale to a final buyer; a simple example will show how value is added at each stage of the production process.

First, assume that the raw materials necessary to make the car are sold to an automobile manufacturer for $3,000. The automaker then uses the raw material to fabricate and assemble a car which an automobile dealer buys for $8,000. Finally, the car is serviced and is sold to a family for $10,000.

How much GNP has been generated by the manufacture of the automobile? One might be tempted to add together the $3,000 worth of raw materials, the $8,000 that the dealer paid the car producer, and the $10,000 paid the dealer by the consumer for a total of $21,000. However, to do this would involve considerable double counting; the value of the raw materials, for example, would be counted three times—first in the $3,000, again as part of the $8,000, and also as part of the $10,000.

This multiple counting of the value of an intermediate product can be avoided by using the value-added method. The raw materials producers are the first stage of production, and it is assumed that they purchase nothing from other firms. Therefore, the $3,000 represents value added in stage 1. At the next stage, value added is $5,000, which is derived by subtracting the raw materials purchases of $3,000 from the auto manufacturer's selling price of $8,000. In a similar manner, value added in the final stage is obviously $2,000 ($10,000 − $8,000). If the values added are summed, the total is $10,000 ($3,000 + $5,000 + $2,000) which is exactly the same as the final selling price of the car and is also equivalent to the total income generated in the production of the car.

At each stage of the production process, incomes are paid to the factors of production which have been used to make the product. In the GNP statement presented in Table 13-1, returns to each of the factors of production—wages, interest, profit, and rent—are listed on the right side under the income approach which focuses on the production of each of the nation's business firms.[2] Taken together, the values added (or incomes generated) by these enterprises comprise the bulk of Gross National Product.[3]

We have seen that the income approach focuses on the production process and on the income generated by business firms. GNP measurement can also be considered from an expenditures perspective. In the value-added example in the preceding section, a car was man-

---

[2] Rent in the GNP accounts is not entirely analogous to the economic concept of rent as a return to the "nature-made" stock of wealth. For the most part, rent in the GNP accounts reflects an imputed value given to owner-occupied houses. The capital consumption allowances category consists primarily of depreciation, and indirect business taxes include sales, excise, and property taxes.

[3] In the United States most value added originates in private business firms. Thus totaling the value added from each of our nation's businesses would account for most of the country's output. However, some production originates in the government sector and some also in households (primarily in the form of the services of domestic servants).

TABLE 13-1
Gross National Product, 1979—expenditures and production approaches
($billions)

Expenditures on new goods and services plus inventory change				Income components of GNP	
Personal consumption expenditures:		$1,509.8 (63.7%)		Capital consumption allowances:	$243.0 (10.3%)
Durable goods	$213.0			Indirect business taxes plus other minor items:	200.2 (8.4%)
Nondurable goods	596.9			Rental income of persons:	26.9 (1.1%)
Services	699.9			Net interest:	129.7 (5.5%)
				Proprietors' income:	130.8 (5.5%)
				Corporate profits:	179.0 (7.6%)
Gross private domestic investment:		387.2 (16.4%)	=	Compensation of employees:	$1,459.2 (61.6%)
Business structures	92.6				
Business equipment	162.2				
Residential structures	114.1				
Business inventory change	18.3				
Government purchases of goods and services:		476.4 (20.1%)			
Federal	166.6				
State and local	309.8				
Net exports of goods and services: (Exports - imports: 257.5 - 262.1)		-4.6 (-0.2%)			
Gross National Product:		$2,368.8 (100.0%)		Gross National Product:	$2,368.8 (100.0%)

ufactured in three stages of production. The sum of the values added was $10,000, which was also the price paid for the car. When the expenditures approach is used to calculate Gross National Product, it is the final selling price of the new goods and services that is included in GNP.

The expenditures method of calculating GNP categorizes spending into four major components according to the type of buyer. The four categories are as follows:

1. Households—consumption expenditures (C).
2. Businesses—investment expenditures (I).
3. Government—government expenditures on new goods and services (G).
4. Foreign sector—net exports (exports minus imports or X − M).

The analysis of the causes of fluctuations of GNP covered in this and later chapters will initially concentrate on the domestic economy, and not until the final section of the book will the foreign sector be discussed. Therefore, from time to time we refer to a "C + I + G" model which takes its name from the three domestic spending categories.

Household consumption (C) represents all consumer expenditures on new goods and services except purchases of houses and mobile homes which, along with purchases of new business plant and equipment and inventory change, are included in investment *(I)*. Government (federal, state, and local) spending on new goods and services *(G)* counts purchases of defense goods and wages and salaries of government employees, among other things. It should be emphasized that the federal spending component of GNP differs considerably from the total spending component of the federal budget. For example, in 1979, total federal spending was $509.0 billion, while federal spending on new goods and services was $166.6 billion. The difference in the two figures is due primarily to the fact that total federal spending includes transfer payments such as unemployment payments and veteran's benefits, while the federal spending component of GNP does not. Finally, total imports are subtracted from total exports to obtain net exports *(X − M)*. When net exports are positive, our sales of goods and services to foreigners exceed our purchases from other nations; the reverse is true when net exports are negative. Figures for the four expenditure categories are given on the left side of Table 13–1.[4]

Two additional national income accounting concepts are presented in Table 13–2. On the left, the sum of payments to the factors of production (from the lower right-hand side of Table 13–1) is designated national income ($1,925.6 billion). These payments can be thought of as earned income, gross of income, and social security taxes. On the right side of Table 13–2, disposable (personal) income is derived; disposable income is the spendable, aftertax income of households. To obtain disposable income, several adjustments are made to national income. First, personal and corporate income taxes and social security taxes are subtracted from national income. Retained corporate profits are likewise removed, since they are not distributed to households and are therefore not available as spendable income. Finally, unearned income (transfer payments) is added and other adjustments are included, giving a disposable income total of $1,629.3 billion. In 1979, households used $1,509.8 billion of their disposable income for consumption; $73.8 billion was saved; and $45.7 billion went for other personal outlays such as payment of loan interest, which the Department of Commerce treats as a separate category.

WHAT IS AGGREGATE DEMAND, AND WHY IS IT IMPORTANT?

The term *aggregate demand* refers to total intended spending on new goods and services by the various categories of purchasers. In

---

[4] Another national income accounting measure, net national product or NNP, can be derived by subtracting capital consumption allowances (depreciation) from GNP.

TABLE 13-2
National income and disposable personal income, 1979 ($billions)

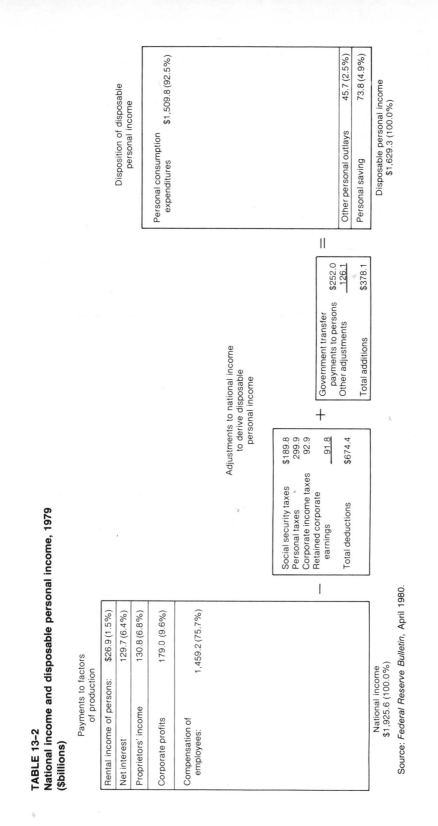

Payments to factors
of production

Rental income of persons:	$26.9 (1.5%)
Net interest	129.7 (6.4%)
Proprietors' income	130.8 (6.8%)
Corporate profits	179.0 (9.6%)
Compensation of employees:	1,459.2 (75.7%)

National income
$1,925.6 (100.0%)

−

Adjustments to national income
to derive disposable
personal income

Social security taxes	$189.8
Personal taxes	299.9
Corporate income taxes	92.9
Retained corporate earnings	91.8
Total deductions	$674.4

+

Government transfer payments to persons	$252.0
Other adjustments	126.1
Total additions	$378.1

=

Disposition of disposable
personal income

Personal consumption expenditures	$1,509.8 (92.5%)
Other personal outlays	45.7 (2.5%)
Personal saving	73.8 (4.9%)

Disposable personal income
$1,629.3 (100.0%)

Source: *Federal Reserve Bulletin*, April 1980.

the remaining sections of this chapter, we develop a simple model of the economy in which the driving force is aggregate demand. In any particular time period, there is assumed to be an upper limit to real aggregate production which we will refer to as potential GNP. Potential GNP is determined primarily by the size of the labor force, the stock of capital, the level of technology, and the level of education and training. Since the factors that determine potential GNP tend to change rather slowly, we assume that potential GNP is fixed in the short run, the time span covered by our analysis.

As is shown later, the relationship between aggregate production and aggregate demand determines whether GNP has a tendency to rise, fall, or remain constant. Regardless of aggregate demand, real GNP cannot rise beyond potential GNP. Since aggregate demand is the critical element in the determination of the level of GNP, it is important that we try to understand what influences determine the desired levels of consumption, investment, and government spending. Initially the model is made as simple as possible by making the following assumptions:

1. The economy is a closed system; that is, there is no foreign trade.
2. The relevant time horizon is the short run; this assumption is implicit in our use of the notion of potential GNP as an upper production limit.
3. All variables are expressed in real terms; that is, inflation and deflation are excluded (monetary influences in general are ignored).

As the analysis proceeds, some of these assumptions are relaxed, while others concerning particular components of the model are introduced at the appropriate time.

Since aggregate demand consists of the desired levels of personal consumption expenditures, investment, and government spending on new goods and services, each of these spending components is discussed in turn. Because consumption accounts for over 60 percent of GNP, it is given the most attention. Investment, while much smaller in absolute terms, is very volatile, and changes in the level of investment spending can produce sizable swings in GNP. Government spending accounts for around 20 percent of GNP, a rather large amount, and is of added significance since it is sometimes altered in an attempt to influence Gross National Product. Control of government spending along with tax changes constitute what is known as fiscal policy.

Consumption

As we explained in Chapter 1, economists usually formulate generalizations about the economy and how it functions based on observations of the behavior of persons and groups and on facts pertaining to whatever they are studying. An initial hypothesis may be very general—for example, "consumption is influenced by income." At some point, however, the economist will usually try to test the hypothesis, and to do so will almost certainly lead to collection and use of data. If preliminary analysis of the data suggests that the hypothesis may be valid, the next step is to try to use the data to determine the specific functional relationship that is most consistent with known values of the variables involved. In the case of consumption, income-consumption statistics may suggest that the two variables are related and that changes in income seem to produce changes in consumption. The remainder of this section on consumption is an elaboration of this methodology.

Generally, consumption hypotheses are formulated for both the household level and the aggregate level, and a complete theory of consumption should contain a logical bridge between household and aggregate consumption. However, our discussion will deal only with aggregate consumption for the sake of brevity. Aggregate consumption is influenced by many forces, some more important than others. Equation 13–1 includes four variables that might logically be expected to have some influence on consumption—disposable income (Y_d), the interest rate (i), credit availability (a), and wealth (w):

$$(13\text{-}1) \qquad C = h(Y_d, i, a, w, \ldots n).$$

The n on the right side of the equation indicates that there are other unspecified forces that affect the level of consumption in addition to the four that are listed in (13–1).[5]

The statistical and analytical difficulties involved in specifying cause-and-effect relationships grow rapidly as the number of variables is increased. Therefore, whenever possible we focus on a limited number of the most important influences. When a single independent variable explains a large proportion of the fluctuations in the dependent variable, the results may not warrant the added com-

---

[5] The h on the right-hand side of Equation (13–1) means "a function of." Therefore, $C = h(Y_d, i, c, w, \ldots, n)$ is read "consumption (C) is a function of (depends on) disposable income (Y_d), the interest rate (i), etc." In the remainder of this book we shall adopt the convention of using the functional notation h when there are two or more independent variables. In two-variable equations, an f will be used when the relationship between the variables is assumed to be positive and a g when the relationship is inverse (negative).

plications that arise from using several explanatory variables. So, while many variables can be used to explain the level of aggregate consumption expenditures, the consumption function employed in this chapter contains only one important explanatory variable—disposable income. Thus we can simplify Equation (13–1), using instead

(13–2) $C = f(Y_d)$,

which posits that disposable income (Y_d) determines the level of consumption (C); the functional notation f indicates that a positive relation is assumed between the two variables.

We now turn to data on consumption and income to help determine more precisely the nature of the income-consumption relation. Table 13–3 lists data for 1959–78 on aggregate consumption and disposable income for the United States; disposable income appears in column (2) and consumption in column (3). Even a casual glance at these two columns suggests that income and consumption are related.

TABLE 13–3
Aggregate disposable income and consumption for the United States, 1959–1978
(billions of 1972 dollars)

(1) Year	(2) Real disposable income (Y_d)	(3) Real consumption (C)	(4) Average propensity to consume $APC = C/Y_d$	(5) Marginal propensity to consume: $MPC = \Delta C/\Delta Y_d$
1959	$477.4	$441.5	0.925	—
1960	487.3	453.0	0.930	1.162
1961	500.6	462.2	0.923	0.748
1962	521.6	482.9	0.926	0.986
1963	539.2	501.4	0.930	0.995
1964	577.3	528.7	0.916	0.717
1965	612.4	558.1	0.911	0.838
1966	643.6	586.1	0.911	1.026
1967	669.8	603.2	0.901	0.653
1968	695.2	633.4	0.911	1.189
1969	712.3	655.4	0.920	1.287
1970	741.6	668.9	0.902	0.461
1971	769.0	691.9	0.900	0.810
1972	801.3	733.0	0.915	1.272
1973	854.7	767.7	0.898	0.650
1974	842.0	760.7	0.903	0.551
1975	859.7	774.6	0.901	0.785
1976	890.1	819.4	0.921	1.427
1977	926.3	857.7	0.926	1.058
1978	965.6	891.2	0.923	0.855

Source: *Economic Report of the President,* 1979.

Columns (4) and (5) contain information which helps us understand the nature of the income-consumption relation. Column (4) lists the average propensity to consume (the APC) based on the observed income and consumption totals for each year during the 1959–78 period. The APC is derived by dividing total consumption by total disposable income; therefore, the APC represents the proportion of total disposable income used for consumption.[6] Note that the APC has fluctuated within rather narrow limits, ranging from a low of 0.898 in 1973 to a high of 0.930 in 1960 and 1963. Column (5) contains the marginal propensity to consume (MPC), which is the change in consumption divided by the change in disposable income. For the economic forecaster, the MPC is of greater relevance than the APC since the analyst usually seeks to predict how much, if any, consumption will change in coming time periods.

The MPC fluctuates quite widely—ranging from 0.461 in 1970 to 1.427 in 1976—which suggests that disposable income alone does not adequately explain year-to-year changes in consumption. Some of the other influences on consumption were listed earlier and are probably among the forces causing changes in consumption and the MPC. It follows, then, that inclusion of additional variables would improve our ability to explain changes in consumption. Disaggregating consumption into more homogeneous groupings may also be beneficial. For instance, consumption data show that purchases of durable goods—because they are often postponable—fluctuate more widely than purchases of nondurables or services; hence, deriving functions for various categories of consumption might improve the reliability of consumption forecasts.

The next step in specifying an income-consumption function is to derive a formula based on the income data in column (2) and the consumption figures in column (3) of Table 13–3. We begin by plotting consumption (C) against disposable income (Y_d) in Figure 13–2.[7] There is an income-consumption coordinate for each year appearing in Table 13–3, and since our observations run for 20 years—1959 to 1978—there are 20 coordinates plotted in Figure 13–2.

---

[6] The average propensity to save (APS) can be found by subtracting the APC from 1.00 since, by definition, disposable income must be used either for consumption or for saving; that is, APC + APS = 1.00. Also, changes in income must be used for either saving or consumption; therefore, MPC + MPS = 1.00, and MPS = 1.00 − MPC.

[7] The scale of the y-axis in Figure 13–2 and similar diagrams that follow is the same as the scale of the x-axis. Therefore, the 45-degree line in Figure 13–2 is a reference line where any point on the line represents an equality between the dependent variable (consumption) and the independent variable (disposable income).

FIGURE 13-2
An income-consumption function for the United States, 1959–1978
(billions of 1972 dollars)

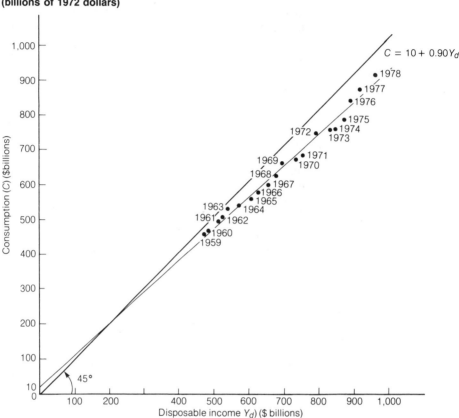

Whenever possible, a linear relation in the form of Equation (13–3),

(13–3) $$C = a + bY_d,$$

is used in simple economic models. The reason for using a linear equation is that such equations are easy to derive statistically and simple to manipulate mathematically. Now, having located the coordinates in Figure 13–2, we can describe two methods of obtaining an income-consumption equation. First, a ruler can be used to draw a "line of best fit" through or as close as possible to each coordinate. If all the coordinates fall on the line of best it, there is a perfect linear relation between the variables; this is not the case for our data set since all 20 points do not fall on a single straight line.[8]

---

[8] If a perfect linear relation existed, then all the MPC figures in column (5) of Table 13–3 would be the same.

When all coordinates fall on or very close to the line of best fit, the method we have just described is acceptable. However, when the coordinates are widely scattered, different analysts would draw varied lines of best fit because the technique depends on the judgment of the person drawing the line. Fortunately we can avoid this problem by using a statistical technique known as linear regression analysis, which is a method for statistically deriving a line of best fit and is preferable to the previous method. We obtain the following regression equation from the data in Table 13-3:

$$(13-4) \qquad C = 10 + 0.90Y_d$$

where 10 is the value for a in Equation (13-3), and 0.90 is the value for b. The reader is probably aware that a is the y-intercept, the point where the consumption function crosses the y-axis, and b is the slope of the line.[9] The value for b, 0.90, is not only the slope of the line but also represents the MPC.

It should be stressed that the main purpose in deriving an income-consumption relation such as this is to illustrate a common technique of economic analysis. As was indicated previously, adequately explaining consumption requires more than simply applying Equation (13-4). For example, while our formula indicates that the MPC is 0.90, we know from column (5) of Table 13-3 that the year-to-year deviations around this value have been rather large.

Investment

Investment is the most volatile of the spending components; this volatility can be illustrated by comparing fluctuations in GNP to changes in investment. Over the period 1970-79, there were three years—1970, 1974, and 1975—when GNP and investment declined and seven years when they increased. For the three years of contraction, the average annual decline was 1.0 percent and 13.9 percent for GNP and investment, respectively. During the expansion years, the annual increase in real GNP averaged 4.4 percent, while the average increase in investment was 10.3 percent annually. Furthermore, though investment is a much smaller total than GNP (see Table 13-1), in the three years during the 1970s when real GNP fell, the average decline in real investment exceeded the average fall in GNP by $14 billion.

Investment is comprised of three major categories: (1) business investment in plant and equipment, (2) construction of residential structures, and (3) inventory change. Some inventory adjustments

---

[9] Given a consumption function in the form $C = a + bY_d$, the saving function can be obtained from $S = -a + (1 - b)Y_d$. Thus, from Equation (13-4), $S = -10 + 0.10Y_d$.

are planned in order to keep inventories in line with anticipated sales; on the other hand, other inventory change is unintentional, the result of sales falling short of or exceeding anticipated levels. Thus category (3) may be subdivided into desired and unintended inventory change, or I_d and I_u respectively. This distinction leads to another classification of investment—desired investment, which includes not only intended inventory change but also categories (1) and (2) above, and undesired investment, which is that portion of category (3) which is unintended. Summarizing, we have

(13-5) $$I = I_d + I_u,$$

where I_d represents business investment in plant and equipment, residential construction, and desired inventory change, and I_u is undesired inventory change.

Investment has been one of the most perplexing economic magnitudes with which economists have had to deal. As with consumer durable purchases, investment can often be postponed. An old piece of equipment can be repaired; installation of more technologically advanced equipment can be delayed; construction of a new plant in a new location can wait a while longer. Thus investment may rise or fall sharply from year to year. The state of mind of investors, a highly subjective matter, is very important in determining the level of investment activity. If companies feel good about the business climate, their optimism may translate into a large increase in aggregate investment. On the other hand, a gloomy outlook can produce a dramatic decline.

Economists have studied a number of variables in trying to explain the level of investment. Equation (13-6) shows desired investment as a function of the interest rate (i), the level of GNP (Y), and changes in GNP (ΔY):

(13-6) $$I_d = h(i, Y, \Delta Y, \ldots n).$$

Elaborate and complex investment models have been formulated in order to explain investment spending. Unfortunately the results have been so poor as to prompt Gardner Ackley's assessment that "macroeconomics . . . lacks an acceptable theory of investment. . . ."[10]

In the remainder of the present chapter we shall assume that investment is an exogenous variable; that is, changes in investment emanate from outside the system. This assumption is expressed in Equation (13-7), where

[10] Gardner Ackley, *Macroeconomics: Theory and Policy* (New York: Macmillan, 1978), p. 666.

$$(13\text{-}7) \qquad\qquad I_d = \overline{I}_d.$$

The bar over the right-hand expression shows that investment is assumed to be some constant amount that is determined exogenously. If the value of an exogenous variable changes, it is due to some force operating outside the model. Making investment an exogenous variable means that the model does not explain why a change in investment occurs; however, the effect of an investment change on GNP can and will be considered.

In later chapters, the model is made more realistic by relating investment to the interest rate as expressed in Equation (13–8):

$$(13\text{-}8) \qquad\qquad I_d = g(i),$$

with the functional notation g indicating that investment and the interest rate are inversely related. The logic of the investment–interest rate relation is straightforward. Interest is the price that businesses must pay to borrow money to finance a new investment project. As interest rates rise, more and more projects are unprofitable due to the high costs of financing them; therefore they will not be undertaken.[11] A falling interest rate has the opposite effect; that is, there is a tendency for the level of investment activity to rise. We shall have more to say about the investment-interest rate function, but for the time being, investment will be treated as an exogenous variable as reflected in Equation (13–7).

Government spending

Like investment, government spending is assumed to be determined exogenously, so that

$$(13\text{-}9) \qquad\qquad G = \overline{G}.$$

The rationale for treating government spending as an exogenous variable is that decisions of Congress and the president for the most part determine the level of government expenditures. Finally, we assume that at least a portion of government expenditures is financed via tax collections (T) and that all taxes come from a proportional income tax of the form

$$(13\text{-}10) \qquad\qquad T = tY,$$

---

[11] Even if funds are available to the firm internally out of retained earnings, a rising interest rate will discourage investment in plant and equipment because, rather than being used for investment, funds can be used to purchase financial assets—bonds, for example—bearing a more attractive return. Firms also can increase dividends if the rate that can be earned on new investments is less than what stockholders require.

where T is the dollar amount of taxes collected, t is the tax rate, and Y represents GNP.

WHAT IS MEANT BY EQUILIBRIUM IN AGGREGATE PRODUCTION?

In this section a simple model of GNP determination is presented which assumes that equilibrium exists when aggregate demand equals aggregate production.[12] Here, aggregate demand is defined to mean consumption (C) plus that portion of investment spending which is planned or desired (I_d) plus government spending on new goods and services (G); thus aggregate demand is equal to $C + I_d + G$. Obviously, if aggregate demand equals aggregate production, inventories are not unexpectedly rising or falling $(I_u = 0)$. If, however, production exceeds aggregate demand (inventories are rising unexpectedly), then there is a tendency for producers to decrease production in order to halt the inventory buildup. Clearly, there will be a tendency for GNP to rise—at least up to potential GNP (Y)—if aggregate demand exceeds total production.

Now that the three spending components have been discussed and macroequilibrium has been defined, only a few final touches are needed to complete a basic macroeconomic model. Thus far, we have the following general equations for consumption, investment, government spending, and taxes:

(13–3) $$C = a + bY_d;$$

(13–7) $$I_d = \overline{I}_d;$$

(13–9) $$G = \overline{G};$$

(13–10) $$T = tY.$$

We continue to assume that $a = 10$ and $b = 0.90$; the tax rate (t) is 0.20, I_d is \$165, and G is \$525.[13] Therefore,

(13–4) $$C = 10 + 0.90\ Y_d;$$

(13–11) $$T = 0.20Y;$$

(13–12) $$\overline{I}_d = 165;$$

(13–13) $$\overline{G} = 525.$$

---

[12] We are assuming at this point that the monetary sector is in equilibrium. Also, it should be noted that there is nothing inherently good or bad about equilibrium as it is defined here; for instance, GNP may be in equilibrium, yet the economy may be operating well below its capacity.

[13] All dollar figures are in billions.

One further manipulation is necessary before the equilibrium level of GNP (Y) can be determined. If disposable income (Y_d) is defined as GNP minus taxes (T), then

(13–14) $$Y_d = Y - T,$$

and

(13–15) $$C = 10 + 0.90(Y - 0.20Y).$$

Finally, simplifying (13–15), we obtain

(13–16) $$C = 10 + 0.72Y.$$

Equation (13–4) can now be thought of as the Y_d form of the consumption function since the relation indicates that disposable income determines consumption; on the other hand, (13–16) is the Y form in that it expresses consumption as a function of GNP or total income.

Since we are defining macroeconomic equilibrium as a situation where total production (Y) is equal to aggregate demand $(C + I_d + G)$, the following equation will hold when the economy is in equilibrium:

(13–17) $$Y = C + I_d + G.$$

Next, Equations (13–16), (13–12), and (13–13) are substituted for C, I_d, and G in (13–17) in order to obtain

(13–18) $$Y = 10 + 0.72Y + 165 + 525.$$

Solving Equation (13–18) for Y, equilibrium GNP is \$2,500. Once at \$2,500, GNP will tend to remain at that level until one of the exogenous variables $(I_d$ and $G)$ or a parameter $(a, b,$ or $t)$ changes.

The reader can verify that \$2,500 is an equilibrium value by first substituting \$2,500 for Y in the consumption function which gives C = \$1,810. Adding C to investment of \$165 and government spending of \$525, aggregate demand is \$2,500, which verifies that this is the equilibrium value of Y. A useful exercise for the reader would be to assume that aggregate production (Y) is temporarily at some other value than \$2,500, say \$2,000 or \$3,000, and compute and compare aggregate demand at those levels of production. Remember that, if aggregate demand $(C + I_d + G)$ exceeds total production (Y), inventories are being unintentionally depleted, and there is a tendency for Y to rise. The opposite is true when total production is greater than aggregate demand.

Figure 13–3 is a graph of the aggregate demand components, $C + I_d + G$, and illustrates the concept of macroeconomic equilibrium.

FIGURE 13-3
The C + I + G model: A graphical representation

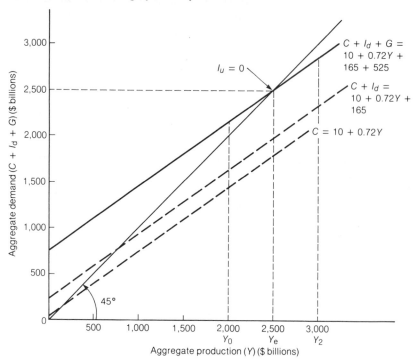

The 45-degree line is a reference line representing all possible equilibrium levels of GNP. Aggregate demand $(C + I_d + G)$ equals total production (Y), and unintended inventory change is zero where the $C + I_d + G$ function crosses the 45-degree line; therefore, in the above example, equilibrium exists at $Y = C + I_d + G = \$2,500$. At GNP levels below Y_e, \$2,000 for example, aggregate demand exceeds total production, inventories are being unintentionally depleted, and GNP will tend to rise until Y_e is attained. At GNP levels larger that Y_e, say \$3,000, production exceeds demand, unwanted inventories are being accumulated, and GNP will tend to fall.

WHAT IS THE MULTIPLIER PROCESS?

One of the more interesting aspects of macroeconomic analysis is the multiplier process. The multiplier deals with what happens if there is a change in one of the exogenous variables. For example, if investment (I_d) or government spending (G) rises, what will happen to equilibrium GNP? In a model such as the one developed above,

FIGURE 13-4
The multiplier effect: A graphical illustration

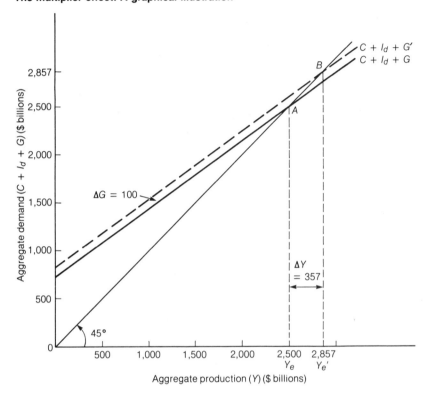

Aggregate production (Y) ($ billions)

and assuming that actual GNP is less than potential GNP, the result is an increase in Y that is larger than the original change in I_d or G. Since the change in Y exceeds the change in I_d or G, there is a multiplier process at work.[14]

To illustrate why the multiplier effect occurs and the forces that determine its size, assume that government spending (G) increases by $100 from the original level of $525 to $625.[15] In Figure 13-4 the solid $C + I_d + G$ aggregate demand line, which intersects the 45-

---

[14] Also, in our model a change in the value of a in the consumption function, which is referred to as autonomous consumption, will produce a multiplier effect. Autonomous consumption might increase because of inflation, which promotes a "buy now" attitude. On the other hand, fear of an impending recession might cause autonomous consumption to decline. If a is larger, the consumption function shifts upward and vice versa.

[15] In this chapter there is no discussion of the sources of government revenue, that is, whether the spending was financed by new taxes, borrowing, or printing money. This important consideration is covered in Chapters 15 and 16.

degree line at point A, represents the original demand levels where equilibrium was $2,500, and the broken line reflects the increase in government spending. Therefore, the original curve is shifted upward by $100, and the new aggregate demand line crosses the 45-degree line at B, where the new equilibrium is $2,857.

The new equilibrium of $2,857 could be calculated in the same manner as the original equilibrium; however, the discussion of the multiplier is aided by developing a slightly different procedure. We begin by substituting the consumption function into the equilibrium condition (Equation 13–17) to obtain

$$(13\text{–}19) \qquad Y = a + b(Y - tY) + I_d + G.$$

Solving for Y, the equilibrium condition can be written in a more general form:

$$(13\text{–}20) \qquad Y = \frac{1}{1 - b + bt}(a + I_d + G).$$

Now if the appropriate values for a, b, t, I_d, and G are substituted into (13–20), equilibrium Y can be calculated. With $G = 625$ and the other values remaining as they were originally, equilibrium production is $2,857.

Equation (13–20) can also be modified to show how a change in a, I_d, or G affects Y. For instance, if a change in government spending (ΔG) occurs, then the change in Y (ΔY) can be obtained using Equation (13–21), where

$$(13\text{–}21) \qquad \Delta Y = \frac{1}{1 - b + bt} \times \Delta G.$$

If investment (I_d) or autonomous consumption (a) change instead of G, then ΔI_d or Δa would be substituted for ΔG in (13–21).

Equation (13–21) indicates that ΔY is equal to ΔG times the expression,

$$\frac{1}{1 - b + bt},$$

which is the multiplier. Using m to designate the multiplier,

$$(13\text{–}22) \qquad m = \frac{1}{1 - b + bt},$$

and using the values assigned previously, the value of the multiplier is

$$m = \frac{1}{1 - 0.90 + (0.90)(0.20)} = 3.57$$

So, given $\Delta G = \$100$, ΔY is \$357 ($m \times \Delta G = 3.57 \times \$100$). Adding \$357 to the original equilibrium value of \$2,500 gives the new equilibrium of \$2,857.

Our model is too crude to yield a reliable multiplier value; however, the multiplier concept can be used to explain why an increase in government spending or investment may generate a change in GNP that is a multiple of the original increment in spending. The multiplier process represents the notion that the impact of the original spending change generates a ripple effect. In the above example, the increased government spending was assumed to be permanent, that is, not a one-time change; otherwise, the increase in GNP would also be temporary.

Imagine that the increased spending goes to purchase new defense goods such as airplanes, tanks, and other weapons. To fill the new orders, defense contractors will have to increase production.[16] As production is increased, the factors of production will simultaneously begin to receive increased wages, interest, and profits. (Remember that as goods are made, there is increased value added in the form of increased income to the factors of production.) The increase in income produces the ripples alluded to in the previous paragraph. What happens to the extra \$100 billion in factor income generated by the purchase of new defense goods? Some money will certainly be used by the income recipients to buy new goods and services. However, in our model, taxes are collected at a rate of \$0.20 for each dollar of income. Therefore, consumers do not receive an extra \$100 billion in spendable (disposable) income; their disposable income increases by only \$80 billion. Thus taxes are a leakage that reduces the expansionary impact of the increased government spending.

Will the second-round increase in consumption spending be the full \$80 billion? It will not, because, while disposable income has risen by \$80 billion, the MPC is only 0.90 (the MPS is 0.10); therefore, only 0.90 times \$80 or \$72 billion will be added to consumption in the second round. Thus savings, another leakage, further diminish the additional impact of the increased government spending. However, the extra consumption of \$72 billion will generate a third-round impact as new incomes are generated in the process of increasing output by \$72 billion. The third-round impact on spending and production will amount to \$72 billion minus the leakages going into taxes and savings.

How long will this process continue? Not forever, since in successive rounds, saving and tax leakages reduce the amount of additional

---

[16] Firms may temporarily fill new orders by drawing down inventories, but we assume that producers will soon adjust production to satisfy the increased demand.

consumption and production. But the process of expansion, though it grows at a slower rate, will continue through many rounds until leakages reduce the increase in spending to an inconsequential amount. At this time the economy will have reached a new equilibrium; in our model the system will have settled at point B in Figure 13-4, where equilibrium GNP is $2,857. At $2,857 a permanent increase in production of $357 has occurred which reflects the initial (permanent) increase of government spending of $100 and a multiplier of 3.57.

The nature of the multiplier concept should now be clear: Increased spending generates increased production leading to higher incomes and, subsequently, more spending; however, the expansion process becomes weaker in successive spending rounds due to leakages. The role of leakages in the multiplier process can be better understood by analyzing the multiplier formula, Equation (13-22). The formula indicates that a lower value for the tax rate (t) will increase the multiplier since a leakage has been reduced. A higher value for b (the MPC) also results in a larger multiplier (the MPS declines when the MPC rises).

WHAT ARE THE USES AND LIMITATIONS OF THE $C + I + G$ MODEL?

The model of the economy developed in this chapter is a crude attempt to explain how the nonfinancial sector of the macroeconomy functions. Nonetheless, it offers valuable insight about how economists construct models of the economy. Also, the system helps us understand something about consumer behavior, the concept of macroeconomic equilibrium, and the impact of a spending change which disturbs equilibrium and sets off a process of adjustment to a new equilibrium.

The model offers our first glimpse of the use of fiscal policy to stimulate or reduce the level of economic activity. Our discussion indicated that an increase in government spending is expansionary, and it should be obvious that a decrease is contractionary. Tax policy, which is the other component of fiscal policy, tends to be expansionary when taxes are lowered and contractionary when they are raised. To demonstrate the impact of a tax cut, assume that the original tax rate of 0.20 is reduced to 0.15. Substituting the new tax rate into Equation (13-20) and using the original values of the other variables, the new equilibrium is $2,979. Thus in our model a tax cut that reduces the tax rate from 0.20 to 0.15 increases GNP from $2,500 to $2,979.

Figure 13-5 shows graphically the effect of the tax reduction.

FIGURE 13–5
The impact of a tax cut: A graphical illustration

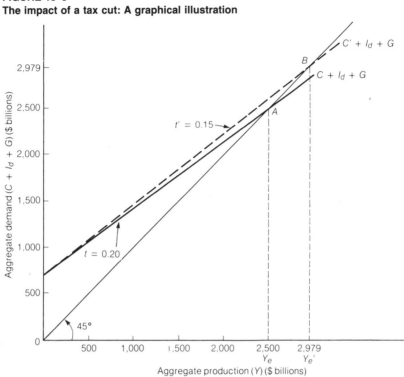

Notice that the lower tax rate rotates the original $C + I_d + G$ line upward. At GNP = 0, a tax cut is meaningless since no taxes are being collected. However, as GNP increases, the gap between the solid $C + I_d + G$ line and the broken $C + I_d + G$ line grows larger and larger because the absolute dollar impact of a tax rate reduction is greater at high GNP levels than at low levels of GNP. In reality the effects of both tax and government spending changes are more complex than the $C + I_d + G$ model implies, and Chapters 15 and 16 deal in more detail with the impact of policy changes.

In much of the remainder of the book, we attempt to add realism to the simple $C + I + G$ structure. Monetary influences are considered in the following chapter, and a formal model that includes a monetary sector (an IS-LM model) is developed in Chapter 15. Financing federal spending is discussed in the context of the analysis of fiscal policy in Chapters 15 and 16. Chapters 17 and 18 focus on the problem of inflation, and the final three chapters deal with international economic influences.

SUMMARY

Gross National Product (GNP) is a measure of new production and is often used as a proxy for aggregate economic activity. GNP can be calculated using the value-added approach, which sums the values added at each stage of the production process; the value-added approach focuses on the incomes (wages, profit, and so forth) of those who produce new goods and services. On the other hand, GNP measurement can be approached from the perspective of those who purchase new products. Total expenditures are comprised of consumption (C), investment (I), government spending (G), and net exports $(X - M)$.

Aggregate demand in an economy without foreign trade is comprised of consumption, desired investment, and government spending $(C + I_d + G)$. In the simple $C + I + G$ macro model developed in this chapter, aggregate demand is the determinant of the level of economic activity; aggregate production, subject to capacity limitations, adjusts to changes in aggregate demand. Thus it is important to understand the determinants of aggregate demand. In our analysis, consumption is a function of disposable income, and government spending and investment are treated as exogenous variables. Equilibrium GNP occurs when aggregate demand equals total production (unintended inventory change is zero). When this condition exists, there is no unanticipated inventory build-up or depletion, and the system is in balance. Moreover, until something outside the model disturbs the balance, equilibrium is maintained. However, if the balance is disturbed by a change in government spending, then the system seeks a new equilibrium. Because of the multiplier process, a change in government spending (G) produces a change in GNP which is a multiple of the original change in G.

The model developed in this chapter is indicative of the methodology that economists commonly employ to understand how the aggregate economy functions, to formulate macroeconomic policies, and to forecast macroeconomic activity. The $C + I + G$ model is simple and has many limitations. In the succeeding chapters, some of these limitations are removed, and the model is made more realistic and more useful.

REVIEW QUESTIONS

1. Discuss the relationship between aggregate production and aggregate spending flows. For a particular time period, must the two be equal? When GNP is measured separately from the production and spending perspectives, what assures that the dollar totals of the two are equal?

2. Using a recent *Federal Reserve Bulletin,* update Tables 13–1 and 13–2. Are there any significant changes in the relative shares of the various GNP components—government spending, for example?

3. Discuss the role of aggregate demand in the $C + I + G$ model. Compare the importance of aggregate demand and aggregate production in determining potential and actual levels of output.

4. What is an income-consumption function? Given $C = 100 + 0.80 \, Y$, what is the MPC? the MPS? If $Y_d = 1{,}500$, what is the APC? the APS? What happens to the MPC as income rises (falls)? to the APC?

5. Is the investment function as stable as the consumption function? Why or why not?

6. Define the concept of macroeconomic equilibrium as it is expressed in the $C + I + G$ model. Distinguish between the necessary equality of total production and spending in an accounting sense versus the equality of aggregate production and demand in an equilibrium sense.

7. Given the following information:
   a. $C = 100 + 0.80 Y_d$
   b. $T = 0.25Y$
   c. $I_d = 200$
   d. $G = 200.$
   What is equilibrium GNP (Y_e)? At Y_e level of output, what is C?

8. Assume that G in the previous problem increases from $200 to $300. What is the new Y_e? C? I_d? G? T? Use the multiplier formula to calculate the multiplier. Is the result consistent with your finding for the new equilibrium level of GNP?

9. Assume that the tax rate in Question 7 falls from 0.25 to 0.20. Recalculate Y_e, C, I_d, G, and T.

10. Show the model given in question 7 graphically.

11. Indicate the impact of the following on the $C + I_d + G$ line in Question 10.
    a. The change listed in Problem 8.
    b. The change listed in Problem 9.

12. Explain how the multiplier process works.

13. What are the more serious limitations of the $C + I + G$ model?

SUGGESTIONS FOR ADDITIONAL READING

Ando, Albert, and Modigliani, Franco. "The 'Life Cycle' Hypothesis of Saving: Aggregate Implications and Tests." *American Economic Review,* vol. 53 (March 1963), pp. 55–84.

Ferber, Robert. "Consumer Economics, a Survey." *Journal of Economic Literature,* vol. 11 (December 1973), pp. 1303–42.

Friedman, Milton. *A Theory of the Consumption Function.* Princeton, N.J.: Princeton University Press, 1957.

Keynes, John Maynard. *The General Theory of Employment, Interest, and Money.* New York: Harcourt, Brace, & World, 1936, chap. 8–10.

Samuelson, P. A. "The Simple Mathematics of Income Determination." In *Income, Employment, and Public Policy.* New York: W. W. Norton & Co., 1948, pp. 133–55.

14

Money and aggregate economic activity

WARM-UP: *Outline and questions to consider as you read*

What is the quantity theory of money, and how has it evolved?
   The velocity approach of Irving Fisher.
   The Cambridge cash balances equation.
How do changes in the money supply affect economic activity in the basic Keynesian model?
   The demand for money.
   The effects of money-supply changes.
What are the channels of monetary influence according to the monetarists?
   The relative-price channel.
   The wealth-effect channel.
How is equilibrium in the monetary sector determined?
   The process of attaining equilibrium: An example.
   Interest elasticity of the demand for money.

NEW TERMS

Interest elasticity of the demand for money: a measure of the degree to which the quantity of money demanded varies with a change in interest rates.

Liquidity preference function: the term used by Keynes to denote the demand for money function.

Liquidity trap: the possibility raised by Keynes that under certain conditions, any increase in the money supply would be hoarded.

Marginal efficiency of capital: the expected rate of return on additional units of capital.

Monetary equilibrium: a state of balance in the monetary sector where money demand (M_d) is equal to money supply (M_s).

Portfolio balance: a condition in which economic units are satisfied with the various asset forms in which their wealth is held.

Precautionary demand for money: money balances held in anticipation of possible emergencies.

Quantity theory of money: a theory that originally held that a change in the money supply would cause prices to change proportionately.

Relative-price channel: the impact of a money-supply change working through changes in interest rates and the associated changes in asset prices.

Speculative demand for money: the demand for money balances arising out of the risk associated with holding wealth in nonmoney form.

Transactions demand for money: the demand for money balances to be used in purchasing goods and services.

Wealth effect: changes in aggregate demand resulting from changes in wealth.

In the previous chapter we looked at some of the forces that determine the level of economic activity, but our survey of these forces was incomplete in that the role of money was not included. This chapter focuses on the different theories of how money affects the level of economic activity. Elements of two current views of the role of money are presented, and important developments in each are traced. For background we begin this discussion with one of the earliest theories of the role of money—the quantity theory.

WHAT IS THE QUANTITY THEORY OF MONEY, AND HOW HAS IT EVOLVED?

The velocity approach of Irving Fisher

Even before economics had been established as a separate discipline, writers had begun to analyze the relationship between money and economic activity. An early result of this analysis was the belief that changes in the supply (quantity) of money led to proportional changes in the level of prices. This belief came to be known as the quantity theory of money, and while there are numerous expressions of it, Irving Fisher's is the best known.[1]

Fisher, one of the first widely known American economists, taught at Yale University and published several notable works from the 1890s to the 1930s.[2] Fisher began with a simple identity: The total value of items sold and the total amount of money spent must be equal. Fisher expressed this relationship in a four-variable equation known as the equation of exchange:[3]

$$(14\text{--}1) \qquad\qquad MV = PQ.$$

In this equation, M is the average quantity of money in circulation, and V is the velocity of money or the average number of times a unit of money is spent. The product of M and V is total money expenditures during the period. P is a price index reflecting the weighted average price of all goods traded during the time period in question; Q is the number of items purchased; and the product of P and Q is the value of all sales in the economy during that time.[4]

---

[1] The French economist Jean Bodin (1520–96) is often credited with originating the quantity theory.

[2] Particularly relevant is Irving Fisher, *The Purchasing Power of Money* (New York: Macmillan, 1911), chaps. 2, 3, and 8.

[3] This is a widely used adaptation of Fisher's original equation which used T instead of Q and differentiated between different types of money such as currency and demand deposits.

[4] The exact nature of P and Q may be seen by letting p_i equal the price of the i'th good and q_i equal the quantity of good i sold; then

$$p_1q_1 + p_2q_2 + \cdots + p_nq_n = \sum_{i=1}^{n} p_iq_i.$$

If P is defined as the average price of each item sold (or each transaction in Fisher's terminology), then we may write

$$p_1q_1 + p_2q_2 - \cdots + p_nq_n = Pq_1 + Pq_2 + \cdots + Pq_n$$

$$= P(q_1 + q_2 + \cdots + q_n) = P\sum_{i=1}^{n} q_i = PQ,$$

where

$$Q = \sum_{i=1}^{n} q_i.$$

Depending on how the variables in Equation (14–1) are defined, the equation of exchange is either an identity or an equilibrium condition. If V is defined as the residual, (PQ)/M, then the equation is properly referred to as an identity in the sense that the two sides must always be equal; on the other hand, if V is interpreted as a variable determined by certain institutional and behavioral factors, then the identity is converted into an equilibrium condition. Furthermore, if M is fixed by the monetary authorities and Q is taken as given, then Equation (14–1) can be expressed as

(14-2)
$$P = \frac{MV}{Q}.$$

In this form, the equation of exchange may be viewed as an equilibrium condition reflecting the influence of the primary factors which determine the price level in the economy.

An obvious implication of Equation (14–2) is that the price level will vary proportionately with the quantity of money in the economy. For example, consider an economy in which the authorities provide a constant money supply of $100 billion. Furthermore, suppose that 10 billion items are purchased (sold) during a given time period and that each unit of money is spent an average of four times during that period. Under these conditions, the average price level in the economy will have to be

$$\frac{(\$100 \text{ billion})(4)}{10 \text{ billion}} = \$40$$

However, if the money supply doubles to $200 billion while V and Q remain constant, then the average price level will double to $80. Thus a change in the money supply leads to a proportional change in the level of prices, and money has no permanent affect on other important economic variables such as the levels of production and employment. This relationship is the essence of earlier or crude versions of the quantity theory of money.

As we noted in Chapter 2, economists have modified the quantity theory equation presented above in order to focus on expenditures for currently produced goods and services rather than on all purchases (including financial assets and items produced in past time periods). When the focus is on currently produced goods and services, the PQ in Equation 14–2 is equivalent to nominal Gross National Product, and the equation is then referred to as the income version of the quantity theory. In this case, P must be reinterpreted as the price index of currently produced goods and services and Q as output of new goods and services.

As Fisher himself recognized, the conclusions of the quantity theory rest upon several assumptions, assumptions that he and most other economists of his time believed were generally correct. Foremost was the belief that M and V are independent; that is, changes in the money supply do not have a significant effect on the velocity of money. The importance of this condition led Fisher and other quantity theorists to study the factors that determined the velocity of money. Their conclusion was that the primary determinants of V were institutional factors such as the rapidity of transport and communication, how often workers are paid, and the extent to which credit is used. It was believed that these factors changed slowly over time and were not affected by the quantity of money in circulation.

An equally important aspect of the early quantity theory was the belief that Q, the quantity of goods and services, was fixed independently of M. At any given time, Q was determined by the available supplies of capital, natural resources, labor, and the state of technology. Furthermore, except for temporary outside or exogenous disturbances, which were assumed to be automatically corrected, Q was the full-employment level of output. However, despite charges by some critics, Fisher was not blind to the possibilities of output variations. In fact, he explicitly recognized that changes in the quantity of money could lead to temporary changes in the volume of trade (Q) as well as the velocity of money. But, he explained, such effects occurred only during "transition periods," and his interest in such temporary conditions was secondary.[5] Primary concern was focused on the permanent effects, that is, the values of the variables M, V, Q, and P, after the economy had adjusted fully to changes in the money supply. In short, he was interested in the long-run equilibrium values of the variables.

Equilibrium values are sometimes referred to as long-run values, and the quantity theorists' neglect of transitional values in order to predict long-run results has been the source of considerable criticism. Keynes's comment that "in the long run, we are all dead" emphasized the danger of ignoring the short run.

The Cambridge cash balances equation

For many years American economists following Fisher's lead couched their analysis in terms of the velocity of money; thus the natural focus of their analysis was on the rate at which money is spent and the forces that govern that rate. On the other hand, at Cambridge University in England, quantity theorists formulated

---

[5] Fisher, *Purchasing Power*, p. 161.

their analysis in a different manner, focusing their attention on the demand for money.[6] Time has proven the latter approach to be more fruitful. The Cambridge economists, under the leadership of Alfred Marshall and A. C. Pigou, developed the following equation:

$$(14-3) \qquad\qquad M = kY = kPQ.$$

Equation (14–3) is known as the Cambridge Equation, in which Y is the level of national income and is equivalent to PQ in the income version of Fisher's equation of exchange, M is the quantity of money, and k represents the proportion of money income that the public wishes to hold as money balances.

The Cambridge Equation, like Fisher's formula, is nothing more than an identity if k is interpreted as a residual in the sense that it takes on whatever value is necessary to generate equality between M and kY. However, if k is interpreted as the public's preferred or desired ratio of money balances to money income, then the Cambridge Equation is a condition for equilibrium between the supply of and demand for money, and the term kY represents the demand for money balances. In either case, k is the reciprocal of Fisher's V.

Suppose that individuals, businesses, and other economic units wish to hold money balances equal to 25 percent of their annual income; that is, $k = 0.25$. If the level of money income is $100 billion, then the aggregate amount of money that economic units wish to hold will be $25 billion according to (14–3). If the money supply equals $25 billion, then the monetary sector of the economy is in equilibrium. On the other hand, if the supply of money is $20 billion, economic units are holding smaller money balances than they desire, and the economy is out of equilibrium. Within the framework of the Cambridge Equation, the effects of money on economic activity are linked to the adjustments that occur when there is monetary disequilibrium—that is, when the supply and demand for money are not equal.

In the following sections we shall explore these adjustments, first in the context of a simple Keynesian model and then in a monetarist framework. Many of the implications and conclusions drawn by Pigou and others from the Cambridge version of the quantity theory were essentially the same as those drawn by Fisher from his version. However, the Cambridge approach concentrates attention on the behavioral factors that determine an economic unit's demand for money; money is viewed as performing services that generate utility. Therefore, as a useful good, money has its own demand function. By

---

[6] A. C. Pigou, "The Value of Money," *Quarterly Journal of Economics*, vol. 32 (December 1917), pp. 38–65.

drawing attention to the demand for money, the Cambridge Equation led to important developments in monetary theory.

Like Fisher, the Cambridge economists believed that money-supply changes had no permanent effects on k or Q; hence, the permanent effect of such changes was a proportional change in prices. The Cambridge k, like V, was assumed to be determined by factors such as the length of salary and wage payment periods and the extent of credit use. Yet the Cambridge economists recognized that expectations regarding prices and returns on investments could also affect k. Consequently, k was viewed as somewhat less rigid than V, and the Cambridge approach resulted in less emphasis on strict proportionality between money and prices than did Fisher's approach.

HOW DO CHANGES IN THE MONEY SUPPLY AFFECT ECONOMIC ACTIVITY IN THE BASIC KEYNESIAN MODEL?

John Maynard Keynes was one of the economists associated with the Cambridge Equation version of the quantity theory. However, as Keynes's ideas developed and emerged in his famous 1936 work, *The General Theory of Employment, Interest, and Money,* he ignited a revolution in economic theory in general, and monetary theory in particular. In the *General Theory,* Keynes dropped many of the assumptions of the quantity theorists and dealt a death blow to the idea that the primary impact of a change in the money supply was invariably a proportional change in prices. The demand for money, or *liquidity preference* as he called it, as well as the money supply were recognized as important economic variables that could influence not only the price level but the levels of output and employment as well.

Writing in the midst of the Great Depression, Keynes was particularly interested in such economic variables as output and employment, which most earlier economists had ignored by assuming that the economy would automatically and quickly adjust to any deviations from the full-employment level of output. Recall from Chapter 13 that Keynes emphasized the role of aggregate demand—the sum of consumption, investment, and government spending—as the major determinant of changes in the level of economic activity. According to Keynes, consumption spending was largely determined by the level of income and what he called the propensity to consume; government spending was policy determined; and investment spending was governed by expected returns (the *marginal efficiency of capital* in Keynes's terminology) and the interest rate. Moreover, the money supply could affect aggregate demand by influencing interest rates, which in turn influenced investment spending. Consequently, through aggregate demand, money could affect not only prices but important real variables such as output and employment as well. The linkage between money and economic activity in the basic Keynesian model is illustrated in Figure 14–1.

Keynes's view that money could be an important determinant of more than just the price level was indeed revolutionary; ironically, however, this idea subsequently gave birth to the belief that monetary policy was an impotent weapon in the battle against declines in employment and output. Nevertheless, it was Keynes's ideas that provided the foundation for subsequent developments in monetary theory. For our purposes the most important of these ideas was his demand for money function.

The demand for money

As noted earlier the Cambridge Equation had begun to direct attention toward the demand for money. Keynes, however, examined the demand for money in much more detail than had his predecessors. As the basis for his analysis, Keynes identified three general motives for holding money balances; he called them the transactions motive, the precautionary motive, and the speculative motive.

Transactions demand. The primary function of money is to serve as a medium of exchange; the more transactions (exchanges) to

FIGURE 14–1
Major linkages in the basic Keynesian model

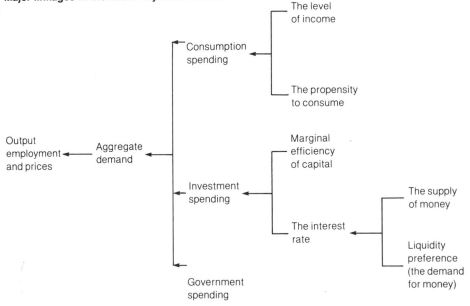

be engaged in, the more money that will be needed. Thus at least part of the demand for money can be traced to a desire or plan to make purchases or engage in transactions. The fact that money serves as a medium of exchange is not sufficient to ensure a transactions demand; transactions demand results when receipts of income and purchases of goods and services do not coincide. Since it is impossible to switch immediately and costlessly between money and interest-earning liquid assets, there is of necessity an interval of time during which economic units must hold money they intend to use for transactions purposes. Thus it is this gap between the receipt of money income and the expenditures for goods, services, or assets that necessitates the holding of transactions balances.

The transactions demand for money is a function of such factors as the timing and mode of payments in the economy, the level of income or the volume of transactions to be undertaken, the level of prices, and other, less-important factors. The transactions motive of Keynes was nothing new; it was essentially the same motive described as basic by Fisher and the Cambridge quantity theorists. Like his predecessors, Keynes believed that the transactions demand for money was proportional to the level of income.[7]

Precautionary demand. Keynes argued that a second motive for holding money was the precautionary motive, stemming from a desire to be prepared for emergencies. The possibilities of such unpredictable events as loss of a job, permanent disability, illness, or financial reverses are reasons for holding precautionary money balances. Keynes believed that the main determinant of the amount of money held to satisfy the precautionary motive was the level of income. Hence, Keynes's identification of the precautionary demand did little to expand monetary theory beyond the earlier developments of the quantity theorists.

Speculative demand. Both the transactions demand and the precautionary demand for money balances arise when money is being held to perform the medium-of-exchange function, and money held for this purpose is sometimes referred to as active balances. Economic units have no choice but to hold money if they want a medium of exchange, but money is not unique in its capacity to perform the store-of-value function. In fact, as a store of value, money typically is inferior to several other kinds of assets in terms of

---

[7] In subsequent years Keynesians have made the case that the transactions demand for money depends in an important way on interest rates; see William J. Baumol, "The Transactions Demand for Cash: An Inventory Theoretic Approach," *Quarterly Journal of Economics,* vol. 66 (November 1952), pp. 545–56. Also, see James Tobin, "The Interest Elasticity of the Transactions Demand for Cash," *Review of Economics and Statistics,* vol. 38 (August 1956), pp. 241–47.

yield. In some respects, however, money may be a superior store of value, thereby generating what is sometimes referred to as the asset demand for money or the demand for idle money balances. Keynes referred to this motive for holding money as the speculative motive.

The speculative demand for money arises out of the desire to avoid losses on those assets whose money prices are expected to fall. In particular Keynes argued that the possibility of fluctuations in bond prices greatly influenced the demand for money. Recall from Chapter 6 that there is an inverse relationship between bond prices and interest rates; rising interest rates tend to drive bond prices down and vice versa. Keynes reasoned that expectations of rising interest rates (falling bond prices) would induce investors to hold money instead of bonds; that is, under such circumstances economic units would prefer to store value in liquid form. Thus Keynes reasoned that there is a speculative demand for money, a preference for liquidity, that is related to interest rates in the following manner:

| High interest rates | → | Expectations that interest rates will fall (that bond prices will rise) | → | Investors attempt to move out of money into bonds, |
| Low interest rates | → | Expectations that interest rates will rise (that bond prices will fall) | → | Investors attempt to move out of bonds into money. |

Because of the influence of interest rates on the speculative demand for money, Keynes viewed the total demand for money as inversely related to interest rates.[8] In subsequent years, the relationship between the demand for money and interest rates became one of the most important and controversial issues in monetary theory.

The foregoing summary is a simplification of the richness and complexity of Keynes's analysis, but it contains the essential elements that are needed to trace the Keynesian view of the effect of money on economic activity. A major contribution of Keynes was the idea that the demand for money is a function of interest rates as well as the level of income. In short, a simplified version of the Keynesian money demand function (liquidity preference function) can be written as follows:

$$(14\text{-}4) \qquad\qquad M_d = kY + g(i)$$

---

[8] While Keynes's formulation of the speculative demand for money was dependent on the idea of normal levels of interest rates and expectations about future rates, James Tobin has shown that the demand for money can be a function of interest rates even when there are no expectations of above- or below-normal rates. See James Tobin, "Liquidity Preference as Behavior towards Risk," *Review of Economic Studies*, vol. 25 (February 1958), pp. 65–86.

FIGURE 14-2
Keynesian demand for money function

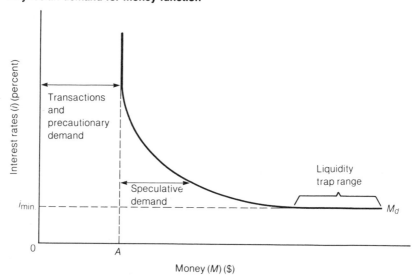

where Y is the level of money income; k is the proportion of income that economic units desire to hold in money form; i is the interest rate; and $g(i)$ denotes an unspecified inverse relationship between interest rates and the demand for money. Thus the demand for money is proportional to the level of income (Y) and inversely related to interest rates. A graphic representation of the Keynesian demand for money function is shown in Figure 14-2.

In Figure 14-2, the demand for money balances is shown as increasing when the interest rate falls. Part of the total demand for money—the transactions and precautionary components—is determined by the level of income, not the interest rate, and this amount is not affected by interest rate changes. Transactions and precautionary demand are depicted as the distance $0A$ in Figure 14-2. The horizontal difference between $0A$ and the M_d curve reflects the speculative demand and indicates that falling interest rates increase the speculative demand for money balances.

Keynes believed that the money demand curve became flat (infinitely interest elastic) at some very low rate of interest; he referred to this situation as a *liquidity trap*. If the economy is in a liquidity trap, economic units will hoard any additions to the money supply. No one expects the interest rate to fall further; therefore, everyone anticipates falling bond prices and prefers to hold additional money rather than purchase bonds. While the liquidity trap has been the subject of much discussion by economists, a considerable body of empirical work has cast doubt upon its existence.[9]

The effects of money-supply changes

By making the demand for money a function of interest rates, Keynes invalidated the quantity theory, or at least those versions that made prices proportional to the quantity of money. Money became a variable that affects not only prices but interest rates as well; in fact, Keynes's demand-for-money function led to a new theory of interest rates—the liquidity preference theory. Monetary equilibrium requires that the money balances demanded be equal to the supply of money. If the money supply is treated as a policy-determined constant, then equilibrium in the monetary sector can be depicted by a graph of money supply and money demand as in Figure 14–3.

Given fixed levels of income and a money supply of M_s, the amount of money balances that economic units wish to hold will be equal to the supply of money only if the interest rate is equal to i_0. If the monetary authorities increased the money supply to M'_s, interest rates would have to fall to i' before monetary equilibrium could be reestablished. At the original interest rate, i_0, economic units would be holding more money balances than they desired. As long as income did not change, there would be no need for additional transactions balances. Thus those economic units with excess money balances could respond by purchasing bonds (or other financial assets). Collectively, this response would be unsuccessful since it merely transfers money balances without reducing the total. The additional demand for bonds would, however, drive bond prices up and yields (interest rates) down.

The process cannot end here, however. By linking money demand to interest rates, Keynes also linked money-supply changes to other economic variables. In particular, investment spending, the I_d portion of the $C + I_d + G$ aggregate demand function of Chapter 13, is affected by interest rates. Keynes believed that capital investment spending by business occurred whenever the expected yield on capital (the *marginal efficiency of capital*) exceeded the rate of interest. When the monetary authorities increase the money supply, and thus drive interest rates down, more and more investment projects become profitable, and the amount of investment spending in-

---

[9] A summary of these works can be found in Thomas M. Havrilesky and John T. Boorman, *Monetary Macroeconomics* (Arlington Heights, Ill.: AHM Publishing Co., 1978), pp. 195–99.

FIGURE 14–3
Keynesian view of monetary equilibrium

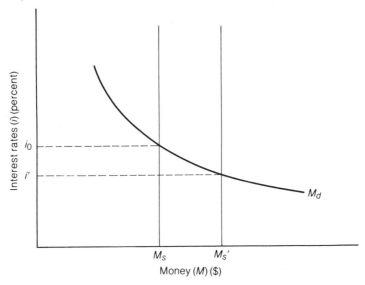

creases. Thus money-supply changes stimulate aggregate demand, which in turn stimulates output, employment, and perhaps prices.

The consequences of a money-supply change such as that depicted in Figure 14–3 are shown in Figure 14–4. The initial effect of the increased money supply is to lower interest rates, to say i_1. At that rate, M_d is equal to the larger money supply M'_s; however, the lower interest rate will stimulate investment and, therefore, aggregate demand. Consequently, the level of income rises, say from Y_0 to Y_2, which produces a need for more transactions balances. Over time, this increased transactions demand will shift the total money-demand function to M'_d which reflects the use of more money balances for transaction purposes at a higher level of income, Y_2. Thus the interest rate i_1 cannot be maintained since, as M_d shifts toward M'_d, money demand will exceed money supply. Excess demand for money will be corrected as bondholders sell bonds, thereby driving bond prices down and interest rates up. Ultimately equilibrium will be restored at interest rate i_2.

Thus as Keynes saw the monetary economy, the interest rate is the variable by which the effects of changes in the money supply are transmitted to the real sector of the economy—to output and employment. Furthermore, by making the demand for money at least partially dependent upon interest rates, Keynes raised a serious

FIGURE 14-4
Effect of changes in money supply

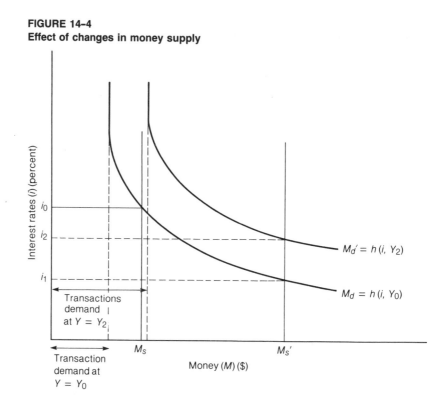

question about the short-run stability of velocity.[10] Money was no longer a neutral variable that affected only the price level. The quantity theory of money, at least in its earlier and simpler form, was dealt a serious intellectual blow. It would be difficult to continue to argue that changes in M would not be accompanied by changes in V and Q as well as P.

The implications of Keynes's work went even further; his belief that the demand curve for money became flatter or more interest elastic at lower interest rates (and could possibly approach a liquidity trap) cast doubt upon the effectiveness of monetary policy as a weapon against a deep recession. To be effective, Keynes felt, money-supply increases had to lower interest rates and stimulate

---

[10] To see this, substitute the demand for money function, $M_d = kY + g(i)$, into the monetary sector equilibrium condition, $M = M_d$. Substituting the result for M in Fisher's version of quantity theory and solving for V, the result is

$$(kY + g(i)) V = PQ, \text{ or } V = \frac{PQ}{kY + g(i)}.$$

Hence, V now depends on interest rates.

investment, but even massive doses of new money were likely to be ineffective under conditions such as those existing in the Great Depression when rates were already very low.

Another implication of Keynes's analysis was the elevation of the government budget to the position of primary policy instrument in the battle against economic instability. Given the possibility that monetary policy was weak or useless during a deep recession, a more effective method of increasing aggregate demand seemed to be an increase in government spending unaccompanied by tax increases. Similar results could also be achieved by cutting taxes (thus increasing consumption spending) while holding the level of government expenditures constant. Either approach called for deficit financing. Thus the major burden of managing the macroeconomy was assigned to the administration and Congress via fiscal policy. The era of large, uninterrupted deficits was born.

WHAT ARE THE CHANNELS OF MONETARY INFLUENCE ACCORDING TO THE MONETARISTS?

The Keynesian view of the links between money and economic activity emphasizes that the major transmission of monetary sector disturbances (disequilibrium between the demand and supply of money) occurs through interest rates in the following manner:

Monetary disturbance $(M_d \gtrless M_s)$ $\rightarrow$ Interest rate changes $\rightarrow$ Investment spending changes $\rightarrow$ Aggregate demand changes $\rightarrow$ Output, employment, and/or price changes.

While followers of Keynes have refined and extended his basic model, another group of economists known as monetarists have also contributed to the theory of how money works. The monetarists' model is in some respects less definite than the basic Keynesian model. As Thomas Mayer puts it,

. . . monetarism is not a clear-cut doctrine set forth in one particular place; it has no General Theory. Indeed it comprises a set of propositions held to a greater or lesser extent by a group of economists who are far from forming a monolithic school.[11]

As with the Keynesian model, we shall not attempt to cover all the facets of monetarism; rather, our focus here will continue to be the mechanism(s) linking money to economic activity. The works of Milton Friedman are often cited as representative of the monetarist

---

[11] Thomas Mayer, The Structure of Monetarism (New York: W. W. Norton & Co., 1978), p. i.

position; however, as Mayer's statement attests, there are many variants of monetarism, some of which are not always consistent with positions taken by Friedman.[12] Friedman's work has been very controversial, and a number of his conclusions have been sharply disputed. There is general consensus, however, that Friedman's original approach to formulating the demand-for-money function was an important advancement in monetary economics which established the foundation for subsequent developments in monetarist doctrine.

Friedman treated the demand for money in a manner similar to that used by economists in analyzing the demand for other goods. He focused attention not on the motives for holding money but on the variables that affect the amount of money economic units wish to hold. Friedman's demand-for-money function was the most detailed developed to that time. Like Keynes, he recognized that interest rates should have an effect on the demand for money (although in later work, he denied the importance of interest rates on empirical grounds). Unlike earlier quantity theorists, he emphasized wealth over income as a primary determinant of money demand; moreover, his wealth variable was complex and included the capitalized value of human labor or what he referred to as human wealth. The rates of return on capital goods or equities and the rate of price change were also included as variables affecting the demand for money.[13]

A very important implication of Friedman's formulation of the demand for money is that money is a substitute for a relatively wide range of assets, and that relative yields on a broad range of assets are important in transmitting monetary disturbances to the rest of the economy. According to Friedman, for money to influence economic activity, its effects do not have to be transmitted through the relatively narrow Keynesian channel of interest rates to investment spending to aggregate demand. Other monetarists have also emphasized the relatively broad channels through which monetary impulses are transmitted, and even Keynesians have extended the basic Keynesian model, many times in ways parallel to the monetarists', so that today there is a much better, though more complex, understanding of how money works. Today most monetarists and Keynesians believe that monetary disturbances can affect the economy through several channels, the most important being the relative-price (or portfolio balance) and the wealth-effect channels.

---

[12] The most cited statement of Friedman's view of the demand for money is found in his "The Quantity Theory of Money: A Restatement," in Milton Friedman, ed., *Studies in the Quantity Theory of Money* (Chicago: University of Chicago Press, 1956), pp. 1–21.

[13] Ibid.

None of these channels are as obvious as the basic Keynesian money-interest rate-investment spending channel discussed earlier. Nevertheless, there is widespread agreement among economists that monetary disturbances operate through these channels.

The relative-price channel

The term *relative price* refers to the ratio of one price to another. It is important to remember that there is an inverse relationship between the market price of any income-producing asset and the return or yield on that asset. If the prices of such assets rise, yields fall; likewise, a rise in yields is accompanied by a fall in price.[14] In the discussion that follows, the terms *relative price* and *relative yield* are often used interchangeably.

To understand how the relative-price mechanism transmits monetary impulses throughout the economy, consider an economic unit that has elected to hold wealth in several forms: money, short-term financial assets such as corporate and government bonds, common stocks, direct ownership of real capital goods such as businesses, and durable and nondurable consumer goods.

The proportions of each type of asset held by each economic unit are not random variables; rather each economic unit holds a portfolio that balances the expected returns and risks from each asset at the margin, In other words, when the economy is in equilibrium, each economic unit believes that it has achieved an optimum asset mix. When all portfolios are in balance, the marginal returns, adjusted for risk, are the same for each type of asset in the portfolio. If this were not the case, it would be rational for economic units to adjust their portfolios. For example, if the expected yield from holding additional Treasury bills (adjusted for any additional risk) exceeds the expected "yield" from holding money balances, economic units will switch some wealth out of money form and into Treasury bills. Therfore, portfolio balance implies that all economic units are holding desired proportions of the various assets denoted earlier.

Let us assume that the money supply is increased so that the quantity of money supplied is greater than the existing demand. The initial effect of monetary disequilibrium is to disturb the portfolio balance of economic units. Given the existing levels of prices, income, wealth, and the marginal returns on various wealth forms,

---

[14] This is most obvious in the case of bonds (see the bond example in Chapter 6), but it applies to all other assets that generate income streams.

economic units now hold excess money balances; portfolios are out of balance. At the individual level, adjustments can be made by converting excess money balances into competing wealth forms such as bonds, stocks, real capital, and consumer durable or nondurable goods. The monetarists envision a chain of events similar to that depicted in Figure 14–5.

Attempts by individual economic units to restore equilibrium to their portfolios will only shift the excess money balances rather than removing them from the economy as a whole; that is, the nominal money supply cannot be reduced. However, the attempts by individual economic units to dispose of their own excess balances initiates a process of portfolio adjustment that leads to falling yields and rising asset prices. If, for example, some economic units use their excess money balances to purchase Treasury bills, such purchases will cause Treasury bill prices to rise and yields to fall. Other economic units may now be dissatisfied with the relatively lower yields on bills and may seek higher yields by purchasing long-term government bonds, commercial paper, corporate bonds, or municipal securities.

As investors shift into these assets, their prices rise (yields fall), and the process will spread; for example, as stock prices rise, investors shift funds into equities to obtain capital gains. The combination of falling bond rates and rising stock prices will make it easier for companies to finance new investment projects, and capital spending will rise. Some economic units will dispose of their excess money

FIGURE 14–5
Effects of excess supply of money as transmitted through the relative price channel: A monetarist view

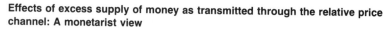
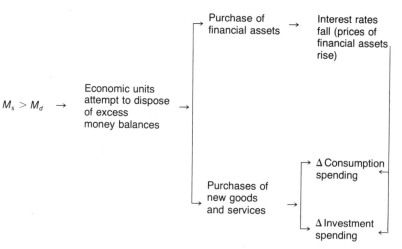

balances and financial assets by purchasing consumer goods. Before the chain reaction ends, the effects of the excess money supply will be transmitted into all sectors of the economy, thus causing aggregate demand to increase which, in turn, causes output, employment, and perhaps prices to rise.

The preceding survey is a general summary of how monetarists see changes in the money supply as affecting economic activity through the relative-price channel or portfolio adjustment mechanism. It should be emphasized, however, that this adjustment process is very much akin to the neo-Keynesian adjustment mechanism in which interest rate changes play a key role in spreading the effects of money-supply changes.[15] Furthermore, prominent Keynesian economists have made important theoretical contributions in the area of analyzing the portfolio process.[16]

Thus monetarists and Keynesians do not differ drastically in their views of the broad elements of the monetary adjustment process. On the other hand, important differences do exist, especially with respect to the uniqueness of money in the process. Keynesians stress that an increase (decrease) in the supply of any asset will initiate a portfolio adjustment process which may affect economic activity, and that the effects of money are not unique. Monetarists would tend to agree with this in principle but would stress that changes in the supply of (demand for) other assets are unlikely to occur independently of changes in the supply of money; thus, to monetarists, money is the central variable in the economy and should therefore receive the bulk of attention. In terms of Figure 14-4, monetarists would have more confidence than Keynesians in the existence of the linkage between money and consumer spending. Other key differences between these two groups will be addressed in more detail in subsequent sections.

The wealth-effect channel

Another channel through which monetary actions may affect economic activity is the wealth-effect channel through which monetary disequilibrium alters the wealth of economic units, thereby influencing their spending. Three ways have been identified by which monetary disturbances may affect wealth: They are through (1) the

---

[15] Warren L. Smith, "A Neo-Keynesian View of Monetary Policy," in Federal Reserve Bank of Boston, *Controlling Monetary Aggregates*, Proceedings of a conference held in June 1969 (Boston; 1969), pp. 105–26.

[16] James Tobin, a neo-Keynesian, is responsible for much of the work on the portfolio balance approach. See James Tobin, "Money, Capital, and Other Stores of Value," *American Economic Review*, vol. 51, no. 2 (May 1961), pp. 26–37.

value of equities, (2) the value of debt, and (3) the value of real balances.

The net wealth of the private sector is viewed as a variable that influences aggregate demand, particularly the consumption component. Net private wealth (excluding human wealth) is generally thought to be comprised of three components:

1. The value of equities or titles to the existing stock of real capital.
2. That part of the money supply which is not a liability of private-sector economic units.
3. The market value of outstanding government debt to the extent that the public does not consider the debt a liability in the form of future taxes.

Since monetary disturbances may affect these wealth components, they are the basis of the wealth-effect channel of monetary influence.

Equities effect.　Equities are securities that represent an ownership interest in the income streams generated by real capital. We noted earlier that money-supply changes are likely to initiate a portfolio adjustment process by economic units. The substitutions that occur because of relative price and yield changes can affect the prices of equity securities. For example, if the supply of money is less than the demand for money and economic units attempt to increase their money balances by selling debt instruments, the prices of bonds will fall (yields will rise). Since debt instruments and equities are to some extent substitute forms of holding wealth, the higher yields on debt instruments will cause a shift out of stocks and into bonds. This will drive stock prices down, resulting in decreases in wealth for stockholders. The decline in wealth will decrease consumption, according to proponents of this view, since wealth is one of the variables in the consumption function. The lower stock prices may also affect aggregate demand by decreasing capital spending. Companies that had planned to finance new investment by issuing stocks are likely to abandon or postpone planned projects until more favorable market conditions prevail. The opposite set of reactions would occur if there were an excess of money balances in the economy.[17]

Debt effects.　Wealth effects arising out of changes in outstanding government debt will occur if members of the public ignore the

---

[17] There is some empirical evidence that the equities effect has a significant influence on economic activity. See Frank DeLeeuw and Edward M. Gramlich, "The Channels of Monetary Policy," *Federal Reserve Bulletin*, vol. 55 (June 1969), pp. 472–91. Also, see Franco Modigliani, "Monetary Policy and Consumption: Linkages via the Interest Rate and Wealth Effects in the FMP Model," in Federal Reserve Bank of Boston, *Consumer Spending and Monetary Policy: The Linkages*, Proceedings of a conference held in June 1971 (Boston: Federal Reserve Bank of Boston, 1971), pp. 9–84.

fact that they are implicitly liable (in the form of future taxes) for the outstanding government securities. Note that the important consideration here is not whether future taxes will ever be levied or whether the debt will ever be repaid but whether individual economic units view their proportionate share of the debt as a liability on their balance sheets. To the extent that they do not, the market value of publicly held government debt constitutes part of private sector net wealth.

Net wealth in the form of government debt is altered by the effects monetary actions have on interest rates. If increases in the money supply drive interest rates down, bond prices rise, and holders of government securities feel wealthier; consequently, they increase their spending. The opposite effects occur if the money supply is increased. Thus there is an interest-induced wealth effect (via government debt) on consumption.

Real-balance effect. Real balances are nominal balances divided by the price index. The real-balance effect was the first of the wealth effects developed as a link between money and economic activity and was initially called the Pigou effect because the English economist A. C. Pigou (noted earlier in connection with his work on the Cambridge version of the quantity theory) was the first to postulate that one component of wealth that affected consumption spending was the real-money balances of economic units. Real balances will increase if the money supply increases faster than prices or if prices fall while the nominal money supply remains unchanged. Thus if the authorities increase the money supply and prices remain constant or increase less than proportionally, real money balances, and hence wealth, will increase. This increase in wealth will stimulate consumption spending and cause aggregate demand and economic activity to increase.

Only a portion of the money supply is included in total net wealth. Part of the money supply, demand deposits (or some near-money items depending on the definition of money), is wealth to the owners and at the same time a liability of the issuer.[18] Thus real-balance effects can be generated only through changes (relative to the price level) in that part of the country's money supply that is not a debt of economic units in the private sector—that is, only through privately held, government-issued money.

The real-balance effect is not thought to be important by most

---

[18] It can be argued that demand deposits are a non-interest-bearing liability of the bank and its stockholders; therefore, an increase in demand deposits will increase the wealth of the bank's owners. Under such circumstances, the demand deposit component of the money supply may transmit a wealth effect. See Boris P. Pesek and Thomas M. Saving, *Money, Wealth, and Economic Activity* (New York: Macmillan, 1967), chap. 4.

economists and has probably generated theoretical interest out of proportion to its practical implications. As a theoretical construct, the real-balance effect allowed non-Keynesians to refute the Keynesian idea that the economy could remain in equilibrium at less than full employment even if prices and wages were flexible. Given flexible prices and wages in an economy with substantial unemployment, the real value of existing money balances will rise and generate a wealth effect capable of eventually stimulating aggregate demand and restoring full employment.

HOW IS EQUILIBRIUM IN THE MONETARY SECTOR DETERMINED?

The process of attaining equilibrium: An example

Let us briefly look at a case of monetary disequilibrium, at the resulting effects on economic activity, at how equilibrium is restored, and at the major aspects of the process on which monetarists and Keynesians are likely to disagree. Suppose the quantity of money in the economy exceeds the amount of money balances demanded and that the demand for money is a function of wealth (W), prices (P), rates of return on various financial assets (r_f), and the return on real capital (r_k). In short,

$$(14-6) \qquad M_d = h(W, P, r_f, r_k).$$

The demand for money is positively related to the wealth and price variables, and inversely related to the interest rate or yield variables. With an excess supply of money, both Keynesians and monetarists would expect economic units to shift out of money, but collectively this is impossible if the monetary authorities maintain the higher nominal money supply permanently. The attempts to reduce money balances will cause economic units to rearrange their portfolios which will initiate the adjustment process.

The resulting portfolio adjustments and their consequences were described earlier and will only be summarized here. The initial effects will occur in the money market as yields begin to fall and prices rise; these changes will be transmitted to longer-term securities and to equities; banks will be willing to lend more, and borrowers will be willing to borrow more; and wealth effects will be generated that will increase consumption. Consequently aggregate demand will rise and production, income, employment, and prices will subsequently increase.

As the above events transpire, equilibrium between the amount of real money balances demanded and supplied will be restored. How? The initial decline in interest rates will cause some increase in the demand for money which will be reinforced by the increases in income and wealth. To the extent that price increases occur, they will reduce the real money supply. Eventually as a result of all of these reactions, equilibrium in the monetary sector will be restored.

Several versions of the preceding scenario are possible. The specific results of monetary disequilibrium will depend on initial conditions in the economy, that is, the extent of excess capacity and unemployment, expectations about price changes, investor optimism and pessimism, the influences of international economic transactions and economic conditions abroad, feedback effects from the real sector to the monetary sector, and the manner in which the excess money balances are initially injected into the economy. At this point, however, we want to focus on one aspect of the adjustment process that is crucial to some of the key differences between Keynesians and monetarists—the interest elasticity of the demand for money.

Interest elasticity of the demand for money

The interest elasticity of the demand for money refers to the sensitivity of the demand for money to interest rate changes. The more that the demand for money changes in response to interest rate changes, the greater the interest elasticity. More precisely, the interest elasticity of the demand for money is the ratio of the percentage change in the demand for money to a percentage change in interest rates. For example, if the interest elasticity is -0.5, then an increase of, say, 20 percent in interest rates results in a 10 percent decrease in money balances demanded. A negative value for the interest elasticity of money, such as was indicated above, indicates that the demand for money changes in the direction opposite to changes in interest rates.

To understand why the interest elasticity of the demand for money is so important, consider the above example, in which monetary equilibrium was restored after the stock of money exceeded the quantity demanded. Suppose that the demand for money is highly interest elastic (the Keynesian liquidity trap would be the extreme of such a situation). Recall that an initial effect of the excess money balances is a decline in interest rates. With a highly interest elastic demand for money, it will only require a small drop in interest rates to induce economic units to hold the excess money balances. Consequently, when the adjustment to monetary disequilibrium is complete, most of the effect will have occurred in the financial sector; aggregate demand and, hence, production, income, and employment will be affected very little or perhaps not at all.

Now suppose that the interest elasticity is very small or even zero, an extreme position attributed to some monetarists including Friedman. Again consider our case of monetary disequilibrium in which there is an excess of money. Even if the resulting transactions by economic units have a considerable impact on interest rates, there will be little effect on the amount of money balances demanded. Only after the adjustment has spread to the real sector (and economic activity has increased so as to increase income, wealth, and/or prices) will the amount of money demanded increase so as to eliminate the excess supply of money balances and restore equilibrium. Under such conditions, money supply changes have a powerful effect on economic activity with most of the adjustment to monetary disequilibrium occurring in the real sector. Whether the final effects are increased production and employment or increased prices depends upon the degree of excess capacity, expectations, and other factors.

The degree of interest elasticity of the demand for money is of course an empirical question, and a considerable body of evidence has been gathered concerning this question. On some points, the evidence is clear; for example, the demand for money is sensitive to interest rate changes. However, the degree of measured responsiveness varies with how money is defined and with the interest rate(s) used. Studies also suggest that the relationship between money and interest rates is relatively stable over time.[19] However, there are many statistical difficulties encountered in demand-for-money studies, and much work remains to be done in this area.

SUMMARY

Early economists viewing the relationship between money and economic activity came to the conclusion that the primary role of money was to serve as a medium of exchange. The store-of-value function of money was given little consideration, and money was thought to have no effect on such real variables as the levels of production and employment. The essence of the dominant early view of the role of money was captured by the quantity theory of money as set forth by Irving Fisher in the United States and a group of English economists working at Cambridge University. Fisher emphasized the velocity of money, while the Cambridge economists made an important contribution by turning attention toward the

---

[19] A good summary of empirical work on the demand for money is found in David E. W. Laidler, *The Demand for Money: Theories and Evidence*, 2d ed. (New York: Dun-Donnelley, 1977), pp. 101–52.

holding of money. Both believed that, except during "transitional periods," a change in the money supply would lead to a proportional change in prices.

That at least some elements of the quantity theory of money were unsatisfactory was evident in the Great Depression of the 1930s. The shortcomings of the quantity theory were highlighted in the work of Keynes as he focused attention on the components of aggregate demand and their determinants. Keynes extended our understanding of the role of money in the economy and, particularly, its role as a store of value. According to Keynes, the interest rate influences the demand for money; furthermore, by affecting interest rates, changes in the supply of money could affect the level of employment and output in the economy.

Followers of Keynes as well as the monetarists (intellectual descendants of the quantity theorists) extended Keynes's work on the demand for money and the connection between money and economic activity. As a result of these efforts, economists now believe there are several channels through which money may affect economic activity.

In recent years, differences between monetarists and Keynesians have narrowed: both schools of thought argue that money matters; neither school believes that money affects only prices, or that prices always vary in proportion to changes in the money supply; both argue that the demand for money is influenced by interest rates and that interest rates are part of the mechanism by which monetary disturbances are transmitted to the real sector. Yet important differences remain: monetarists tend to believe that monetary policy is more potent than fiscal policy in the short run, but that in the long run neither is able to cause permanent changes in the level of employment. Keynesians are not confident that the nominal money supply can be controlled within narrow limits by the monetary authorities, while monetarists are likely to feel that the authorities can control the nominal supply very closely. These differences continue to lead to disputes between the two groups with respect to many policy questions.

REVIEW QUESTIONS

1. What is the relationship between k in the Cambridge version of the quantity theory and velocity in Fisher's version?
2. Given: (1) $MV = PQ$; (2) the demand for money is a function of both income and interest rates, $M_d = h(Y,i)$; and (3) equilibrium requires that the money supply, M_s, equal money balances demanded, M_d. Explain why prices will not always vary in proportion to the supply of money.

3. How does the relative-price channel operate to transmit monetary disturbances to aggregate demand?

4. Why is the interest elasticity of the demand for money so important?

5. What is the real-balance effect, and how might it transmit an increase in the money supply into an increase in output and employment?

6. If the money supply exceeds the quantity of money demanded, explain how equilibrium in the monetary sector would be restored in the basic Keynesian model? In a monetarist model?

SUGGESTIONS FOR ADDITIONAL READING

DeLeeuw, Frank, and Gramlich, Edward M. "The Channels of Monetary Policy." *Federal Reserve Bulletin,* vol. 55, no. 6 (June 1969), pp. 472–91.

Fisher, Irving. *The Purchasing Power of Money.* New York: Macmillan, 1911.

Friedman, Milton. "The Quantity Theory of Money: A Restatement." In Milton Friedman, ed., *Studies in the Quantity Theory of Money.* Chicago: University of Chicago Press, 1952, pp. 3–21.

Keynes, John Maynard. *The General Theory of Employment, Interest, and Money.* New York: Harcourt, Brace & World, 1936.

Laidler, David E. W. *The Demand for Money: Theories and Evidence.* 2d ed. New York: Dun-Donnelley, 1977.

Smith, Warren L. "A Neo-Keynesian View of Monetary Policy." in Federal Reserve Bank of Boston, *Controlling Monetary Aggregates,* (proceedings of a conference held in June 1969), Boston, 1969, pp. 105–17.

15

The IS-LM framework: A macroeconomic model with money

WARM-UP: *Outline and questions to consider as you read*

What is the IS curve?
    Derivation of the IS curve.
    Shifts in the IS curve.
What is the LM curve?
    Derivation of the LM curve.
    Shifts in the LM curve.
IS-LM equilibrium: What does it mean?
How are policy changes reflected in the IS-LM
    system?
    Monetary policy.
    Fiscal policy.
    Monetarist and Keynesian special cases.
What does the IS-LM model tell us about the
    process of inflation?

NEW TERMS

Comparative statics model: a model that can be used to solve for equilibrium values at given points in time yet which is essentially timeless in that the adjustment process and its speed are not described.

Crowding-out effect: the hypothesis that an increase in government spending under certain conditions tends to be offset by a reduction in spending in the private sector.

Government budget constraint: the fact that government expenditures must be financed either by printing money, issuing bonds, or collecting taxes.

IS curve: a curve depicting those interest rate-GNP combinations which would produce product-sector equilibrium.

IS-LM equilibrium: the particular interest rate-GNP combination that produces simultaneous equilibrium in both the product and monetary sectors.

LM curve: a curve depicting those interest rate-GNP combinations which would produce monetary-sector equilibrium.

In Chapter 13 we constructed a simple Keynesian model known as a $C + I + G$ model because aggregate demand, which is composed of consumption (C), desired investment (I_d), and government purchases of new goods and services (G), determines equilibrium aggregate supply (GNP). The $C + I + G$ model has several deficiencies, among them the absence of a monetary sector. In Chapter 14 we analyzed the role of money in the macroeconomy, paying particular attention to Keynesian and monetarist differences. Part of the discussion about money and aggregate economic activity showed how monetary influences are transmitted to the real sector. In this chapter we present a more formal integration of the product and monetary sectors that is basically a Keynesian system known as the IS-LM model.

The first step in the derivation of the IS-LM system is to modify the $C + I + G$ framework by changing investment from an exogenous variable to a function of the interest rate which thereby transforms the unique equilibrium solution of the $C + I + G$ model into a function expressing numerous product sector equilibria. Next, a monetary-sector equilibrium function is obtained, and then the monetary and product sectors are integrated to form a determinate system. Subsequently, there is an analysis of how the effects of monetary and fiscal policy actions are portrayed by the IS-LM model.[1]

WHAT IS THE *IS* CURVE?

In the $C + I + G$ model, equilibrium is said to exist when aggregate demand and total production are equal (unintended inventory

---

[1] We continue to assume that the economy is closed to foreign trade. Also, in most of this chapter, price-level changes are kept in the background; however, in the final section inflation is considered in the context of the IS-LM framework, and later, in Chapters 17 and 18, inflation is analyzed in detail.

change (I_u) is zero); the expanded model developed in this chapter retains this concept of product-sector equilibrium. However, when investment is changed from an exogenous variable to a function of the interest rate, the depiction of product-sector equilibrium becomes somewhat more involved.

We observed in Chapters 13 and 14 that investment is influenced by interest rates, though other forces such as the state of business confidence frequently swamp the effect of interest rates on investment spending and make the interest rate-investment function unstable. Thus while it is an improvement to introduce an interest rate-investment relationship of the form

$$(15\text{--}1) \qquad\qquad I_d = g(i),$$

the results are by no means completely satisfactory. Figure 15–1 shows an interest rate–investment function of the form denoted by Equation (15–1) which uses the functional notation g to indicate that investment and interest rates are inversely related. Thus, at high rates of interest such as i_2, investment spending is low (I_{d_2}), while at lower interest rates $(i_1$ or $i_0)$, it is greater $(I_{d_1}$ or $I_{d_0})$. With an interest rate-investment relation that is unstable, the curve will frequently shift; if the business community became more optimistic, the function would shift outward, and at a given interest rate, investment would be greater, while the reverse would be true if the state of business confidence declined.

FIGURE 15–1
An interest rate–investment function

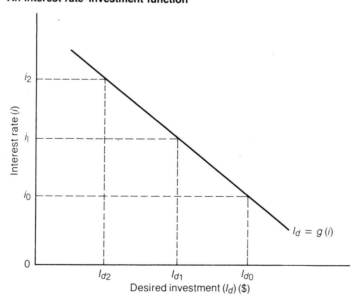

Derivation of the IS curve

How does changing the investment function from an exogenous variable to a function of interest rates affect the $C + I + G$ model? Figure 15-2 illustrates the impact of making investment depend on interest rates. Since investment now varies with the rate of interest, there is a different $C + I_d + G$ line for each possible interest rate; in Figure 15-2 we have shown three $C + I_d + G$ lines out of an infinite number of possibilities; that is, there is a different $C + I_d + G$ function for each and every possible interest rate.

Consider carefully the relation between Figure 15-1 and Figure 15-2. In the first figure, as interest rates decline, the level of investment rises because investment and interest rates are inversely related. Thus to draw a specific $C + I_d + G$ curve, one must now know the interest rate because interest rates determine the level of investment; investment, along with the consumption function and government spending, determines the location of the $C + I_d + G$ line. To illustrate, if $i = i_2$ in Figure 15-1, then investment is I_{d_2}. Given i_2 and I_{d_2}, the associated total spending function is depicted in Figure 15-2 as $C + I_{d_2} + G$. If the interest rate were lower, say i_1, then investment

FIGURE 15-2
The $C + I_d + G$ diagram with investment a function of the rate of interest

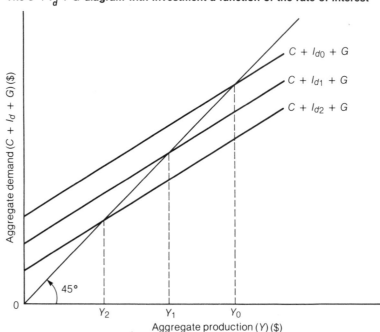

$C + I_{d0} + G$

$C + I_{d1} + G$

$C + I_{d2} + G$

Aggregate demand $(C + I_d + G)$ ($)

45°

0

Y_2 Y_1 Y_0

Aggregate production (Y) ($)

would be greater—I_{d_1} rather than I_{d_2}—and the $C + I_d + G$ function would likewise be different—$C + I_{d_1} + G$ in Figure 15-2.

So, for each and every interest rate, there is an associated level of investment, and for every level of investment there is a different $C + I_d + G$ function, three of which are shown in Figure 15-2. Making investment a function of the interest rate has made the model indeterminate; now there are an infinite number of equilibria, one for each possible rate of interest.

In Figure 15-3, part A is a reproduction of Figure 15-1; part B is

FIGURE 15-3
Derivation of the IS curve

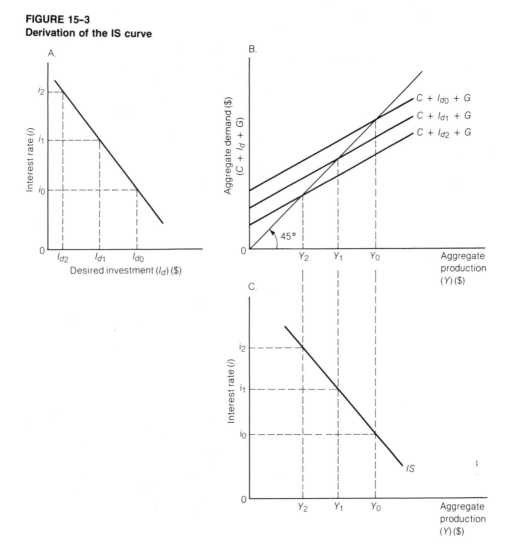

taken from Figure 15-2; and parts A and B are used to derive part C, which depicts a product-market equilibrium curve known, in short, as an IS curve.[2] The derivation of the IS curve begins with the investment function shown in part A. Three particular interest rates (i_0, i_1, and i_2) are depicted with their associated levels of investment (I_{d_0}, I_{d_1}, and I_{d_2}); for each interest rate-investment combination—i_0-I_{d_0}, i_2-I_{d_1}, i_2-I_{d_2};—there is an associated $C + I_d + G$ function (see part B). In part C of Figure 15-3, the IS curve indicates that product sector equilibrium would exist if $i = i_0$ and $Y = Y_0$, or if $i = i_1$ and $Y = Y_1$, or if $i = i_2$ and $Y = Y_2$, and so forth. Obviously, there are an infinite number of such combinations; we have simply focused on three. Since all the functions are linear, the IS curve will also be linear, and only two coordinates would be necessary to determine its location.

To reiterate, the IS curve represents various equilibrium interest rate-GNP combinations which produce equilibrium in the product market. Instead of the single GNP equilibrium of the $C + I + G$ model, there are now an infinite number of possibilities. The system has been made indeterminate, and not until the monetary sector is added is it possible to determine which interest rate-GNP combination on the IS curve is the relevant one.

The IS curve shown in Figure 15-3 slopes downward from left to right. To understand why, look at the i_2-Y_2 equilibrium combination and compare it to i_0-Y_0. If $i = i_2$, the level of investment is relatively small (I_{d_2} in part A of Figure 15-3). Given a low level of investment, the associated $C + I_{d_2} + G$ line intersects the 45° line in part B of Figure 15-3 at a low level of GNP (Y_2). On the other hand if $i = i_0$, investment will be higher (I_{d_0} in part A, and the $C + I_{d_0} + G$ curve will intersect the 45° line at a higher GNP level (Y_0). Thus product sector equilibria occur at combinations of high interest rates and low GNP, and of low interest rates and high GNP.

This section can now be concluded with an algebraic representation of the IS function. We use Equations (15-2) and (15-3), which were derived in Chapter 13,

(15-2) $$C = \$10 + 0.72Y$$
and

(15-3) $$G = \$525,$$

---

[2] The curve is labeled an IS curve because in a model without government, product-market equilibrium exists when desired investment (I) and saving (S) are equal. We have emphasized the relation between total spending and total production rather than investment and saving. Thus from our viewpoint the IS curve could be more appropriately called an "AD-AS" curve since it represents the equilibrium condition that Aggregate Demand equals Aggregate Supply.

and specify investment as a function of the interest rate:

(15–4) $I_d = \$305 - 1,400i.$

(As in Chapter 13, dollar figures are in billions.) Therefore, product sector equilibrium is given by Equation (15–5):

(15–5) $Y = 10 + 0.72Y + 305 - 1,400i + 525.$

Solving for i, the result is

(15–6) $i = 0.60 - 0.0002Y.$

Equation (15–6) is depicted graphically in Figure 15–4 as the IS curve. The reader viewing Equation (15–6) or the curve in Figure 15–4 will recognize the indeterminacy of the system since there two unknowns, Y and i, but only one equation.

Shifts in the IS curve

The IS curve may shift inward or outward (and also change slope) for a variety of reasons; for the most part, we shall concentrate on

FIGURE 15–4
The IS curve for Equation (15–6)
($ billions)

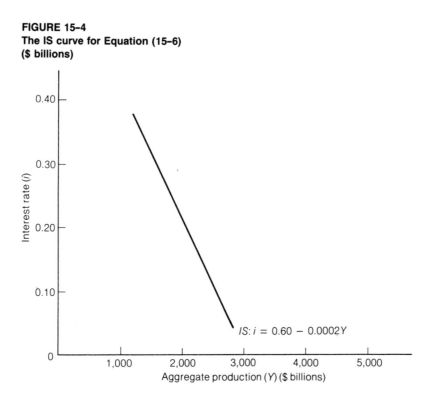

IS: $i = 0.60 - 0.0002Y$

how fiscal policy changes affect its location. If government spending is changed, for example, the IS curve will shift. To understand why, look at Figure 15-5 where increased government spending has shifted each $C + I_d + G$ line upward by ΔG so that G is now G' as the broken lines indicate. Now for any given interest rate, say i_0, the associated level of GNP is higher—Y_0' instead of Y_0; consequently,

FIGURE 15-5
The effect of increased government spending on the IS curve

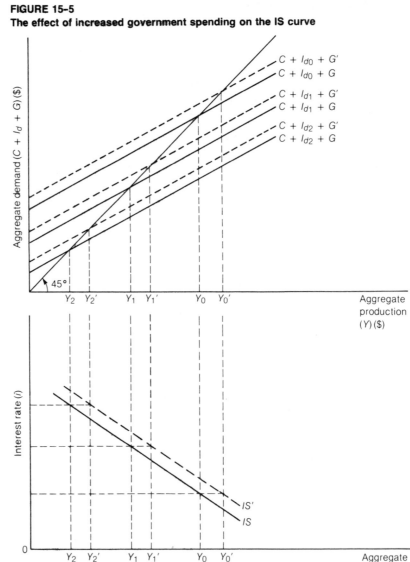

the IS curve shifts to IS'. This result can also be demonstrated by increasing G from \$525 to say \$625 in Equation (15–4). With this change the equation for the IS curve becomes

(15–7) $$i = 0.67 - 0.0002Y.$$

The reader should have no trouble understanding that a reduction in government spending will be contractionary and will shift the IS curve inward to the left.

A change in the tax rate will also cause the IS curve to shift. In Chapter 13, it was shown that a lower tax rate would rotate the consumption function upward. This result is depicted in the upper panel of Figure 15–6 where the broken $C' + I_d + G$ lines represent total spending after the tax rate reduction. (In order to keep the diagram as simple as possible, $C + I_d + G$ functions are depicted for only two interest rates, i_0 and i_2.) The effect of lowering tax rates is to shift the IS curve outward, which reflects the rotation of the $C + I_d + G$ lines. This result can also be shown algebraically. In Chapter 13, the tax rate, t, was originally set at 0.20; changing t to 0.15 increases the slope of the consumption function.[3] Rewriting Equation (15–2) to reflect the lower tax rates gives

(15–8) $$C = 10 - 0.765Y,$$

and substituting (15–8) into (15–5), we obtain the following IS equation:

(15–9) $$i = 0.60 - 0.00017Y.$$

Thus the slope of the IS curve changes from -0.0002 to -0.00017.

Finally, shifts of the IS curve may result from other, nonfiscal policy forces that affect the investment or consumption functions. Increased business optimism or improvements in technology would shift the investment function outward and in turn move the IS curve to the right. Or a "buy now" attitude by consumers, perhaps in anticipation or higher prices, would shift the consumption function upward, producing an outward movement of the IS line.

WHAT IS THE LM CURVE?

While converting investment to an endogenous variable determined by the interest rate makes the investment function more realistic, it is impossible to determine which of many possible levels

---

[3] The reader may need to refer to the discussion in Chapter 13 on how to convert $C = f(Y_d)$ to $C = f(Y)$. By setting $Y_d = Y - T$ and $T = tY$, $C = a + bY_d$ can be converted to $C = a + b(Y - tY)$, which was done to derive (15–8).

FIGURE15–6
The effect of a lower tax rate on the IS curve

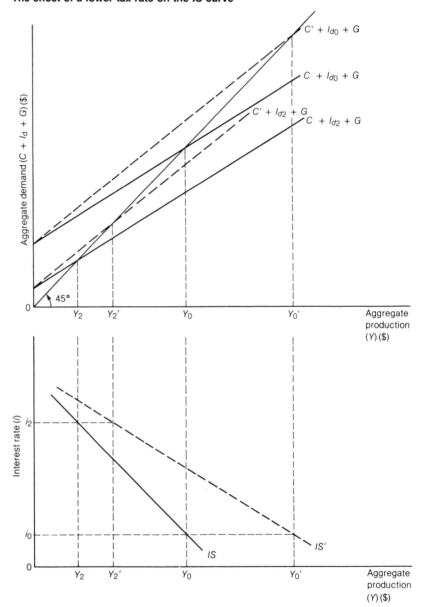

of income will be the equilibrium level (unless the interest rate is known). In this section, several functional relationships dealing with the supply and demand for money are introduced. These relationships are then incorporated into what is known as the LM curve. The discussion (in Chapters 8–11) of how the Federal Reserve controls the money supply and the discussion of money in the previous chapter will provide most of the background material for this section. At this point these elements are merely drawn together to construct a simple model of the monetary sector. Later, the system is made determinant by combining the product- and monetary-sector equilibria functions (the IS and LM curves).

Derivation of the LM curve

The description of the Federal Reserve indicated that the Fed uses open-market operations, and to a lesser extent, reserve requirements and discount rate policy to manage the nation's supply of money and credit. Though we used a mechanistic approach to describe the process of monetary control, the last section of Chapter 9 was devoted to showing how certain variables relating to the behavior of the public and the banking system could alter the relation between the variables under Federal Reserve control—the monetary base and reserve requirements—and the money supply. However, most observers believe that the Fed can control the money stock within fairly narrow limits, particularly if the time span is a quarter, six months, or a year rather than a shorter time period. In other words, in the very short run, due to random influences, varying response lags, and so forth, the Fed's control of the money supply may not be as good as one would like, but for a longer period, the money stock can be managed within tolerable limits. If it is assumed that the money supply is under Federal Reserve System control, the money stock can be treated as an exogenous variable as is indicated by

(15–10) $$M_s = \overline{M}_s.$$

On the demand side of the money market, assume that the demand for money varies inversely with the interest rate (i) and is a positive function of Gross National Product (Y) as indicated by Equation (15–11):

(15–11) $$M_d = h(i, Y).$$

The concept of money-market equilibrium is similar to the equilibrium condition for the product market. In the product market, equilibrium exists when aggregate demand for new goods and services equals aggregate supply. In a similar vein, money-market equilibrium exists when aggregate money demand is equal to the money supply, which can be expressed as

(15–12) $$\overline{M}_s = M_d$$

or

$$\overline{M}_s = h(i, Y).$$

The foregoing money market relationships are shown in Figure 15–7 where the upper panel is similar to Figure 14–4. The money supply is fixed at $\overline{M}_s$ by the monetary authorities, and money demand, M_d, is a function of interest rates (i) and income (Y). The three different money demand curves depicted slope downward from left to right, indicating that interest rates and demand for money balances are inversely related. Since income and money demand are directly related, higher levels of Y will produce a larger demand for money balances. In Figure 15–7 the income-related money demand is represented by the distance between the y-axis and the vertical portion of the M_d curves. Thus when Y is Y_0, income-related money demand is equal to distance $0A$; when $Y = Y_1$, it is $0B$; and when $Y = Y_2$, it is $0C$.

Given some income level, say Y_0, total demand for money is given by the curve labeled $M_d = h(i, Y_0)$; money-market equilibrium can exist only if i is i_0 since that is the only interest rate which would generate a level of money demand $(0A + AD)$ equal to the fixed money supply $(0D)$ at income level Y_0. The i_0–Y_0 coordinate and two other i–Y combinations $(i_1$–Y_1 and i_2–$Y_2)$ that also produce money market equilibrium are plotted in the lower panel of Figure 15–7. When the three points are connected, the result is an LM (money market equilibrium) curve.

Observe that the LM curve slopes upward from left to right; low interest rates are associated in equilibrium with low levels of GNP, and high interest rates are associated with high levels of GNP. The logic of the positively sloped LM curve can be understood by analyzing two interest rate–GNP combinations. First, if interest rates are low, say i_0, idle money balances will be relatively large (AD) since holding money does not involve the sacrifice of a large return. Given a fixed supply of money, income-determined money demand must therefore be relatively small $(0A)$ if the total demand $(0A + AD)$ is to equal the fixed money supply. Thus in the monetary sector, low interest rates are associated in equilibrium with low levels of income. On the other hand, if the interest rate is high, say i_2, being liquid involves a high opportunity cost in the form of foregone interest which results in a low demand for idle money balances (CD). If total money demand is to be equal to the available money supply,

FIGURE 15–7
Derivation of the LM curve

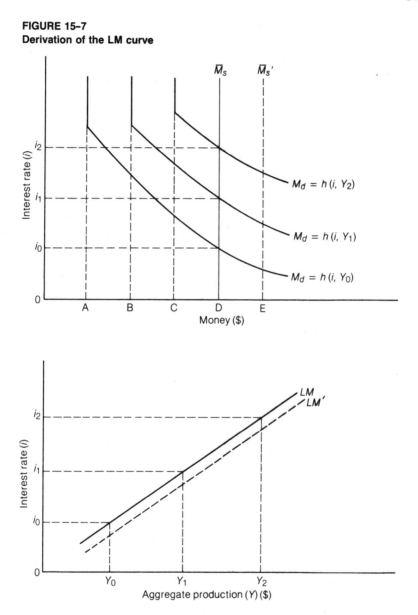

GNP must be high in order to generate a large demand for active money balances (0C).

To derive an algebraic version of the LM curve, assume that M_d is a linear function of income (Y) and the interest rate (i); consequently,

(15–13) $$M_d = d - ei + kY.$$

Specifying values for d, e, and k of \$150, 1,000, and 0.20, respectively, and assuming that the money stock is \$550 billion, in equilibrium

(15–14) $$550 = 150 - 1{,}000i + 0.20Y.$$

Solving for i gives the following expression:

(15–15) $$i = -0.40 + 0.0002Y.$$

Equation (15–15) is shown graphically in Figure 15–8 as the LM curve.[4]

Shifts in the LM curve

Shifts in the LM curve occur if there is a change in the exogenously determined stock of money $(\overline{M}_s)$ or if there is a change in one of the money demand parameters d, e, or k. First, consider an increased supply of money, such as depicted by M_s' in Figure 15–7. For any particular level of GNP, say Y_2 in Figure 15–7, the interest rate

FIGURE 15–8
A specific LM curve: Graphical representation of Equation (15–15)

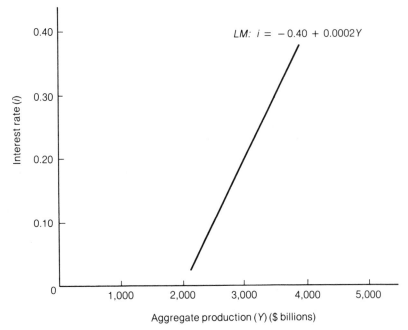

---

[4] Frequently, demand for money is denoted by the letter L instead of M_d; consequently, the money market equilibrium curve is referred to as an LM curve.

must be lower in order to generate the increase in money demanded that is required for monetary-sector equilibrium. Thus the larger money supply produces an outward and downward shift in the LM curve to LM', since monetary-sector equilibrium requires that various levels of GNP now be associated with lower interest rates.

Second, a shift in the LM curve will occur if the one or more of the money demand parameters—d, e, and k in Equation (15–14)—change. The demand for money (M_d) will decline if d or k decrease or if e, the interest rate parameter, increases. A decline in money demand is equivalent to an increase in the velocity of money because the reduction in desired money balances causes the money stock to turn over more rapidly.[5] A decrease in money demand (increase in velocity) affects the LM curve in a manner similar to an increase in the money stock; that is, the LM shifts outward and downward.

IS-LM EQUILIBRIUM: WHAT DOES IT MEAN?

Those students familiar with ordinary supply-demand analysis have probably already anticipated the next step in the study of the IS-LM framework. We have a curve representing product-sector equilibrium—an IS curve—and another representing monetary-sector equilibrium—an LM curve—and there are an infinite number of equilibrium i–Y combinations on the IS curve and also on the LM curve. But there is only one i–Y combination that produces equilibrium in both sectors; graphically that combination corresponds to the intersection of the IS and LM curve.

Figure 15–9 depicts the specific IS and LM functions derived earlier from Equations (15–7) and (15–15), respectively:

(15–7) $$\text{IS: } i = 0.60 - 0.0002Y,$$

and

(15–15) $$\text{LM: } i = -0.40 + 0.0002Y.$$

Setting the right-hand side of (15–7) equal to the right side of (15–15) permits us to find the equilibrium value of Y, which is $2,500. Substituting $2,500 for Y in either (15–7) or (15–15), equilibrium i is 0.10, or 10.0 percent. These equilibrium values are shown in Figure 15–9 where it is apparent that only when the interest rate is 0.10 and GNP is $2,500 will both markets be in equilibrium. At any other i–Y combination either the monetary sector, the product sector, or both will be out of equilibrium.

---

[5] The relation between measured money velocity and holdings of money balances was introduced in Chapter 2; that chapter contains data on the velocity of money for the United States economy for selected years beginning in 1960.

FIGURE 15-9
IS-LM equilibrium

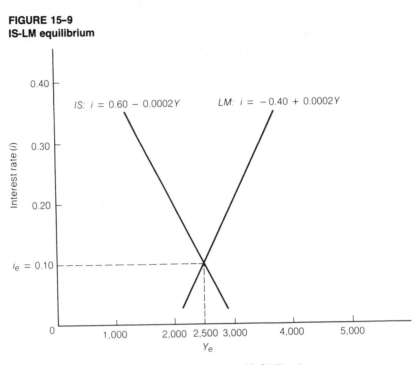

Aggregate production (Y) ($ billions)

An important consideration is the matter of how the system adjusts if it is out of equilibrium. While a detailed discussion of this subject is beyond the scope of this book, an outline of the adjustment process is presented. Assume that i is not equal to 10 percent and Y is not equal to $2,500. Under these circumstances, we would expect pressures to emerge that would eventually cause Y and/or i to change. On the product sector side, being out of equilibrium and off the IS curve means that aggregate demand is not equal to total production. The analysis of the $C + I + G$ model showed that, when aggregate demand and production are not equal, Y tends to rise or fall. This explanation still holds; the desire to halt unanticipated inventory accumulation or depletion would create pressures that would restore product sector equilibrium.

On the monetary sector side, being off the LM curve means that money demand is not equal to the fixed money supply. If money demand exceeds money supply, downward pressure is exerted on GNP because money holders will be scrambling to increase money balances, and in the process spending will fall, thereby putting downward pressure on GNP and moving the economy in the direction of equilibrium. Also, when money demand exceeds the money supply, interest rates tend to rise because asset holders will sell nonmonetary interest-bearing assets to try to build up their money holdings; in the process the prices of these assets will fall and interest rates will rise. Of course, rising interest rates will reduce M_d which helps eliminate the excess demand for money. If money demand is less than the money supply, similar forces will operate in the opposite direction to restore monetary-sector equilibrium.

The IS-LM system is a comparative statics model; that is, the adjustment process is timeless. With a static model it is possible to derive equilibrium values of the variables included in the analysis; one may also change the value of an exogenous variable, G or M_s for instance, or change the value of a parameter, say a in the consumption function, and derive new equilibrium values. In doing so, the original equilibrium values can be compared with the new ones, and thus we have the term *comparative statics* model. Since static models are timeless, the model itself does not describe the process of movement from one equilibrium to another. Our description of the sequence of events that tend to move the system to equilibrium is therefore not a part of the formal IS-LM model but an analysis of what logically might be expected to happen to the economy after some disturbance such as an increase in the money stock has occurred.

We have listed in column (2) of Table 15–1 the original equilibrium values for the variables contained in the model. At the top of the table, the specific equations for the product and monetary sectors are included as a ready reference. In the next section, we consider how certain policy changes influence IS-LM equilibrium, and columns (3), (4), and (5) of Table 15–1 show their impacts. As the discussion proceeds, the student may wish to refer back to Table 15–1 to trace the effects of policy changes on the values derived initially.

HOW ARE POLICY CHANGES REFLECTED IN THE IS-LM SYSTEM?

Monetary policy

The first illustration of how policy changes affect IS-LM equilibrium deals with monetary policy. Assume that the Federal Reserve System wishes to stimulate the economy and therefore purchases U.S. government securities in order to enlarge the monetary base and ultimately the money stock. Figure 15–10 depicts the impact of a $50 billion increase in the money supply ($\Delta \overline{M}_s = \$50$). Note that as the LM curve shifts outward to the right, equilibrium GNP rises from $2,500 ($Y$) to $2,625 ($Y'$), and the interest rate declines from 0.10 (i_e) to 0.075 (i_e'). The new equilibrium is found by the same method used

TABLE 15–1
IS-LM equilibrium: Comparison of values before and after policy changes
($billions)

Specific equations—original values	
Product sector	**Monetary sector**
$\overline{G} = \$525$ $T = 0.20Y$ $I_d = 305 - 1,400i$ $C = 10 + 0.72Y$	$\overline{M}_s = \$550$ $M_d = 150 - 1,000i + 0.20Y$
Equilibrium condition: $Y = C + I_d + G$	Equilibrium condition: $\overline{M}_s = M_d$

(1) IS-LM variables	(2) Original values	(3) Increase in the money supply $\Delta M = \$50$	(4) Increase in government spending $\Delta G = \$100$	(5) Reduction in the tax rate $t' = 0.15$
GNP and the interest rate:				
$Y_e =$	$2,500	$2,625	$2,677	$2,703
$i_e =$	0.10	0.075	0.135	0.141
Product sector:				
$\overline{G} =$	$ 525	$ 525	$ 625	$ 525
$T =$	$ 500	$ 525	$ 535	$ 405
$I_d =$	$ 165	$ 200	$ 115	$ 108
$C =$	$1,810	$1,900	$1,937	$2,070
$C + I_d + G =$	1,810 + 165 + 525 $2,500	1,900 + 200 + 525 $2,625	1,937 + 115 + 625 $2,677	2,070 + 108 + 525 $2,703
Monetary sector:				
$\overline{M}_s =$	$ 550	$ 600	$ 550	$ 550
$M_d =$	$ 550	$ 600	$ 550	$ 550

FIGURE 15–10
IS-LM equilibrium: The impact of a $50 billion increase in the money stock

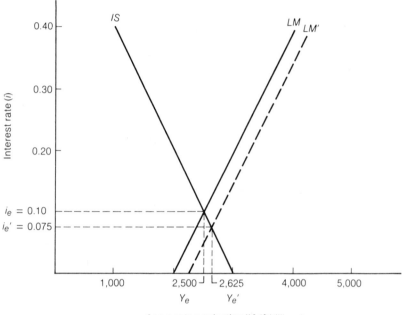

Aggregate production (Y) ($ billions)

to calculate the original values.[6] The final results of the money supply increase can be seen by comparing column (3) of Table 15–1, which lists the new equilibrium values, with column (2), where the original equilibrium values are shown.

Consider why the increase in the money supply generates this expansionary impact. When M is increased from $550 to $600, there is initially an excess supply of money, which tends to drive interest rates down. At this point the initial disturbance in the monetary sector begins to spill over into the product sector since falling interest rates will stimulate investment. As investment rises, GNP also begins to expand which in turn causes consumption to rise. How long will this process continue? Until the rising level of GNP and falling interest rates increase money demand (M_d) to a level equal to the new money supply.

---

[6] The new LM curve is $i = -0.45 + 0.0002Y$ instead of $i = -0.40 + 0.0002Y$. Setting the right-hand side of the new LM equation equal to the right side of the IS curve and solving for Y gives $Y = $2,625$. Substituting $2,625 for Y in either the IS or LM equation, the value of i is determined to be 0.075.

Inflation and interest rates. At this point it is worthwhile to consider some possible complications concerning the relationship between monetary growth and interest rates. In the context of the IS-LM system, the analysis indicates that expansion of the money supply is associated with falling interest rates and rising income while a contraction of the money stock generates higher rates of interest and lower levels of income. What, then, accounts for the frequently observed situation where interest rates rise during a period of sustained, rapid monetary expansion?

Rising interest rates as a consequence of monetary expansion may occur if inflation is incorporated into the IS-LM framework; that is, if monetary growth is too rapid, a decline in interest rates may be only temporary when the effects of a rising price level are considered. Such a result is possible since inflation reduces the *real* quantity of money (M_s/P). In other words, an increase in the price level is equivalent to a reduction in the nominal money supply (M_s); thus inflation—or a decrease in the money supply—will shift the LM curve to the left, thereby causing interest rates to rise. Whether the final interest rate is higher or lower than the original level depends on the extent of the rise in prices.

Furthermore, if borrowers and lenders expect inflation in the future, then lenders will desire (and borrowers will be willing to pay) higher interest rates since both believe that money loaned (borrowed) now will be repaid with less valuable dollars. Though our presentation of the IS-LM system has not incorporated price expectations, it is possible to include the impact of this factor. For example, expectations of higher prices would shift the IS curve outward if a "buy now" attitude increases aggregate demand. Of course, when the IS curve shifts outward, interest rates rise. For the remainder of this chapter we set these complications aside and assume that money supply increases do not generate inflation; thus we retain the result that interest rates fall when the money stock is increased.

The liquidity trap. One further matter involving the effectiveness of monetary policy needs to be mentioned. In the *General Theory*, Keynes indicated that there is a possibility that monetary policy might be ineffective because "liquidity-preference may become virtually absolute in the sense that almost everyone prefers cash to holding a debt which yields so low a rate of interest."[7] This phenomenon has been labeled the liquidity trap, a term descriptive of the possibility that, in a depression when interest rates are abnormally low, it may become impossible to induce people to purchase

---

[7] John Maynard Keynes, *The General Theory of Employment, Interest, and Money* (New York: Harcourt, Brace & World, 1936), p. 207.

bonds. As noted in Chapter 14, this reluctance to buy bonds is due to the risk associated with holding bonds when interest rates are unusually low and bond prices therefore are exceptionally high. (The reader may refer to Figure 14–2 for a diagrammatic representation of the liquidity trap.) Given these conditions, the downside risk that bond prices will fall and cause losses for bondholders discourages investors from purchasing bonds.

In the context of the IS-LM model, a liquidity trap would be reflected by an LM curve that is horizontal at the interest rate where liquidity preference is, in Keynes's words, "virtually absolute." The implications of a liquidity trap for monetary policy are very important: The monetary authorities cannot lower interest rates if the economy is in a liquidity trap; hence, monetary policy will not influence the level of economic activity. An increase in the money stock no longer reduces interest rates because any more money injected into the system by the monetary authorities is hoarded, that is, none of it is used to purchase bonds. Thus bond prices cannot rise, and interest rates will not fall. Since the increased money supply, by failing to lower interest rates, does not stimulate investment, monetary policy has no impact on the economy.

The possible existence of a liquidity trap, along with some other assumed shortcomings of monetary policy, led many economists to conclude that monetary policy was unreliable and that fiscal policy was the more dependable means of managing aggregate economic activity. However, monetarists have insisted that changes in the money stock do in fact have a reliable and powerful impact on economic activity. Few if any economists are now willing to ignore monetary policy altogether, and the debate continues to wage between monetarists and others regarding the relative effectiveness of monetary and fiscal policy. Even Keynes, after raising the possibility that liquidity preference may become virtually absolute, went on to say, "But whilst this limiting case might become practically important in the future, I know of no example of it hitherto."[8]

The rationale for the Keynesian liquidity trap is the high degree of interest-rate risk perceived by investors when interest rates are unusually low. In the world of the 1930s, Keynes was essentially correct in viewing investor alternatives as money or long-term bonds subject to a high degree of interest-rate risk. Today a wide range of short-term assets with little or no interest-rate risk are available as alternatives to holding money: NOW accounts, share drafts, money market funds, and Treasury bills are examples. Thus it is questionable that any basis for a liquidity trap exists today even if it did in the

[8] Ibid., p. 207.

1930s. Nonetheless, in the final part of this section the liquidity trap situation is presented as a special case in the context of the monetarist-Keynesian debate over the relative effectiveness of monetary and fiscal policy.

Fiscal policy

Government spending changes. The effects of fiscal policy in the IS-LM model can be illustrated by first considering an increase in government spending and then a decrease in the tax rate. Assume that, in our model, government spending, which was initially $525, now is increased by $100 to $625. Figure 15–11 illustrates the impact of a spending increase showing the IS curve shifting outward to IS'. The level of GNP rises from $2,500 to $2,677, an increase of $177, and the interest rate rises from 0.10 to 0.135. Thus both the equilibrium GNP and the equilibrium interest rate go up.

Column (4) of Table 15–1 shows the effect of the increase in government spending on the IS-LM variables. Note that as a result of the $100 increase in government spending, equilibrium GNP rises by $177, from $2,500 originally to $2,677. The reader may recall from Chapter 13 that in the simple $C + I + G$ model, the multiplier (m) was

FIGURE 15–11
IS-LM equilibrium: The impact of a $100 billion increase in government spending

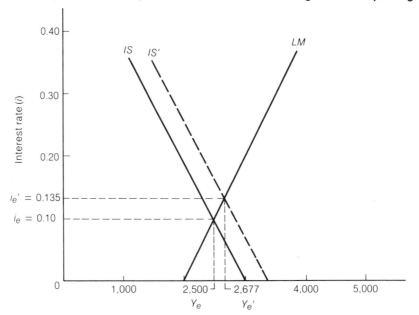

Aggregate production (Y) ($ billions)

3.57; therefore, in that model an increase in government spending would have generated a $357 change in equilibrium GNP, not the $177 increase calculated in the IS-LM model.

The lower multiplier is the result of including a monetary sector and an interest-sensitive investment function. In the $C + I + G$ system there was no monetary sector. Now the money stock and the velocity of money in combination set an upper limit to aggregate production. Therefore, given a fixed supply of money and holding the parameters of the money demand function constant, a rise in GNP which will lead to an increase in desired money balances can be maintained with a fixed money supply only if interest rates rise and thereby produce an offsetting decline in desired money balances.

As interest rates rise, however, investment (I_d) declines; this decline in spending in the private sector resulting from forces generated by the increase in government spending is sometimes referred to as the *crowding-out effect*. Comparing columns (2) and (4) of Table 15-1, the increase in G of $100 is accompanied by a decrease in I_d from $165 to $115 or a decline of $50. Obviously the more interest sensitive the investment function, the more crowding out there will be.

A possibility that would render fiscal policy ineffective is one raised primarily by monetarists. In a study of the demand for money published in 1959, Milton Friedman found no statistically significant relation between interest rates and money demand.[9] As Friedman later pointed out, this finding is not equivalent to saying that there is not a relationship between interest rates and money demand, but merely indicates that, based on the empirical evidence, one could not conclude that such a relation exists.[10] Nonetheless, some monetarists have taken the position that money demand is not sensitive to interest rate changes, an assumption that leads to the conclusion that fiscal policy will be ineffective.

If money demand is interest insensitive, then the rise in interest rates occasioned by the increase in government spending will not encourage more intensive use of money balances to support a higher level of GNP. Thus the fixed money stock times the velocity of money continually sets an upper limit for GNP. In this situation, an increase in government spending with a constant money supply would crowd out an equal amount of investment, and GNP would remain constant. However, considerable study of the influence of interest rates on money demand has been done since Friedman's

---

[9] Milton Friedman, "The Demand for Money: Some Theoretical and Empirical Results," *Journal of Political Economy*, vol. 67 (June 1959), pp. 327–51.

[10] Milton Friedman, "Interest Rates and the Demand for Money," *Journal of Law and Economics*, vol. 9 (October 1966), pp. 71–85.

study in 1959, and the results have established that money demand is interest sensitive.[11] The interest-inelastic-demand-for-money function is treated as a monetarist special case later in this chapter.

The government budget constraint.   There is another important consideration relating to a change in government spending—the so-called government budget constraint. The government budget constraint refers to the method of financing an increase in government spending. In our example, the government increased its spending by $100 from $525 to $625. New expenditures are financed using one or more of three methods—collecting more taxes, printing new money, or issuing new bonds.

In our model, tax collections are a function of GNP and the tax rate; as GNP rises from $2,500 to $2,677, tax revenues increase by the tax rate (0.20) times the change in GNP ($177) or by $35.4 billion. Therefore, at the new equilibrium GNP, the per period difference of $64.6 between the spending increase of $100 and the tax increase of $35.4 must be financed by increasing the supply of money and/or by issuing new government debt (borrowing).

In the United States, the government does not simply print new money and use that money to cover its deficit. If this method were employed, the LM curve would initially shift outward, reflecting the increase in M_s necessary to cover the difference between the increased government spending and the increase in tax collections generated by the rise in GNP. But that would not be the end of the story. Government spending is a flow, while the money supply is a stock. In the next period, new money would once again have to be issued to finance a deficit, and the LM would shift outward once more. Would this process ever end? The answer is yes because the increase in M would have an additional effect of raising GNP thereby causing tax collections to rise also. Eventually the LM curve would move outward far enough so that tax revenues would be sufficient to finance the higher level of G, and no further additions to the money stock would be necessary.

Monetary management and federal spending are by and large administered separately in this country. Therefore, if increases in the money supply are to be envisioned as a way of financing government expenditures, the process must be indirect. The Federal Reserve is severely limited in the amount of bonds that it can purchase directly from the U.S. Treasury. In the absence of such a limitation, bonds purchased directly would be paid for by increasing the Treasury's checking account at the Federal Reserve which is equivalent to

---

[11] A good summary of this issue can be found in David Laidler's *The Demand for Money: Theory and Evidence*, 2d ed. (New York: Dun-Donnelley, 1977), chap. 7.

printing new money. Since this direct method of purchasing bonds is for practical purposes closed to the Fed, a roundabout procedure is used.

The Federal Reserve purchases most of its U.S. government securities from investors who have bought the bonds from the Treasury. These Federal Reserve open-market purchases make it easier for the Treasury to sell new bonds, thereby providing indirect assistance. Also, we know from Chapters 9 and 10 that open-market purchases ultimately increase the money stock, which increases GNP and generates more tax revenue. Without intervention by the Fed, debt-financed government expenditures would drive up interest rates and reduce investment. As noted earlier, this effect is known as crowding out.

In reality, increased government spending is financed by a combination of the methods we have mentioned. Typically, when government spending is increased, the accompanying growth of GNP generates new tax revenue. (On occasion tax rates may be raised to help finance new expenditures.) Any difference between tax collections and spending is usually covered initially by issuing bonds.[12] But as we have seen, bond financing tends to increase interest rates and crowd out some spending in the private sector. At this point the Fed frequently steps in and tries to mitigate the interest rate increase through open-market bond purchases. Such purchases lead to an increase in the money stock which causes GNP to grow, thereby enlarging tax revenues. When this sequence of events occurs, it is difficult to separate the fiscal policy effects on the economy from the monetary policy effects; this relationship between monetary and fiscal policy will be further explored in the following chapters of this section.

Tax rate changes. Now consider how lowering the tax rate (while holding government spending constant) will affect the variables in an IS-LM system. Figure 15–12 shows the IS curve rotating outward because the tax rate has been reduced, from 0.20 to 0.15. GNP rises from $2,500 to a new equilibrium of $2,703, and the interest rate also increases from 0.10 to 0.141. The rise in interest rates occurs because the lower tax rate reduces tax collections (T) even though the tax base (GNP) has risen (the increase in the tax base is not large enough to offset the loss of revenue due to lower tax rates).

---

[12] William L. Silber has pointed out that changes in bond supply and demand functions logically would be expected to shift both the LM curve and the IS curve. For simplicity, we choose to ignore these effects. For a discussion of the impact of changes in the bond market on the IS-LM model, see William L. Silber, "Fiscal Policy in IS-LM Analysis: A Correction," *Journal of Money, Credit, and Banking,* vol. 2 (November 1970), pp. 461–72.

FIGURE 15–12
IS-LM equilibrium: The impact of reducing the tax rate from 20 to 15 percent

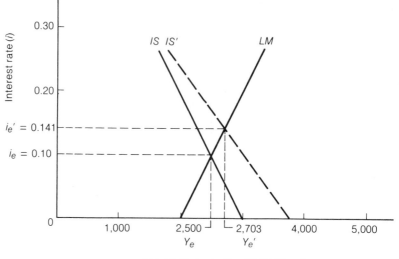

Aggregate production (Y) ($ billions)

With government spending held constant, smaller tax collections must be offset with issuance of new bonds which pushes the interest rate up. Column (5) of Table 15–1 shows the final impact of the lower tax rate.

Monetarist and Keynesian special cases

Several times in this section on monetary and fiscal policy and in previous chapters we have discussed the policy debate between monetarists and Keynesians over the relative effectiveness of fiscal and monetary policy. Here we use the IS-LM model to illustrate the differences between certain Keynesian and monetarist special cases.[13] At the outset it should be noted that very few economists adhere to these extremes, and that the analysis is useful primarily as a means of illustrating conditions under which monetary and fiscal policies are more or less effective.

The extreme Keynesian position is that "money doesn't matter." This statement implies that monetary policy is completely ineffective in producing a change in real GNP. As mentioned previously,

---

[13] The main purpose of this section is to discuss the specific issue of the interest elasticity of the demand for money. There are other more fundamental differences separating the two camps which are discussed in Chapters 14 and 19.

the existence of a liquidity trap would render monetary policy useless. Part A of Figure 15–13 depicts a horizontal LM curve which would result if there were a liquidity trap. We have already discussed the implication of the liquidity trap for monetary policy. In the liquidity trap situation, an increase in the money supply would not shift the horizontal LM curve since the new money balances would be hoarded. Consequently, LM′, which represents the effect of an increase in the money stock, is identical to LM. Clearly, increasing the money supply has no impact on aggregate production if there is a liquidity trap, and consequently, "money doesn't matter."

On the other hand, the horizontal LM curve implies that fiscal policy will be highly effective. Since the liquidity trap indicates the existence of relatively large idle money balances, government spending (and borrowing) can be accomplished without driving up interest rates. The existence of this pool of liquidity which can be tapped to finance new government spending prevents any crowding out of investment spending. An increase in government spending, which shifts the IS curve to IS′, results in the full multiplier effect of the simple $C + I + G$ model rather than the smaller impact depicted by the version of the IS-LM model presented earlier in this chapter.

As noted earlier, Keynes raised the possibility of a liquidity trap only when the economy was depressed and interest rates had fallen to a very low level (bond prices would be unusually high). Therefore, the LM curve shown in part A of Figure 15–13 would, even in the Keynesian case, begin to rise eventually. However, the point to remember is that the *more* interest elastic the demand for money, the *less* effective is monetary policy and the *more* effective is fiscal policy. The extreme exists when money demand is infinitely interest

FIGURE 15–13
IS-LM analysis: Monetarist and Keynesian special cases

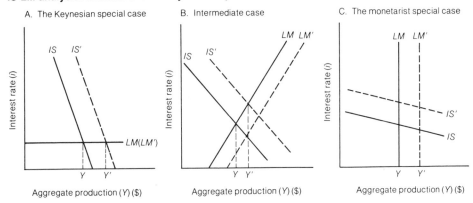

A. The Keynesian special case   B. Intermediate case   C. The monetarist special case

elastic (the liquidity trap); then monetary policy is useless and fiscal policy is of maximum effectiveness.[14]

Finally, Keynesians also question the efficacy of monetary policy on the grounds that money's channel of influence is narrow. In the Keynesian world, monetary policy works by reducing interest rates and thereby stimulating investment. If the investment function is interest inelastic, thereby producing a steep IS curve as in Figure 15-13A, then monetary policy would be weakened. Furthermore, if influences other than the interest rate have a significant effect on investment (the interest rate–investment function is unstable), then these influences may offset at least part of the impact of interest rates and thereby diminish the effectiveness of monetary policy. The foregoing assessment of monetary policy is obviously far from optimistic. In the Keynesian world, use of monetary policy is, at best, risky business. However, monetarists have reached much different conclusions about the relative effectiveness of monetary and fiscal policies.

Figure 15-13C shows the extreme monetarist position. The LM curve is vertical indicating that the demand for money is perfectly interest inelastic, and the IS curve is relatively flat, which reflects the assumption that aggregate spending is very interest sensitive. When the LM curve is vertical, then "money alone matters"; that is, monetary policy is very powerful, and fiscal policy is completely ineffective. Monetary policy is very powerful because an injection of new money balances has no impact on desired average money balances and velocity. Even though interest rates will fall when the LM curve shifts to LM', people will not decrease the intensity of their use of money balances, and hence, the velocity of money remains constant. Consequently, an increase in the money supply will increase GNP by an amount equal to the unchanged velocity of money times the change in the money stock.

Fiscal policy is useless in this situation because the money supply, coupled with the velocity of money, sets an upper limit on aggregate spending. If government spending is increased, thereby shifting the IS curve to IS', there is no change in Y. Since money balances are constant and will not be used more intensively, the increase in government spending simply crowds out an equal amount of private sector spending via higher interest rates.

As we noted earlier, monetarists reject the engine of analysis of

---

[14] The interest elasticity of the demand for money is related to the (absolute) value of the interest rate coefficient, e, in Equation (15–13) which is a demand-for-money function; e can range between zero and infinity with the former value representing the monetarist special case and the latter value the Keynesian liquidity trap situation.

the Keynesian approach and argue that the channel of influence of money is much broader than the interest rate–investment mechanism. There are several ways that money could influence aggregate spending which in the IS-LM model would result in a shift in the IS curve in addition to the shift of the LM function. The key point here, however, is that the *less* interest elastic the demand for money, the *more* effective is monetary policy and the *less* effective is fiscal policy. In the extreme, when money demand has zero interest elasticity, monetary policy will be very powerful and fiscal policy useless.

The version of the IS-LM model presented in this chapter reflects the idea that "money matters" but not exclusively. Figure 15–13B once again shows an IS-LM model that reflects this view. Once out of the extreme Keynesian and monetarist situations, both monetary and fiscal policy are effective, and their relative importance will depend on the slopes of the curves. Thus we can make the curves more monetarist or more Keynesian by changing their slopes to conform more closely to the extremes discussed in this section. The following chapter deals with some empirical evidence related to the monetary versus fiscal policy controversy.

WHAT DOES THE IS-LM SYSTEM TELL US ABOUT THE PROCESS OF INFLATION?

To this point, price level changes have been relegated to the background in that the IS-LM model has been formulated in real terms. But by using the potential output concept introduced in Chapter 13, some insights into the inflationary process are possible. As previously explained, the potential level of output cannot in practice be identified precisely. For pedagogical purposes, we shall ignore this problem and assume that there is a strictly defined ceiling on aggregate real production and that as this ceiling is approached, output increases become more and more difficult to achieve.

Figure 15–14 depicts the original IS and LM curves derived earlier; equilibrium GNP is $2,500, and the equilibrium interest rate is 10 percent. The vertical line in Figure 15–14 represents the upper limit to real output which is designated as Y_p and is assumed to be $3,000. Therefore, if aggregate demand is greater than $3,000, prices will rise, since real production capacity is limited to $3,000 at current prices. For instance, if the monetary authorities create so much new money that the LM curve intersects the IS curve beyond Y_p, or fiscal policymakers cause the IS curve to shift similarly, then prices are bound to rise. This type of process is known as excess-demand inflation.

FIGURE 15-14
Actual and potential GNP

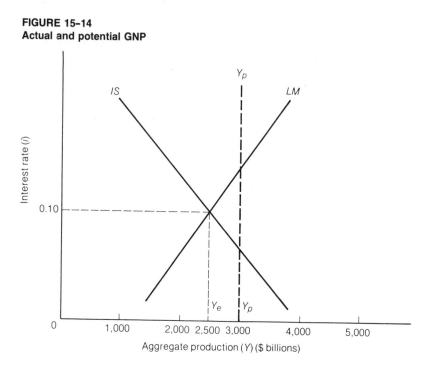

Past experience with inflation shows that price increases are possible even before the level of potential GNP is reached. The likelihood of inflation depends on how close actual GNP is to potential output and on the rate at which the economy is expanding. If there is a large gap between actual and potential GNP, then inflationary pressure is not likely to be large. On the other hand, as the gap narrows, certain industries will begin to reach capacity, and even though aggregate output has not reached its maximum, firms in these industries will begin to raise prices. The nearer the economy to capacity, the more likely such price increases become.

The other critical element is the speed at which the economy is expanding toward full employment. If the process is not too rapid, firms will have time to expand their output levels by adding to their capacity to produce.[15] These adjustments take time, however, and if aggregate demand is growing too fast, producers will not have adequate time to increase output and will therefore raise prices.

There are certain policy implications to this discussion. First,

---

[15] Adding new capacity will shift Y_p to a higher level. Policies designed to stimulate aggregate supply are covered in Chapter 19.

policymakers must be especially cautious as the economy reaches the neighborhood of full employment. Creating too much aggregate demand under those circumstances will produce inflation. Furthermore, if the economy is in a recovery phase, timing is critical. If policymakers are impatient and try to expand the economy too rapidly, then the likelihood of inflation rises. Further analysis of the inflationary process and of policies to deal with the problem is undertaken in the chapters that follow.

SUMMARY

In this chapter we have constructed a formal model that embodies many of the concepts developed in Chapters 13 and 14. First, the $C + I + G$ model of the product sector was modified to include an interest rate–investment function; the result is a product-sector equilibrium curve known as an IS curve. Second, many of the ideas on money from Chapter 14 were incorporated into a monetary-sector equilibrium function referred to as an LM curve. Included among the more important causes of shifts in the IS curve were changes in government spending and tax rates; on the monetary sector side, changes in the money supply and forces operating through the demand for money may shift the LM curve. Finally, the intersection of the IS and LM curves presents a unique interest rate–GNP combination that produces equilibrium in both sectors.

Economic policy can be used to influence the level of GNP. For example, government spending can be increased or tax rates reduced in order to stimulate the level of economic activity. The exact effect of an increase in government spending depends on whether the expenditures are financed by issuing new bonds, printing new money, and/or collecting new taxes. Also, the supply of money can be changed in order to influence the economy. The final impact of a policy change is determined by several factors including the interest elasticity of money demand.

REVIEW QUESTIONS

1. Write your own definition for the IS curve, and explain why it is downward sloping.
2. Write your own definition for the LM curve, and explain why it is upward sloping.
3. Using an IS-LM model, illustrate the effect of each of the following changes on equilibrium GNP and equilibrium i.
   a. A decrease in the money supply.

b. An increase in government spending financed by increases in the money supply (also assume that the higher levels of GNP generate some new taxes).

c. An increase in government spending financed entirely by new taxes.

d. A decrease in the velocity of money.

e. An increase in the interest sensitivity of money demand.

4. Given a money-demand function, $M_d = 100 - 1,000i + 0.40Y$, and a money supply of $210, derive an equation for the LM curve. How does the equation change if the money supply is reduced to $180? Depict the original and the new LM curves graphically.

5. Given an investment function, $I_d = 300 - 2,000i$, a consumption function, $C = 0.80Y_d$, government spending of $200, and a tax function, $T = 0.25Y$, derive the equation for the IS curve. Depict the function graphically.

6. Combine the original LM function from Question 4 with the IS equation of Question 5 in the same graph. What is the equilibrium value for Y? for i? Check these results algebraically.

7. If the information in Question 5 were changed so that investment were an exogenous variable equal to $400 and the monetary sector were ignored, what would be the value of the simple $C + I + G$ multiplier? If G were increased by $100 in the context of the IS-LM framework, would the multiplier effect be larger or smaller? Why?

8. Discuss the effectiveness of monetary policy in the context of the IS-LM model. How important is the possibility of a liquidity trap? an interest insensitive investment function? Explain.

SUGGESTIONS FOR ADDITIONAL READING

Hicks, J. R. "Mr. Keynes and the 'Classics'; A Suggested Interpretation." *Econometrica*, vol. 5 (April 1937), pp. 147–59.

Silber, William L. "Fiscal Policy in the IS-LM Analysis: A Correction." *Journal of Money, Credit, and Banking*, vol. 2 (November 1970), pp. 461–72.

Smith, Warren L. "A Graphical Exposition of the Complete Keynesian System." *Southern Economic Journal*, vol. 23, no. 2 (October 1956), pp. 115–25.

16 Fiscal policy in the monetary economy

WARM-UP: *Outline and questions to consider as you read*

What are the major objectives of the federal budget?

What are the more important budget trends of recent years?

Who has primary responsibility for the federal budget-making process?

What is the impact of fiscal policy on economic activity?

Measures of fiscal policy impact.

The effectiveness of fiscal policy.

Are federal budget deficits inevitable?

What are the major problems encountered by fiscal policymakers?

NEW TERMS

Administrative lag: the time elapsing between recognition of a problem and when action is taken to deal with it.

Effect lag: the time elapsing between implementation of a policy and when that policy has a significant impact on the economy.

Fine tuning: small economic policy adjustments made frequently in an attempt to maintain economic stability.

337

Government transfer payments: government spending, such as unemployment compensation, for which recipients have not performed current-period productive services.

High-employment federal budget: the levels of federal spending and revenues that would exist if the economy were operating at its potential.

Office of Management and Budget (OMB): the government agency that has primary responsibility for federal budget planning, preparation, and control.

Public good: a good, such as a lighthouse, that tends to be underproduced by the private sector because there is no practical way to levy charges on its users.

Recognition lag: the time elapsing between the occurrence of a problem and its recognition.

Thus far in Chapters 12–15 of this section, "Theory and Policy in the Monetary Economy," we have (1) surveyed the major elements of the macroeconomy, (2) developed a simple macromodel without money (a $C + I + G$ model), (3) analyzed money's relation to aggregate economic activity, and (4) constructed a macroeconomic framework with money known as an IS-LM model. Furthermore, the first three parts of the book dealt with the money-supply process including many of the elements involved in the conduct of monetary policy. The discussion has also touched on the use of fiscal policy to influence the level of economic activity, with most of the analysis in the context of the macromodels of Chapters 13 and 15; that is, the description of fiscal policymaking has focused on how equilibrium values of the models are affected by changes in government spending and taxes. In this chapter the impact of fiscal policy is examined more closely as are the mechanics of the federal budgetary process.

The first three parts of the chapter describe some of the pertinent facts and processes relating to the federal budget.[1] Since the focus of this text is the monetary framework, the discussion of the mechanics of fiscal policy is relatively brief. However we do think that at least a cursory knowledge of the federal budgetary process is vital if one is to understand fiscal policy and its relation to monetary policy actions. The remaining parts of this chapter consider (a) the effectiveness of fiscal policy, (b) historical trends relating to the thrust of fiscal policy, and (c) the major problems involved in administering fiscal policy.

---

[1] Throughout most of this chapter, we are concerned only with the federal budget and ignore state and local governments. The rationale for this procedure is that fiscal policy is primarily a federal government responsibility.

WHAT ARE THE MAJOR OBJECTIVES OF THE FEDERAL BUDGET?

Each year as Congress and the president work to shape the federal government's budget for the upcoming fiscal year, they are involved in an arduous process. Several of the budgetary problems are covered in the final section of this chapter; in this part we wish only to list some of the major objectives of the federal budget and to identify one of these objectives as the focus of this chapter.

One important federal governmental function is to promote a hospitable legal, social, and economic environment; activities of the federal judiciary would be included in this category as would ad-ministration of housing, health, and environmental standards, and enforcement of antitrust legislation. Antitrust laws, for instance, are directed at promoting a competitive business environment in which goods and services can be produced as efficiently as possible. It goes almost without saying that many of the mandates handed down by various regulatory bodies are not always an unmitigated blessing. The health regulations of the Occupational Safety and Health Ad-ministration (OSHA) and the environmental controls of the En-vironmental Protection Agency (EPA) have improved health and en-vironmental conditions but not without costs. Many authorities at-tribute part of the drop in productivity increases in the United States during the 1970s to the growing network of government regulatory activity.

Second, a considerable portion of the federal budget goes to pro-vide *public goods*. It is the nature of public goods that they would be underproduced by the private sector.[2] Therefore, the federal gov-ernment provides funds for national defense, for highways, and for other such goods. During the early years of this nation's existence, providing public goods and engaging in a few activities included in the legal-social-economic environment category were considered the chief budgetary functions of the federal government.

Two additional areas of federal government responsibility have become increasingly important—redistributing income and using the budget for fiscal policy purposes. The first of these involves use of the power to tax and to spend in order to transfer income among individuals. In simple terms, federal income tax collections are transferred to those who are eligible for funds under a multitude of federal programs such as Social Security, unemployment insurance, Medicare, and Medicaid. The last objective, stabilization of the

---

[2] Typically, public goods would be underproduced by the private sector because there is no effective mechanism through which the private-sector producers could collect payment from all users. The classic case of a public good is the lighthouse which benefits all ships that pass by. Private enterprise would not construct the lighthouse, however, because there is no effective mechanism for collecting from those who use it.

economy, became increasingly important during and following the Great Depression of the 1930s. Fiscal policy seeks to promote short-run economic stability and long-term economic growth through manipulation of federal expenditures and tax collections.

Obviously the four broad objectives listed above are interrelated in the budget-making process. One logical view of the budget is that the expenditure side of the budget should be determined on the basis of the funds required (1) to create a hospitable legal, social, and economic framework, (2) to furnish public goods, and (3) to establish an equitable distribution of income via various transfer programs; these are the first three objectives listed above. Then, given the level of federal spending so determined, tax rates would be set so as to apply the proper amount of fiscal stimulus or restraint in order to stabilize the economy in the short run and to promote its growth in the long run. In fact, decisions about government spending and tax collections are not based on a simple formula but rather reflect a multitude of interacting political, social, and economic forces.

WHAT ARE THE MORE IMPORTANT BUDGET TRENDS OF RECENT YEARS?

Within the last decade or so the structure of the federal budget has changed considerably. On the spending side, national defense spending as a percent of total federal expenditures has declined while the relative importance of transfer payments has risen sharply. As for receipts, the most notable trend has been the increasing importance of payroll (primarily Social Security) taxes.

Table 16–1 presents a condensed version of the federal budget for fiscal years 1969 and 1979.[3] Observe in the upper panel of Table 16–1 the declining proportion of total expenditures devoted to national defense—43.5 percent of total expenditures in 1969 compared to 23.8 percent in 1979. (Putting defense spending in real terms would indicate a decline in real national defense expenditures between 1969 and 1979). On the other hand, funding for education and training, health, and income security has come to occupy a more prominent place in the federal budget, rising from a total of 30.3 percent of total federal expenditures in 1969 to 48.6 percent in 1979. Interest on the federal debt increased from $15.8 billion in 1969 to $52.6 billion in 1979, but the relative importance of interest payments increased just two percentage points, from 8.6 percent to 10.6

---

[3] The federal government fiscal year begins October 1 and ends September 30.

TABLE 16-1
Federal government expenditures and receipts, fiscal 1969 and 1979
($billions)

Budget item	1969		1979	
Expenditures				
National defense .... $ 80.2		43.5%	$117.7	23.8%
Education and training 6.9		3.7	29.7	6.0
Health 11.8		6.4	49.6	10.1
Income security 37.3		20.2	160.2	32.5
Interest on federal debt 15.8		8.6	52.6	10.6
Other outlays 32.5		17.6	83.9	17.0
Total expenditures $184.5		100.0%	$493.7	100.0%
Receipts				
Individual income taxes ......$ 87.2		46.4%	$217.8	46.7%
Corporate income taxes 36.7		19.5	71.4	15.3
Payroll taxes 39.7		21.1	141.6	30.4
Excise taxes 10.6		5.6	18.7	4.0
Other receipts 13.6		7.2	16.4	3.5
Total receipts $187.8		99.8%*	$465.9	99.9%*

* Total not equal to 100.0 percent due to rounding.
Source: *Federal Reserve Bulletin.*

percent; the growth in interest payments by the federal government reflects a larger debt and higher interest rates.[4]

The lower panel of Table 16-1 lists federal government receipts. The most obvious trend has been the growth of payroll taxes, from 21.2 percent of receipts in 1969 to 30.4 percent in 1979. Social Security tax rates have been raised as has the upper income limit on which Social Security taxes must be paid. Corporate income taxes have declined in relative importance, individual income taxes have remained at about 46 percent of total receipts, and the other receipts categories have declined in relative importance.

Finally, the reader should compare total expenditures and receipts for 1969 and 1979.[5] In 1969, total expenditures were $184.5 billion and total receipts were $187.8 billion; thus receipts exceeded expenditures by $3.3 billion, thereby generating a budget surplus. By 1979 total expenditures were $493.7 billion, and receipts totaled $465.9 billion, resulting in a deficit of $28.7 billion. This and other deficits had to be financed by borrowing which pushed the debt total

---

[4] The gross federal debt rose from less than $400 billion in 1970 to over $850 billion by early 1980.

[5] Total federal expenditures were 20.5 and 21.9 percent of GNP in fiscal 1969 and 1979 respectively.

to over $830 billion at the end of fiscal 1979. Taking the 20 fiscal years ending with 1979, in 2 of those years the government budget was in surplus, and in 18 it was in deficit.

WHO HAS PRIMARY RESPONSIBILITY FOR THE FEDERAL BUDGET-MAKING PROCESS?

Each year's final federal budget emerges as the end product of a complex set of economic, social, and political forces. The size of the current budget is mind-boggling; expenditures for fiscal 1979 were almost $500 billion. In addition to the tremendous size of the budget, the large number of budgeted items, the executive and legislative budget machinery, and the multitude of budget objectives and pressures all contribute to make the budgetary process complicated. The budget that is finally adopted contains a set of compromises that pleases hardly anyone. As former Federal Reserve chairman Arthur Burns has commented, "Budgets in this country have just happened. They certainly have not been planned."

Executive fiscal planning, execution, and control are embodied in the Department of Treasury, the Office of Management and Budget (OMB), and the Council of Economic Advisors (CEA).[6] All of these agencies are active in analyzing economic data, preparing forecasts on which to base projections of tax collections, supervising preparation of the budget, and advocating executive branch economic philosophies that are inherent in the president's budget recommendations.

The executive office most involved in the federal budget is the Office of Management and Budget. The president's budget proposal, which is submitted to Congress, is the executive branch's financial plan for the federal government. The OMB's preparation of a budget begins about 9 months before the budget is submitted to Congress in January and approximately 18 months in advance of the beginning of the fiscal year covered by the budget proposal. In the spring, agencies are asked to evaluate their programs and make budgetary projections. These projections are subsequently revised by OMB and by the president.

Simultaneous with the expenditures planning, the Council of Economic Advisors, the Treasury, and the OMB prepare tax estimates based on forecasts of the economy. By fall or early winter, tentative spending targets for the coming fiscal year are sent back to the various federal agencies to aid their planning. Finally, a last

---

[6] There are other executive branch agencies which take part in the budget process, but the ones listed are the most important.

review is made by the OMB, and a draft of the budget is presented to the president for last-minute revisions. The president makes final changes and submits the proposed budget to Congress in January with his annual budget address.

When the budget is submitted to Congress in January, a revision process begins, and the final budget will differ considerably from the president's original proposal. Until 1975 Congress handled the budget on a piecemeal basis. No total expenditure–total revenue targets were adopted, and the final balance resulted from a series of separate actions rather than a planned attempt to achieve an overall fiscal target in line with the existing state of the economy. In 1975, however, Congress began implementation of the 1974 Budget Control Act. This law requires that Congress complete action on a first concurrent budget resolution by May 15 and on a final one by September 15; these resolutions target total expenditure and revenue levels for the fiscal year beginning October 1.

Months later, after Congress has acted on the budget, the executive branch is responsible for budget execution and control—tasks supervised by OMB. Budget review and audit comprise the final stage of the budget process, and the OMB participates in this phase along with the General Accounting Office (GAO). The GAO conducts an ongoing program of audit, examination, and evaluation of federal government financial activities.

WHAT IS THE IMPACT OF FISCAL POLICY ON ECONOMIC ACTIVITY?

Measures of fiscal policy impact

Gauging the impact of fiscal policy on the economy can be approached in terms of how a change in government spending or a change in tax rates influences certain key economic variables such as GNP, employment, and prices. Or the total federal budget can be viewed as an entity, focusing attention on the budget balance and its impact on the economy. The macromodels used in this text have expounded the first approach. Given a change in government spending (ΔG) or a change in the tax rate (Δt), the models allow us to predict the effect on equilibrium GNP. Changing government spending or tax rates with the intent of managing the level of economic activity is known as active fiscal policy. Our description in earlier chapters of how fiscal policy works indicated that an increase in government spending has a multiplier effect on the level of Gross National Product and that a tax rate decrease also causes an increase in the level of economic activity.

One difficulty in measuring the impact of fiscal policy on GNP is that a two-way relation exists between GNP and tax collections and between GNP and government spending. That is, not only can a change in government spending cause a change in GNP, but a change in GNP can also cause a change in government spending; the same is also true for taxes and GNP. Another difficulty in gauging the effect of fiscal policy arises out of the government budget constraint—that is, the method of financing expenditures.

To illustrate the first difficulty, assume that an increase in investment spending produces a rise in GNP. As income increases, tax collections go up (the two-way street), and there may also be a reduction in government spending as unemployment compensation and other income-related transfer payments decline. In this situation, the fiscal policy variables are working as automatic stabilizers. If, instead of rising, investment initially had fallen, the ensuing decline in GNP would have resulted in lower tax collections and more government spending, again helping automatically to stabilize the economy. Gauging the impact of fiscal policy is complicated by this two-way street between the economy and the fiscal policy variables.

As we mentioned at the outset of this section, the overall budget balance can be used to gauge the impact of fiscal policy. In essence this procedure includes both elements of fiscal policy—spending and revenues—and tries to indicate how the entire fiscal package influences economic activity. This approach focuses on the impact of the budget surplus or deficit for a particular fiscal year. The first inclination would be to conclude that a deficit (G greater than T) represents expansionary fiscal policy, that a surplus (G less than T) indicates contractionary fiscal policy, and that a balanced budget (G equal to T) means that fiscal policy is neutral.

Unfortunately this interpretation of the effect of fiscal policy is not as straightforward as it might seem on the surface. Say, for instance, that the economy is presently at full employment and the government budget is in balance. Now assume that investment spending declines, causing the level of GNP to fall also. Simultaneously the fiscal policy variables will be affected; that is, the fall in GNP will lower tax collections and result in an increase in government spending. Since tax collections are more sensitive to changes in GNP than is government spending, the fall in T will exceed the rise in G; consequently, the government budget will move from balance to deficit. Can we therefore conclude that fiscal policy is expansionary? The answer is no because the deficit is not the consequence of active fiscal policy but is due to the slump in economic activity which in turn influences government spending and taxes. We have again encountered the two-way street that connects GNP and the fiscal policy variables. From this example it should now be apparent that the budget balance can be a misleading indicator of whether fiscal policy as summarized by the budget balance is expansionary, contractionary, or neutral.

Is there another way of more accurately gauging the impact of fiscal policy? One possibility is to estimate what is known as the high-employment budget and to use the high-employment budget balance as an indicator of the thrust of fiscal policy. The high-employment budget is an estimate of what government spending, tax collections, and the associated budget balance would be if the economy were operating at full employment. This budget requires an estimate of potential GNP, which is the level of aggregate production that would occur if the economy were at full employment. We have already discussed some of the difficulties of computing potential GNP in Chapter 12, where it was noted that data on potential GNP are by no means precise; consequently, neither are figures on the high-employment budget.

If the conceptual problems that plague the calculation of potential GNP are ignored, then that estimate is the basis for deriving the high-employment budget. High-employment government spending is the level of expenditures that would exist if the economy were operating at capacity. If unemployment exists, then high-employment expenditures would be less than actual spending because certain expenditures such as unemployment benefits are lower when the economy is at full employment. High-employment tax receipts, on the other hand, would be more than actual receipts because income levels would be greater. Given estimates of high-employment government spending and tax receipts, the high-employment budget depicts the budget balance that would occur if the economy were operating at capacity.

In the example discussed previously, we assumed that from an initial position of full employment and budget balance, an economic decline occurred which produced a budget deficit. We argued that in this case the deficit did not represent active fiscal policy but rather the influence of the economy on the fiscal policy variables. If the impact of fiscal policy influence had been measured by the high-employment budget balance—which does not vary with the level of economic activity—the possible misinterpretation could have been avoided. For instance, if the high-employment budget were balanced, fiscal policy would be taken to be neutral, regardless of movements in the level of economic activity.

Does this mean that the high-employment budget is an infallible gauge of the impact of fiscal policy? Because of certain problems with the high-employment budget concept, it does not. One of these difficulties is the previously mentioned problem of having to estimate potential (full-employment) GNP in order to derive the high-employment budget. Furthermore, there is the possibility that the high-employment budget is balanced initially but goes into surplus as potential GNP grows, implying that active fiscal policy has become restrictive; in fact, the surplus is a result of the change in GNP. The high-employment budget is a useful device to help evaluate fiscal policy, but it, like the actual budget, has limitations.[7]

The effectiveness of fiscal policy

After the *General Theory* was published in 1936, fiscal policy began to assume a central role in macroeconomic policymaking. Keynesian analysis indicated that fiscal policy could be used to influence the level of economic activity, and the simple Keynesian models portrayed a world where changes in government spending and tax collections led to considerably greater changes in GNP via the multiplier process. For instance, in Chapter 13 our model without money represented an economy with a powerful response to fiscal policy influence. Even in Keynesian-type models containing a monetary sector and considering the financing of new government spending, fiscal policy is commonly depicted as a powerful tool capable of having a great influence on the level of economic activity.

There have always been those suspicious of these policy implications. Many economists were uncomfortable with the minor role given monetary policy by the early interpreters of Keynesian theory, and there were some who doubted that fiscal policy was quite as powerful as many Keynesians argued that it was. The most persistent of these skeptics united under the banner of monetarism with the main policy theme being that monetary policy is extremely powerful while fiscal policy has little or no lasting influence on economic activity.

In a 1958 article Milton Friedman set forth the theoretical underpinning of what came to be called monetarism.[8] The monetarist framework has undergone considerable refinement since then, and a good presentation of present-day monetarism can be found in *The*

---

[7] There are other approaches to measuring the impact of fiscal policy that attempt to correct some of the problems with the measures of fiscal policy impact discussed in this section. For example, Alan S. Blinder and Robert M. Solow derive what they call the "weighted standardized surplus." For a discussion of this particular measure of fiscal influence, see their "Analytical Foundations of Fiscal Policy," *The Economics of Public Finance* (Washington, D.C.: The Brookings Institution, 1974), pp. 3–115.

[8] Milton Friedman, "The Quantity Theory of Money: A Restatement," in Milton Friedman, ed., *Studies in the Quantity Theory of Money* (Chicago: University of Chicago Press, 1956), pp. 3–21.

Structure of Monetarism by Thomas Mayer.[9] Since most of the theoretical elements of the monetarist model were surveyed in Chapter 14, here we shall concentrate on (1) the empirical work of monetarists relating to fiscal policy, (2) rebuttals of these studies, and (3) other statistical evidence concerning the effectiveness of fiscal policy. Our survey is by no means comprehensive and is intended only as a summary of the debate on the effectiveness of fiscal policy.

In 1963, Friedman and David Meiselman published an article that stirred a lengthy debate.[10] Their work compared the effectiveness of fiscal and monetary policy based on empirical evidence for the United States economy for the period 1897–1958. They concluded from their analysis of the statistical record that "on the evidence so far, the stock of money is unquestionably far more critical in interpreting movements in income than is autonomous expenditures."[11] Or in other words, monetary policy is much more effective than fiscal policy.

The Friedman-Meiselman article generated considerable criticism of their findings. A particularly biting analysis of the study can be found in an article by Albert Ando and Franco Modigliani, who contend that the Friedman-Meiselman study is deficient for several reasons.[12] Theirs and other criticism raised considerable doubt about the conclusions reached by Friedman and Meiselman, and the majority of economists remained unconvinced that fiscal policy was ineffective in controlling economic activity.

But the controversy was not over, and the debate was rejoined in 1968 with the publication of an article by Leonall Andersen and Jerry Jordan in the *Review of the Federal Reserve Bank of St. Louis.*[13] They concluded on the basis of empirical evidence for the period 1952–68 that ". . . the finding that the response of total spending to changes in government expenditures is small compared with the response of spending to monetary actions strongly suggests that it

[9] Thomas Mayer, *The Structure of Monetarism* (New York: W. W. Norton & Co., 1978).

[10] Milton Friedman and David Meiselman, "The Relative Stability of Monetary Velocity and the Investment Multiplier in the United States, 1897–1958," in Commission on Money and Credit, *Stabilization Policies* (Englewood Cliffs, N.J.: Prentice-Hall, Inc., 1963), pp. 165–268.

[11] Ibid., p. 188.

[12] Albert Ando and Franco Modigliani, "The Relative Stability of Monetary Velocity and the Investment Multiplier," *American Economic Review*, vol. 55 (September 1965), pp. 693–728.

[13] Leonall Andersen and Jerry Jordan, "Monetary and Fiscal Actions: A Test of Their Relative Importance in Economic Stabilization," *Review of the Federal Reserve Bank of St. Louis*, vol. 50 (November 1968), pp. 11–24.

would be more appropriate to place greater reliance on the latter form of stabilization action."[14] Thus the model developed by economists at the Saint Louis Federal Reserve Bank offered new evidence in support of the premise that monetary policy was powerful and fiscal policy virtually impotent.

Again evidence was offered to rebut this finding and show that fiscal policy is much more powerful than the Saint Louis model indicated. The article by Blinder and Solow cited in the previous section provides a good summary of the effectiveness of fiscal policy as depicted by several econometric models.[15] The very small expenditures multiplier of the Saint Louis model contrasts with the other models named in the Blinder-Solow paper: after 12 quarters of sustained increase in nominal nondefense government spending, the multiplier effect on nominal GNP is 0.1 in the Saint Louis model but ranges from about 1.5 to 3.0 in the six other models included in the comparison.

What then can be concluded about the effectiveness of fiscal policy? A majority of economists continue to hold the position that changes in government spending and taxes will influence the level of economic activity; very few of any persuasion including monetarists would accept the extreme monetarist position that "money alone matters." Therefore, the extreme monetarists have not convinced the majority of their colleagues that fiscal policy has little influence on the economy; they have, however, generated a reevaluation of economic policymaking. Fiscal policy has not been cast aside as the result of monetarist analysis, but its sway over policymaking has diminished while monetary policy has come to be viewed more favorably.

ARE FEDERAL BUDGET DEFICITS INEVITABLE?

After publication of the *General Theory*, Keynesian policy prescriptions came to dominate macroeconomic policymaking. The Employment Act of 1946 represents a committment to use economic policy for stabilization purposes. Macroeconomic policymaking did not come of age, though, until the early 1960s under presidents Kennedy and Johnson. Walter Heller, chairman of the Council of Economic Advisors from 1961 to 1964, actively promoted the use of fiscal policy to reduce unemployment and stimulate economic growth. His efforts were instrumental in the passage of the Kennedy-Johnson tax reduction bill of 1964 which is credited by some

---

[14] Ibid., p. 22.

[15] Blinder and Solow, "Analytical Foundations of Fiscal Policy."

economists as the key to the impressive performance of the U.S. economy during the mid-to-late 1960s.[16]

During the 1950s and early 1960s, economists promoted the idea that government spending increases, lower taxes, and deficits are useful ways of promoting a stable economy. This concept represented a sharp turnabout from the days when fiscal responsibility and a balanced budget were one and the same. By the mid-1960s many economists were convinced, and politicians by and large agreed, that the formula for uninterrupted prosperity had been found; all that needed to be done was to apply what was already known about policymaking.

The record with respect to federal deficits is indicative of the extent to which the concept of active fiscal policymaking has been applied. Taking successive five-year periods beginning with 1950–54 and ending with 1975–79, the average annual deficit grew from $1.24 billion in 1950–54 to $46.54 billion in 1975–79. For the first half of the entire 1950–79 period, there were four surplus years and ten other years when the deficit was less than $10 billion; during the second half of that era, there was a surplus in one year and only five years when the deficit was less than $10 billion. Thus the tendency to accept deficits as part of the quest for economic stability is obvious. Also, one cannot help but observe that deficits have ballooned during presidential election years. In 1968 the deficit was $25.2 billion, which at that time was $12 billion more than the deficit for any year since World War II. In 1972 the deficit was $23.4 billion, and in 1976 it was $66.5 billion. These figures certainly arouse suspicion that political expediency may be more important than economic urgency, at least during the period immediately preceding elections.

The tendency for deficits to be the rule rather than the exception and for politics to impinge unduly on fiscal policymaking has promoted a movement for a constitutional amendment that would require an annually balanced budget. This proposal and certain of its variations are discussed in Chapter 19.

WHAT ARE THE MAJOR PROBLEMS ENCOUNTERED BY FISCAL POLICYMAKERS?

In this section we conclude the discussion of fiscal policy by enumerating some difficulties involved in its administration. The following problems are covered.

---

[16] Other economists would stress the role of monetary policy, particularly the rate of growth of the money supply, as the key factor.

1. Uncertainty about the size and timing of the impact of fiscal policy.
2. Lags and forecasting.
3. Political considerations.
4. Difficulties related to financing expenditures.

Some of these topics were introduced earlier, while others are being discussed for the first time.

We have already described the controversy regarding the magnitude of the impact of fiscal policy. Monetarists take a dismal view of its influence while Keynesians—or perhaps a slightly more apt title here is fiscalists—think that fiscal policy is effective. Even among fiscalists, though, there is differing opinion about the degree to which fiscal policy is effective. Remember that in the models mentioned earlier (with the exception of the Saint Louis Model), the expenditures multiplier ranged from 1.5 to 3.0 as measured 12 quarters after the increase in government spending. Obviously, a policymaker trying to decide how much fiscal stimulus to apply faces considerable uncertainty. Also, the use of fiscal policy is complex because the speed at which fiscal policy is expected to affect the economy not only varies from model to model but in fact seems to change from one situation to another; thus the timing of policy actions is critical.

The timing of fiscal policy impact is related to the second problem listed above—lags and the need for accurate forecasting. There may be considerable delay between the occurrence of a problem—a downturn in GNP, for instance—and the full impact of the policy applied to remedy the situation. Three lags have been identified in connection with policy—the recognition lag, the administrative lag, and the effect lag. These lags apply to both monetary and fiscal policymaking, and the following description is therefore related to both.

As a simplified example of the lag problem, assume that during the first quarter of the year the pace of economic activity begins to slow. This situation is shown in Figure 16–1 at t_1 point in time. The problem will not be recognized immediately since it takes time to collect and analyze data that verify the slowdown. Assume that by the beginning of the second quarter (t_2 in Figure 16–1), a downturn is apparent. So, some time has elapsed between the initial occurrence of the problem and when it is generally recognized; this interval is known as the recognition lag. Since monetary and fiscal policymakers have access to essentially the same data, the recognition lag should be approximately the same for both policies.

Now, having recognized that a problem exists, a course of action must be determined. In the case of fiscal policy, new expenditures

FIGURE 16-1
Lags in fiscal and monetary policymaking

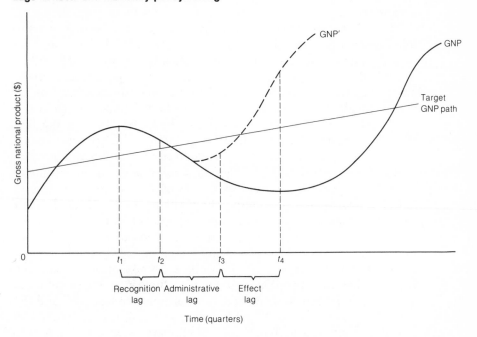

programs or tax revisions take time to pass and implement. Assume that action is taken to stimulate the economy by cutting taxes at the end of the fourth quarter; this action is depicted as occurring at t_3 in Figure 16-1. The time that passes between recognition of a problem and implementation of policy to combat the situation is known as the administrative lag. The administrative lag associated with monetary policy would normally be shorter than for fiscal policy since the Board of Governors and the Federal Open Market Committee can institute policy changes quickly and with fewer complications.

Finally, it takes time for policy to have an effect, and this lag between implementation of policy and its impact on the economy (at t_4 in the figure) is known as the effect lag. Thus the total lag between when a problem arises and when the effect is felt may be well over a year. Note that in the example of Figure 16-1, the impact of policy occurs when the solid line representing GNP is still declining, thereby indicating that the timing of the policy was correct.

Various studies have found different lags for monetary and fiscal policy, and the time periods used in the example and depicted in Figure 16-1 must be thought of as rough approximations. Furthermore, there is some evidence that indicates that the time span for each of the three lags is variable. Variability of lags would, of course, further complicate policymaking since policymakers could not be sure when the main impact of policy changes would occur.

The existence of lags obviously increases the importance of accurate forecasting; if good forecasts of the course of the economy are available several quarters in advance, then policy results should be much better. Ability to forecast accurately would permit policymakers to react in advance of problems, thus moderating cyclical fluctuations. Ideally, policymakers would like to eliminate the cycle and have GNP grow at a steady rate shown in Figure 16–1 by the line labeled "Target GNP path" which is what nominal GNP would be, assuming that full employment and stable prices were maintained.

But if forecasting is faulty, then lags are a more serious problem. Consider, for example, the consequences of inaccurate forecasting in a situation where expansionary policy is being applied to deal with a slowdown that has just recently been recognized. Moreover, suppose that the economy has already begun to rebound on its own, but forecasters fail to predict the upturn. Under these circumstances, expansionary policy would probably be inappropriate since the economy has already rebounded. Such a situation is shown in Figure 16–1 where the relevant GNP curve is assumed to be GNP', and the impact of the expansionary policy at t_4 would further stimulate an already expanding and perhaps inflationary economy. Such possibilities account for the fact that many economists have now come to view fine tuning the economy with frequent policy adjustments with considerable misgivings. Also, those who advocate adoption of monetary and fiscal policy rules rather than relying on the discretion of policymakers share the same concern. According to rules proponents, lags and their variability make it virtually impossible for policymakers to respond correctly to cyclical changes in economic activity given the present state of the art of forecasting.

The third problem associated with fiscal policymaking is the political pressure involved in the budget-making process. It is often more popular to increase governmental programs and to cut taxes than to spend less and collect more taxes. So a tendency exists to run deficits even in years when a balanced budget or a surplus is clearly in order. This tendency has become glaringly apparent during election years as noted in the previous section.

A final consideration concerning the use of fiscal policy is the method chosen to finance an increase in expenditures. Financing a spending increase by collecting more taxes is less expansionary than issuing new debt or creating new money. There is a natural inclination to view tax-financed expenditures as neutral with respect to GNP since the increase in spending would seem to be offset by a decrease in aggregate demand occasioned by the new tax collections. However, it is possible that a rise in tax payments will not be matched by an equal drop in spending. As disposable (aftertax) income declines, consumption will decrease but not as much as taxes since some of the increased taxes will come at the expense of saving. Consequently, the *direct* effect of a tax-financed increase in government spending is a net gain in aggregate demand. The complete effect is less clear, however, since the fall in saving will reduce the availability of loanable funds and, hence, exert upward pressure on interest rates. The higher interest rates will, in turn, cause a decline in aggregate demand.

It is more common that some portion of the increased level of spending will be financed by issuing new government debt. Since the new borrowing increases the demand for loanable funds, there will be upward pressure on interest rates, and subsequently some private spending will be crowded out. Of course, the impact of fiscal policy under these circumstances will be diminished.

It is at this point that monetary policy often enters the picture. To increase the funds available to the government and to hold down interest rates, the Fed may purchase government securities on the open market, thereby setting the stage for an expansion of the money supply. Fiscal and monetary policies are obviously not independent of each other but are clearly interrelated.

It is obvious that policymaking is seldom a simple process; consequently, doubts regarding the possibility of fine tuning the economy through frequent applications of monetary and fiscal policy have been raised. One thing seems certain—an economic myopia seems to have plagued policymaking for the past two decades. Unwilling or unable to look farther ahead than the next election, policymakers have often sacrificed long-term stability for the expediency of the short run. Gradually, many people are coming to recognize that only when rational policies are applied consistently over a long period will they be successful.

SUMMARY

This chapter has explored the use of fiscal policy to influence the level of economic activity. Managing the economy, however, is not the only federal budget objective; others include providing a hospitable legal, social, and economic environment, producing or supervising the production of public goods, and redistributing income.

The structure of the federal budget has changed significantly during the past decade or so. In the late 1960s spending on national defense accounted for over 40 percent of the federal budget, while today the defense budget is less than 25 percent of total spending.

On the other hand, transfer programs have expanded rapidly and presently are about one half of all federal expenditures, compared to about 30 percent at the end of the 1960s. On the revenue side, individual income taxes provide most federal revenue, but payroll taxes have increased most rapidly during the past decade.

Gauging the impact of fiscal policy is not simple. The effect on economic activity of changes in government spending and taxes is difficult to discern because a two-way relation exists between GNP and the fiscal policy variables. The federal budget balance may be used to gauge the influence of fiscal policy, but the actual balance often has misleading implications. The high-employment budget is in some respects a better indicator of fiscal policy influence, but even the high-employment budget is deficient in several respects.

The effectiveness of fiscal policy is a matter of some debate. Monetarists argue that fiscal policy has at best a minor impact on economic activity and believe that monetary policy is much more powerful. Keynesians, or fiscalists, contend that fiscal policy has a significant influence on the level of economic activity. Presently most economists believe that both fiscal and monetary policy can be used to influence the economy, but there is still considerable disagreement over the relative effectiveness of each.

There is evidence that use of fiscal policy has become more active since World War II. Budget deficits have become more common, and the magnitude of deficits has increased relative to GNP. Fiscal policy was the centerpiece of fine tuning which was advocated by many economists during the 1960s, but the idea that the economy can be fine tuned by continually making small adjustments to economic policy is no longer viewed with much optimism.

There are numerous problems involved with efficiently administering fiscal and monetary policy including (1) uncertainty regarding the impact and timing of fiscal policy, (2) lags, (3) political considerations, and (4) the choice of how to finance new federal expenditures.

REVIEW QUESTIONS

1. Consult a recent *Federal Reserve Bulletin* and update Table 16–1. Are there any discernable trends in the relative importance of any of the expenditures or receipts totals?

2. Why may the actual budget balance be a poor guide to the thrust of fiscal policy?

3. Is the high-employment budget balance a better indicator of the thrust of fiscal policy than the actual budget balance? Why or why not?

4. Summarize the monetarist position on the effectiveness of monetary policy. Offer some counterarguments.

5. What are the three lags associated with fiscal (and monetary) policymaking? Use a hypothetical situation to illustrate the three lags. (You might assume, as a starting point, that the economy recently reached the peak of the cycle.)

6. Are fiscal and monetary policy related to one another? In what manner?

7. Some argue that fiscal policy should be used to fine tune the economy, while others contend that fiscal policy should be put more or less on automatic pilot—for example, by requiring a balanced budget. What is your opinion about these two approaches?

8. Consult the most recent *Economic Report of the President*. What is the current administration's fiscal policy plan for the near future?

SUGGESTIONS FOR ADDITIONAL READING

Andersen, Leonall C., and Jordan, Jerry L. "Monetary and Fiscal Actions: A Test of Their Relative Importance in Economic Stabilization." *Review of the Federal Reserve Bank of St. Louis,* vol. 50, no. 11 (November 1968), pp. 11–24.

Blinder, Alan S., and Solow, Robert M. "Analytical Foundations of Fiscal Policy." In *The Economics of Public Finance.* Washington, D.C.: The Brookings Institution, 1974, pp. 3–115.

Economic Report of the President, recent issues.

Fellner, William A. *Towards a Reconstruction of Macroeconomics.* Washington, D.C.: American Enterprise Institute for Public Policy Research, 1976, especially chap. 7.

Lerner, Abba P. "Functional Finance and the Federal Debt." *Social Research,* vol. 10 (February 1943), pp. 38–51.

Tax Foundation, Inc. *Facts and Figures on Government Finance.* Washington, D.C.: The Tax Foundation, Inc., annual.

U.S., Office of Management and Budget. *The Budget of the United States Government.* Washington, D.C.: U.S. Government Printing Office, annual.

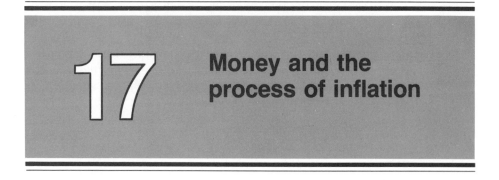

17

Money and the process of inflation

WARM-UP: *Outline and questions to consider as you read*

What is inflation, and why is it a problem?
> The burden of inflation on individual economic units.
> The burden of inflation on society.

What are the causes of inflation?
> Money and inflation.
> Government deficits, money, and inflation.
> Excess-demand or cost-push inflation.

What are the dynamics of the inflationary process?

NEW TERMS

Cost-push inflation: inflation resulting from increased costs of production such as higher wages or materials costs.

Excess-demand inflation: inflation resulting from too much aggregate demand.

Price-information costs: the extra costs generated during a period of inflation by the necessity of making frequent price adjustments and future price estimates.

Relative prices: the price ratios of different products and resources which are the basis for income and resource allocation decisions.

As of this writing, public opinion surveys in the United States reveal that inflation is viewed as the number one economic problem in the country. Furthermore, the inflation problem is not unique to the United States or to the current time period. There have been many historical episodes of inflation, but, until recently, inflation in this country was generally associated with wartime periods. While the origins of the current inflation are usually attributed to the Vietnam war, the postwar persistence and severity of the problem are without parallel. Figure 17–1 shows that throughout U.S. history, wartime

FIGURE 17–1
Prices in The United States, 1800–1979

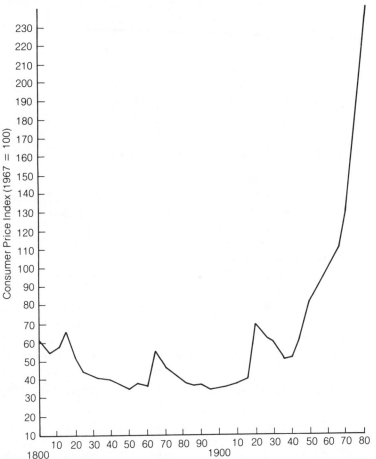

Sources: U.S. Department of Commerce, *Historical Statistics of The United States, Colonial Times to 1970*, pt. 1, pp. 210–11; *Economic Report of the President*, 1978; and Board of Governors of the Federal Reserve System, *Federal Reserve Bulletin*, vol. 66, no. 2 (February 1980), p. A51.

periods of inflation have been followed by periods of falling prices. The absence of price declines after World War II is often attributed to the market power of big labor and big business and to an expansionary bias in public policy toward aggregate demand management.

In the early 1960s, the country experienced considerable optimism regarding our ability to manage the economy so as to achieve the major macroeconomic goals of full employment, stable prices, and economic growth. Events in the 1970s have greatly diminished this optimism, and, in fact, there now exists an air of pessimism regarding our ability to deal with inflation. What is the nature of this inflation plague? How harmful is it? Is the recent inflation some new and uncontrollable mutation of older varieties of inflation? Is economic policy capable of dealing with inflation? What would be the consequences of measures strong enough to subdue today's inflation? These and related questions are the subject of this and the following chapter. While the economics profession is not unanimous in its answers to these questions, we believe that the discussion presented in the following pages reflects the general direction toward which the consensus of opinion is moving.[1]

WHAT IS INFLATION, AND WHY IS IT A PROBLEM?

Inflation can be defined as (1) a declining value of the monetary unit, or equivalently as (2) a continuing rise in the general level of prices.[2] These simple definitions have several important, but often neglected, implications. Inflation is by nature a monetary phenomenon; it makes no sense to talk of inflation in a barter economy. Hence, a monetary economy is a necessary, but not sufficient, condition for inflation. Also, inflation is a continuing process; rising prices, not high prices, constitute inflation. Finally, a rise in the price of one, several, or even many goods does not necessarily signify inflation. If these price increases are accompanied by price declines of other products, the general level of prices may remain unchanged. The situation would be one of changing relative prices rather than of a general change in prices. It is only when prices of most goods are rising and are not accompanied by offsetting declines

---

[1] The reader may wish to consult Helmut Frish's summary of the state of inflation theory in "Inflation Theory, 1963–1975: A 'Second Generation' Survey," *Journal of Economic Literature*, vol. 15, no. 4 (December 1977), pp. 1289–1317. More detailed and somewhat less technical summaries are found in Samuel A. Morley, *Inflation and Unemployment*, 2d ed. (Hinsdale, Ill.: The Dryden Press, 1979) and David C. Colander, ed., *Solutions to Inflation* (New York: Harcourt, Brace, Jovanovich, Inc., 1979).

[2] For a discussion of price indexes and the measurement of inflation, the reader may wish to review the relevant sections of Chapters 2 and 12.

TABLE 17-1
Inflation rates in selected countries, 1972–1978

Country	Average annual percentage change in prices	Country	Average annual percentage change in prices
Argentina.................	197.3	Italy	19.1
Australia	14.8	Japan.....................	13.8
Austria	8.4	Mexico....................	22.9
Belgium...................	10.7	New Zealand	15.6
Brazil	39.3	Norway	11.2
Canada	10.8	Peru	35.7
Chile......................	302.0	Portugal...................	23.2
Columbia..................	28.1	Saudi Arabia..............	22.2
Denmark	13.0	South Africa	13.6
Finland....................	16.1	Spain	21.1
France	12.2	Sweden	11.6
Germany, West	5.7	Switzerland	5.7
Greece....................	19.0	Turkey	29.4
Iceland....................	45.3	United Kingdom	18.3
India	10.3	United States	7.7
Iran	17.7	Uruguay	85.3
Ireland	17.8	Venezuela	9.0

Source: International Monetary Fund, *International Financial Statistics*, vol. 32, no. 7 (July 1979).

in other prices that the value of the monetary unit is falling, and only when the value of the monetary unit is falling do we have inflation.

Recent (1972–78) rates of inflation in 33 major countries as shown in Table 17–1 confirm that inflation is not unique to the United States. These data indicate that average annual rates of inflation of 10 to 20 percent are not uncommon, and that some countries have experienced annual rates of inflation in excess of 100 percent. However, these recent cases of inflation are quite mild compared to several earlier inflationary episodes such as the German inflation of 1921–23 and the Hungarian inflation of 1945–46. From August 1922 through November 1923, the German price level rose an average of 322 percent per month. Prices at the end of that period were approximately 7,320,000,000 times higher than at the beginning of the period. This was a mini-inflation, however, compared to the Hungarian case in which price increases averaged 19,800 percent per month between August 1945 and July 1946.[3]

The burden of inflation on individual economic units

The existence of inflation creates great concern, which implies that people are somehow harmed by inflation, and indeed that is

---

[3] Phillip Cagan, "The Monetary Dynamics of Hyperinflation," in Milton Friedman, ed., *Studies in the Quantity Theory of Money* (Chicago: University of Chicago Press, 1956), chap. 2.

often the case. Two types of inflationary effects may be identified: (1) a redistribution of income from which some people benefit while others lose even though the economy as a whole may not suffer and (2) a reduction in the well-being of society as a whole through a lowering of output levels due to resource misallocations.

The extent to which inflation can inflict harm upon individual economic units is often dependent upon whether or not inflation is anticipated. Consider two individuals, a debtor and a creditor. The debtor borrows $1,000 from the creditor and promises to repay the $1,000 plus 5 percent interest at the end of one year with both parties assuming that there will be no inflation during the year. Let us assume, however, that unanticipated inflation does occur at an annual rate of 20 percent. At the end of the year the borrower will repay the lender $1,050 as agreed. In the above case, the borrower has gained at the expense of the creditor due to the unanticipated inflation which has reduced the purchasing power of the lender's proceeds to the point where it will now take $1,200 to purchase what the original $1,000 would have purchased one year earlier. Put another way, the $1,050 that the borrower pays the lender is equivalent in purchasing power to only $875 as compared to the $1,000 that the lender originally gave the borrower.[4]

The money rate of interest that lenders earn is sometimes referred to as the nominal rate of interest. In terms of purchasing power, the nominal rate of interest is a deceptive measure of what creditors earn on loans during periods of inflation. To reflect the effects of inflation, the nominal interest rate is converted to a real rate of interest by subtracting the rate of inflation, or adding the rate of deflation if prices are falling. Thus, in the above example, the creditor earned a nominal rate of interest of 5 percent, but the real rate of interest was negative after adjusting for the 20 percent inflation rate.

An obvious question arises at this point: Why would anyone be willing to lend money at a rate of interest that is lower than the rate of inflation? In fact, lenders reduce their lending if rates remain below the anticipated rate of price increase. Let us go back to the above example and change one assumption so that both debtors and creditors correctly anticipate the 20 percent rate of inflation. Anticipating a 20 percent rate of inflation, creditors will realize that they must have a 25 percent nominal return in order to realize a 5 percent real return. Likewise, debtors will be willing to pay a 25 percent nominal rate of interest because the dollars they borrow have

---

[4] This number is obtained by deflating the end-of-year figure ($1,050) by the price index (120) based on the beginning of the year as the base period. Thus,

$$\frac{\$1,050}{120} \times 100 = \$875.$$

considerably more purchasing power than the dollars they repay. Thus to the extent that inflation is correctly anticipated, the nominal rate of interest will rise to offset the anticipated rate of inflation. The empirical evidence indicates that borrowers and lenders do not always correctly anticipate the rate of inflation, but during periods of sustained inflation, anticipation of continued price increases causes the nominal rate of interest to adjust upward to offset a major portion of the inflation.

Borrowers and lenders are not the only groups whose welfare can be affected by unanticipated inflation. Consider a group of workers who agree to a long-term (three-year) wage contract at the then-prevailing wage rate of, say, $5 per hour without any anticipation of inflation during the three-year period. Suppose that inflation occurs at an annual rate of 10 percent. By the end of the third year of the contract, prices will be approximately one-third higher than when the contract was negotiated, and workers will have suffered a one-third drop in their real wages. To the extent that the employer's prices are flexible, the prices of products produced by the workers can be increased. Thus when inflation is unanticipated, prices are likely to rise faster than wages, but to the extent that workers come to anticipate inflation, they will demand sufficient wage increases over the life of a contract to offset the expected decline in the purchasing power of their wages. Again much of the redistribution of income from inflation can be avoided if the rate of price rise is correctly anticipated.

The burden of inflation on society

The fact that unanticipated inflation redistributes wealth is not sufficient grounds for concluding that the aggregate effect of inflation is harmful. To society in general, inflation may be only an inconvenience resulting from the illusion created by focusing attention on price increases while ignoring the accompanying income increases. In fact, if there is a permanent trade-off between inflation and unemployment as some believe, total production and the aggregate standard of living may be higher with inflation that without it.

From society's standpoint, however, inflation does create at least one serious problem—a misallocation of resources that can diminish the productivity and growth rate of the economy and, in the long run, make everyone worse off. Inflation tends to diminish productivity and lessen economic growth in several ways:

1. By reducing the incentive to save.
2. By biasing personal and business investment decisions toward unproductive or less-productive investments.

3. By distorting the price signals that guide the market economy toward efficient resource allocation.
4. By causing economic units to devote extra resources to gathering information and making decisions in situations where the outcome is sensitive to the inflation rate.

Diminished incentive to save. Inflation can reduce the incentive to save if economic units learn by experience that saving results in diminished real wealth. Savers will find their real wealth diminishing if the rate of inflation is not correctly anticipated, or if legal constraints hold the nominal rate of interest below the inflation rate. Under these conditions, channeling savings into forms having fixed monetary values results in a loss of wealth. In recent years, interest controls such as Regulation Q have resulted in negative real rates of interest to many savers. Some savers avoid these ceilings through disintermediation—the process whereby funds are withdrawn from the financial intermediaries and used to purchase primary financial claims such as Treasury bills, commercial paper, and corporate bonds. The recent regulatory changes that permit thrift institutions to offer money market certificates paying interest at market-determined rates have allowed some savers to fare better during inflation, and the phasing out of Regulation Q should also prove to be a beneficial step.

What are the alternatives for those savers who are too small to take advantage of higher-yielding financial assets but who seek to protect their savings from inflation? One alternative is to save less and consume more. In fact, if inflation is severe, there will be a scramble to consume before prices increase. The lower savings rate and increased consumption ultimately require that more of the economy's productive capacity be devoted to consumption goods and less to capital formation. In the long run, this results in a lower rate of economic growth.

Investment in nonproductive assets. Not only is inflation likely to create a bias toward more consumption, but it also biases business investment decisions toward nonproductive asset forms. Rather than investing in new and more productive plant and equipment, firms purchase raw materials and invest in inventories, or they may invest in foreign currency rather than new capital goods. Furthermore, completely new types of businesses spring up that utilize society's resources to supply the objects of the growing speculative fever. For example, even in relatively mild inflations, additional resources are quickly channeled into the marketing of gold, silver, other precious metals, and other commodities.

Relative-price distortions. During inflation, prices of different items do not adjust at the same rate. Price changes for some items (fresh produce, for example) can be made quickly, while prices of other items (new automobiles) are adjusted rather infrequently. Because of the differential effects of inflation on the prices of individual items, relative prices can become distorted in any given time period. In a market economy, relative prices guide resource-use decisions; therefore, if current relative prices are "wrong," and future relative prices are more difficult than ever to forecast, resource misallocations occur. Furthermore, if resources are used inefficiently, aggregate production and economic growth are at less than optimum rates.

Price-information costs. As economic units come to anticipate further inflation, they begin to devote resources to predicting the amounts and timing of price increases and to coping with the effects of those increases. Information that would not be needed or wanted if prices were stable must be gathered and disseminated when prices are unstable: list prices must be constantly updated; stockclerks must stamp new prices over old ones; new catalogues must be issued more frequently; and more time must be devoted to projecting future prices. All these activities raise opportunity costs and ultimately reduce output because resources must be transferred from some other use. Since the occurrence of these types of activities increases as inflation increases, output losses rise along with the rate of inflation.

Inflation gives people an incentive to economize on their holdings of money and other assets with fixed monetary values. This incentive is weak if the rate of inflation is low, but it strengthens as the rate of inflation increases. Consequently, when there is extremely rapid price change, a situation known as hyperinflation, workers demand to be paid more and more often, and immediately upon receiving wages, they hurriedly make purchases of goods, foreign currencies, or anything tangible before their purchasing power is eroded. Small business proprietors may even close their doors several times a day so that they can spend the day's proceeds before prices increase further. Time and resources are expended in minimizing money holdings. Such a use of time and resources precludes their use in more productive ways so that productivity and growth must suffer.

WHAT ARE THE CAUSES OF INFLATION?

Money and inflation

Is inflation caused by excessive growth of the money supply, by government deficits, by big labor unions, by oligopolistic corporations, by OPEC, or by all of the above? There is rather widespread agreement that continued and significant inflation cannot occur in the absence of excessive increases in the money supply. More precisely, if the supply of money is maintained in excess of the demand for money, then the necessary and sufficient condition for inflation will exist. There is disagreement, however, concerning the importance of certain other factors and their precise role in the inflationary process. We are not asserting that changes in the money supply are the only cause of inflation; for example, several factors could cause a decline in the demand for money while the money supply remains unchanged with the result being a rising level of prices. One is hard pressed, however, to find historical instances where such factors induced significant price changes, and there are no historical cases of sizable inflations that were not accompanied by increases in the money supply.

Data on inflation and money supply growth for 33 countries during the 1972–78 period are presented in Figure 17–2. The data indicate a strong correlation (but not necessarily a cause-and-effect relationship) between the rate of growth of a country's money supply and the rate of price increase (as measured by the consumer price index) for that country.[5]

While changes in the supply of money relative to the demand for money are both necessary and sufficient to bring about significant and prolonged inflation, the cause of inflation is not fully explained until there is a description of how and why these money supply increases occur. Historically, many instances of inflationary increases in the money supply (increases in excess of the growth of demand for money) have occurred because governments needed to finance wars and were not able or willing to do so by raising the revenue through taxes. The advent of paper money made financing through issuance of money an easy approach for governments. Examples from the U.S. experience include the paper dollars issued by the Continental Congress to help finance the Revolutionary War, and the "greenbacks" issued by the Union during the Civil War.

Historical examples of money-supply expansions on a scale large enough to cause inflation are by no means confined to paper money cases. Even under metallic standards, where the primary circulating medium is made of some precious metal, governments have generated significant supply increases by debasing the currency—a process whereby the amount of precious metal in the coins is reduced. Again, examples of coinage debasements are usually associated with wartime periods. An early example of such occurred in

---

[5] A perfect correlation between money supply changes and inflation would exist if all points had fallen on the 45-degree line.

FIGURE 17-2
Inflation and money supply changes for selected countries, 1977-78*

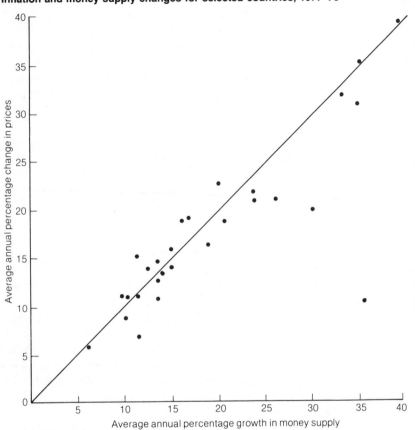

*Includes those countries in Table 17-1 which had inflation rates of less than 40 percent.
Source: International Monetary Fund, *International Financial Statistics,* vol. 32, no. 7 (July 1979).

Rome during the Punic Wars when the copper content of the major Roman coin, the *as,* was reduced from 12 ounces to ½ ounce in a series of debasements. Apart from war-related expansion of the money supply, historical examples of money-supply increases that set off inflationary periods can be found any time large new discoveries of gold and silver were made. The classic example is the increase in the European gold supply, particularly in Spain, associated with the discovery of the New World.

Government deficits, money, and inflation

In early episodes of paper money–induced inflation, national governments simply ran the printing presses and then used the new money to purchase goods and services. More recently in the United States and in many other countries, the central bank has been responsible for managing the country's money supply, and most modern governments recognize that it is the height of fiscal irresponsibility to "run the printing presses" in order to finance the government's expenditures. This does not mean, however, that governments are no longer instrumental in generating inflationary increases in the money supply. The classic example is the post–World War I government of Germany.

Suffering from defeat at the hands of the Allies and reeling under the heavy burden of reparations, the German government was unable to raise sufficient tax revenues to finance its expenditures. It began to borrow, and much of this borrowing was done by selling treasury bills. Initially these treasury bills were sold primarily to the public, but eventually the government could not sell sufficient quantities, so it began discounting them (selling them) to the German central bank, the Reichsbank. The Reichsbank paid for the bonds by printing new marks (the German monetary unit) which the government promptly spent, thereby increasing the German money supply. The process had exactly the same effect as if the German government had resorted to the printing presses.

The alert reader will recognize that the Federal Reserve engages in precisely this type of operation when it enters the government securities market as a net buyer of outstanding securities in order to keep interest rates from rising when the government sells additional bonds. This process is referred to as monetizing the public debt, and if it occurs on a large scale or at the wrong time, it is almost certain to be inflationary.

Recognition of an association between government deficits and growth of the money supply has led many people to view government deficits as the source of inflation. This is not necessarily the case; if the deficit is financed by selling bonds to the public, new money creation will not be inevitable. The dollars supplied to the government by deficit financing can be used to acquire goods and services without bidding up prices since the public has given up command over an equivalent value of goods and services by purchasing the government bonds. In the process, interest rates will rise as the government attracts funds in the financial markets, and the higher rates force some potential private borrowers to postpone or cancel their planned purchases.

However, if the Federal Reserve purchases bonds in the open market in order to moderate pressures on interest rates, the amount of money and credit available to the public will not be reduced. Consequently, price increases are likely to occur as the public and the government compete to purchase goods and services. Furthermore, since the Fed's open-market purchases increase the monetary base, the stage is set for a further increase in the money supply. Even in this case, however, the deficit financed by the central banks is not a sufficient condition for inflation. If adequate idle resources and excess capacity exist in the economy, the result simply may be a case of monetary and fiscal policy acting to expand aggregate demand, employment, and output. On the other hand, when the economy is operating near full capacity, deficit financing leading to money supply growth rates in excess of output growth rates is virtually certain to be inflationary.

Responsible governments do not continuously finance their expenditures by printing new money or by exerting pressure on the central bank to purchase government bonds. Neither do responsible independent central banks purchase government debt under such circumstances. Yet, in the United States and other countries, we do observe central banks purchasing government debt in quantities that lead to inflationary increases in the money supply. Part of the reason for this can be attributed to the growing degree to which governments have engaged in aggregate demand management since World War II. This practice has meant that government taxing and spending patterns and monetary policy actions are adjusted to stimulate or contract aggregate demand in an attempt to achieve major macroeconomic goals. Thus deficit financing coupled with accommodating monetary policy—monetary policy that expands bank reserves and the money supply sufficiently to keep interest rates low—is usually a deliberate course of action when unemployment is unacceptably high and the economy is operating at less than capacity.

Consider the possibility that the economy is operating at less than full capacity: Will expansionary monetary and fiscal policies lead to output increases instead of price increases? There are a number of problems associated with monetary and fiscal policy that may cause well-meaning government and central bank authorities to pursue policies that turn out to be inflationary.

The timing and magnitude problems. Recall from Chapter 16 that neither fiscal nor monetary policy can be instantaneously applied, and once applied, there is some delay before the economy feels the full effect of whatever policy actions are taken. If the forecasts of the size and timing of an economic problem are wrong, then policy actions could have an adverse effect. Another practical problem with which monetary and fiscal policymakers must deal is the question of the degree of action to be taken. Even if the forecasts of recession are correct and the timing problem is avoided, an overly expansionary budget deficit and /or money-supply increase can cause the economy to overshoot its mark. The policymakers then end up curing the recession but causing (or worsening) inflation in the process.

The conflicting objectives problem. A common view during the 1960s was that the goals of low unemployment and stable prices might conflict. That is, if the unemployment rate were unacceptably high, lowering it would entail a trade-off in the form of rising prices. This notion was embodied in the Phillips Curve which depicted a stable, inverse association between the unemployment rate and the rate of inflation; thus the choices available would be low unemployment with rising prices or higher unemployment with more stable prices. On the basis of this presumed trade-off, policymakers were able to rationalize inflationary policies on the basis that full employment was a more important objective than price stability. Therefore, the tendency of policymakers to overstimulate the economy in recent years has to a great extent been based on the trade-off assumption. The discussion in the following chapter indicates, however, that the Phillips Curve hypothesis is not as widely accepted as it once was.

Excess-demand or cost-push inflation

The essence of the explanation of inflation up to this point may be stated simply: Excessively rapid monetary growth that is often linked to fiscal policy raises aggregate demand faster than the real output of the economy can be increased. Since the real value of output at existing prices cannot increase fast enough to accommodate aggregate demand, prices must increase enough so that the monetary value of real output at the new higher prices absorbs the aggregate demand for output. This view of inflation is often referred to as excess-demand inflation. We would expect that such inflation would be most likely to occur in a full- or high-employment economy. However, episodes of rising prices have been observed during periods when resources have not been fully utilized. It appears only reasonable, therefore, to conclude that excess aggregate demand is not the cause of at least some episodes of inflation and that perhaps more than one type of inflation is possible. In fact, during the 1950s and 1960s, economists commonly distinguished between excess-demand (sometimes called demand-pull) inflation and cost-push inflation, with the latter term referring to those inflationary episodes occurring at less than full employment.

Cost-push inflation is the term used to describe inflationary periods in which cost-of-production increases force business firms to raise prices. Powerful labor unions capable of demanding and receiving wage increases in excess of productivity gains usually are cited as the cause of the cost increases. Such excessive wage settlements increase per unit production costs and force the firms involved to raise prices. Obviously this view carries an implicit indictment of unions. They, in turn, react by arguing that this view of the cause of inflation is unfair and inaccurate. A more accurate explanation, they contend, takes account of the fact that union wage demands are in excess of productivity gains only because workers are rightfully attempting to recoup purchasing power lost to inflation. Unions, therefore, should not be charged with being the original or ultimate source of inflation. Under the cost-push view of inflation, other causes of cost increases could be rising materials costs or increases in profit margins obtained by businesses in oligopolistic or monopolistic industries.

The cost-push view of inflation seems plausible for those periods when the economy is operating with some unemployment along with inflation. However, a serious problem with the cost-push view of inflation is its failure to explain adequately an acceleration in the rate of inflation such as occurred in the United States and many other countries in the 1970s. Furthermore, excessive aggregate demand appears to be a prerequisite for cost-push inflation; that is, significant cost-push inflation will not occur in the absence of monetary and fiscal policies that have overstimulated the economy and have initiated or fueled the inflation process.

Cost-push theories can also be criticized at a more fundamental level. The exercise of market power by large unions or oligopolistic businesses merely leads to high prices, not rising prices. Therefore, since inflation is a process of rising prices, cost-push theories require that unions and business gain more and more market power to keep pushing prices upward. There is now a considerable body of theoretical and empirical work on the role of expectations; this work provides the basis for an alternative explanation of the unemployment-inflation relationships for which the cost-push view had previously offered the only satisfactory explanation. Thus economists today are less inclined than in the past to view cost-push inflation and demand-pull inflation as separate varieties of inflation. Rather, an inflationary period is seen as having different phases which may contain elements of both cost and excess-demand pressures.

Economists of Keynesian persuasion have tended to view the causes of inflation somewhat differently than those with a monetarist leaning. Early monetarist versions, as a general rule, viewed the cause of all inflations as excess demand resulting from a rapidly expanding money supply. Earlier Keynesian views of inflation were also based on excess demand in the economy, but Keynesians also believed that the excess demand might originate in the real sector of the economy independently of excessive money-supply growth; that is, excessive consumption, investment, or government spending could touch off inflation with no change in the money supply. Keynesians could logically hold this view since they believed that the demand for money (velocity) was unstable. Thus, even if money-supply increases accompanied inflation, Keynesians were likely to view these increases as accommodating inflation rather than initiating it.

Keynesian economists are also more prone than monetarists to believe that inflation may be caused by forces other than excessive aggregate demand. Hence, they are more likely to accept the cost-push explanation as valid. Keynesians believe that money-supply changes are often generated by changes in aggregate demand, while monetarists see the causation running in the other direction. Thus the widely found association between money-supply changes and price-level changes is seen by both groups as consistent with their own views. The two camps are also likely to differ in their policy prescriptions, with the monetarists having much more faith than Keynesians that monetary policy alone can halt inflation. Monetarists reject the idea that there is a permanent trade-off between unemployment and inflation; that is, they believe that, except temporarily, policymakers cannot buy a lower unemployment rate with higher rates of inflation. Therefore, policy recommendations of monetarists, unlike those of Keynesians, do not reflect concern over this trade-off. Yet there is an emerging consensus in recent years that the differences between the two schools of thought have probably been overemphasized and that the emphasis on their disagreements has diverted attention from their agreement on some essential aspects of inflation.

In recent years the theory of inflation has been extended by a considerable amount of theoretical and empirical work. Economists have been particularly interested in unraveling the relationships between expectations and inflation and vice versa. Several important generalizations are emerging from these efforts.

1. Inflation cannot be adequately explained by either excess-demand or cost-push (supply-side) factors alone. Rather, there is mounting evidence that an explanation of inflation must view rising prices as a process that is affected at times by excess aggregate demand and at times by aggregate supply considerations.

2. Increases in the money supply are an essential ingredient in creating and sustaining the excess aggregate demand that plays a role in the inflationary process.

3.   The extent to which inflation is anticipated determines the reaction of and final impact on an economic unit. These reactions, in turn, may have an influence on the rate of inflation itself.

In the following pages we present a view of inflation that reflects these developments.

WHAT ARE THE DYNAMICS OF THE INFLATIONARY PROCESS?

A complex but useful way of viewing inflation is as a process whereby the economy moves from one equilibrium level of general prices to another equilibrium level at which prices are higher. The process normally starts when aggregate demand begins to exceed potential GNP. This situation may be the result of overly stimulative monetary and fiscal policies carried out in an attempt to reduce unemployment to unsustainable levels, or it may have been made necessary by wartime conditions. The present U.S. inflationary process is generally believed to have begun in the latter 1960s when the government tried to finance both the Vietnam War and an expanding menu of social programs without an increase in taxes. In the economist's jargon, we tried to have both guns and butter.

Excess demand is not the only way in which an inflationary spiral can start; for instance, an outside shock such as higher petroleum prices can put upward pressure on prices from the cost side. In order to preserve employment in the face of such situations, policymakers may follow with stimulative aggregate demand policies. Otherwise, the cost-initiated inflation will die out, but perhaps at the expense of a temporary increase in unemployment.

Once inflation is under way for any length of time, economic units begin to anticipate further inflation. These expectations of inflation show up in higher interest rates and, particularly, in workers' demands for wage increases. The original flare-up of inflation, if it is not quickly extinguished, tends to generate more intense inflationary pressures of a cost-push type. These expectations of further inflation can put upward pressure on prices regardless of the state of aggregate demand. If aggregate demand is restricted at this time by monetary and fiscal policy, wages and prices in our economy are unlikely to fall. Therefore, much of the deficiency in aggregate demand will be translated into a drop in output and employment. Under such conditions, we are, for a time, likely to observe increasing prices—the result of the cost-push pressures being generated by expectations based on past inflation experience—and (for a while) increasing unemployment—the result of policies designed to restrict aggregate demand and curb inflation in an economy characterized by resistance to price declines.

A scenario similar to that described above usually develops only

after several years of inflation. That is, only when inflation is anticipated will workers begin to demand wage increases in line with the
expected rate of inflation. Meanwhile, the government, under pressure to stop inflation, will be forced to institute restrictive monetary
and fiscal policy measures so that the growth of aggregate demand is
halted and maybe even reversed. Yet prices and wages will continue
rising even as inadequate aggregate demand results in a decline in
output and employment. These stagflationary conditions, especially
if they occur near an election year, put pressure on the government
to reverse its monetary and fiscal policies in an attempt to combat
unemployment. If fiscal and monetary policies are reversed and
aggregate demand is stimulated again, overexpansion often results,
and excess demand reappears to again put upward pressure on
prices and reinforce expectations on inflation.

If policymakers are lucky or wise (or both), and monetary and
fiscal policy actions do not continue to create excess aggregate demand conditions, the inflationary expectations that exert upward
pressure on wages, costs, and prices will eventually begin to diminish. The rate of inflation will slow, and if outside shocks can be
avoided, the economy can return to a condition of relatively stable
prices. However, once inflationary expectations become strongly
engrained, it appears impossible to halt inflation quickly through
the use of restrictive monetary and fiscal policy. A quick solution
under those conditions would entail massive unemployment and
output losses.

To date we have little empirical evidence on how large and how
lasting a recession is needed to eliminate the effects of inflationary
expectations. To the extent that the 1973–75 recession is representative, the implications are not good. This recession was the worst
since the Great Depression of the 1930s; the unemployment rate of
9.2 percent in May 1975 was accompanied by an inflation rate in
excess of 7 percent. (The inflation rate did decline with some lag to
less than 5 percent in 1976.) It may be argued that this experience is
not representative since the economy was subjected to the effects of
worldwide crop failures, the Arab oil embargo, and higher energy
prices at the same time as the recession was getting under way.
However, even under more favorable circumstances, inflation, once
established, cannot be cured easily. The following chapter is devoted to the policies that have been used or recommended as solutions to the inflation problem.

SUMMARY

Inflation, which is the process of rising prices, is not a recent
phenomenon, nor is it unique to the United States. Inflation creates

two types of problems for an economy: (1) it creates a burden for certain individuals in that it redistributes wealth away from them to others in society; and (2) prolonged and rapid inflation can result in lower rates of production and growth.

Inflation is a complex process involving both demand- and supply-side forces. Ultimately, inflation can be linked to excessive money creation which can occur for several reasons, the primary one being deficit spending by the federal government for the purpose of waging war or, in more recent years, stimulating the economy. The cost of curbing inflation through a tight-money policy can be quite high in terms of lost output and employment. The real objective of anti-inflationary policy, therefore, is to achieve the desired level of price stability at a minimum cost in terms of lost output and employment. Because inflation is so difficult and costly to control once it becomes established, the best anti-inflationary policy is one of prevention rather than cure. The following chapter explores the policy alternatives for curing inflation. However, our review of past attempts to control inflation does not lead to optimism regarding a quick solution to the problem.

REVIEW QUESTIONS

1. How is excessive money creation linked to government deficits if the government has not resorted to printing money to finance those deficits?
2. Explain why governments may persist in deficit spending even though it may lead to inflation.
3. If the Federal Reserve can control the money supply, why has the Fed caused the growth of the U.S. money supply to be so rapid as to be inflationary?
4. How are Keynesians and monetarists likely to differ in their assessment of the inflationary process?
5. Give examples of how various groups in the economy would suffer or benefit by inflation. What patterns emerge? How does it matter that inflation is anticipated?
6. Are cost-push and excess-demand inflation related? If so, in what manner?
7. Discuss the role of each of the following in terms of U.S. inflation of recent years: powerful labor unions, big businesses, OPEC, the Federal Reserve, and Congress.

SUGGESTIONS FOR ADDITIONAL READING

Bresciani-Turroni, Costantino. *The Economics of Inflation: A Study of Currency Depreciation in Post-War Germany.* Translated by Millicent E. Sayers with a foreword by Lionel Robbins. London: George Allen & Unwin, Ltd., 1937.

Frisch, Helmut. "Inflation Theory 1963–1975: A Second Generation Survey." *Journal of Economic Literature,* vol. 15, no. 4 (December 1977), pp. 1289–1317.

Griffiths, Brian. *Inflation: The Price of Prosperity.* New York: Holmes and Meier Publishers, Inc., 1976.

Jianakoplos, Nancy Ammon. "Are You Protected from Inflation?" *Review of the Federal Reserve Bank of St. Louis,* vol. 59, no. 1 (January 1977), pp. 2–9

Morley, Samuel A. *Inflation and Unemployment.* 2d ed. Hinsdale, Ill.: The Dryden Press, 1979.

Solow, Robert M. "The Intelligent Citizen's Guide to Inflation." *The Public Interest,* no. 38 (Winter 1975), pp. 30–66.

18 Inflation and economic policy

WARM-UP: *Outline and questions to consider as you read*

What is the trade-off between inflation and unemployment?

What measures have been tried in the fight against inflation?

Can inflation be controlled?

The choices before us.

The outlook.

NEW TERMS

Incomes policies: attempts to reduce inflation using various types of wage and price controls.

Indexing: a technique whereby contracts for future payments (receipts) are adjusted for inflation so that the purchasing power of the payments (receipts) remains constant.

Modified incomes policies: the use of incentives to induce firms and individuals to avoid inflationary increases in wages and prices.

Phillips Curve: a graph depicting the rate of inflation associated with different unemployment rates.

Supply-side economics: an approach also referred to as incentive economics which emphasizes policies that encourage more work and investment thereby stimulating production.

375

Tax-based incomes policy (TIP):   a modified incomes policy under which taxes would be increased or decreased for companies and workers according to whether or not their wage settlements exceeded or fell short of some government standard.

In Chapter 17, inflation was identified as a process of rising prices that is ultimately linked to the money supply; however, this linkage is dynamic and complex. Moreover, the role of excessive money in creating inflation is often tied to government fiscal policy; thus the role of monetary policy in causing and controlling inflation cannot be analyzed adequately apart from fiscal policy. In this chapter, we examine the record of interrelated attempts at using monetary and fiscal policy to combat recent United States inflation. Since the record indicates that past efforts have been less than successful, we also examine some alternative courses of action.

WHAT IS THE TRADE-OFF BETWEEN INFLATION AND UNEMPLOYMENT?

An important factor behind the apparent tendency of governments to pursue inflationary monetary and fiscal policies is found in what is known as the Phillips Curve relationship. In 1958, A. W. Phillips published the results of his study of historical wage-rate changes and unemployment in the United Kingdom. His study indicated a stable negative relationship between the rate of growth of money wages and the unemployment rate. A graphical presentation of this relationship is known as the Phillips Curve. Since wage rates account for the greater portion of most prices, it was very logical that the original Phillips Curve would be modified in later studies to indicate a relationship between the rate of growth of prices and the unemployment rate. An example of such a modified Phillips Curve is shown in Figure 18–1 which is based on U.S. data for the period 1960–69.

If there is a stable relationship between unemployment rates and inflation rates such as that illustrated in Figure 18–1, then there is a conflict between two of the most important of our macroeconomic goals—full employment and stable prices. Higher rates of inflation must be tolerated in order to achieve lower rates of unemployment. For example, given the data in Figure 18–1, if the situation were one of 6 percent unemployment and 1 percent inflation, and the 6 percent unemployment rate was considered unacceptable, the government might try to lower the unemployment rate to 4 percent by using monetary and fiscal policy to expand aggregate demand. However, the inflation rate associated with such an increase in aggregate de-

FIGURE 18–1
Inflation and unemployment rates in the United States, 1960–1969

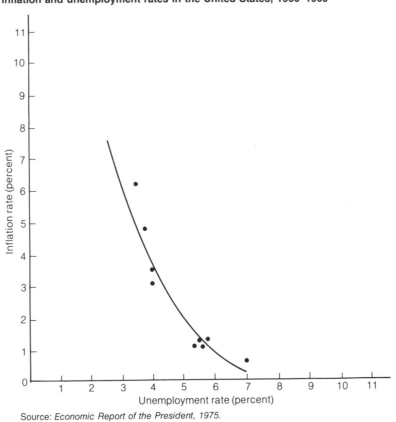

Source: *Economic Report of the President, 1975.*

mand is 3 percent in Figure 18–1; a two-percentage-point increase in the inflation rate could be traded for a two-percentage-point reduction in the unemployment rate. It is safe to say that the Phillips Curve concept caused governments to view inflation as the cost of reducing unemployment and to resist policies that might reduce demand and slow inflation out of a fear that the cost in terms of unemployment would be excessive.

The belief that there is a stable relationship between the unemployment rate and the rate of inflation (and that this relationship can be empirically estimated and depicted as a Phillips Curve) was shaken by the unemployment rate–inflation rate figures for the 1970s. By 1974 it was obvious that higher rates of inflation did not always "buy" lower unemployment rates. In terms of Figure 18–1, an acceleration of the inflation rates to 6 percent did not necessarily result in lowering the unemployment rate. Monetarist economists explained this result by arguing that the downward-sloping Phillips Curve is a temporary, short-run phenomenon dependent on differences in the actual and expected rates of inflation and that the long-run Phillips Curve is a vertical line, U_n, as shown in Figure 18-2. In short, they hold that there is a natural rate of unemployment to which the economy will adjust regardless of the rate of inflation. Thus an inflationary increase in aggregate demand will only temporarily reduce unemployment, and to reduce the unemployment rate below the natural rate for any length of time would require ever-increasing rates of inflation. A short-run trade-off exists only so long as the actual rate of inflation is more than the expected rate; only when the expected rate of inflation (which adjusts to the actual rate over time) equals the actual rate will the unemployment rate be at its natural level, U_n. While not all economists accept the monetarist explanation, the experience of the 1970s has cast serious doubt on the original Phillips Curve hypothesis that there is a permanent trade-off between inflation and unemployment.

FIGURE 18-2
Monetarist view of Phillips Curve relationships

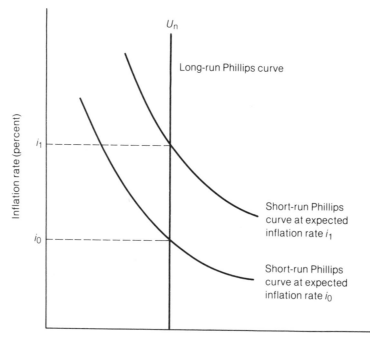

U_n

Long-run Phillips curve

Inflation rate (percent)

i_1

i_0

Short-run Phillips curve at expected inflation rate i_1

Short-run Phillips curve at expected inflation rate i_0

Unemployment rate (percent)

WHAT MEASURES HAVE BEEN TRIED IN THE FIGHT AGAINST INFLATION?

Control of inflation is likely to be small in cost and easy to accomplish in situations where the inflation rate is low and not well established—that is, in those economies where anticipation of further inflation is not widely held (or, at least, the expected rate of inflation is low). Thus the Swiss and West Germans are likely to find controlling inflation much easier than the Argentines, Brazilians, and Israelis (or Americans).

In countries where the inflation rate has been high for long periods of time, the cost of stopping it may come to be viewed as greater than the cost of the inflation itself. Inflation policy in such countries consists primarily of finding ways to minimize the harm caused by rising prices. For example, automatic cost-of-living adjustments (accelerator clauses) become widespread as a part of wage contracts; bond principal and interest payments are tied to some price index; income tax rates are periodically adjusted to allow for the growing divergence between real and nominal income; and government and private pensions may be tied to the price index so that recipients do not suffer unduly from inflation. Policies such as these are often collectively referred to as indexing, and such policies are common in countries with a well-established history of relatively high rates of inflation. Israel and Argentina are two examples of countries which practice indexing on a wide scale. The persistence of inflation in the United States has created a climate that is more and more conducive to the growth of indexing practices. Accelerator clauses in labor contracts are becoming more common, and some prominent economists are now calling for widespread use of indexing. It should be stressed, however, that indexing is not a solution to inflation but a mechanism for mitigating some of the undesirable effects of inflation. Also, indexing is not without some disadvantages, and economists are currently debating its relative merits and demerits.[1] In any case, it is likely that various forms of indexing will become more common in the United States in the next few years.

Many countries which have high and well-established inflation rates have concluded that they must live with inflation because they view the cost of controlling it as greater than its damage. Most countries, perhaps including the United States, probably fall in this cate-

---

[1] Jai-Hoo Yang, "The Case for and against Indexation: An Attempt at Perspective," *Review of the Federal Reserve Bank of St. Louis,* vol. 56, no. 10 (October 1974), pp. 2–11.

gory. With this background it is instructive to review attempts to combat the recent inflationary process in the United States.

From 1952 through 1967, the annual inflation rates ranged from −0.5 percent in 1954 to 3.4 percent in 1966; the average annual increase for the period as a whole was less than 1.6 percent. For the period 1968 through 1979, the range of yearly inflation rates was 3.4 percent in 1971 and 1972 (years in which prices were partially controlled) to over 13 percent in 1979. The average annual rate of price increase for the 1968–1979 period was in excess of 7.0 percent. In this section we shall look at some of the policy actions that have been undertaken in an attempt to halt this upward trend in prices. The following review, which begins with the 1961–65 period, should prove helpful in assessing our chances of controlling inflation in the future.

The years 1961 to 1965 represented one of those rare periods when the economy appeared to achieve all of the major macroeconomic goals. After coming out of a mild recession in 1960 and 1961, the economy performed in textbook fashion, and by the end of 1965, the annual unemployment rate was below 4 percent—a figure that most economist viewed as full employment. During this same period prices were climbing only moderately, and economists spoke of "creeping" inflation. The annual rate of increase in prices as measured by the CPI never exceeded 1.7 percent between 1961 and 1965, and real GNP grew at an average annual rate of 5.2 percent. As for macroeconomic policy, from 1961 to 1965 the cumulative government deficit was only $11.6 billion, and the largest deficit in any one year was $4.2 billion in fiscal 1962. The money supply as measured by M-1 grew at an average rate of 3.5 percent per year between December 1960 and December 1965.[2]

With the economy operating at virtually full capacity, monetary and fiscal policies should be applied judiciously; unfortunately, policy became overexpansionary, and the economy was pushed from its position of relatively high employment and stable prices into an inflationary situation. During the period 1966 through 1968, federal government expenditures increased by $58 billion, an annual rate of growth of 13.7 percent, and the cumulative deficit was over $20 billion. The Federal Reserve helped the Treasury finance this deficit by increasing its holdings of government securities by almost $12 billion. The rate of growth of the money supply (M-1) increased from an average annual rate of 3.5 percent in the 1961–65 period to a 5.6 percent annual rate during the 1966–68 period. The result of these ex-

---

[2] The M-1 measure of money was used by the Fed prior to 1980 and was very similar to the present M-1A.

pansionary monetary and fiscal actions was entirely predictable; by 1968 the rate of inflation was 4.7 percent, the highest for any year since the Korean War.

What went wrong in the 1966–68 period? Part of the answer lies in the government's attempts to wage an expanding war and an expanding program of social services without increasing taxes and at a time when the economy was operating with virtually all resources employed. During these years, defense expenditures jumped by almost $31 billion (62 percent) and expenditures for four major social programs—community development and housing, education and manpower, health, and income security—increased by 42 percent or $22 billion. If the government tries to preempt a larger portion of the economy's output, then the private sector must consume less, or the economy must produce more. Since the economy was operating at full capacity, the latter approach was not possible, at least not in the short run.

Nevertheless, inflation can be avoided in such situations if the government finances its increased purchases by taxing its citizens and thereby transfers resources and output from private use to public use. Or, if the government borrows the funds to finance its added purchases by selling bonds to private-sector investors, interest rates will rise, private-sector borrowing will decline, and the necessary transfer of resources can be accomplished with little change in prices. There is only one other approach that may be taken, and it leads to inflation. If the government views higher taxes as politically unpopular and issues bonds to finance its expenditures, there will be upward pressure on interest rates, and if, in order to moderate the rise in interest rates, the Fed purchases government securities in the open market, the result will be equivalent to printing new money. In this case the government spending component of aggregate demand increases without a corresponding decline in private-sector aggregate demand. Since output cannot rise to meet the increased demand, prices will rise, and inflation will result from the attempt to transfer resources from private to government use without an accompanying increase in taxes.

The above scenario may be somewhat oversimplified, but it reflects the basic process that pushed the American economy into an inflationary episode from which we have not yet escaped. Government economists warned of inflation in 1966, and a tax increase was recommended, but to no avail. Not until 1967 did President Johnson recommend a tax increase in the form of a temporary income tax surcharge requiring each taxpayer to add 10 percent to ordinary tax liability. The bill providing for the tax increase was not signed until June 1968 and is a good example of the timing problem referred to in earlier chapters. With the advantage of hindsight, we can see that the tax increase probably should have been enacted at least two years earlier. In addition to its timing, the tax increase had another shortcoming as a weapon against inflation—it was temporary, and members of the public did not view it as requiring a permanent reduction in their consumption patterns. They reacted by reducing saving, and the tax had only a moderate effect on immediate consumption. (The reduction in saving put upward pressure on interest rates and made it more difficult for the monetary authorities to resist expansionary increases in the money supply.) In retrospect, it would not be correct to conclude that fiscal policy failed to prevent inflation; a more accurate conclusion would be that an appropriate policy was not applied.

What about monetary policy during this period? The monetary authorities are thought to be less subject to political pressures than the fiscal authorities; if so, they should be able to respond more quickly to inflationary conditions. Indeed, the monetary authorities recognized the need for restraint, and the growth of the money supply was curtailed in 1966. During that year, the annual rate of growth of the money supply dropped to 2.6 percent from 4.7 percent a year earlier. In fact, as far as monetary policy is concerned, 1966 might well be divided into two periods. During the first part of 1966, the authorities induced a sharp decline in the money supply; however, later in the year they reversed this policy and allowed M-1 to grow sharply enough so that by year-end the rate of increase for the year was 2.6 percent.

By the end of 1966, interest rates were rising, and the economy was slowing. There was some fear that monetary policy had been and was overly restrictive. The Fed was unwilling to risk pushing the economy into a recession; rather it hoped to pursue a moderate policy that would keep the economy strong without adding unneeded stimulus to aggregate demand. Had the Fed pursued a restrictive policy, a recession would have been likely. However, at that time, inflationary expectations were not strongly entrenched, and a mild recession might have ended the inflation. Our conclusion is not that the Fed should have created a recession, but that it was overly expansionary in attempting to avoid one. Like fiscal policy, monetary policy during this period would be better described as misapplied rather than impotent. Had the Fed pursued a more moderate approach when it restricted monetary growth earlier in the year and a more moderate approach when it expanded monetary growth later in the year, subsequent years of worsening inflation might well have been prevented.

After 1966, there appears to have been no other serious effort to use monetary policy to curb inflation until 1969. In 1967, the money supply (M-1) grew by 6.6 percent, and in 1968, the rate of growth of money increased to 8.1 percent. The rate of inflation continued to accelerate, and by the end of 1968, prices were rising at an annual rate of more than 4 percent. In 1969, both monetary and fiscal policy again turned restrictive. During that year, the annual rate of growth of the money supply (M-1) dropped from 8.1 percent to 3.2 percent, and the federal budget recorded a surplus of $8.5 billion. The result was predictable but not immediate; the economy slowed markedly in 1970. Real GNP declined slightly, and the unemployment rate (seasonally adjusted) was 6.0 percent in December compared to only 3.9 percent at the beginning of the year. (The 4.9 percent average unemployment rate for the year was the highest since 1964.) Clearly the restrictive monetary and fiscal policies of 1969 were being felt.

The impact of the downturn in economic activity on the rate of inflation was disappointing. The trade-off between unemployment and inflation predicted by the Phillips Curve models did not materialize. The Consumer Price Index increased by 5.9 percent during 1970 as compared to 5.4 percent a year earlier. However, analysis of the progress of inflation throughout the year indicates that some slowing did occur. From February through June, prices increased at an annual rate of 6.4 percent, but in the last six months of 1970, the rate of inflation dropped to 4.8 percent. Inflation (as reflected in the CPI) continued to slow in the first half of 1971, but the reduction was disappointing considering the extent of unemployment in the economy. (The unemployment rate averaged 6 percent during the first six months of 1971.)

With an election year approaching, policymakers had to decide whether to continue the fight against inflation by restricting aggregate demand at the risk of higher unemployment and lost production. The cost appeared high considering the slow pace at which inflation was abating. In trying to determine the appropriate course of action, economists were faced with explaining why restrictive monetary and fiscal policies had not been more successful. A major part of the explanation was that inflationary expectations had become well established in the minds and plans of economic units throughout the country. These expectations were exerting cost-push pressure on prices and wages even though GNP was running below its potential. Such inflationary expectations, coupled with resistance to reductions in wages and prices, were preventing traditional monetary and fiscal policy actions from having an immediate impact on inflation. In the meantime, the cost in terms of unemployment and lost output was unacceptably high.

The problems facing economic policymakers became more complex in 1971 as the country's balance of payments position began to deteriorate sharply. Faced with serious international and domestic economic problems, the Nixon administration introduced wage and price controls in August 1971 and prohibited foreign central banks from converting dollars into gold. Simultaneously a package of tax reductions was proposed in an attempt to stimulate the economy. According to the *Economic Report of the President*, the program was "designed to create conditions in which a more stimulative budget policy would be safer and more effective."[3]

With the wage and price controls suppressing inflationary pressures, fiscal and monetary policy turned expansionary in an attempt to reduce unemployment. The high-employment budget was in deficit by $8.5 billion for 1971 as a whole. The money supply grew by 6.5 percent. In 1972, a presidential election year, fiscal and monetary policy were even more expansionary with the high-employment budget showing a deficit of $16.7 billion and the money supply growing in excess of 9 percent. The expansionary monetary and fiscal actions were supposed to nudge the economy back to full employment, while the wage and price controls would reduce the inflationary expectations that were putting upward pressure on prices.

If price and wage controls are to control inflation, they can do so only by dampening those price increases associated with inflationary expectations (and then only if the controls are accompanied by appropriate monetary and fiscal policies). However, price and wage controls lead only to shortages and frustration if they are accompanied by excessive stimulation of aggregate demand.

Furthermore, wage and price controls are costly in terms of lost output because they restrict the ability of the pricing system to provide the signals needed for efficient resource allocation. Hence, most control programs are not designed to be permanent. The Nixon administration program went through four phases: phase 1, which froze most wages and prices, lasted from August 15, 1971, to November 15, 1971; phase 2 then went into effect through January 11, 1972. Thus during 1972 we were operating under phase 2, which allowed some increases in both wages and prices. The immediate results of the above policy package appeared promising, but over the longer run, the degree of fiscal and monetary stimulus appears to have been excessive. Held in check by wage and price controls, the rate of inflation declined to only 3.3 percent for 1972; total employment grew by 3.3 percent, the largest gain since 1956, and real GNP

---

[3] *Economic Report of the President*, 1972, p. 24.

grew by 5.7 percent. The administration's policy appeared to have been successful on all fronts.

Phase 3 of the wage and price control program went into effect in January 1973 with the introduction of "voluntary" controls. This phase lasted only until August, and the year was marked by shifting developments in both policy and performance. The rate of inflation jumped to 6.2 percent for the year as a whole, but there was some good news in that the unemployment rate continued to decline so that the average rate for the year was only 4.9 percent. The expansionary impact of monetary and fiscal policies was moderated as the high-employment budget deficit declined from $16.7 billion in 1972 to $6.7 billion in 1973, and the annual rate of growth of the money supply declined to 6.0 percent compared to 9.1 percent in the previous year.

What happened in 1973 to cause the jump in the inflation rate? Was the degree of expansion created by monetary and fiscal actions too great? Were prices simply adjusting to reflect pressures that had been suppressed by the mandatory price and wage controls? Were inflationary expectations still prevalent in the economy, or did some outside shock create upward pressure on prices? Any one or even two of the above factors acting alone probably would have resulted in only a moderate effect on prices, but the misfortune of facing all four adverse developments simultaneously resulted in a surge in prices. Outside shocks played an important role: the Arab oil embargo in October created shortages that led to higher energy-related prices; a bad crop year worldwide put upward pressure on food and agricultural products; finally, a devaluation of the dollar made imported goods more costly and raised demand for American goods abroad, which increased domestic prices.

In August 1973, the phase 3 price control program was revised, and a more restrictive phase 4 program was instituted. Both monetary and fiscal policy became considerably less expansionary in the latter half of the year. The unemployment rate declined slightly during the first half of the year but was rising by the end of the year as real GNP declined sharply during the fourth quarter. By the end of the year, the economy was obviously in a downturn; production was running considerably ahead of final sales, and business inventories built up sharply, setting the stage for layoffs and production cutbacks. Even with the more restrictive phase 4 controls, prices continued to rise sharply due to cost pass-through provisions and the exemption of some industries from the controls.

The economy entered 1974 with declining production and sharply rising prices, a situation sometimes referred to as stagflation.

By now, fiscal policy was only slightly expansionary. The high-employment budget for the first quarter had a deficit of only $1.3 billion on an annual basis, a sharp contrast to the $13 billion deficit that characterized the first quarter of 1973. The monetary authorities permitted the money supply to grow at a 6 percent annual rate during the first half of the year but only at a 3 percent rate during the latter half of the year. Interest rates climbed to record levels, and, for the first time, the rate of inflation reached double-digit levels (12.2 percent). By the end of the year, the unemployment rate exceeded 7 percent, and from the fourth quarter of 1973 through the fourth quarter of 1974, real GNP declined by 4.6 percent.

With a serious recession and a worsening rate of inflation, policymakers again faced the choice of stimulating aggregate demand in an attempt to reduce unemployment or of continuing to restrict demand in an effort to combat inflation. The choice was made early in 1975—President Ford asked for a $16 billion tax cut, and Congress granted $21 billion. Fiscal policy turned strongly expansionary with a high-employment budget deficit for the year of $31 billion. Monetary policy was accommodating; the rate of growth of the money supply during the first six months of 1975 was 8.7 percent on an annual basis, but during the latter half of 1975 it slowed considerably.

The unemployment rate peaked at 9.2 percent, then fell slowly as the decline in real GNP was finally reversed in early 1975. Furthermore, the rate of inflation for the year was down to 7 percent compared to over 12 percent for the previous year. However, both unemployment and inflation remained unacceptably high despite the improvements during the year. Nevertheless, the cumulative damage done by events of 1973–75 was great. Not only had the nation suffered a severe loss of output, but the continuation of high rates of inflation renewed and strengthened inflationary expectations and probably reversed any dampening effect on expectations that may have been achieved by the price and wage controls which, except for traces in particular industries (most notably, those producing or selling petroleum products), had been quietly dropped.

There were no sharp changes in monetary and fiscal policy in 1976, 1977, and 1978. Fiscal policy remained quite stimulative with the high-employment budget showing deficits of $27 billion, $35 billion and $23 billion in 1976, 1977, and 1978 respectively. The money supply as measured by M-1 grew at an average annual rate of approximately 7 percent over the three-year period; total employment increased by over 7 million persons in the period, and real GNP increased at an average annual rate of 4.8 percent. These data indicate that the period was one of strong expansion; yet the unemployment rate remained exasperatingly high, averaging 7.7, 7.0, and 6.0 percent in 1976, 1977, and 1978 respectively.

The rate of inflation continued to moderate during 1976, but in 1977 inflation began to accelerate once again. The consumer price index rose by 5.8 percent in 1976, 6.5 percent in 1977, and 9.0 percent in 1978. Although the seriousness of the inflation problem was officially recognized, both monetary and fiscal policy remained expansionary. The pressures of considerable unemployment in the economy undoubtedly prompted policymakers to continue stimulating the economy. Inflationary expectations were reinforced, making it doubtful that restrictive demand policies could achieve a rapid reduction in prices without inducing a severe recession. Again, with the advantage of hindsight it is apparent that a more moderate fiscal policy in 1977 and 1978 would have been more conducive to a healthy economy.

During 1979, the inflationary problem continued to worsen as prices rose by more than 13 percent. The economy was again subjected to outside shocks via shortages of petroleum and rising energy-related costs. Furthermore, economic activity slowed in early 1979, although it recovered in the final two quarters. The unemployment rate hovered around 6 percent all year. The Carter administration tried to persuade business and labor to restrain prices and wages voluntarily, but the approach met with only limited success, and by early 1980, more and more calls for mandatory controls were being heard.

CAN INFLATION BE CONTROLLED?

The choices before us

If controlling inflation were the only objective of economic policymakers, the answer to the question, Can inflation be controlled? would be a simple yes. By pursuing restrictive policies for a sufficiently long period of time, inflation could eventually be halted, but the cost in terms of lost output and employment might well be unacceptably high. Thus we pose a more relevant question: Can inflation be controlled at an acceptable cost in terms of lost output and employment? When the question is phrased in this manner, the answer is no longer simple because a successful anti-inflation program is likely to entail sacrifices; furthermore, since failure to curb inflation is also costly, the relevant goal of anti-inflation policy should be to return the economy to an acceptable rate of price increase with the least possible cost in terms of lost output and employment during the transition period.

With this goal in mind, we examine four approaches to controlling inflation. They are as follows:

1. Restrictive monetary and fiscal policies.
2. Wage and price controls (income policies).
3. Modified incomes policies.
4. Production- and efficiency-oriented approaches.

Restrictive monetary and fiscal policies. Since a number of earlier chapters have dealt extensively with monetary and fiscal policymaking, the following comments are very brief. If the experience of the 1960s and 1970s is representative, then the application of restrictive monetary and fiscal policies in an attempt to curb inflation can be costly, and the only viable approach seems to be a gradual and moderate application of restrictive policies. Thus, while traditional demand-management policies are not a quick fix for established inflation, it is imperative to avoid improper or badly timed policies. Furthermore, none of the other approaches to fighting inflation is likely to meet with a significant degree of success in the absence of appropriate monetary and fiscal policies. In short, monetary and fiscal policy must play a role in any attempt to curb inflation.

Wage and price controls. Mandatory wage and price controls alone are not a solution to inflation although they may temporarily treat the symptoms and may create an environment in which other policies can be utilized more effectively. Various degrees of restraint are possible, ranging from a freeze on prices and wages (as under phase 1 of the Nixon controls) to a program with liberal upper limits and cost pass-through provisions. Controls often have a wide appeal, but they are not without potentially serious costs in the form of distorted price signals, inefficiencies due to resource misallocation, and shortages. The costs of controls vary directly with their duration and stringency and inversely with the extent of excess capacity in the economy.

The usefulness of controls is not so much in suppressing inflation as in destroying expectations of continuing or accelerating inflation. For example, the imposition of strict controls during a time when the economy was operating at or near capacity accompanied by highly expansionary monetary policy would be an exercise in frustration and futility. Bottlenecks and shortages would develop; black markets would be encouraged; enforcement of the controls would become difficult; and eventually they would have to be dropped. On the other hand, if there were adequate supplies of goods and resources available in the economy (as in a recession or the early stages of a recovery), or if monetary and fiscal policy did not create excessive growth of aggregate demand, then wage and price controls might dampen inflationary expectations. Wage and price controls might also make a useful contribution as a supplement to restrictive monetary and fiscal policies. By curbing inflationary expectations, controls free monetary and fiscal policy to be restrictive without creating extensive employment and output declines. In the absence of controls, inflationary expectations boost wages and prices so that aggregate demand must continue to expand in order to prevent unemployment and lost output.

Modified incomes policies. The shortcomings of wage and price controls, or incomes policies as they are sometimes called, have caused economists to search for more effective approaches to controlling price and wage increases. One approach, often referred to as "jawboning," is the use of voluntary controls or guidelines. The likelihood that such an approach will be effective is small; however, some economists see promise in two relatively new variations of incomes policies that attempt to address the dilemma of controlling prices while allowing enough flexibility for prices to perform their rationing and signaling functions effectively. The essence of both approaches is the same—they attempt to provide individual economic units with an incentive to avoid inflationary actions. The difference in the two is that one, the tax-based incomes policy (TIP), would provide an incentive through the tax system, while the other approach, referred to as market-based incomes policy (MIP) or market anti-inflation plan (MAP), attempts to impose a cost for inflationary actions (and a reward for anti-inflationary actions) by setting up a market pricing mechanism under which firms pay for the right to increase prices. Only the first approach is discussed here as it has existed longer and appears to have a wider appeal.[4]

The tax-based incomes policy (TIP) approach has been advocated by some of the country's leading economists including Henry Wallich of the Federal Reserve's Board of Governors and the late Arthur Okun, a former chairman of the Council of Economic Advisors. The essence of the approach is to legislate a tax system that would impose higher taxes for businesses that grant wage increases in excess of some government-set standard; the standard would be gradually lowered until the inflationary element was eliminated. Companies and workers holding wage increases below the standard would be eligible for tax-rate reductions or refunds. Price controls would not be needed, it is argued, since historical evidence indicates that

---

[4] For more details on the MAP approach, see Abba Lerner and David C. Colander, "MAP: A Cure of Inflation," in David C. Colander, ed., *Solutions to Inflation* (New York: Harcourt, Brace, Jovanovich, Inc., 1979), pp. 210–20.

prices reflect a constant markup over labor costs. Thus by holding labor costs down, the TIP would supposedly hold prices down. The advantages of the plan is its built-in flexibility. Where demand for a product is strong and labor is badly needed (because of high demand), companies could exceed the standard rate and recoup the extra tax costs by raising prices. But such price increases are exactly the type that should occur in a market-oriented economy but could not under typical wage and price control programs. The tax refunds resulting from wage settlements below the standard would encourage firms in industries with slack demand to seek settlements below the standard.

Numerous variations of TIP have been proposed by different economists, and while each has its own advantages and disadvantages, some economists question the feasibility of the TIP plans in general. For example, it is questionable whether unions would accept TIP in view of the possibility that firms could increase prices even if wages were restrained. Also, numerous administrative problems would be encountered in applying and monitoring the performance of thousands of firms in hundreds of different industries and settings. However, while the TIP approach does not eliminate the need to consider and allow for a multitude of administrative details, it does recognize the importance of control without rigidity and attempts to provide it. The frustration currently felt because of the inability to deal effectively with worsening inflation may well lead policymakers to a "let's try something" attitude. That something may be a tax-based income policy.

Efficiency oriented approaches.   Several approaches that have been recommended as solutions to the inflation problem may be grouped together in that the common thrust of each is to increase the efficiency of the economy. The policies are sometimes referred to as supply-side approaches. Examples of such actions include:

1. The repeal of inflationary special interest legislation such as fair-trade laws, import quotas, or other competition-restraining statutes.
2. Measures designed to stimulate business spending on new capital improvements that will increase efficiency (investment tax credits, more liberal depreciation allowances, and an easing of the capital gains tax rates, for example).
3. Actions, such as lower marginal tax rates, that would increase work incentives.

There is a growing consensus that more attention should be given by policymakers to these and other actions that would increase supply. Policy actions that increase the rate of growth of output allow a greater increase in aggregate demand to be accommodated before inflationary pressures are generated.

Policies that would increase output and growth are desirable in their own right and would prove beneficial in the fight against inflation. Such policies by themselves, however, are unlikely to be the complete solution to inflation. Many of the suggested actions would generate a one-time effect that would shift some prices downward but leave unaltered the process of rising prices that represents inflation. Also, even the one-time effect of some of the measures would probably be quite small. These shortcomings should not be taken to mean that efficiency-increasing activities are irrelevant. They should be pursued, but to view them alone as the solution to inflation is overly optimistic.

The outlook

There is room for both optimism and pessimism concerning future rates of inflation. On an optimistic note, there is no evidence that the U.S. situation is in imminent danger of deteriorating into hyperinflation. Historically, two conditions appear to be necessary for moderate inflation to accelerate into hyperinflation: (1) the political situation must be unstable, and (2) the government's ability to generate tax revenues must be impaired severely. Neither condition appears to be present in the United States.

The outlook is pessimistic, on the other hand, with respect to the likelihood that the current high rates of inflation will be reduced significantly within a relatively short period of time. Unless we are willing to pay a high cost in terms of lost output and employment, the most that can be expected is a gradual reduction in the rate of inflation over a period of several years. In any case, whatever success or failure is achieved will be to a great extent determined by the type of monetary policies pursued by the Federal Reserve. Furthermore, the monetary policies that are pursued will depend in large measure on the fiscal policy stance of the federal government.

SUMMARY

Monetary and fiscal policies that have ultimately resulted in inflation can be traced, at least in part, to the Phillips Curve concept that inflation is the cost of maintaining low levels of unemployment. While there is some evidence that the Phillips Curve trade-off is not a reliable guide, there is also considerable evidence that, once established, inflation is difficult to curtail without incurring substantial output and employment losses.

The record of anti-inflationary economic policy in the United States over the last 20 years is examined in this chapter; that record indicates a distinct lack of success and confirms both the difficulty and the costliness of stopping inflation through restrictive monetary and fiscal policies. This conclusion does not imply, however, that monetary and fiscal policies have no role to play in the battle against inflation; no approach to solving the inflation problem can prove successful if appropriate monetary and fiscal policies are not also applied.

Alternatives (or additions) to restrictive monetary and fiscal policies as weapons against inflation have been proposed; they are (1) wage and price controls or incomes policies, (2) modified incomes policies such as the tax-based incomes policy, and (3) approaches designed to increase output and efficiency. Each is examined in this chapter, and it is concluded that none of these approaches, acting alone, appears capable of solving the inflation problem; however, each has some potential. Furthermore, each category has a growing number of advocates and may play a role in future anti-inflation strategy in this country.

REVIEW QUESTIONS

1. From the latest issue of the *Economic Report of the President*, obtain annual data on the average unemployment and inflation rates for the 1970s and the 1960s. Plot the data on separate graphs, one for the 1960s and one for the 1970s. What conclusions do you draw? Can you explain the differences between the two graphs?

2. Given the hindsight provided by the summary of economic policy in the United States over the decades of the 1960s and 1970s, what do you think policymakers should have done differently? Cite specific time periods and explain.

3. Can wage and price controls make a useful contribution in the fight against inflation? Explain by weighing their advantages and disadvantages.

4. In what respects are the tax-based incomes policies superior to regular wage and price controls? What are the shortcomings of TIP?

5. During the 1966–68 period, what were the roles of both monetary and fiscal policy in creating inflation in the United States?

6. Does the U.S. experience with wage and price controls in 1971–74 indicate that they are helpful? Useless? Evaluate the accompanying monetary and fiscal policies. What do you think was the rationale behind these policies?

SUGGESTIONS FOR ADDITIONAL READING

The Conference on Inflation (proceedings of a conference held at the request of President Gerald R. Ford and the Congress of the United States, September 27–28, 1974). Washington, D.C.: U.S. Government Printing Office, 1974.

Okun, Arthur. "An Efficient Strategy to Combat Inflation." *The Brookings Bulletin*, vol. 15, no. 4 (Spring 1979), pp. 1–5.

Perry, George L., ed. *Curing Chronic Inflation*. Washington, D.C.: The Brookings Institution, 1978.

Samuelson, Paul A., and Solow, Robert M. "Analytic Aspects of Anti-Inflation Theory." *American Economic Review*, vol. 50, no. 2 (May 1960), pp. 179–94.

Schultz, George P., and Aliber, Robert Z., eds. *Guidelines, Informal Controls, and the Market Place*. Chicago: University of Chicago Press, 1966.

Tucker, James F., and Weber, Warren E. "Indexation as a Response to Inflation: An Examination." *Economic Review*, Federal Reserve Bank of Richmond, vol. 60 (November /December 1974), pp. 17–21.

Ture, Norman B. "Tax-Based Incomes Policy: Pain or Pleasure in Pursuit of Price Stability?" *Tax Review*, vol. 39, no. 6 (June 1978), pp. 23–30.

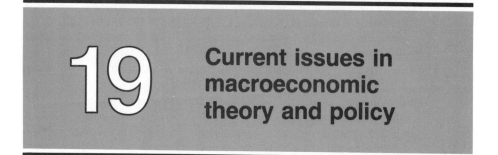

19

Current issues in macroeconomic theory and policy

WARM-UP: *Outline and questions to consider as you read*

Why do monetarist and Keynesian macroeconomic
  policy prescriptions differ?
  The classical (pre-Keynesian) approach.
  The Keynesian approach.
  The monetarist approach.
Should the discretionary powers of macroeconomic
  policymakers be limited?
Can supply-side economic policy revitalize the U.S.
  economy?
  Causes of declining productivity growth.
  The Laffer curve
  Supply-side solutions.

NEW TERMS

Classical model: an assortment of pre-Keynesian concepts which
have been combined to form a model of macroeconomic activity.

Laffer curve: a graph depicting the idea that government efforts to
increase tax revenues by increasing tax rates are eventually counterproductive.

Negative income tax: an income tax scheme whereby low-income
families receive a government subsidy (negative income tax) when
their income falls below a specified level.

Rational expectations: a theory which asserts that based on past experience, people are able to anticipate the true effect of economic policies and accordingly take action, thereby greatly hastening the occurrence of the ultimate outcome.

Say's Law: a theory, formulated by French economist Jean Baptiste Say (1767–1832), which asserts that aggregate supply creates an equal amount of aggregate demand.

This chapter deals with three related issues that are indicative of the state of turmoil presently surrounding macroeconomic theory and policymaking. The current unrest is to a large extent the consequence of the stagflation that plagued the economy in the 1970s: inflation was rampant; unemployment rose to a post–World War II peak; and productivity gains diminished, which retarded the growth of output. Not only was there a deterioration of economic performance in the 1970s compared to the 1950s and 1960s, but problems also seemed to become more persistent and perplexing than ever. Consequently, new approaches to theory and policy have emerged and will continue to do so, and these developments may well affect the application of monetary and fiscal policy.

The first issue is the Keynesian-monetarist debate which has been in progress for over two decades. Much of the controversy between the two camps has been described in previous chapters. Here we provide some background to the debate by discussing the evolution of macroeconomics from the classical system to the Keynesian and the monetarist models. The analysis highlights some crucial differences between the two modern approaches, particularly with respect to policy prescriptions.

The second issue, which is related to the first, deals with two opposing philosophies of macroeconomic policymaking. In the view of many economists, the poor economic performance in the 1970s was not so much the result of flawed economic models as it was the consequence of failing to devise policies consistent with the models. In other words, the policy implications of the models were simply ignored, and the result was endemic inflation and sluggish growth. The question we shall explore is whether policymakers—monetary and fiscal—should be fettered by a strict set of rules or granted discretionary policymaking power. The combatants in this controversy tend to be divided along Keynesian-monetarist lines.

Both the monetarist and the Keynesian models stress the role of aggregate demand and assume that the level of short-run aggregate supply is constrained by factors such as the labor supply, the stock of capital, and the level of technology. Consequently, economic activity has been viewed by both groups as depending primarily on aggregate demand. The third issue explores a new direction in macroeconomics which does not view aggregate supply as fixed. Instead, the supply-side approach focuses on the forces determining aggregate supply and on policies that encourage higher levels of output. Supply-side economics is sometimes referred to as incentive economics.

WHY DO MONETARIST AND KEYNESIAN MACROECONOMIC POLICY PRESCRIPTIONS DIFFER?

In previous chapters we have discussed Keynesian and monetarist theories and policies. Chapter 13 features a truncated Keynesian system—that is, a model without money—which was labeled a $C + I + G$ model. Chapter 14 introduced money and explained elements of both the Keynesian and the monetarist systems. Chapter 15 presents the IS-LM system which, in fact, weds classical (pre-Keynesian) and Keynesian elements. Chapter 16 covers fiscal policy, while Chapters 17 and 18 explore inflation and the use of fiscal and monetary policies to control it; Keynesian and monetarist disagreements about the causes of inflation and how to deal with it are a prominent feature of the discussion in these chapters.

The classical (pre-Keynesian) approach

The present-day Keynesian-monetarist controversy can be put into perspective by surveying the classical model of the macroeconomy. Since macroeconomics as a separate endeavor originated with Keynes's General Theory, the classical model actually represents a loose body of pre-Keynesian concepts that have been molded together into a unified system by post-Keynesian macrotheorists. As will become apparent, both the Keynesian and monetarist approaches have utilized various elements of classical doctrine.

A cornerstone of classical macroeconomics was Say's Law, which in essence is an assertion that aggregate supply creates its own aggregate demand.[1] That is, the wages and other factor income generated in the production process create sufficient purchasing power to clear all markets. As for individual markets, flexible prices (wages in labor markets) guarantee that shortages and gluts will be temporary.

A possible hitch in Say's Law is the existence of saving; that is, a portion of income earned in the process of production is not used by

---

[1] The origin of this idea is attributed to the French economist Jean Baptiste Say (1767–1832).

FIGURE 19-1
The classical saving-investment mechanism

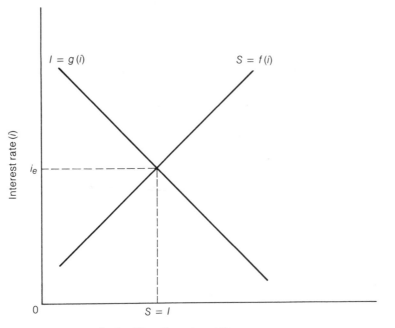

Saving (S) and investment (I)

the income recipient to purchase goods and services. Classical writers, however, solved this problem by asserting that income recipients could only be induced to trade present consumption for future consumption—that is, save—if they were paid interest; therefore, the flow of savings depends on the interest rate. On the other hand, businesses invest according to the expected profitability of a project which hinges in part on the rate of interest. These relationships are shown in Figure 19-1 which shows saving and investment as positive and negative functions of the interest rate, respectively. As long as the interest rate is free to fluctuate, the quantities of desired saving and investment will be equal. In this manner, income not consumed (saved) is returned to the spending stream via the investment process with no adverse impact on aggregate demand.

In the classical system, money functions only as a medium of exchange; people do not hoard money (hold it as a store of value). After all, the argument went, why would a rational person hold money, which does not pay interest, when alternative interest-earning investments are available?[2] Consequently, the only mac-

---

[2] Today it is recognized that money might be held as a store of value because it is liquid and is therefore safe and convenient.

roeconomic role played by money is to determine the general level of prices (P). Recall from Chapter 14 that the equation of exchange,

$$(19\text{--}1) \qquad\qquad MV = PQ,$$

can be used to illustrate how the quantity of money would determine the price level. According to the classical quantity theory of money, both velocity (V) and output (Q) are fixed in the shortrun; velocity is determined by the financial network of institutions, instruments, and customs which evolve slowly, and Q is at or near full employment as the result of the operation of Say's Law and the flexibile wage-price mechanism. With V and Q constant, a change in the money stock (M) will produce a proportional change (in the same direction) in prices (P).

The various elements of the classical model combine to produce full-employment levels of output automatically. Thus there is no need to use fiscal policy to stabilize output; price stability could be achieved by steadily increasing the money stock at a rate equal to the growth of the economy. Therefore, the classical approach to policymaking was one of nonintervention.

The Keynesian approach

The Great Depression of the 1930s shattered confidence in the classical concept of an automatically adjusting economy and the attendant role of policy. Either the classical view of how the macroeconomy functioned was seriously flawed, or policy had been badly misapplied. Keynes developed an alternative view of the economy with policy implications that differed radically from those of the classical system.

Keynes attacked the classical view—that the system was self-stabilizing and that output would be automatically maintained at or near full-employment levels—by questioning a major classical premise—wage and price flexibility. According to Keynes, certain institutional rigidities exist that make price and wage reductions unlikely. For instance, trade unions may prevent wage reductions, and large corporations may possess sufficient market power to resist price decreases. Consequently, even if there is considerable unemployment, wages and prices may not fall enough to restore full employment, or at the very least, wage-price rigidities may delay adjustments beyond a reasonable period of time. As for Say's Law, Keynes argued that saving was a function primarily of income and not of interest rates; therefore, the automatic adjustment mechanism assuring equality of investment and saving in the classical system was inoperative. It was possible, according to Keynes, for intended saving to exceed intended investment, thereby causing insufficient aggregate demand; furthermore, this situation might persist for a lengthy period of time.

Aggregate demand is the driving force in Keynesian analysis and determines whether there is a gap between actual and potential output. Potential output is determined by forces such as the size of the labor force, the stock of capital, and the level of technology. Since these factors cannot be altered in the short run, potential output is not the focus of policymaking. Aggregate demand is the critical factor in the Keynesian model in that the total of consumption, investment, and government spending determines the level of output (up to the economy's potential). The simple $C + I + G$ model of Chapter 13 incorporates the concept that aggregate demand determines aggregate supply; this view is the opposite of Say's Law.

Given the key role played by aggregate demand and the conclusion that inadequate demand is responsible for unemployment, government should focus on managing aggregate demand through fiscal and monetary policy actions. A tax reduction (to increase consumption), more government spending, and a higher money growth rate can be used to stimulate aggregate demand in order to produce an increase in output and employment. In summary, the Keynesian world is one where the private sector is basically unstable and where it is impractical to wait for such automatic forces as might exist to produce full employment. In this world there is a permanent need for government demand management using fiscal and monetary policy; this conclusion is obviously 180 degrees away from the hands-off role assigned to policy by classical theory.

In some respects, however, Keynes borrowed from the classical model. The IS-LM system discussed in Chapter 15 is, in fact, a synthesis of concepts developed by Keynes and elements taken from classical theory. Gardner Ackley aptly makes the point:

> To this synthesis Keynesian theory brings (a) the distinction between actual and potential output; (b) the aggregate demand approach to the explanation of actual output; together with (c) the consumption function as the determinant of the largest element of aggregate demand. In the synthesis, these elements are, in one way or another, married to theories of the interest rate, investment, money, and the determination of wages and prices, partly or largely derived from classical ideas.[3]

The Keynesian framework has dominated macroeconomic theory and policy during the post–World War II era. Policymakers applied Keynesian concepts, and during the 1960s, the United States experi-

---

[3] Gardner Ackley, *Macroeconomic Theory and Policy* (New York: Macmillan, 1978), p. 283.

enced its longest expansion on record. The Kennedy-Johnson tax cut of 1964 is viewed by Keynesians as a milestone in fiscal policymaking, marking the first time that a tax cut was enacted with the primary purpose of stimulating the economy.[4] The 1960s were a time of almost unbridled optimism: it was widely believed that business cycles could be virtually eliminated by applying existing knowledge—the age of "fine tuning" had arrived.

The optimism of the 1960s began to fade by the end of the decade. Spending on the Vietnam War coupled with a refusal to curtail domestic programs produced excessive aggregate demand. Economists now discovered that politicians were far less eager to raise taxes and reduce spending. As a result of too little action taken too late, the inflationary process became engrained in the economy and the "age of Keynes" seemed less than the salvation it had earlier. In 1936, when he wrote the *General Theory*, Keynes had little concern for inflation, and many economists now believe that Keynesian analysis is inadequate during periods of inflation. Reducing aggregate demand to combat inflation is almost certain to involve slower economic growth and higher unemployment at least for an interim period until most or all of the inflationary psychology has been eliminated. Politically, such action has proved distasteful. Even during the time when Keynesianism was at its pinnacle, there was never unanimous acceptance of the Keynesian framework and its policy prescriptions. By the early 1960s Milton Friedman had begun to win converts to a new macroeconomic approach that became known as monetarism. The monetarist model blends Keynesian and classical elements with certain new concepts. Like the Keynesian system, the monetarist approach focuses on the relationship of aggregate demand to potential output. In many respects, however, the Keynesian and monetarist systems are quite different.

The monetarist approach

The monetarist view of short-run movements in the economy varies considerably from the Keynesian interpretation. Monetarists believe that the economy is fundamentally stable—a proposition of the classical system—and that fluctuations in economic activity result primarily from inept government policymaking, particularly monetary mismanagement. The monetarist would, for example, point to the reduction of the money stock by one third during the

---

[4] Keynesians give a great deal of credit to the tax reduction for generating the exceptionally good economic performance of the 1960s; on the other hand, monetarists point to accomodative monetary policy as the primary cause of the expansion.

first four years of the Great Depression as the primary cause of the collapse and to the acceleration of money-supply growth in the 1970s as the primary cause of recent inflation. Keynesians, on the other hand, while conceding that economic policy can be a de-stabilizing influence, would also argue that the economy is not as stable as monetarists think it is; therefore, there is a need to use economic policy to offset the economy's inherent instability.

The monetarist's engine of analysis is the classical equation of exchange and a modern (monetarist) version of the quantity theory of money. Recall from Chapter 14 that the equation of exchange,

$$(19\text{--}2) \qquad\qquad M = kPQ,$$

(where k is the reciprocal of velocity) is the basis of the modern (monetarist) quantity theory of money. The monetarists believe that the rate of change of the money stock (M) dominates short-run changes in nominal GNP and, furthermore, that changes in M have a highly predictable impact. The predictability of this money sup-ply–GNP relationship stems from the belief that the demand-for-money function is stable. That is, the influences that determine k in Equation (19–2) are discernable and can be used to forecast k. If k (the reciprocal of velocity) can be anticipated, then obviously the effect on GNP (PQ) of a change in M can be forecast. Notice that it is not argued that P and Q can be predicted separately, given a change in M. Rather, the monetarist model contains a causal arrow running from M to PQ and not from M to P (or Q) only; in this sense, the monetarist model departs from its classical ancestry.

If the demand for money is stable, a change in the money stock is transmitted to the real sector in the following manner.[5] Starting from equilibrium, an increase in M creates an excess of money supply over money demand; consequently, money holders have excess money balances relative to all assets (real assets included). In an attempt to rid itself of these balances, the public spends money on other financial assets such as bonds and real assets including capital and consumer goods. As a total, the public cannot reduce its money balances, but in attempting to do so, a process of adjustment is set in motion. (For instance, bond prices will be bid up [interest rates will fall] which induces people to want to hold larger money balances.) The monetary transmission process is broad and works directly on consumption and investment as well as indirectly through lower interest rates; however, the monetarists stress the direct effects.

The Keynesian transmission mechanism focuses on the interest

---

[5] A detailed discussion of the monetary transmission mechanism of the monetarist model is contained in Chapter 14.

rate effect of an increase in the money supply. Since consumption is assumed to be rather interest insensitive, Keynesians view the impact of money as operating almost exclusively on investment. Thus monetary effects are transmitted through a narrower channel; coupling this view with the Keynesian supposition that the investment function may be relatively interest inelastic and unstable, one can easily understand the Keynesian tendency to conclude that monetary policy may be ineffective or unreliable. Furthermore, Keynesians view the demand-for-money function as unstable. Consequently, an increase in the stock of money might produce offsetting changes in the velocity of money. This controversy over the interest elasticity of money demand was discussed in Chapters 14 and 15.

Many of the disagreements between Keynesians and monetarists over macroeconomic policy have been discussed previously. For reasons that should now be apparent, monetarists emphasize the strength of monetary policy relative to fiscal policy, arguing that expansionary fiscal policy unaccompanied by changes in the money stock crowds out private expenditures and has little effect on the aggregate level of economic activity. Nonetheless, monetarists are concerned that uncontrolled deficit spending puts pressure on the Federal Reserve to expand the money supply excessively in order to hold down interest rates. Thus as long as the propensity exists for government to run deficits, it is unlikely that monetary policy can be conducted judiciously. Monetarists generally believe that the Federal Reserve has caused the money stock to grow too rapidly and to fluctuate too widely. They would remedy the problem by requiring the Fed to increase the money supply within some narrow range of growth, say, 3 to 5 percent each year. The next section is to a large extent a continuation of the monetarist-Keynesian controversy, dealing with the issue of the proper amount of discretionary power that should be granted to both fiscal and monetary policymakers.

SHOULD THE DISCRETIONARY POWERS OF MACROECONOMIC POLICYMAKERS BE LIMITED?

There are many economists who feel that economic policymaking is increasingly out of control and that the discretionary power of policymakers should be limited. To buttress their contention, advocates of limiting policymaking power cite evidence that, in their opinion, indicates poor performance particularly in the 1970s. Specifically, critics argue that fiscal and monetary policy in recent years has consistently been overly expansionary; furthermore, they say that political realities are such that the only effective way to rationalize the process is to limit the discretionary power of policymakers.

A review of the record points to the fact that policy has become increasingly expansionary. There have been federal budget deficits in every year from 1970 to 1979; in the 1960s there were budget deficits in seven of ten years while in the 1950s there were five surpluses and five deficits. Furthermore, the federal debt grew about $450 billion in the 1970s, and the $160 billion debt increase in 1975–76 was about $50 billion more than for the entire 1950–69 period.

Not only has there been a tendency in the post–World War II era for federal deficits to become more common and to grow larger in absolute terms, but they have also risen relative to GNP. The deficit was a peacetime record 4.6 percent of GNP in 1975 and exceeded 2.0 percent of GNP in three other years of the 1970s. From 1950 to 1969 the federal deficit exceeded 2.0 percent of GNP only in 1958.

Turning to monetary policy, growth of the money supply was higher in the 1970s than in the previous two decades. The average annual growth rate of M-1A was 6.1 percent in the 1970s, 3.9 percent in the 1960s, and 2.6 percent in the 1950s. Moreover, as reflected in Figure 19–2, monetary growth has varied considerably within these periods. This variability has been criticized, particularly by monetarists, as a source of economic instability.

We have observed in earlier chapters that there has been a noticeable propensity for policymakers to throw caution to the winds in

FIGURE 19–2
Annual change in money supply, 1959–1979

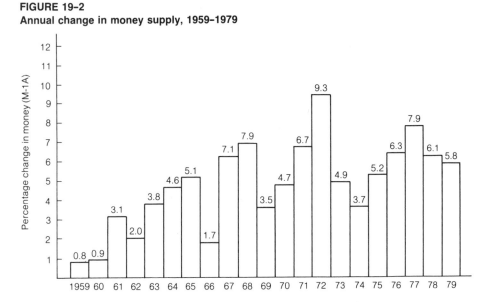

presidential election years. The growth rate of money in 1968 was 7.9 percent, and the federal deficit was a then peacetime record of $25.2 billion. In 1972 monetary growth spurted to 9.3 percent, and the deficit was $23.4 billion. Four years later the deficit was a staggering $66.5 billion and monetary growth was 6.3 percent. These figures strongly suggest that political considerations are frequently an important factor in the economic policymaking process.

The most predictable consequence of excessive fiscal and monetary stimulus is inflation. Ten times since 1950, the annual inflation rate has exceeded 4.0 percent, once in both the 1950s and 1960s, and eight times in the past decade. Twice—in 1974 and 1979—prices rose more than 10.0 percent. The average annual rate of inflation was 7.2 percent in the 1970s compared to 2.7 and 2.1 percent in the 1960s and 1950s, respectively.

Unfortunately, the poor performance on the price-level front was not accompanied by better results in other key areas. The average annual unemployment rate in the 1970s, like the rate of inflation, compares unfavorably to rates in the two previous decades. The average yearly rate was 4.5 percent in the 1950s, 4.8 percent in the 1960s, and 6.2 percent in the 1970s. The highest unemployment rate—9.2 percent—occurred in May 1975 and reflected the severity of the 1973–75 recession, the worst slowdown since the Great Depression. From 1970 to 79 the average annual growth rate of real GNP was 3.2 percent; in the 1960s and 1950s the rates were 3.9 and 3.3 percent, respectively. Other evidence of faltering macroeconomic performance could be cited, but the figures on inflation, unemployment, and GNP are sufficient to demonstrate that the economy has not performed in recent years as well as it should have.

Linking these and other problems to inept policymaking, a growing number of economists advocate limiting the power of policymakers. This viewpoint is responsible for the rules-versus-authority debate that was discussed in the last part of Chapter 3; the reader may find it useful to reread that section. Briefly, many rules advocates want to require that the Federal Reserve keep monetary growth within specified limits, say 3 to 5 percent a year. According to proponents of a monetary rule, the monetary authorities have badly mismanaged monetary policy and must be restrained if further damage is to be avoided. On the other hand, those favoring a discretionary approach say that it would be unwise to tie the Federal Reserve's hands with an inflexible rule and that the Fed's policymaking record will improve as it learns from its mistakes.

Monetary policymakers are not alone in facing efforts to curb their discretionary power. In the remainder of this section, a proposal to limit the authority of fiscal policymakers is explored. Various proposals to amend the Constitution that have received a great deal of attention would require the federal government to balance its budget annually. For instance, Senate Joint Resolution 126, which was debated in 1980, states in part, "The Congress shall adopt for each year a budget, which shall set forth the total receipts and expenditures of the United States. No budget in which expenditures exceed receipts shall be adopted, unless three-fifths of each House of Congress approve such budget by a roll call vote directed solely to that subject." This seemingly simple proposition and others similar to it are considerably more complex than they might seem at first glance.

First, the budget is actually an estimate of expenditures and receipts for the upcoming fiscal year, and the level of receipts depends not only on tax rates and tax regulations but also on the level of economic activity. Furthermore, actual spending may or may not be equal to the estimate included in the budget. If the proposed amendment were adopted, what would happen if GNP turned out to be smaller than estimated and a shortfall of tax receipts produced a budget deficit? Would taxes have to be raised or expenditures reduced and, if so, according to what formula? Or would any action be required as long as estimates of expenditures did not exceed estimated receipts?

There are also other complications. For instance, adoption of a balanced-budget amendment would make it tempting to shift more spending to the off-budget category.[6] Off-budget programs are the main reason that increases in the federal debt are larger than federal budget deficits; for instance, in fiscal 1979 the deficit was $27 billion, but the debt rose $53 billion. While Congress could require that expenditures be defined to include off-budget items, even that inclusion would not cover loan guarantee programs which have exploded in recent years. There are other mechanical problems that could be mentioned, but it should be clear that implementation and enforcement of a balanced budget amendment would not be a simple matter.

Another problem, the impact of requiring a balanced budget regardless of the state of the economy, is perhaps even more serious. If there is a high level of unemployment and the level of aggregate output is declining, fiscal policy would normally be used in order to reverse the decline. The conventional approach is to cut taxes and /or to increase expenditures. Since these actions would in all likelihood unbalance the budget, they would be prohibited under a balanced-budget amendment. Figure 19–3 illustrates the situation just described. Government spending (G) and taxes (T) are shown as a function of GNP. Note that G declines slightly as GNP increases,

---

[6] Off-budget federal outlays include those of federal entities such as the Postal Service fund and outlays of government-sponsored enterprises which are privately owned but may receive federal funds because they carry out federally sponsored programs (Federal Home Loans Banks are an example).

FIGURE 19-3
A balanced budget at the current level of Gross National Product

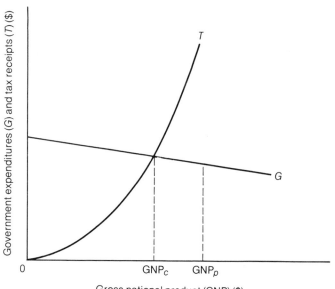

reflecting the fact that spending on programs such as unemployment compensation falls as the economy approaches potential Gross National Product (GNP$_p$ in Figure 19-3).[7] Taxes, on the other hand, are more sensitive to the level of GNP, increasing progressively as GNP rises.

Assume the economy is currently at GNP$_c$ which involves a considerable level of unemployment since there is a large gap between GNP$_c$ and potential GNP (GNP$_p$). Given the requirement that the budget be balanced, policymakers would have to adopt some combination of tax rates and regulations and government spending so that receipts would equal outlays. One such combination is shown in Figure 19-3. Moreover, there are any number of combinations of G and T that would result in a balanced budget when GNP is at GNP$_c$.

Consider the balanced budget combination of G and T which is illustrated in Figure 19-3. If the economy begins to recover and GNP starts to expand toward GNP$_p$, a restraining influence from the government sector would occur. This is apparent from the figure because when GNP rises beyond GNP$_c$, T becomes larger than G, and the accompanying budget surplus retards the expansionary process. This impact will be moderated to the extent that the government channels the surplus into the financial markets, thus making addi-

---

[7] In earlier chapters, for simplicity, it was assumed that G did not vary with GNP. In that case the line representing G in Figure 19-3 would be horizontal.

tional funds available to private borrowers. Nevertheless, some believe that the requirement to balance the budget may be flawed with respect to the countercyclical policy objective since a slack economy is not stimulated with a balanced budget.

Concern about monetary and fiscal policy has prompted many proposals to limit the discretion of policymakers. The odds that any of these proposals will be passed are probably less than 50–50. While there is widespread agreement that macroeconomic policy has not worked adequately, it is difficult to agree on specific actions to remedy the problems. One fact is clear, however; monetary and fiscal policy are so interrelated that if either is badly mismanaged, the other cannot be expected to salvage the overall policy package.

Whether policymaking is conducted according to rules or discretion, the public will typically respond to policy measures—good or bad—in a manner that will further their own self-interests. The *theory of rational expectations* hypothesizes that people learn what the ultimate impact of policy actions will be from past experience and on that basis act accordingly. Therefore, policymakers who attempt to produce temporary short-run results inconsistent with what is possible in the long term eventually will be frustrated by the reaction of the public. For example, if the monetary authorities attempt to reduce unemployment with large injections of money, the public, understanding the inflationary impact of such actions, will act accordingly in its own self-interest; consequently, the inflationary impact of the policy will occur very rapidly, and, according to the theory of rational expectations, the desired effect on unemployment will be frustrated. Thus, for policy to be effective, it must be geared to sustainable results over the long run.

In conclusion, it should be noted that the contestants in the debate over whether to limit policymakers' authority tend to be divided along Keynesian-monetarist lines. Remember that the Keynesian view of the macroeconomy is that it is basically unstable. Therefore, Keynesians generally oppose placing limits on policymakers since to do so would hamper their efforts at stabilization. On the other hand, the monetarist model portrays a system that is inherently stable; consequently, the role of policy is to avoid imposing destabilizing influences, especially in the form of rapid money-supply changes. From this perspective it is easy to understand why monetarists would wish to limit the power of policymakers.

CAN SUPPLY-SIDE ECONOMIC POLICY REVITALIZE THE U.S. ECONOMY?

The combination of serious inflation and declining productivity growth in the 1970s is known as stagflation. Some economists have expressed concern that neither the Keynesian nor the monetarist approach is sufficient since it is possible that even optimal demand management policies will not bring inflation under control and simultaneously generate more vigorous productivity growth. Therefore, demand management may need to be supplemented with other policies; that is, an improved policy package may result by adding other tools to the arsenal. Presently, policies generated by what is known as supply-side economics are believed by some to have great potential for improving economic performance.

Supply-side, or incentive, economics focuses on ways of increasing productivity and providing increased incentives to produce, which, according to proponents, not only mitigates the problem of stagnation but also relieves inflationary pressure. In the remainder of this section our attention is directed at the causes of and cures for the slowdown of growth of productivity and production. We do not discuss demand management policies to control inflation or stimulate production since they have been analyzed elsewhere.

Causes of declining productivity growth

Economists have offered several explanations for the decline in the rates of growth of productivity and output experienced in recent years.

1. The saving rate in the United States has declined: as a percent of disposable income, saving has historically been between 5 and 8 percent; however, the rate dropped to 5 percent or less for most of 1977–79, and in the final quarter of 1979, the saving rate was only 3.5 percent, the lowest ever recorded for this country. The rate in other countries where productivity growth has been more vigorous is much higher. For instance, in Germany, saving typically runs about 15 percent of disposable income; the rate is usually in the neighborhood of 25 percent in Japan. When the desire to save is weak, loanable funds to finance new plants and equipment may be inadequate to promote vigorous productivity growth.

2. Productivity gains have been slowed by the imposition of a host of regulations. The environmental, safety, and health standards administered by the Environmental Protection Agency (EPA) and the Occupational Safety and Health Administration (OSHA) are cases in point since, to meet the regulations, firms must divert funds that might otherwise be used to purchase output-increasing plant and equipment.[8]

---

[8] The effect on productivity should not be the sole criterion for judging the appropriateness of regulations; regulations typically entail benefits as well as costs.

3.   There are a multitude of other restrictions that foster inefficiencies of one kind or another; examples include tariffs, quotas, and subsidies. These protective measures isolate firms from competitive pressures and permit inefficient firms to continue to operate; otherwise, many enterprises would have to become more efficient or else be forced out of business.

4.   Because some workers are ill-trained and /or have little formal education, they remain in unproductive occupations unless training is made available. Also, certain workers may have skills that are being underutilized because they live in an area where there is no market for the particular skills that they possess.

5.   The services components of GNP have been growing faster than GNP itself, causing the share of services in GNP to rise. Because productivity gains are less likely in the services areas than in agriculture, construction, transportation, mining, and manufacturing, the overall rate of growth of productivity is reduced as services come to occupy a larger proportion of GNP.

6.   From 1972 to 1979, the "fuels and related products, and power" component of the Producer Price Index rose from 119 to more than 480, an increase of over 300 percent.[9] The soaring cost of energy has forced firms to spend money on energy-saving equipment instead of purchasing equipment that would raise output. Also, high-priced energy may have induced some firms to substitute labor for capital in order to conserve fuel.

7.   Our tax and transfer system often generates production disincentives. In the case of transfer payments, unemployment compensation and other government programs soften the impact of being unemployed. Therefore, the search for a job may be less intense than otherwise, and the unemployed workers may find it easier to wait to find just the right job. Also, since income earned on the job reduces eligibility for most transfer programs, the net gain in income that results from taking a new job may be small.

The Laffer Curve

Imposition of taxes on income results in a "wedge" being driven between the wage that employers pay and the net (aftertax) wage received by workers. Before taxes are imposed, the wage rate paid by an employer and that received by the worker are identical. When an income tax of say 10 percent is levied on workers' earnings, the

---

[9] The increase in energy prices has contributed to the high rate of inflation in the United States. However, other nations more dependent than we on foreign fuel, such as West Germany, have had lower inflation rates than ours, which suggests that inflationary forces other than energy have been at work in the United States.

supply of labor will decrease because net income is smaller; consequently, workers will substitute leisure for work because leisure involves a smaller sacrifice of income than previously. This decrease in the supply of labor means that firms must now pay higher wages to obtain the same quantities of labor as before the imposition of taxes; therefore, the quantity of labor demanded will fall. Hence, levying a tax on income results in a smaller supply of labor and a reduction in employment.

The disincentive effect of taxes is the basis of the Laffer Curve popularized by Professor Arthur Laffer. Figure 19–4 depicts the notion that high tax rates discourage production. Remember that actual tax collections (T) are the product of tax rates (t) and income (Y); that is,

$$(19–3) \qquad\qquad\qquad T = tY.$$

Assuming that taxes are a disincentive, continuing to raise tax rates would eventually result in lower income.[10] There is some tax rate, t_0 in Figure 19–4, that produces a maximum level of tax revenues, T_0. If tax rates are raised above t_0, the disincentive effect on income (Y), causes the total level of tax collections (T) to decline; raising tax rates above t_0 is clearly counterproductive.

Supply-side solutions

There are a large number of proposals to stimulate productivity and growth including exempting all or part of interest income on savings from taxation. Lowering taxes on savings would raise the effective interest rate and would provide incentive for savers to opt for future consumption rather than buying goods and services now. Tax incentives can also be extended to businesses to encourage investment. Accelerating depreciation and allowing companies to deduct a portion of the investment purchase price from their tax liabilities as a tax credit in the year of the purchase are means of stimulating investment spending. These devices have been and still are being used and can be liberalized to help spur investment activity.

Deregulation and removal of tariffs, quotas, and subsidies would increase efficiency and cause production to rise. Regulations usually provide benefits, cleaner air for example, but are costly to implement and enforce. These benefits and costs should be compared prior to

---

[10] The initial imposition of taxes may actually cause income to rise since the resulting tax collections can be used to provide essential public goods such as defense, law and order, and a transportation infrastructure.

FIGURE 19–4
The Laffer Curve

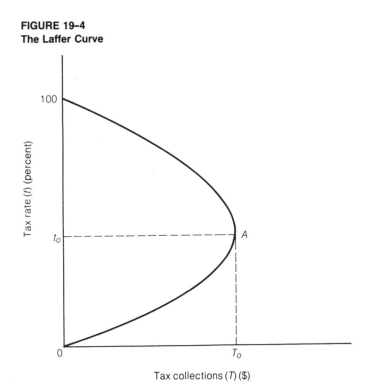

Tax collections (*T*) ($)

imposing new regulatory requirements. Lower tariffs, quotas, and subsidies would subject domestic firms to more intense competitive pressure necessitating that they become more productive.

Training programs can be used to increase worker skills. Unfortunately, the training projects undertaken in the past have met with mixed success. For some, the training has been the key to a better future; for others, the program has merely provided an income subsidy during participation in the program, with no discernable long-term impact. Past attempts at subsidized relocation met with some success as unemployed workers were given money to move to another place where their skills were needed. However, subsidized relocation projects are no longer operating in the United States.

A proposal to eliminate some of the built-in disincentives of the present welfare program is the negative income tax. As was indicated earlier, some income subsidy programs are so designed that transfer payments are reduced by an amount approximately equal to the increase in income, meaning, in effect, that the marginal tax rate on new income is 100 percent. One proposal to remedy this situation is the negative income tax, which can be designed so that low-income families receive a subsidy (a negative income tax) that would decline as income rises, but not on a dollar-for-dollar basis. That is, a $1.00 increase in income might reduce the subsidy by say $0.40. Of course, at some level of income the subsidy would be zero; above that point the tax rate would then be positive. Thus if the negative income tax replaced most other welfare programs, there is the advantage that it could be designed to produce a relatively small disincentive effect.[11]

Probably the most radical of the proposals to stimulate aggregate supply is the Kemp-Roth tax reduction plan. In 1977 Congressman Jack Kemp and Senator William Roth introduced a bill that included the following provisions:

1. A tax-rate reduction in excess of 30 percent over a three-year period; the range of tax rates would have been lowered from 14–70 to 8–50 percent.
2. Reduction of the corporate tax rate from 48 to 45 percent, also over a three-year period.
3. An increase in the corporate surtax exemption from $50,000 to $100,000.

Congress failed to pass the legislation, but sentiment for a massive tax cut still exists.

All of the proposals mentioned above have been met with opposition that ranges from mild to vehement. For example, opponents of the proposal to exempt interest income from taxation argue that there is no clear-cut evidence on the interest elasticity of saving. Thus a rise in the effective yield on savings may produce very little increase in the total amount saved. It is unlikely, but nonetheless possible, that a rise in interest rates would reduce savings, since a smaller amount of saving would then be needed to achieve a given savings objective. The determinants of saving are complex, however, and the effect of a change in interest rates may be relatively unimportant.

Critics of the negative income tax point out several problems with implementing and administering the system. Some argue that it is unlikely that existing welfare programs will be dismantled and that the negative income tax will simply be added to the current maze of welfare programs. While the existing tax collections system could be used to administer the negative income tax, more people would be needed to do so, especially if the government sent low-income families negative-income-tax checks on a monthly or quarterly basis.

---

[11] For further explanation of the negative income tax and a numerical example, the reader may refer to Richard H. Leftwich, *A Basic Framework for Economics* (Dallas: Business Publications, 1980), pp. 328–30.© Business Publications, Inc., 1980.

Despite its potential problems, many economists feel that the negative-income-tax idea offers the best chance of rationalizing what is today a very cumbersome welfare system.

Opponents of the Kemp-Roth tax reduction proposal are also dubious that the benefits envisioned from the tax cut will materialize. Proponents of a large tax reduction point to past episodes when the economy responded vigorously to a cut in taxes. They argue, for instance, that the Kennedy-Johnson tax bill of 1964 propelled the economy into an expansion that lasted until 1970. But those opposing a large tax cut argue that the Kennedy-Johnson legislation had its effect through stimulating aggregate demand which in 1964 was well below potential GNP. Recently, on the other hand, aggregate demand, if anything, has pressed too heavily on potential output, thereby creating inflationary pressure. Thus it is argued that a large tax cut would overstimulate the economy and generate a still more rapid rise in prices.

In the final analysis, the new interest in incentive economics is more likely to supplement than supplant present macroeconomic theory. While it is clear that macroeconomic policy has not succeeded completely and is to a large extent responsible for the acceleration of inflation in the 1970s, it is also obvious that aggregate demand management cannot be ignored while experiments with supply-side approaches are tried.

SUMMARY

In the 1930s the depressed state of the economy seemed to require new policies to deal with massive unemployment and low levels of output. The classical (pre-Keynesian) view that the economy was inherently stable was questioned. In particular, Keynes developed a new approach explaining how the macroeconomy functioned. In the Keynesian world, stability was not automatic; instead economic policy needed to be applied continuously to stimulate aggregate demand and keep workers employed and output near its potential.

The monetarist approach pioneered by Milton Friedman also focused on aggregate demand, using a modern version of the quantity theory of money as its chief instrument of analysis. Monetarists more or less hold the classical view that the economy is stable. The monetarists see monetary influences as more powerful than fiscal changes, to which they assign a secondary role. In the monetarist approach, however, both fiscal and monetary policy should be applied carefully; otherwise, economic policy may be a destabilizing influence.

There are at present a number of proposals to limit the power of macroeconomic policymakers. In this chapter, proposals to limit fiscal policymakers were discussed. In particular, we considered the merits of a balanced-budget amendment to the Constitution. The propensity of the federal government to spend in excess of tax revenues has prompted a call for such an amendment, but there are a number of mechanical problems that would make application of the requirement difficult.

The twin problems of declining productivity growth and inflation which plagued the United Stated economy during the 1970s do not seem amenable to solution with traditional monetary and fiscal policies. Consequently, a host of ideas that deal with aggregate supply have been proposed to combat the stagflation situation. Supply-side, or incentive, economics will not eliminate the controversy over how to administer monetary and fiscal policy, nor will it answer the question about the relative effectiveness of the two types of macro-policy. Nonetheless, supply-side policies may offer a supplement for solving the present inflation–slow growth dilemma.

REVIEW QUESTIONS

1. Do the policy prescriptions of the classical system have more in common with the Keynesian or the monetarist view of the policymaking? Explain.
2. In view of the current state of the economy, recommend a policy package consistent with the monetarist approach. Do the same but for the Keynesian approach.
3. Research the federal budget and the monetary growth rate for the past five years. Do you believe that a balanced budget and a stable growth rate of money of 3 percent would have produced better or worse results?
4. Explain the meaning of the Laffer Curve. What problems do you see in using the concept for policymaking purposes? Explain.
5. List and discuss some possible cures for the declining rate of productivity growth.
6. Relate the theory of rational expectations to the Phillips Curve debate covered in Chapter 18.

SUGGESTIONS FOR ADDITIONAL READING

Fellner, William. *Towards a Reconstruction of Macroeconomics: Problems of Theory and Policy.* Washington, D.C.: American Enterprise Institute for Public Policy Research, 1976.

Laffer, Arthur. "Two Views of the Kemp-Roth Bill." *American Enterprise Institute Economist* (July 1978).

Maclaury, Bruce K. "Proposals to Limit Federal Spending and Balance the Budget." In Joseph A. Pechman, ed., *Setting National Priorities: The 1980 Budget.* Washington, D.C.: The Brookings Institution, 1979, pp. 213–24.

Mayer, Thomas B. *The Structure of Monetarism.* New York: W. W. Norton & Co., 1978.

Peterson, Wallace C. *Emerging Approaches to Macroeconomics.* Bureau of Business Research, University of Nebraska, Faculty Working Paper no. 63 (November 1978).

V

INTERNATIONAL TRANSACTIONS IN THE MONETARY ECONOMY

20 International economic transactions: An introduction

NEW TERMS

Balance of payments: the record of all economic transactions occurring during a given time period between economic units in a particular country and economic units in all other countries.

Bill of exchange: an unconditional written order by one party requiring a second party to pay a specified sum of money to a third party.

Capital account: the record of international transactions involving financial assets.

Current account: the record of international transactions involving goods, services, and gifts.

Devaluation: a reduction in the official exchange value of a country's currency.

Exchange rate: the price paid for foreign currency on the foreign exchange market.

Foreign exchange: currencies available for use in international transactions.

Forward exchange rate: the price paid for foreign currency to be delivered at a future date.

Spot exchange rate: the price paid for foreign currency to be delivered immediately.

In the previous chapters, it was assumed that economic units in one country did not engage in economic transactions with economic units in other countries. That assumption is dropped in this section, and attention is focused on international or foreign transactions which are defined here as economic transactions between economies using different monetary units or currencies. International economic transactions are similar in many important respects to economic transactions between domestic economic units. For example, nations, like individuals, can benefit greatly from specialization and exchange; the principle of comparative advantage provides a compelling argument for the position that international trade is beneficial to all trading partners.

However, the nature of the benefits of international trade is often misunderstood. This misunderstanding is a result of a confusing of means and ends and a failure to look beyond special interests to national interests. Thus the rhetoric and debate surrounding international trade sometimes creates the impression that exports are the benefits of international trade, and imports are to be avoided if possible. Actually, the opposite would be close to the truth if it could be permanently achieved; that is, a country's imports are its benefits from trade, while its exports are its cost (its means of paying for the imports).

Despite considerable variation in the institutional frameworks of different countries, many of the propositions relating to the role and theory of money remain applicable across national boundaries. Like domestic transactions, international transactions may be carried out on a barter basis or through the use of money. As in the domestic case, the use of money is far more efficient as a means of affecting international transactions. Furthermore, just as most domestic transactions involve payment by check rather than cash, most international transactions utilize the services of banks and involve the transfer of claims against banks rather than the transfer of currency. In this chapter we explore the nature of international transactions, the mechanisms that have been developed to facilitate payment for them, and some of the ways that international transactions affect domestic economic activity.

WHAT IS THE BALANCE OF PAYMENTS, AND HOW IS IT MEASURED?

There are many types of international economic transactions. Just as individuals and private business firms keep records of their economic transactions in order to appraise their economic condition and to plan and make decisions accordingly, nations keep records of their international economic transactions because such records are essential to many policy decisions made at the national level. The record of all economic transactions during a given time period between economic units in a particular nation and all foreign economic units is known as that nation's *balance of payments*. Because this phrase is the object of considerable attention, concern, confusion, and misunderstanding, the following pages explore it in more detail.

Let us first review in a general manner the types of transactions included in the balance of payments. Since the record is supposed to include all economic transactions with foreign economic units, it will contain transactions by individual consumers, business firms, governmental units, and the nation's official monetary agency which is usually the central bank. These transactions may involve goods (referred to as merchandise transactions), services, transfer payments or gifts, financial assets, foreign currencies, and international reserve assets such as gold.

When analyzing transactions that affect the balance of payments, keep in mind that all transactions are regarded as two-sided; that is, something is purchased or acquired, and, on the other side, that purchase must be financed or paid for by the transfer of something of equivalent value. Therefore, the balance of payments records are based on the principles of double-entry bookkeeping with items being recorded as either debits (payments) or credits (receipts). A country records as debits on its balance of payments those items that result in an outflow of foreign exchange (currency used in foreign transactions). Imports, for example, are recorded as debit or payment items. Credit items, on the other hand, reflect transactions that give rise to an inflow or receipt of foreign exchange. Viewed in this manner, a country's balance of payments reflects its sources and uses of foreign exchange.

The double-entry approach to recording international transactions has two results that should be stressed:

1. The total of all debit entries and the total of all credit entries must balance—in that sense, the balance of payments is always in balance.
2. The value of all debit entries and all credit entries for one, a few, or even several categories of transactions need not balance, and, in fact, are unlikely to balance.

It is the existence of the second possibility that allows us to speak of balance of payment problems in the form of deficits or surpluses. For example, even though in the aggregate the balance of payments must always balance, the particular account "Merchandise trade," which reflects merchandise exports as a credit and merchandise imports as a debit, need not balance. Thus we could speak of a balance of payments surplus with respect to the merchandise trade if merchandise exports exceeded merchandise imports for the time period in question.

The U.S. balance of payments

A useful way of classifying international transactions is reflected in Table 20–1 which is an adaptation of the U.S. balance of payments data for the first quarter of 1979. Transactions are divided into three general categories:

1. Current account transactions which involve flows of merchandise, services, and gifts.
2. Capital account transactions which involve flows of financial assets such as stocks, bonds, bills of exchange, and bank deposits.
3. Transactions conducted by the official monetary authorities of the nation—its central bank, treasury, or an exchange stabilization agency.

TABLE 20–1
Summary of U.S. international transactions, first quarter of 1979
($billions)

Item	Credits (receipts)	Debits (payments)	Cumulative balance
Current account transactions			
Exports of goods	$41.4		
Imports of goods		$47.5	
Balance on merchandise trade		6.1	$− 6.1
Exports of services	23.0		
Imports of services		15.4	
Balance on services	7.6		
Balance on goods and services			+ 1.5
Unilateral transfers (gifts, net)		1.3	
Balance on current account			+ 0.2
Capital account transactions			
Long-term investment			
Direct investment abroad by			
U.S. economic units		6.3	
Direct investment in United States			
by foreign economic units	1.3		
Portfolio investment abroad			
by U.S. economic units		2.1	
Portfolio investment in United States			
by foreign economic units	3.4		
Balance on long-term investments		3.7	
Basic balance			− 3.5
Short-term investment			
Short-term capital investments			
abroad (est.)	5.8		
Short-term capital investments			
in United States (est.)	8.1		
Balance on capital account	10.2		+10.4
Official reserves transactions			
Net change in U.S. official			
reserve asset holdings			
(including new SDR allocations)		2.4	
Net increase or decrease in			
liabilities to foreign central banks		8.5	
Balance on official reserves			
transactions		10.9	− 0.5
Net errors and omissions (statistical discrepancy)	0.5		0.0

Source: Adapted from U.S. Department of Commerce, Bureau of Economic Analysis, *Survey of Current Business,* vol. 59, no. 6 (June 1979), p. 41. The data used in the table are preliminary and subject to revision.

In Table 20–1, the column labeled Credits (receipts) reflects transactions that result in an inflow of foreign exchange to the United States. The column labeled Debits (payments) reflects transactions that require the United States to give up foreign exchange. Note that the United States had a $6.1 billion deficit in its balance on merchandise trade. This indicates that debit items—goods purchased from other countries, or imports—exceeded credit items generated by exports of goods. To pay for these "extra" imports, we had to acquire funds from sources other than exports. The remainder of the balance of payments accounts shows how these funds were acquired.

The balance on merchandise trade reflects only transactions involving merchandise. If, for example, transactions involving services—transportation, hotel accommodations, medical, and other services provided for foreign residents—are included with merchandise transactions, the net difference between debit and credit items is referred to as the balance on goods and services.[1] As the name implies, the balance covers not only all exports and imports of goods but all exports and imports of services also. For the quarter, the United States had a surplus of $1.5 billion in the balance on goods and services. This surplus, in contrast to the deficit on merchandise trade, reflects the fact that U.S. exports of services exceeded U.S. imports of services. The surplus on services, which gave rise to an inflow of foreign exchange, helped finance the excess of merchandise imports over merchandise exports.

The U.S. government, individuals, and many charitable organizations make gifts of goods or money to foreign individuals, organizations, and governments. These are by nature one-way transactions; however, as noted earlier, all international transactions are recorded, according to the principles of double-entry bookkeeping, as both a debit and a credit. An account called "Unilateral transfers" is used so that gifts of goods, currency, or financial assets will have a corresponding entry. For example, if an American charitable organization ships corn to one of the underdeveloped nations, the shipment will show up as a credit to exports and a debit to unilateral transfers. As noted in Table 20–1, Americans' gifts to foreigners exceeded foreign gifts to us by $1.3 billion. Thus when the effects of gifts are considered along with transactions of goods and services, the result is the "Balance on current account." In quarter one of 1979, the United States had a current account surplus of $0.2 billion.

International capital flows may complicate or expedite the financing of current account transactions. Recall that international flows of financial assets are reflected in the capital account transactions which are divided into three categories: (1) direct investment, (2) portfolio investment, and (3) short-term capital flows. As implied by this classification, direct investment and portfolio investment are long term; that is, they involve financial assets with a maturity of

---

[1] For more detail on the items included in the balance of payments accounts in Table 20–1 see U.S. Department of Commerce, Bureau of Economic Analysis, *Survey of Current Business,* vol. 58, no. 6, pt. 2 (June 1978).

more than one year. Short-term capital flows involve financial assets with maturities of less than one year and include (but are not limited to) very liquid assets such as bank deposits and foreign currencies. A long-term capital flow is classified as direct investment if it involves real estate or if the investor exercises direct control of the business involved. Direct control is presumed to exist if various economic units in one country own a total of 50 percent or more of a company located in another country or if a single economic unit (or group of economic units acting in concert) owns 25 percent or more of the voting stock of a company located in another country. Portfolio investment represents long-term capital flows that are presumed not to give investors effective control over the companies involved.

In the first quarter of 1979, direct investment in other countries by U.S. economic units was $6.3 billion, while direct investment in the United States by foreign economic units totaled only $1.3 billion. In terms of portfolio investment, U.S. economic units invested less abroad than foreign economic units invested in the United States. However, the balance on long-term investments was a $3.7 billion deficit. The balance on long-term investments plus the current account balance is often referred to as the basic balance. During this period, the U.S. basic balance was a $3.5 billion deficit. After allowing for short-term capital flows, the cumulative balance with respect to goods, services, gifts, and capital was a $10.4 billion surplus.

How did the United States offset or balance this net inflow of funds? The answer is found in the "Official reserves transactions" balance. Foreign central banks decreased their holdings of dollars and dollar-denominated financial claims on the United States by $8.5 billion, an amount sufficient to offset most of the surplus accumulated by the United States on other international transactions; this amount was supplemented by $2.4 billion as the United States increased its holdings of official reserve assets. Official reserve assets are a country's official holdings of foreign exchange or assets that can be sold for foreign exchange without incurring an offsetting outflow of its own currency. The primary official reserve assets are gold, accumulated holdings of the currencies of other countries, liquid claims on other countries denominated in their currency, and special drawing rights (SDRs) at the International Monetary Fund (IMF).[2]

Note that after the official reserves transactions are considered,

---

[2] Special drawing rights are discussed in more detail in the following chapter. They are in essence deposit liabilities of the International Monetary Fund that are transferable between official monetary agencies.

the cumulative balance is a $0.5 billion deficit which is offset by the last line item, "Net errors and omissions (statistical discrepancy)." This entry is a balancing item that assures that the total debits and credits (payments and receipts) for international transactions are equal. "Net errors and omissions" would not be necessary if accurate data were available on all international transactions. However, complete and errorless data on such a large scale are seldom available because many items are derived from secondary sources. Consequently, errors are inevitable, and the "Net errors and omissions" category measures the net effect of those discrepancies.

Balance of payments problems

If the balance of payments must always balance, how is it that we hear of various countries having balance of payments problems? The answer involves the manner in which the balance is achieved; for example, in 1977, the United States was able to finance its overseas transactions because foreign central banks were willing to acquire and hold dollar-denominated assets. In effect they granted us credit to the tune of $37 billion. This situation is considered to be a problem because a country cannot rely on such a method of financing indefinitely. However, the extent of the problem depends on the reasons foreign central banks were purchasing dollar-denominated assets. If they did so because they considered dollar assets a good form in which to hold their reserves, there is less of a problem than if they bought dollars in order to support the exchange value of the dollar. More will be said about this matter in the discussion of exchange rates.

Just as individuals and businesses cannot continue to spend more than their receipts, nations cannot continually spend more abroad than they can finance. If international credit becomes scarce, or if foreign central banks become hesitant about continued acquisition of dollar-denominated assets, what will happen? This question is explored in more detail later, but in general the answer depends on whether or not we are willing to let the exchange value of our currency decline. Under a flexible exchange rate system, the dollar price of foreign currencies would rise. This decline in the value of the dollar on the foreign exchange market would lead American economic units to curtail foreign expenditures, thus resulting in a lowering of our standard of living. Another result would be greater foreign expenditures in the United States. These changes would probably correct the payments problem, but in the process, the United States would have to give up more of its goods for the same amount of foreign goods or less.

Under a regime of fixed exchange rates, a recurrent U.S. balance of payments problem would put pressure on the Federal Reserve to sell reserve assets—gold, SDRs, and any accumulated foreign currencies. To do this for an extended period would eventually require borrowing from the IMF or foreign central banks. When funds from these sources were no longer available, the dollar would have to be devalued—the official dollar exchange rate lowered—or import restrictions such as tariffs and quotas would be necessary. Such actions might draw retaliatory measures from our trading partners. The other alternative would involve the use of monetary and fiscal policy actions to reduce domestic economic activity in order to reduce imports.

HOW ARE PAYMENTS MADE IN INTERNATIONAL TRANSACTIONS?

National political boundaries by themselves have no meaningful effect on transactions occurring between nations. Rather, it is the fact that different nations have different monetary units that makes international transactions dissimilar to domestic transactions. The mechanisms for handling economic transactions occurring between economic units in New York and California are essentially the same as those used to handle transactions between residents within one of those states. However, if an individual or firm in California or New York wishes to engage in an economic transaction with a firm or individual in West Germany, the procedures used in domestic exchanges are no longer adequate. The political boundaries between states do not create problems because both New York and California use a common currency; likewise, the boundary between New York and Germany would create no special problems if Germany and New York did not use different currencies.

The exchange of currencies in international transactions

Just as individuals within a single country find it more efficient to use money than to engage in barter, trade between individuals and firms in different countries is more efficient if money is used. Thus German auto manufacturers do not try to trade Volkswagens to Americans for computers or wheat. Instead, they sell Volkswagens for money and use money to buy computers and wheat. However, the use of money in international transactions is not as simple as in domestic transactions. German exporters want marks, not U.S. dollars, for their goods since they must pay their workers, suppliers, and stockholders in marks. Likewise, American wheat exporters do not want German money (marks) for their wheat; they want U.S. dollars because that is what they must use in paying their expenses. Thus importers must directly or indirectly (usually indirectly) pay exporters with currency of the exporting country. How do importers obtain the foreign currencies needed to carry out their planned purchases? In most cases, the currency would be purchased in what is known as the foreign exchange market. The seller would probably be a bank with an international department, and the price paid would be referred to as the exchange rate. In the case of a German importer who purchases dollars, the price paid would be the exchange rate between marks and dollars. The dollars obtained and the marks paid would be referred to as foreign exchange.

The term *foreign exchange* refers to funds available for use in international transactions and may include foreign currency, deposits in foreign banks, and other liquid, short-term financial claims payable in foreign currencies. Most payments in international transactions are made or facilitated by trading foreign exchange on the foreign exchange markets. Before we take up the question of how exchange rates—the prices for foreign exchange—are determined, it is helpful to take a brief look at the institutional framework underlying the foreign exchange markets.

Like all markets, foreign exchange markets consist of buyers and sellers; in addition, a middleman often is involved. The buyers of foreign exchange are economic units who wish to acquire goods, services, or financial assets that must be paid for with foreign monies. Governments and central banks may also participate as buyers (or sellers). A seller is anyone who has acquired foreign currency and wishes to exchange it for domestic currency. Most foreign exchange transactions utilize the services of a middleman which is typically a large commercial bank located in a major financial center (such as New York City in the case of the United States). Through deposit and branching relationships, banks throughout the country have access to the foreign exchange market in New York and throughout the world.

Banking relations between countries take several forms:

1. Banks in one country may operate branches in important cities in other countries.
2. Banks in one country may set up correspondent relationships with important domestic banks in other countries.
3. Banks may singly or jointly with other domestic or foreign banks establish or acquire banks in other countries.

These banks, through their branches, correspondents, and subsidiaries, play a vital role in the international payments mechanism.

Consider again a German importer who wishes to purchase American wheat. The importer typically would approach a bank in Germany that maintains an international department and has a correspondent relationship with a New York bank. Consequently, the German bank would maintain a correspondent balance, denominated in dollars, with the New York bank. Under these circumstances, the importer's bank will sell the importer a cable transfer or bank draft payable to the American wheat exporter and drawn by the German bank on its account in the New York bank.[3] The importer could buy the draft from the German bank and mail it directly to the American exporter, or the German bank could cable instructions to the American bank to transfer funds from its account to the American exporter's account.

The check drawn by the German importer to pay the German bank would be denominated in marks; on the other hand, the bank draft would be denominated in dollars. The amount of marks paid by the importer would be determined by the dollar cost of wheat and the exchange rate between marks and dollars. If the exchange rate were 1.8 marks per dollar and the wheat cost $1 million, the importer's check to his bank would be for 1.8 million marks, and the bank draft would be for $1 million. Ignoring slight time lags and assuming that title to the wheat changes hands immediately, the effects of the complete transaction can be seen in the balance sheet changes of the importer, the exporter, and the two banks as shown in Figure 20-1.

The use of a draft or cable transfer is only one way to handle the payment for an international transaction. Another possibility is for the importer to maintain dollar deposits in a U.S. bank upon which checks could be written for purchases in the United States. Of course, such deposits require the importer to purchase dollars at some time, and the cost of these dollars is determined by the exchange rate. However, to hold dollar balances (or any other foreign currency) subjects an importer to the risk of adverse exchange rate fluctuations; that is, exchange rate fluctuations can increase or decrease the value of any foreign currency holdings.

Another commonly used method of making payment for international transactions is by use of a bill of exchange, which is an unconditional order, expressed in writing, by one party—the drawer—requiring a second party—the drawee—to pay a specified sum to a designated third party—the payee or bearer. If the bill is payable immediately when presented to the drawee, it is known as a sight bill; if payable at a later date, it is known as a time bill. Of course one party does not necessarily have to honor another party's

---

[3] A bank draft is an order to pay drawn by one bank on its account in another bank.

FIGURE 20–1
Balance sheet effects of sale of American wheat to German importer

Importer

Title to wheat	+1.8 million marks
Deposit at German bank	−1.8 million marks

German bank

Mark value of dollar deposit at U.S. bank	−1.8 million marks	Deposits of importer	−1.8 million marks

U.S. bank

	Deposits of German bank	−$1 million
	Deposits of exporter	+$1 million

Exporter

Title to wheat	−$1 million
Deposits at U.S. bank	+$1 million

order to pay. Thus such orders usually reflect prior agreements that the order will be honored. To signify an intention to honor the bill, the drawee will write *accepted* across the face with the date and signature. With this, the bill becomes an acceptance, and the drawee has made a legal promise to pay. If the drawee is a bank, the bill is known as a bank acceptance; otherwise, it is known as a trade acceptance. Exporters often draw time bills upon an importer or importer's bank and then discount or sell the bills to another party, thus obtaining funds immediately. The party holding a time bill grants credit until the importer pays the amount of the acceptance. In any case, the importer must at some time make a foreign exchange purchase to acquire the funds needed to honor the acceptance.

The large commercial banks that act as foreign exchange dealers stand ready to buy and sell foreign exchange at all times. They sell bank drafts drawn on their balances in foreign branches or with foreign correspondents and are willing to buy bills of exchange drawn on foreign economic units. The dealer banks usually have a trading room with special traders and an elaborate network of communications equipment that keeps them in direct contact with each other and with various exchange brokers. While dealer banks may take a position in certain currencies (hold large amounts of those currencies), they are more likely to try to cover most of each day's sales with offsetting purchases of the currencies involved. This

TABLE 20–2
Exchange rates between the U.S. dollar and other major currencies,
January 1980

Currency	Price of currency in U.S. dollars	Price of U.S. dollars in foreign currency	
Canadian dollar	$0.85912	1.16398	Canadian dollars
German mark	0.57986	1.72723	marks
Italian lira	0.0012427	804.69944	lire
Japanese yen	0.0042041	237.86303	yen
Mexican peso	0.04378	22.84148	pesos
Swiss franc	0.62693	1.59507	francs
British pound	2.2641	0.44168	pounds

* Average of daily prices at noon in New York.

Source: Board of Governors of the Federal Reserve System, *Federal Reserve Bulletin*, vol. 60, no. 2 (February 1980), p. A-68.

minimizes the risk of exchange variations. In major foreign exchange centers, dealer banks are likely to engage in three types of trans-actions: (1) transactions involving themselves and their customers, (2) transactions with each other through brokers, and (3) transactions with dealer banks in other countries.

Exchange rates

In the exchange market, every country's currency has a unique price or exchange rate in terms of every other country's currency. Thus there are many exchange rates. The relevant exchange rate in the example of the German importer would be the exchange rate between marks and U.S. dollars; that is, the mark price of dollars. Some recent exchange rates between major currencies are shown in Table 20–2. From that table, we can see that, if the international transaction in the above example took place in January 1980, the German importer could obtain U.S. dollars at a cost of 1.7272 marks per dollar. An American Volkswagen importer who must obtain marks in order to pay for the Volkswagen would have to pay $0.5798 for each deutsche mark. Note that exchange rates, like all prices, are ratios relating what must be given up to what is being received. Thus the exchange rate between dollars and marks is the reciprocal of the exchange rate between marks and dollars.

Exchange rates function as a linking mechanism between prices in different countries that use different currencies. Thus the price of Volkswagens in dollars is determined by the price of Volkswagens in marks and the exchange rate between dollars and marks as indicated by Equation (20–1):

(20-1)

| Price in U.S. dollars of Volkswagen sold in United States | = | Exchange rate between dollars and marks | × | Price in marks of Volkswagen sold in Germany. |

For example, if a rise in production costs of Volkswagens were to cause the German automaker to raise domestic prices (in marks), this price increase would be reflected in the dollar price of Volkswagens sold in the United States. However, the dollar price of Volkswagens sold in the United States could also change due to exchange rate variations even in the absence of changes in the mark price of Volkswagens.

Exchange rates may be determined by the market forces of supply and demand, or they may be fixed or controlled by unilateral or consensus agreement of some central authorities. In the latter case, the resulting exchange rates are referred to as fixed, controlled, or pegged.

Free exchange rates. Free exchange rates are determined in the market by private supply and demand forces. There is no intervention on the part of governments or central banks acting as buyers or sellers in an attempt to influence the exchange rate. Thus free exchange rates are sometime referred to as floating rates since they may "float" upward or downward in a free response to private market forces. In cases where there is some official interference in the exchange market, but not enough to keep exchange rates constant, the situation is referred to as a "dirty float" in contrast to a "clean float" which involves no official intervention.

Consider a specific exchange rate—the exchange rate between deutsche marks and U.S. dollars. Remember that the exchange rate between dollars and marks may be expressed as the mark price of dollars (1.7272 in Table 20-2) or the dollar price of marks (0.57986 in Table 20-2). To buy dollars, you would have to pay 1.7272 marks; to buy marks, you would have to pay $0.57986 (or 1/$1.7272). Thus when the mark price of dollars is determined, the dollar price of marks is also determined.

Why was the mark price of dollars 1.7272? In a world of free exchange rates, the answer can be explained in terms of Figure 20-2. If the mark price of dollars were anything other than 1.7272, the quantity of dollars supplied would be more or less than the quantity demanded, and the exchange rate would be bid up or down accordingly. For example, if the mark price of dollars happened to be 1.6500, there would be more dollars demanded (Q_2 in Figure 20-2) than supplied (Q_1 in Figure 20-2). Some buyers would be unable to obtain dollars and would be willing to pay higher rates. A slightly

FIGURE 20-2
Demand and supply of dollars in terms of marks

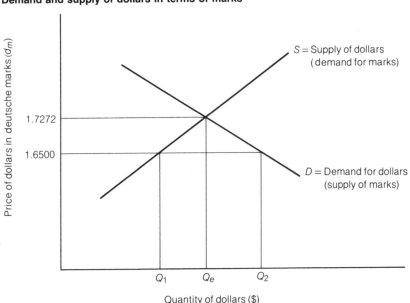

higher rate would result in more dollars being supplied to the foreign exchange markets. Only when the exchange rate reached 1.7272 would the quantity supplied equal the quantity demanded. At that point no upward or downward pressure would be put on the exchange rate. At any exchange rate greater than 1.7272 marks per dollar, there would be a surplus of dollars available, and downward pressure would be put on the exchange value of dollars (mark price of dollars).

Note in Figure 20-2 that the demand curve for dollars is also labeled the supply curve for marks. Demanding dollars is the same as supplying marks. Likewise, the supply curve for dollars is a demand curve for marks. This follows from the fact that the mark price of dollars is simply the reciprocal of the dollar price of marks.

Dollars are supplied to the foreign exchange market because some dollar holders wish to obtain marks. If speculative motives are ignored, the major reason that anyone with dollars would want marks would be a desire to purchase German goods, services, or financial assets. Such purchases must, for the most part, be carried out in marks. Thus the total number of dollars supplied may be viewed as a function of the exchange rate between marks and dollars and the various other factors that affect Americans' desires to purchase German goods. These other factors include such variables as the level of income in the United States, the price of German goods relative to American goods, tastes and preference patterns in the United States, and other factors. In addition to wanting marks to purchase German goods, Americans might also want marks to make financial or capital investments in Germany. American firms, for example, may wish to build plants in Germany, purchase German government bonds, or purchase stock in German corporations. Any of these actions would require marks and would result in dollars being supplied to the foreign exchange market.

The supply and demand curves for foreign exchange as illustrated in Figure 20–2 are like all such curves in that they are a device for focusing attention on two variables—price and quantity—while abstracting from the effects of other variables that influence the quantities supplied and demanded. For example the supply curve for dollars in Figure 20–2 indicates how many dollars will be supplied in the exchange markets at various prices (exchange rates between dollars and marks) allowing for and holding constant the effects of the variables other than the exchange rate.

The reason that the supply curve of dollars is upward-sloping with respect to the exchange value of dollars is that a higher mark price of dollars means fewer dollars are needed by Americans in order to carry out specific purchases of German goods, services, and financial assets. Thus a higher mark price of dollars stimulates American purchases of German goods. Looked at another way, if the mark price of dollars rises, the dollar price of German goods falls, thereby increasing American purchases of those goods and causing Americans to supply more dollars (demand more marks) in the foreign exchange markets.[4]

Suppose an American importer wishes to import Volkswagens, which the manufacturer is willing to sell for 8,000 marks each. The cost in dollars of importing the Volkswagens will depend on the exchange rate between dollars and marks and the mark price of Volkswagens in accordance with Equation (20–1). Thus

$$\begin{array}{ccc} \text{Dollar cost of} & \text{Dollar price} & \text{Mark price} \\ \text{imported} & = & \text{of} & \times & \text{of} \\ \text{Volkswagens} & \text{marks} & \text{Volkswagens.} \end{array}$$

Column (1) of Table 20–3 shows the assumed mark price of each Volkswagen, and in column (3), the American dealer's dollar cost of each Volkswagen is given for the various exchange rates listed in column (2). In column (4) the American dealer's selling price is shown based on an assumed markup of 20 percent. Column (5) re-

---

[4] This assumes that the import demand for German goods is not price inelastic.

TABLE 20-3
Hypothetical relationships among Volkswagen sales in the United States, various exchange rates, and the supply of dollars in foreign exchange markets

(1) Mark price of Volkswagens	(2) Exchange rate (dollar price of marks)	(3) Cost of VWs to dealer in dollars	(4) Selling Price with 20 percent markup	(5) Number of units sold	(6) Total marks demanded by dealer (5) × (1)	(7) Total dollars supplied by dealer to exchange market (2) × (6) or (3) × (5)
8,000	$.65	$5,200	$6,240	10	80,000	$52,000
8,000	.60	4,800	5,760	11	88,000	52,300
8,000	.55	4,400	5,280	13	104,000	57,200
8,000	.50	4,000	4,800	15	120,000	60,000
8,000	.45	3,600	4,320	17	136,000	61,200

flects the increased dealer's sales that are assumed to accompany the various selling prices associated with the exchange rates in column (2) and the dealer's 20 percent markup. Column (6) shows the total number of marks the dealer would demand at the various exchange rates shown in column (2), and column (7) reflects the total dollars supplied by the dealer to the exchange market at the various exchange rates. If column (6) were plotted against column (2), the result would be a demand curve for marks in terms of the dollar price of marks. If column (7) were plotted against the reciprocal of column (2) (the mark price of dollars), the result would be a supply curve of the type shown in Figure 20-2. Thus the supply curve of dollars is equivalent to the demand curve for marks with the exchange rate expressed in an alternate manner.

The demand for dollars is dependent upon those factors that cause Germans to wish to purchase American goods, services, and financial assets. These factors include prices of American goods relative to similar goods produced in Germany and other countries (a reflection of the exchange rate and American domestic prices), the tastes and preferences of Germans for American goods, interest rates and investment opportunities in the United States relative to interest rates and investment opportunities in Germany, and other factors. If all of the foregoing factors except exchange rates are held constant, the demand for dollars can be plotted against the exchange rate to produce a demand curve similar to that shown in Figure 20-2. A change in one or more of the other factors discussed above would cause the demand curve for dollars to shift, resulting in a new exchange rate.

In a world of free exchange rates, the rates vary as supply and demand forces shift. In general anything that causes an increase in the supply of dollars (a shift to the right of the S curve) will put downward pressure on the value of dollars in the foreign exchange markets. This is illustrated in Figure 20-3 by the shift of the S curve to S' and a decline in the exchange rate from E_0 to E_1.

An outward shift in the supply curve of dollars could have several causes. One example, which mirrors the experience of recent years, would be a greater rate of inflation in the United States than in Germany. The lower inflation rate in Germany would make German goods relatively attractive and would increase U.S. imports of such goods, causing additional dollars to be supplied in exchange for marks. This process could be depicted by a shift of the supply curve for dollars to the right from S to S' in Figure 20-3. Other factors that could cause a similar shift are an increased American preference for German goods, a rise in interest rates in Germany relative to interest rates in the United States, and increases in incomes in the United

FIGURE 20-3
Effects of shifting supply and demand curves on the mark price of dollars

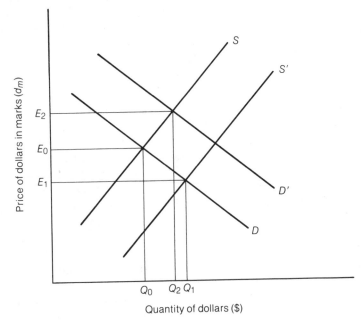

States. If these changes were in the opposite direction, the S curve would shift to the left, and the exchange rate would rise. The exchange rate would also change if anything caused the demand curve for dollars to shift. For example, if the level of disposable income in Germany were to rise, some of this increased income would probably be spent on imported American goods, thereby shifting the demand curve for dollars to the right (for example, from D to D' in Figure 20-3) and causing the mark price of dollars to increase from E_0 to E_2.

Spot rates and forward rates. Economic units wishing to engage in international transactions may purchase foreign currency for immediate delivery (usually 2 days after the day of trade), or they may contract for delivery of the currency at some future date. The price paid for currency to be delivered immediately or "on the spot" is referred to as the *spot rate*. The rates shown in Table 20-2 are spot rates. The price paid for foreign currency to be delivered, say in 90 days, is referred to as the forward rate, or in this case, the 90-day forward rate. Forward rates in the foreign exchange market are functionally analogous to futures prices in commodities markets. Just as it is possible to purchase a futures contract for wheat, a futures contract for marks or yen can also be purchased in the forward exchange market. For example, on May 14, 1979, at 3:00 P.M. in New York, the spot rate for West German marks was $0.5265; the 30-day forward rate was $0.5290, the 90-day forward rate was $0.5332, and the 180-day forward rate was $0.5392. When the forward rate is above the spot rate, as in this case, the forward rate is said to be at a premium. When the spot rate exceeds the forward rate, the forward rate is said to be at a discount. Forward purchases of currencies can be used for protection against exchange rate variations, or they can be used to speculate on exchange rate variations.

Fixed exchange rates.   There has been considerable debate over whether or not a system of free, or cleanly floating, exchange rates is superior to a system of fixed exchange rates. In 1944, at the Bretton Woods Conference, the major trading nations of the world set up a system of fixed exchange rates that was to be the basis of postwar trade. The major provisions of this system were centered around the International Monetary Fund which is discussed in the following chapter. However, at this point we merely note that the fixed exchange rate system had some advantages, but it had some severe disadvantages. By 1973, the cumulative effect of these disadvantages had become so great that fixed exchange rates could no longer be maintained. When the United States suspended convertibility of the dollar into gold in August 1971, the demise of the fixed-rate system was inevitable. Thus a consideration of fixed exchange rates may not be as timely as in the past. Nevertheless, there are those who view such a system as preferable; therefore, it is pertinent to consider the nature of a system of fixed rates.

Under the Bretton Woods Agreement, the value of the United States dollar was defined in terms of gold. Gold would be exchanged for dollars and vice versa at the price of $35 per ounce. The exchange rates of other currencies were set within very narrow ranges in terms of gold and dollars, and each nation set up a stabilization fund to be used to intervene in the exchange market, buying or selling that nation's currency as necessary to maintain the value at the agreed-upon rate. Suppose, for example, that the exchange rate between marks and dollars had been set at four marks per dollar. If for some reason the rate began to rise above four, the German central bank would, under the terms of the agreement, go into the exchange market as a purchaser of marks to prevent a fall in the exchange value of the mark; likewise, the Federal Reserve could intervene as a seller of dollars.

The primary advantage claimed for fixed rates is that they prevent uncertainty and thus encourage foreign trade. Under fixed exchange rates, both importers and exporters can plan international purchases and sales without fear of losses due to possible exchange-rate variations. This presumably leads to a greater volume of international trade. The system, as outlined above, works well when temporary balance of payment deficits or surpluses cause temporary pressures on exchange rates. However, some balance of payments deficits are of a chronic or recurring nature. Such deficits create continuing problems in a fixed-exchange-rate system because no nation has enough international reserves in its stabilization fund to continue supporting its currency indefinitely. To maintain the fixed exchange rate in the face of such problems, nations would have to resort to various restrictions on imports in the form of tariffs, quotas, and exchange controls which have the effect of restricting trade and, therefore, are considered undesirable. To avoid these restrictions, there were provisions for changing the fixed rates when nations were faced with chronic balance of payments problems under the existing rates. The corrective mechanism was to be the setting of a new fixed exchange rate for the problem currency. In such cases, the fixed exchange value of the currency would be revised downward, an action referred to as *devaluation*. Given the provisions for periodic adjustments, the system came to be known as an "adjustable peg system."

The corrective mechanism of devaluation will not necessarily be a permanent solution to a country's balance of payments problems if the underlying causes of the currency's declining value are not corrected. For example, if overly expansionary monetary and fiscal policies were creating a greater rate of inflation in country A than in country B, the value of country A's currency would continue to fall, and devaluation would have to be carried out on a recurring basis. Thus devaluation will not solve basic underlying problems, but it will permit trade to continue without undue restrictions while solutions are sought for more fundamental problems.

Even though occasional devaluations were possible under the fixed-exchange-rate system, the devaluation process was viewed by the countries involved as undesirable. Nations were reluctant to devalue their currencies even when it was obvious that the existing fixed exchange rates were no longer appropriate. Thus the controlled adjustments so necessary in a fixed-rate system often did not take place when needed. Politicians in deficit countries were hesitant about devaluation since it resulted in higher prices of imported goods, a result not likely to be popular. Furthermore, devaluation carried the stigma of an indictment against the government's economic policies.

The system of fixed rates with its attendant problems appears to be dead (but not buried) for now; however, central banks still try to maintain "orderly" markets for their currencies. Consequently, the

Federal Reserve system often buys or sells dollars to moderate any tendency toward sharp changes in the exchange value of the dollar. Thus while fixed rates have been abandoned, we have not moved completely to free rates, and the present arrangements are often referred to as a "dirty float."

HOW DO INTERNATIONAL TRANSACTIONS AFFECT DOMESTIC ECONOMIC ACTIVITY?

In earlier chapters we explored the basic determinants of national economic activity; for simplicity international transactions were ignored in order to focus attention on important domestic variables. In this section, the channels through which international transactions affect such key domestic variables as prices, production, income, and employment are explored, and in turn, the manner in which key domestic variables affect international transactions is examined. This examination is introduced with a discussion of the international gold standard.

The workings of the international gold standard

That there is a relationship between domestic economic activity and a nation's balance of payments position has been known for hundreds of years. One of the earliest statements of this relationship is that of David Hume, an 18th-century British political economist. Hume's explanation, sometimes referred to as the price-specie-flow mechanism, reflects two related factors:

1. The quantity theory of money, which emphasizes the relation between changes in the money supply and changes in the price level.
2. The link between the domestic money supply and gold which, in turn, links international gold flows and the money supplies of the countries involved.

The workings of the price-specie-flow adjustment mechanism of Hume is best understood in the context of the international gold standard which operated for many years but broke down after World War I. Under the gold standard, each nation's monetary unit was defined in terms of so much gold, and each government would buy or sell gold at that price upon demand. Furthermore, there were no restrictions on gold flows into and out of each country, and under the implicit rules of the game as well as the state of the art of monetary policy, the money-supply effects of international gold flows were not offset by monetary policy actions of the central banks.

Under these conditions the exchange rates between different countries' currencies were fixed by each government's mint price of gold. Thus the ratio of the official gold content of the U.S. dollar to the official gold content of the British pound would give the exchange rate between dollars and pounds; however, slight deviations from this rate could occur due to the costs of shipping gold. Any significant deviation of the market exchange ratio from the mint price ratios could not be maintained in the face of private buying and selling of gold and foreign exchange. If one ounce of gold were worth $20 at the U.S. mint and 10 pounds at the British mint, the exchange rate would be $2 for 1 British pound.

To illustrate why the exchange rate could not deviate (except temporarily) from $2.00, consider the transactions that could occur if the exchange rate were to rise to $2.25 per pound. A crafty Yankee trader (or anyone else) could take $20.00 to the U.S. mint and obtain one ounce of gold. Ignoring transportation and transactions costs, which would be relatively unimportant in large-scale transactions, the trader could take the ounce of gold and sell it to the British government at the British mint price of 10 pounds. The 10 pounds could then be sold (for dollars) in the foreign exchange market to provide a total of $22.50 (10 pounds × the exchange rate of $2.25). The trader has made a profit of $2.50 for his efforts, and this reward will attract others. A continuation of these activities would lead to the following consequences:

1. An increased supply of pounds (demand for dollars) in the foreign exchange markets.
2. An outflow of gold from the United States and an inflow of gold into Britain.
3. Because of (1), a drop in the value of pounds on the foreign exchange markets.

Thus the process would automatically restore the exchange rate to the ratio of mint prices ($2.00 per British pound).

A second feature of the international gold standard was that it automatically led to correction of any balance of payments problems. For example, a balance of payments deficit would mean that the deficit country was not making enough foreign sales to provide the foreign exchange needed to finance imports. To continue to finance their imports, importers would either have to sell gold or bid up the price of foreign exchange (which would, in the manner described above, lead to an outflow of gold). Thus a gold outflow automatically accompanied a balance of payments deficit. Furthermore, under the gold standard, gold outflows would reduce the domestic money supply in the deficit country. In the surplus country, gold inflows would increase the money supply. According to the quantity theory of money, the reduced money supply in the deficit country would result in lower prices there, while the increased money supply in the surplus country would lead to higher prices. These price movements would cause the deficit country's imports to decline and its exports to increase. The opposite results would occur in the surplus country, and the final outcome would be a correction of the balance of payments problem.

Despite its self-adjusting features, the international gold standard broke down after World War I as the worldwide Depression of the 1930s caused countries to isolate their domestic economies from international influences. As the adjustment process of the gold standard was originally believed to operate, the effects of international gold flows were confined to price changes. However, in the face of Keynesian analysis and the Depression of the 1930s, it was realized that a deficit country might also experience a drop in employment and production as part of the adjustment process. The outcome of the adjustment process as far as the balance of payments was concerned would be the same, but the now-apparent side effects were considered intolerable. Thus when the Western nations met near the end of World War II and set about the job of planning the international monetary framework for the postwar period, there was no real desire to go back to the gold standard. While the fixed exchange rates and automatic balance of payment adjustment process of the international gold standard were viewed favorably, no nation was willing to neglect its domestic aggregate demand in order to stabilize its international trade position. Therefore, the Bretton Woods Conference established a system of fixed or pegged rates with provisions for adjusting the fixed rates by devaluation or revaluation in cases of chronic balance of payments problems.

The Bretton Woods system was supposed to provide the benefits of fixed rates but allow enough flexibility to permit nations to isolate the management of their domestic economies from the monetary effects of trade flows. However, as we shall see below, the system was not completely successful in isolating domestic economic activity from outside influences. In the following section, some of the consequences of various balance of payments positions are explored.

Current account transactions and economic activity: Some direct effects

As we saw in Chapter 13, the equilibrium level of GNP is equal to planned levels of consumption spending (C), government spending (G), and desired investment spending (I_d); the sum of these variables was referred to as aggregate demand. However, in an open economy—an economy that engages in international transactions—those international transactions involving goods and services have a direct effect on aggregate demand in the countries involved. Letting X stand for exports of goods and services and M stand for imports of goods and services, then $X - M$ equals the country's balance on goods and services. If there are no unilateral transactions, the balance on goods and services equals the current account balance. In the following pages, $X - M$ will be refererd to as either the current account balance, net exports, or the balance of trade, and will denote the direct effects of international transactions on the demand for currently produced domestic goods and services. With these adjustments, the product sector equilibrium condition in an open economy can be expressed in the following manner:

(20–1) $$Y = C + I_d + G + (X - M).$$

The rationale for adding $(X - M)$ to domestic expenditures is rather clear. Exports represent expenditures by foreign buyers in domestic markets. Thus exports contribute to aggregate demand while imports operate to decrease aggregate demand as domestic economic units make expenditures for foreign rather than domestically produced products. The direct effects of international transactions upon domestic aggregate demand depend upon whether the contractionary effect of imports is outweighed by the expansionary effect of exports. In short, international transactions increase a country's domestic aggregate demand if exports exceed imports—that is, if the country is running a surplus in its balance on goods and services. The general possibilities are illustrated in Figure 20–4.

Figure 20–4 reflects various possible effects of international transactions on GNP. A balance of trade surplus results in total aggregate demand $(C + I_d + G + (X - M)_1)$ which is higher than domestic aggregate demand $(C + I_d + G)$. Thus the direct effect of a trade surplus is upward pressure on GNP $(Y_1$ as opposed to $Y_0)$. Whether or not the increase in GNP is real or inflationary depends upon the present level of production relative to potential GNP. If the economy is operating near full capacity, the direct effect of the balance of trade surplus is likely to be inflationary. On the other hand, a balance of trade deficit has a depressing effect on aggregate demand. This is indicated by the $C + I_d + G + (X - M)_2$ curve which lies below the domestic aggregate demand curve.

The relationship between international transactions and domestic economic activity is not one-way. Current account transactions are determined by several factors, one of which is the level of domestic economic activity. The primary determinants of a country's imports are its aggregate level of income, the value of its currency in the

FIGURE 20–4
Direct effect of a country's balance of trade on aggregate demand

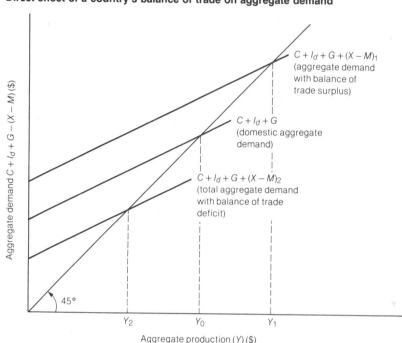

exchange markets, and prices of foreign and domestic goods and services. As a country's national income increases, it will import more goods and services due to the tendency for people to increase their consumption of domestic and foreign goods as incomes rise. When the exchange value of domestic currency rises, the domestic prices of foreign goods decline; therefore, as long as the overall demand for imported goods is elastic, the lower domestic prices of imported goods will result in increased imports. Finally, the desirability of imported goods is increased if their prices fall because of declining prices in the producing country or if their prices fall relative to domestic goods' prices because of a lower relative rate of inflation in the producing country.

A country's exports are determined by prices of its goods relative to prices of goods produced in other countries, the exchange value of other countries' currencies, and the levels of income in other nations. The lower the price of a country's goods in other countries, because of either the exchange rate or the relative domestic prices of these goods, the greater will be that country's exports. Likewise, as foreign countries experience increases in income and consequently increase their expenditures on goods and services, there will be an increase in their imports and, hence, the exports of other countries.

Effects of international capital flows

The direct effects of current account transactions are only part of the story. Capital flows and transactions involving intervention by official monetary authorities must also be considered. These, in turn, may be dependent upon or independent of a country's current account balance. In any case, there can be important indirect effects on aggregate demand and domestic economic activity which will often have feedback effects on the current account transactions.

It was noted above that a deficit in a country's current account transactions is equivalent to a reduction in domestic aggregate demand. However, the very existence of a deficit requires either offsetting capital transactions, interventions by the official monetary authorities in the form of official reserve transactions, or both. Whichever occurs, it is likely that domestic economic variables will be affected. For instance, consider a situation in which a country's current account deficit is financed by foreigners investing in financial assets issued by economic units residing in the deficit country; the form of financial assets purchased—corporate bonds, government securities, corporate equities, or CDs—is not of central importance. In essence, the current account deficit means importers in the deficit country will have to obtain foreign currencies in excess of the amount being supplied by foreign economic units through their purchases of goods and services produced in the deficit country. If the source of this foreign currency is the sale of financial assets to foreign purchasers, no exchange rate changes or official intervention will be required. The excess demand for foreign currencies resulting from the current account deficit will be offset by an excess supply resulting from the capital account surplus.

What will happen in a country experiencing a current account deficit and an offsetting capital account surplus? The direct effects of the current account deficit have already been explained; downward pressure is exerted on aggregate demand which tends to reduce production, income, employment, and prices. These changes may be good or bad depending on whether or not aggregate demand is excessive or insufficient. Furthermore, either monetary policy or fiscal policy may be used to offset the direct effects on aggregate demand. If not offset, the direct effects will exert downward pressure on imports and upward pressure on exports; thus there will be a tendency for the current account imbalance to be self-correcting. However, the country's net inflows from capital transactions (which permit the exchange rate to remain constant while the current account deficit continues) result in additional loanable funds flowing into the financial markets of the deficit (on current account) country. On the other hand, there will be an outward flow of loanable funds from financial markets in those countries with current account surpluses (capital account deficits). These changes will cause interest rates to fall in the capital-surplus country and rise in the capital-deficit countries. To the extent that interest rates affect spending, aggregate demand will rise in the capital-surplus countries and fall in the capital-deficit countries. Thus the effects of the capital account imbalance will tend to moderate the direct effects of the current account imbalance on production, income, employment, and prices. Ultimately, unless the direct effects of the current account imbalance are completely offset by the capital account influences, there will be feedback effects on the current and capital account imbalances which will tend to be corrective.

Official intervention and domestic economic activity

It is unlikely that a current account deficit will be exactly offset by a capital account surplus. What would happen if there were no capital account surplus or if it were too small to offset the current account deficit? (In this section we shall refer to such a situation as a net deficit.) Under such conditions, the quantity of foreign currencies supplied to the exchange market (through foreign purchases of goods and financial assets) will be less than the quantity demanded by economic units in the net-deficit country for the purpose of financing their imports of goods and financial assets. If exchange rates are permitted to fluctuate, this disequilibrium in the exchange market would cause the value of the net-deficit country's currency to decline; however, if the existing exchange rates were fixed, as under the Bretton Woods system, it would be necessary for the net-deficit country's monetary authorities—its central bank—to intervene in the financial markets to supplement the demand for domestic currency in that market.[5] In order to intervene, the authorities must have foreign currency with which to purchase the excess domestic currency. Where does the central bank obtain foreign currency, given that there is already a shortage? Several options are usually available—at least temporarily:

---

[5] Actually, the intervention can occur through the central bank of the net-surplus country which may purchase the net-deficit country's currency and thus create an inflow of the scarce currency to the foreign exchange markets.

1. It may draw down its holding of foreign currencies obtained as a result of past activities.
2. It may sell gold in the open market or to other central banks.
3. It may borrow from other central banks or from commercial banks in other countries.
4. It may be able to borrow from the International Monetary Fund.

Regardless of how the central bank obtains foreign currency, it must use that currency to intervene in the foreign exchange market as a purchaser of domestic currency. As the central bank purchases domestic currency from would-be importers in the net-deficit country, the domestic money supply is reduced. When importers in the net-deficit country spend their newly acquired foreign currency to pay for imported goods and financial assets, the money supply in the surplus country will increase.[6] Thus there are money-supply effects when countries have a disequilibrium in their capital and current account transactions, and the central bank intervenes in order to keep exchange rates fixed. The central bank may or may not choose to use domestic monetary policy to offset these effects.

What are the consequences of these money-supply changes in terms of domestic activity and the balance of payments disequilibrium? Recall from Chapter 14 that there is still some disagreement on the exact channels through which money supply changes affect aggregate demand. Keynesians tend to emphasize the effects of money-supply changes on interest rates, while monetarists emphasize the direct effects on consumption and investment spending that can occur if the supply of money exceeds the demand for money. In any case, the decline in the net-deficit country's money supply resulting from official intervention is likely to lead to higher interest rates.

The rising interest rates in the net-deficit country tend to attract an inflow of additional foreign capital investment, which helps ease the balance of payments deficit. The opposite effects occur in the net-surplus country. In addition, aggregate demand in the net-deficit country (and, therefore, production, income, employment, and prices) tends to decline in the face of these higher interest rates and a declining money supply. Again, the opposite effects would occur in the net-surplus country. Furthermore, the changes in production, income, and prices tend to produce a feedback on the balance of

---

[6] Under most methods of financing intervention, this statement is true. There are exceptions, however; for example, if the deficit country's central bank sells gold to private economic units in the surplus countries who do not monetize it, the money supply in the surplus country would not change.

payments deficit in a manner that tends to correct the imbalance.[7] Thus intervention resulting from a balance of payments net deficit leads to money-supply changes that, if not offset, have the same impact in the deficit country as brought about by the workings of the international gold standard. The domestic economy is subjected to fluctuations due to the country's balance of payments position. However, unlike the situation under the international gold standard, there is no reason why the central bank cannot use monetary policy to offset these effects on domestic economic activity. On the other hand, continued offsetting actions frustrate the working of the forces that are acting to bring about correction of the balance of payments problems. Hence, offsetting activity means continued intervention which, as we saw earlier, cannot be maintained due to limits on the central bank's sources of foreign exchange. Official intervention is likely to be successful, therefore, only in those cases where the balance of payments problem is of a temporary nature.

Domestic effects of flexible exchange rates

Under a system of flexible exchange rates, if a current account deficit cannot be financed by a capital account surplus and official intervention is avoided, exchange rates will adjust so as to correct the payments imbalance. The exchange value of the deficit country's currency will fall, while the value of the surplus country's currency will rise, resulting in more exports by the deficit country and less exports by trading partners of the deficit country. The changes, of course, tend to eliminate the balance of payments disequilibrium and the attendant pressure on exchange rates without inducing changes in domestic production, income, employment, and prices.

There will be, however, changes in the composition of output in both the deficit and surplus countries. Those industries producing for export will enjoy increased business in the deficit country, while those that depend upon imported products will suffer. These changes merely reflect the required adjustments to a balance of payments problem—less consumption of foreign products and more foreign consumption of domestically produced products. The total goods available for consumption in the deficit country must fall unless output can be increased to accommodate the expansion of exports.

Ultimately, correction of fundamental balance of payments prob-

---

[7] Recall the variables affecting exports and imports. A fall in economic activity will reduce imports while leaving exports unchanged or perhaps even increase them.

lems under fixed exchange rates is likely to require adverse adjustments in domestic employment, income, production, and prices, which can be minimized or avoided when exchange rates are allowed to adjust. The flexible exchange rates, rather than changing production, income, employment, and prices, operate to reduce or increase exports and imports of goods and capital so that domestic economic activity is likely to be less sensitive to imbalances in international payments flows.

In conclusion, a country has a balance of payments problem when its expenditures on foreign goods, services, and capital cannot be financed continuously in the current manner. If the current situation cannot be maintained, some adjustment must occur. Why will this adjustment occur, and how will it change the current situation? Looking at the situation from the standpoint of the deficit country, adjustment requires a reduction in purchases of foreign goods, services, and capital and/or an expansion of exports of goods, services, and capital. The changes that are required to correct a balance of payments problem may be induced by one or a combination of four possible factors:

1. Changes in exchange rates.
2. Changes in real income.
3. Changes in domestic price levels.
4. Imposition of barriers to trade.

Another way of looking at the alternatives facing a deficit country is to recognize that a country is able to exercise simultaneous control over no more than three of the following:

1. The exchange value of its currency.
2. The level of the primary domestic economic variables—income, employment, and production.
3. The domestic price level.
4. The free flow of international trade across its borders.

In reality this may overstate the available choices as there is considerable doubt that domestic prices will be flexible in the required downward direction. In short, if a country were to choose not to restrict trade flows and to try to maintain existing exchange rates, that country would find it impossible to obtain balance of payments equilibrium if it tried to use monetary and fiscal policy to keep domestic employment, income, and production from falling. Painful adjustment could then be avoided only if surplus countries allow adjustments to occur in their economies. Such action usually is not possible.

SUMMARY

Every nation maintains a summary record of its international transactions. That record is known as the balance of payments. The balance of payments record of a country reveals how that country finances its international transactions. If its current method of financing is unsustainable, the country cannot maintain its present mix of international transactions and is said to have a balance of payments problem. For purposes of classification, international transactions can be divided into three types: (1) goods, services, and gifts, (2) capital transactions or transactions involving financial assets, and (3) official reserve transactions.

Exchange rates are the prices of foreign currencies. Like all prices they are determined by supply and demand forces, but governments may intervene in the market so that the rate is different from what market forces alone would have determined. When official intervention results in constant exchange rates, we refer to those rates as fixed, or pegged, exchange rates. In the absence of intervention, rates can vary, and such rates are referred to as floating rates or free rates. From the end of World War II to 1971, exchange rates generally were fixed. In recent years, rates have been free to float but not without some intervention by various governments, a situation referred to as a dirty float.

International transactions may affect domestic aggregate demand and, therefore, income, employment, production, and prices. In general, a balance of trade surplus provides a direct stimulus to aggregate demand, while a deficit causes a direct reduction in aggregate demand. However, these direct effects may be offset by indirect effects resulting from money-supply changes and international capital transactions, so that the net effects of international transactions on domestic economic activity are difficult to predict and may be favorable or unfavorable depending upon domestic conditions at that time. Furthermore, monetary and fiscal policy are often used to offset these effects. Thus international transactions create an additional dimension for the monetary economy, a dimension that we will explore in more detail in the following chapters.

REVIEW QUESTIONS

1. In what sense must the balance of payments always balance? In what sense can the balance of payments be out of balance?
2. Would a current account surplus and a capital account surplus have similar effects on economic activity? Would the channels of influence be the same? Explain.

3. What would happen to the exchange rate between dollars and yen (the dollar price of yen) under the following circumstances? (Assume no intervention.)

    a. The rate of inflation in Japan exceeds that in the United States.

    b. American incomes rise faster than Japanese incomes.

    c. Interest rates in the United States begin to exceed Japanese interest rates.

    d. There is a recession in Japan.

    e. Japan lowers it restrictions on imported goods.

4. Illustrate graphically the effects of the events in Question 3 in terms of shifts in the supply and demand curves for yen. Do the graphic results confirm your answers to 3?

5. Can official intervention, by itself, solve a chronic balance of payments problem? Explain.

6. Can a country continuously run a current account deficit? How?

7. Can a country continuously run a current account deficit if its capital account is in balance? Explain. What alternatives are available to it?

8. How would the international gold standard operate to correct a balance of payments deficit in France? A balance of payments surplus in Britain?

SUGGESTIONS FOR ADDITIONAL READING

Fieleke, Norman S. *What is the Balance of Payments?* Boston: Federal Reserve Bank of Boston, 1976.

Holmes, A. R., and Schott, F. H. *The New York Foreign Exchange Market.* New York: Federal Reserve Bank of New York, 1965.

Kemp, Donald S. "Balance-of-Payments Concepts—What Do They Mean?" *Review of the Federal Reserve Bank of St. Louis,* vol. 57, no. 7 (July 1975), pp. 14–23.

Kindleberger, Charles P., and Lindert, Peter M. *International Economics.* Homewood, Ill.: Richard D. Irwin, 1978.

Solomon, R. *The International Monetary System, 1945–1976.* New York: Harper & Row, 1977.

Yeager, Leland B. *International Monetary Relations.* New York: Harper & Row, 1966.

21

The international monetary and financial system: Recent developments

NEW TERMS

Edge Act: federal law that allows the formation of corporations to engage in international banking and financial operations.

Eurobonds: bonds denominated in currencies other than the currency of the country in which they are issued.

Eurodollars: dollar deposit liabilities of banks outside the United States.

Gresham's Law: the idea that bad (cheap) money will drive good (dear) money out of circulation.

International Monetary Fund (IMF): an international agency formed by trading nations for the purpose of promoting international monetary stability through a framework of international cooperation.

International reserve assets: highly liquid assets (usually gold, strong major currencies, or Special Drawing Rights) that can be used to settle international debts.

Special Drawing Rights (SDRs): a form of international money created by the IMF for use by the national monetary authorities of IMF member countries in transactions with each other.

Swap arrangement: an agreement between two or more central banks involving the temporary exchange of currencies.

In this chapter we explore some of the "recent" developments in the international monetary and financial system. Of course, the term *recent* is relative, and here it is used to refer to the period following the end of World War II, a period chosen since it coincides with the creation of the International Monetary Fund (IMF). The chapter begins with a discussion of the IMF and Special Drawing Rights or SDRs, an innovation that some have hailed as the new international money and a replacement for gold. Since one of the major developments in international finance in recent years has been the Eurodollar market, the reasons for this phenomenon as well as some of its implications are explored. In the final section of the chapter, we look at some of the ways in which the Federal Reserve System is affected by international monetary developments.

WHAT IS THE INTERNATIONAL MONETARY FUND?

Background and functions

The International Monetary Fund (IMF) was a creation of the 44 countries whose representatives met in international conference at Bretton Woods, New Hampshire, in 1944. The meeting was an effort to avoid a repeat of the conditions that led to the breakdown of the international gold standard and to the international chaos of the interwar years. The IMF is owned and operated by member countries and is the operational arm for administering the international trade and monetary rules agreed upon by the participants at Bretton

Woods. The primary goals of the IMF were outlined in Article I of its articles of agreement:

1. To promote international monetary cooperation through a permanent institution which provides the machinery for consultation and collaboration on international monetary problems.
2. To facilitate the expansion and balanced growth of international trade, and to contribute thereby to the promotion and maintenance of high levels of employment and real income and to the development of the productive resources of all members. . . .
3. To promote exchange stability, to maintain orderly exchange arrangements among members, and to avoid competitive exchange depreciation.
4. To assist in the establishment of a multilateral system of payments with respect to current transactions between members and in the elimination of foreign exchange restrictions which hamper the growth of world trade.
5. To give confidence to members by making the fund's resources available to them under adequate safeguards thus providing them with the opportunity to correct maladjustments in their balances of payments without resorting to measures destructive of national or international balances of payments of members.

Obviously the emphasis of the IMF was on the promotion of trade through stable exchange rates, international cooperation, and freedom from trade restrictions.

The International Monetary Fund comes closer than any other institution to being an international central bank. While the IMF does not possess all of the powers at the international level that domestic central banks have at the national level, it does perform several central banking–type functions; chief among these are (1) the ability to act as a "lender of last resort" at the international level, (2) the ability, within a limited range, to create international money, and (3) the ability to act as a clearinghouse in the settlement of international deficits and surpluses.

The name International Monetary Fund was derived from the fact that the IMF was to consist of a pool of funds submitted by each of the member countries. Each country was to contribute a certain quota into the pool, with the contribution split into two parts. One part, equal to 25 percent of a country's total quota, was to be paid in gold and is referred to as the country's *gold tranche* position in the IMF. The remaining 75 percent of a country's quota was in the form of its own currency. Each country's quota was based on its importance as a trading nation. With this pool of funds obtained from the contributions of member countries, the IMF was in a position to make loans to countries who needed gold or foreign currency in order to finance payment of international transactions.

Promotion of fixed exchange rates was at the core of the IMF procedures. The participants at Bretton Woods were aware of the chaotic conditions that had accompanied previous national attempts to use exchange rate variations and trade barriers to promote their domestic economies at the expense of other countries. Accordingly, IMF member countries had to agree to establish par values of their currency with respect to gold and, therefore, the U.S. dollar, the value of which was fixed in terms of gold. Each country set up an exchange stabilization fund to intervene in the foreign exchange markets should the exchange value of its currency deviate from its official or par value. Fluctuations were to be confined to within plus or minus 1 percent of the official value.[1]

As noted earlier, a country is limited in its ability to support its exchange rate by the extent of its holding of international reserve assets—assets with immediate liquidity that can be sold to support the exchange rate. In general, a country's international reserves include its gold holdings plus any foreign currency it has accumulated or can borrow. In recent years, the IMF has added to the list a third asset, called SDRs or Special Drawing Rights. The existence of the IMF was supposed to provide a source from which a country could borrow additional reserves in order to support its exchange rate in periods when its international reserve assets might otherwise be insufficient. It was hoped that the use of each country's own international reserve holdings plus access to additional international reserves through borrowing from the IMF would assist the member nations in maintaining the exchange value of their currencies when faced with a temporary balance of payments disequilibrium. Furthermore, the distinction between a temporary balance of payments problem and a fundamental disequilibrium was recognized.

Examples of temporary balance of payments disequilibriums would be trade deficits caused by a poor crop year for a country's primary export crop or a dock strike resulting in a large but temporary decline in exports. In such situations, the country involved could expect to preserve the exchange value of its currency by using its own reserve assets supplemented by borrowing from the IMF until the conditions causing the temporary disequilibrium were removed. However, a country might be suffering from balance of trade deficits and consequent downward pressure on the exchange value of its currency due to more fundamental problems—problems that could not be regarded as temporary. For example, unduly

---

[1] Originally, the permissible range of variation was even smaller.

expansionary monetary and fiscal policy might be causing domestic inflation at a rate in excess of that in other countries; or other countries might have become so much more competitive in international markets that the home country lost its primary export markets. Under such conditions, the currency of the country involved would become overvalued, and continued support of its exchange value would be futile—sooner or later that country's reserves and borrowing capacity would run short.

Recall from the previous chapter that, if a member country of the IMF were suffering from a fundamental balance of payments problem under the Bretton Woods system of fixed exchange rates, its only viable solution—assuming it did not want to contract domestic economic activity—was devaluation of its currency; that is, the par value of its currency in terms of other countries' currencies would be lowered. In an effort to prevent competitive and retaliatory devaluations, member countries were supposed to devalue only after consultation with the IMF. The IMF could not forcibly prevent a devaluation or a revaluation in excess of what was supposed to be a 10 percent maximum; it could, however, declare a country that acted in a contrary manner ineligible for further use of the resources of the IMF. More important, perhaps, was the inability of the fund to force a devaluation when it was considered desirable: limited devaluation was allowed by the rules of the agreement but could not be forced by the IMF. Therefore the fixed exchange rate system was to be truly fixed only in the short run; over the longer run, rates could and did vary but probably not as much as they should have.

Performance and problems

The results of IMF operations and the Bretton Woods approach are mixed. On the plus side, the mechanism for international cooperation, while far from perfect, was a significant improvement over the experience of the 1920s and 1930s. World trade increased at a sharp and steady pace following World War II, and most observers feel that the IMF was a positive force behind this growth in trade. The system of fixed but occasionally adjustable exchange rates might appear to be a perfect compromise between the advantages of fixed rates and free rates; unfortunately, the process did not function so smoothly in practice. One problem was generated by attempts on the part of both Britain and the United States at various times to maintain the exchange value of their currencies when devaluation was clearly warranted. Therefore, needed adjustments in exchange rates did not occur or were delayed to the extent that timely corrections of balance of payment problems did not take place.

The abandonment in 1973 of fixed exchange rates, which were the cornerstone of the Bretton Woods system, appeared to many observers to signal an end to the IMF, but the end did not come. Despite being created to foster the fixed exchange rate system, the IMF has survived and even expanded its role. In the years following 1973, it broadened its lending to member countries; it successfully issued a new form of international money—SDRs; it established what is known as the "oil facility" to help member countries finance the balance of payments deficits resulting from petroleum imports; and it formulated procedures for providing lending assistance to developing countries.[2] A contributing factor in the growing prestige and importance of the IMF was the declining favor with which the dollar came to be viewed as an acceptable international reserve asset. The "suspension" of gold convertibility of the dollar in 1971 and the subsequent decline in its exchange value created a vacuum in the international monetary scene. Most countries had no desire to return to the gold standard, but the problems with a dollar standard were evident. In this vacuum, the IMF was perceived by many to be the only possible solution to their dilemma.

The failure of national governments to utilize procedures for changing the exchange values of their currency was only one of the problems with which the IMF had to wrestle. Another problem was created by large, international, short-term capital movements. The very existence of a large volume of short-term, international capital investments is indicative of a potential for large changes in the supply and demand conditions for any country's currency. The framers of the Bretton Woods system did not anticipate the extent and effect of these capital movements in which billions of dollars of funds could be quickly shifted from country to country in response to interest rate differentials and expected (or feared) adjustments in exchange rates.

The existence of sizable short-term international capital investments provided speculators with the wherewithal to aggravate any country's balance of payment problem—especially if it were a fundamental problem. To the extent that a country persisted in trying to maintain the exchange value of its currency in the face of an obvious need for devaluation, speculators would sell any short-term investments in that country and convert their holdings to other currencies or to assets denominated in other currencies. Furthermore, they faced virtually no risk of loss in the transaction. If devaluation came,

---

[2] See Anthony Scapelanda, "The IMF, An Emerging Central Bank," in John Adams, ed., *The Contemporary International Economy* (New York: St. Martin's Press, 1979), pp. 248–55.

they could shift back at a profit; if not, the fixed exchange rates provided protection against loss. Fixed exchange rates, therefore, encouraged speculative activities by holders of short-term international capital which, in turn, could aggravate the condition of a weak currency and sometimes cause other holders of that currency to sell out of a fear of falling exchange values. Thus the ability to shift large amounts of short-term liquid investments into other currencies magnified the pressures caused by a balance of payments problem.

Consider the case of a German bank that maintained a dollar deposit in a New York bank in order to accommodate its customers in the importing business. Prior to 1971, the bank could expect to be able to shift dollars out of this account into marks at a fixed exchange rate. If in the face of continuing trade deficits, a devaluation of the dollar appeared imminent, the German bank, out of either fear of loss or a hope for speculative gain, would have a strong incentive to convert its dollar holdings back into marks. Such action would put additional downward pressure on the exchange value of the dollar, and if devaluation were to occur, the bank could convert the same amount of marks back into more dollars than it previously held.

Still another problem faced by the IMF in the years following Bretton Woods was the international liquidity problem. International liquidity refers to the total reserve assets held by all countries. Reserve assets were particularly important in the Bretton Woods fixed-exchange-rate system, for they provided a means of supporting fixed exchange rates in the face of temporary balance of payments problems. The international liquidity problem and its possible solutions are discussed in the following section.

WILL SPECIAL DRAWING RIGHTS SOLVE THE INTERNATIONAL LIQUIDITY PROBLEM?

The international liquidity problem

As international trade grew sharply in the years following World War II, the international liquidity problem became more troublesome. Member countries of the IMF used their international reserve assets coupled with borrowings from the IMF to support the exchange values of their currencies in accordance with the plans of Bretton Woods. However, as the volume of international transactions grew for all countries, the size of imbalances grew also. Thus more and more international reserve assets were necessary to support exchange rates in the face of the larger and larger imbalances that occurred from time to time. As noted earlier, the problem was magnified by a growing volume of short-term capital flows. As time passed, it became obvious that international reserve assets could not grow at a pace sufficient to keep up with the need for them. This was the essence of the international liquidity problem.

The nature of international reserve assets requires that they consist of items that are readily acceptable in foreign exchange markets. Prior to 1970, items that met this qualification included gold and strong major currencies. Serving as reserve currencies after World War II were the British pound and the United States dollar. Gold, of course, is very limited in supply, and while new quantities are always being mined, a continual rapid increase in supply was considered unlikely. Thus to a greater and greater extent, the dollar became the primary source of the needed increase in international reserves. Nations augmented their holdings of gold with holdings of foreign currencies, with more and more of the latter consisting of U.S. dollars. In fact, since the United States was willing to convert dollars into gold at a fixed price, the dollars were, in effect, as good as gold.

For the dollar to be a source of increasing international reserves, the United States would have to export dollars continuously (run a deficit on current and capital account transactions). If the U.S. current and capital transactions were in balance or in surplus, foreign countries would need to use their dollar holdings to finance their own current account transactions and would, therefore, be unable to accumulate dollars as part of their international reserve holdings. It follows, then, that an adequate growth of international liquidity required continued U.S. balance of payments deficits. This requirement created a real dilemma: a continued U.S. deficit and a growing supply of foreign-held dollars meant that eventually the United States would no longer be able to convert dollars into gold at the existing price. Confidence in the dollar would fall, and it would cease to be acceptable as an international reserve asset. If dollars could not be counted on to supply needed international liquidity, and an adequate supply of gold was not available, what would be the source of the needed increase in international reserves? This was the dilemma that plagued national monetary authorities and international economic experts during the 1950s and 1960s. The proposed solution that eventually evolved called for the creation of a new international reserve asset to be known as Special Drawing Rights (SDRs). The development of SDRs appears to have reduced concern about the international liquidity problem. Therefore, it is appropriate that we now shift attention to SDRs and their role as an international reserve asset.

Special Drawing Rights

In September 1967, the IMF's Board of Governors adopted an amendment that altered the international monetary framework set up by the Bretton Woods conference. The change involved a plan to allow the IMF to begin issuing Special Drawing Rights. These rights were, in effect, a new form of international money issued by the IMF to participating nations to be used by national monetary authorities in their transactions with each other. The first SDRs were issued by the IMF in January 1970. In the United States, SDRs were seen as a means to add to the nation's existing reserves and thus strengthen the dollar. In other countries, it was hoped that SDRs would reduce world dependence on the dollar as the primary source of international reserves.

Anything that is to serve as money must be readily acceptable; accordingly, for SDRs to become an international reserve asset, countries must be willing to accept and hold them. To assure acceptability, the IMF is required to secure advance approval from IMF member countries in order to create specific amounts of additional reserves in the form of SDRs.[3] By prior agreement, participating countries assure their willingness to accept limited amounts of these SDRs in exchange for their own currencies. This assurance of acceptability helps SDRs serve as an official international money in the absence of any specific "backing" or intrinsic value.

SDRs created by the IMF are allocated to participating countries in proportion to the countries' IMF quotas. The SDRs are not physical monies; rather, they are entries on the books and the computer tapes of the IMF. Originally, each SDR had a value of one United States dollar; however, this valuation procedure has been changed, and now the value of an SDR is based on a weighted average of the exchange rates of the currencies of major IMF member countries.

Rules governing the use of SDRs reflect the importance of maintaining their acceptability as money. For example, no country is obligated to accept SDRs from other countries in an amount greater than twice its own original allocation of SDRs. Furthermore, over a five-year period, each participating country must maintain average holdings of SDRs equal to not less than 30 percent of the total amount of SDRs allocated to it over the period. These provisions help prevent nations from using SDRs to finance continuous deficits in their balance of payments or using SDRs to acquire and hold gold and foreign currencies at the expense of other countries. The rules are designed to prevent the operation of Gresham's Law, which in essence says that people will hold a preferred form of money and use the less preferred form of money in their transactions until ulti-

---

[3] Specifically, countries holding at least 85 percent of the weighted voting power must approve any proposed new issue of SDRs.

mately no one will want to accept the less-preferred money. A country's SDR holdings in excess of its allocation earn interest at the rate of 1½ percent per year while countries holding less than their allocation pay 1½ percent on the difference between their holdings and their allocation.

SDRs represent an attempt to create an international money as a supplement and an alternative to gold. Since there is no real limit on the amount of SDRs that could be issued, they are, in theory at least, a solution to the international liquidity problem. This possibility, however, rests upon their continued acceptance which, in turn, is assured only as long as everyone believes SDRs are generally acceptable. This expectation is the fragile thread upon which the success of SDRs depends. It remains too early to be certain of the eventual outcome of the SDR experiment, as only limited amounts of SDRs have been issued to date. In early 1980, the total allocation of SDRs stood at $16 billion, and SDRs made up approximately 5 percent of the reserve assets of IMF member countries.

There is no question but that SDRs hold the promise of a more stable international monetary system. Widespread acceptance of SDRs would not only solve the liquidity problem but would also allow countries to achieve desired increases in international reserves without pursuing policies designed to create balance of payments surpluses. Pressure to achieve surpluses would be removed or lessened which, in turn, should enhance international trade.

While there is less concern about international liquidity now than in the days prior to SDRs, it is possible that SDRs should not be given complete credit for any alleviation of this problem. The period of SDRs overlaps the period of flexible exchange rates, and the willingness of nations to permit the exchange values of their currencies to fluctuate has reduced their need for reserve assets. Therefore, flexible exchange rates have also contributed to a reduction in the magnitude of the international liquidity problem by reducing the need for liquidity while SDRs have helped alleviate the problem by contributing to the supply of international reserves.

WHAT IS THE EURODOLLAR MARKET?

Origins and nature of Eurodollars

Beginning in the 1950s, banks outside the United States, particularly in Europe, began to hold deposit liabilities denominated in dollars in addition to their regular deposit liabilities denominated in the national currencies of the countries in which they were located. These dollar deposits in banks outside the United States became known as Eurodollars. Eurodollar deposits are believed to have originated with the Russians who were fearful that dollar deposits maintained in United States banks might be confiscated or frozen by the government as payment for old debts. To circumvent this possibility, the dollars were deposited in European banks. In the 1960s, Eurodollar deposits grew in number and importance, and deposits in other currencies also began to show up in banks outside of the home country of the currencies involved. The term Eurocurrencies is now applied to all deposits in banks anywhere in the world which are not denominated in the currency of the country in which the banks are located.

The key to Eurodollar and Eurocurrency deposits is not who owns them but the fact that they are deposits denominated in a foreign currency. Thus the dollar deposit of an American corporation in a West German bank would be a Eurodollar deposit, and, if it were transferred to a German firm, it would still be a Eurodollar deposit. Eurodollar deposits may occur either when foreign currencies are converted into dollars which are then deposited in a bank outside of the United States or when dollar deposits in a U.S. bank are transferred to a bank (or branch) in another country. Note that dollars in currency form need not leave the United States in order for a Eurodollar deposit to be created. Another characteristic of Eurodollar deposits is that they are usually time deposits rather than demand deposits. In the following pages, we trace through a hypothetical example of the creation of a Eurodollar deposit and the subsequent expansion of this deposit.

Suppose that W. W. Traveler, a wealthy entrepreneur, opens a time deposit account for $100,000 in a West German bank by depositing a check written on a demand deposit account at a New York bank. Furthermore, suppose that the West German bank is a large international bank which maintains dollar deposits at the same New York bank. Traveler's deposit in the German bank may be denominated either in marks or in dollars; it will be a Eurodollar deposit only if it is denominated in dollars. In the latter case, Traveler will have a claim against the German bank for $100,000, and the German bank will have a claim against the New York bank for $100,000. If the German bank were to maintain the proceeds of the collected check as an addition to its existing deposit balance at the New York bank, the situation, as reflected by the changes in the balance sheets of Traveler, the German bank, and the New York bank, would appear as follows:

W. W. Traveler

Deposit at New York bank	−$100,000	
Dollar-denominated deposit at German bank	+$100,000	

German bank

Dollar-denominated deposit at New York Bank	+$100,000	Dollar-dominated deposit of Traveler	+$100,000

New York bank

		Deposit of Traveler	−$100,000
		Deposit of German bank	+$100,000

Under the above set of transactions, there has been no decrease in deposits held by U.S. banks although deposit ownership has changed. Eurodollar deposits, however, have increased by $100,000. Contrary to popular belief, the creation of Eurodollar deposits does not necessarily drain money away from the United States.

The story is not likely to end here, for there is an active market for these Eurodollar deposits. Suppose that Traveler's deposit at the German bank is a time deposit that the bank expects to hold for six months. The bank will try to do what it does with all deposits—lend the proceeds at a rate of interest sufficient to cover not only the interest it is paying on the deposits but also other costs incurred in connection with the deposit. Thus the German bank would be willing to lend these dollars at an appropriate interest rate and for an appropriate time period, and there are numerous would-be borrowers looking for such funds. These borrowers could be individuals, foreign or U.S. business firms, banks, or even foreign governments. These borrowed Eurodollars may, in turn, be spent or deposited in other foreign or U.S. banks.

To the extent that additional lending and redepositing takes place outside the United States, the volume of Eurodollar deposits will grow. Suppose that a Swiss bank with customers who wish to borrow dollars arranges to borrow $50,000 from the German bank for a period of six months with the loan proceeds in the form of a check written on the German bank's dollar deposit in the New York bank. For simplicity, we will assume that the Swiss bank also maintains the funds in an account at the same New York bank. The transaction would affect the three balance sheets as follows:

New York bank

	Deposits of German bank	−$50,000
	Deposits of Swiss bank	+$50,000

Swiss bank

Deposits at New York bank	+$50,000	Eurodollar loan from German bank	+$50,000

German bank

| Deposit at New York bank | −$50,000 | | |
| Eurodollar loan to Swiss bank | +$50,000 | | |

Of course, the Swiss bank did not borrow the $50,000 in order to hold it; so we shall assume that the dollars are immediately loaned to one of its customers, Finewatch Corporation, and are credited to its demand deposit account. The Swiss bank's balance sheet and the borrower's balance sheet will be affected as follows:

Swiss bank

Eurodollar loan to Finewatch	+$50,000	Deposit of Finewatch Corporation	+$50,000

Finewatch Corporation

Eurodollar deposit at Swiss bank	+$50,000	Eurodollar loan from Swiss bank	+$50,000

Finewatch Corporation has every intention of spending the Eurodollars, and when it does, someone else will acquire dollars. In the process, the Swiss bank will lose its dollar deposits at the New York bank. However, the recipient of the dollars that Finewatch spends will probably redeposit them in some bank; hence, there is the possibility of continued creation of Eurodollars. At this point the $100,000 deposited in the German bank by Traveler has grown to $150,000 in Eurodollars outstanding, and the process may not be finished. Theoretically, the creation of Eurodollars could continue indefinitely. In practice, this will not happen, because "leakages" occur. For example, one or more of the banks may not lend all of their dollar balances due to a desire to keep some reserves, or some borrowers of Eurodollars may want to keep some reserves or hold or transfer dollars back to the United States. The extent of the leakages determines the size of the Eurodollar multiplier—the amount of Eurodollars that can be created from an initial or primary Eurodollar deposit.

This example illustrates two points about the Eurodollar market: (1) it is largely an interbank market, and (2) such interbank redepositing of an initial Eurodollar deposit does not add to the amount of credit available in financial markets. Only when one of the banks involved makes a loan to a nonbanking economic unit such as an individual, a business, or a government is there an extension of credit. Thus to measure the amount of credit generated in the Eurodollar market, interbank deposits must be excluded.

Eurodollars and escape from Regulation Q

In the 1960s American banks discovered that the Eurodollar market offered them a mechanism for escaping the effects of Regulation Q and the resulting disintermediation that occurred during tight money periods. Consider a situation in which short-term interest rates in the U.S. money market rise above the ceiling rates imposed by Regulation Q on time deposits. Holders of large time deposit accounts in commercial banks would shift funds out of these accounts and invest directly in Treasury bills, commercial paper, longer-term government securities, or Eurodollar deposits. Consequently, banks would experience an outflow of funds. When American banks began to experience these outflows of deposits, they were unable to react by offering higher interest rates due to the Regulation Q ceilings. However, the banks soon discovered they could enter the Eurodollar market as borrowers of dollars with no restrictions upon the rates they could pay. In fact, an American bank would often borrow from one of its foreign branches.

American banks borrowing funds in the Eurodollar market initially did not have to maintain reserves against those funds. Thus more useable funds were acquired per dollar of Eurodollar borrowing than would have been available from one dollar of time or demand deposits. This advantage gave banks an added incentive for going to the Eurodollar market for funds. They were able to compete for funds in periods of high interest rates without running into the Regulation Q ceiling, and more of each borrowed Eurodollar could be converted into earning assets. However, in September 1969, the Fed amended its Regulation M so as to require banks to hold a 10 percent reserve against their overseas dollar borrowings, and in June 1973, Regulation Q ceilings were dropped from large negotiable CDs. These two actions greatly reduced the incentive of American banks to borrow in the Eurodollar market. Reserve requirements against such borrowings were eliminated in 1978 but partially reinstated in 1979.

Virtually all Eurodollar deposits are time deposits. Hence, they cannot serve as a medium of exchange, and if money is defined as transactions balances only (an M-1A or M-1B definition), Eurodollar deposits do not expand the money supply. However, if a broader definition of money (which includes time deposits) is used, Eurodollar deposits are responsible for some increase in the world's money supply. Relative to the total world money supply, however, Eurodollars probably have had very little impact.

In recent years, many of the dollars flowing into the Eurodollar market have come from Middle Eastern oil-exporting countries which have experienced large balance of payments surpluses as a result of their petroleum exports. Channeling the surplus into the Eurodollar market is one of the available alternative uses. The dollars held by these countries have become known as petrodollars, and the amount of petrodollars outstanding has caused considerable discussion and some consternation. In Chapter 22, we shall look at the petrodollar question in more detail.

The Eurodollar market and the exchange value of the dollar

We cannot say with certainty just what impact the Eurodollar market has had on the value of the dollar in foreign exchange markets. One can envision a scenario in which the Eurodollar market contributes to a declining value of the dollar. Suppose conditions are such that speculators believe a decline in the value of the dollar is near. They could enter the Eurodollar market as borrowers of dollars and then use these dollars in the exchange market to purchase strong currencies. Their action of course puts downward pressure on the exchange value of the dollar and, in a fixed-exchange-rate world, could hasten or bring about the expected dollar devaluation. Thus the existence of the Eurodollar market augments the resources available to speculators.

If the speculators are correct in forecasting a decline in the exchange value of the dollar, they can repurchase dollars in the foreign exchange markets to obtain the funds needed to repay their Eurodollar loans. At that point, their activities would exert upward pressure on the exchange value of the dollar so that ultimately, there can be little net effect on the dollar's value. The speculators must make enough on the set of transactions to cover the interest on their Eurodollar loans plus the commissions on two exchange market transactions. If the dollar does not decline on the exchange market, speculators suffer losses in the amount of their costs.

On the other hand, one may argue that the existence of the Eurodollar market has created an alternative investment for holders of dollar balances. The Eurodollar market has resulted in a convenient and efficient mechanism for the temporary investment of dollar balances—an attractive use of funds that is not available for most other currencies; hence, the relative attractiveness and consequently the exchange value of the dollar, it may be argued, has been enhanced by the Eurodollar market.

The existence of the Eurodollar market means that dollars (or claims to dollars) flowing out of the United States do not necessarily affect the supply of dollars in the foreign exchange markets. Dollars (or claims) can be transferred out of the country and invested in the Eurodollar market as dollars rather than being sold in the exchange market for foreign currencies. Since such dollar-denominated flows going directly into the Eurodollar market normally do not enter the foreign exchange markets, they do not depress the dollar's exchange value. In fact, to the extent that dollars going into the Eurodollar market are purchased in the exchange market, the exchange value of the dollar is strengthened. Overall, therefore, the dollar's value in the exchange markets is probably somewhat higher than it would be in the absence of the well-developed Eurodollar market.

The Eurobond market

The term *Eurobond market* refers to the market for bonds denominated in a monetary unit other than the domestic currency of the country in which they are issued. The Eurobond market differs from the Eurodollar market in two respects. First, the financial claims created and traded in the Eurodollar market are short term. In that sense, the Eurodollar market is essentially a money market. Eurobonds, on the other hand, are longer-term claims. Second, whereas the Eurodollar market is based on intermediation, the Eurobond market allows lenders to hold primary claims on the ultimate borrower—the issuer of the Eurobonds. Like the Eurodollar market, the Eurobond market is not confined to a particular location and thereby escapes most of the regulation that occurs in national markets. Eurobonds are "placed" directly with private investors, usually simultaneously, in several countries. The value of Eurobonds outstanding is considerably smaller than the Eurodollar volume, but the market is growing.

HOW ARE FEDERAL RESERVE OPERATIONS INFLUENCED BY INTERNATIONAL MONETARY DEVELOPMENTS?

As we have already observed, the responsibilities of the Federal Reserve System include the promotion of full employment, price stability, and economic growth insofar as these goals are affected by monetary and credit conditions over which the central bank has some control. In Chapter 20 we observed that the important domestic goals are affected by international transactions. Recall, for example, that balance of payments surpluses, if not offset, can increase domestic liquidity, which can be inflationary if they occur at the wrong time. Likewise, a deficit can create recessionary forces which at times could hinder the achievement of the major domestic goals of full employment and economic growth. Even though domestic goals are the Fed's top priority, the monetary authorities must be aware of the interaction between the domestic economy and the international economy.

The dilemma that international conditions can create for the Federal Reserve System is summarized in Table 21–1 which indicates the various combinations of domestic and international economic conditions with which the Fed may have to deal. Of the nine combinations of domestic and international situations, six involve conflicts between the monetary action required by domestic conditions and the action required by international conditions. For example, suppose that domestic conditions are satisfactory, but that the country is suffering from a fundamental balance of payments problem reflected by a falling exchange value of the dollar (if exchange rates are flexible) or continued official settlement deficits (with the exchange value of the dollar being maintained). Monetary policy actions that would improve the international condition would be of a restrictive nature, but such a policy might create a recessionary situation at home. Obviously, a recession at home coupled with a deficit in the balance of payments also calls for opposing monetary policies. In fact, a conflict in policy is avoided only if (1) both domestic and international conditions are satisfactory (situation G); (2) a deficit balance of payments problem occurs during a period of inflation (situation E); or (3) a balance of payments surplus occurs during a period of recession (situation C).

The potential problems faced by the Fed due to conflicting policy requirements are minimized due to the fact that the most likely combinations of domestic and international problems are inflation and a balance of payments deficit. Also, a recession at home tends to coincide with a surplus balance of payments condition. Should conflicting situations arise, the dilemma can be avoided if the exchange

TABLE 21-1
Monetary policy actions required under alternative domestic and international economic conditions

Domestic economic conditions	International economic conditions		
	Satisfactory	Balance of payments deficit	Balance of payments surplus
Recession conditions	Situation A International conditions call for a neutral policy, while domestic conditions call for an expansionary policy.	Situation B Domestic conditions call for expansionary policy, while international conditions call for a restrictive policy.	Situation C Expansionary monetary policy appropriate to both domestic and international situations.
Inflation conditions	Situation D International conditions call for a neutral policy, while domestic conditions call for a restrictive policy.	Situation E Restrictive monetary policy appropriate for both domestic and international situations.	Situation F Domestic conditions call for restrictive policy, while international conditions call for an expansionary policy.
Satisfactory conditions	Situation G Neutral policy called for by both international and domestic conditions.	Situation H Domestic conditions require a neutral policy, while international conditions require a restrictive policy.	Situation I Domestic conditions call for a neutral policy, while international conditions call for an expansionary policy.

rate is allowed to vary. The flexible exchange rates of recent years have made the Fed's job easier in times when domestic conditions and international conditions call for different monetary policy actions.

Integrating the effects of international transactions into monetary policy decisions usually is part of the job of the Federal Open Market Committee (FOMC). Recall that this committee, made up of the Federal Reserve Board of Governors and five Federal Reserve bank presidents, makes the decisions with respect to buying and selling of government securities in the open market. Recall also that open-market operations are the major instrument for carrying out monetary policy. When the FOMC meets, it includes in its considerations the U.S. balance of payments position, its trend, and the effects of the balance of payments on domestic money and credit conditions, exchange rates, and the major economic objectives. Thus the effects of international transactions have an influence on Federal Reserve open-market operations. Moreover, discount rate changes and reserve requirement changes are occasionally made because of balance of payments considerations.

Because banks are involved in international transactions, the regulatory and supervisory functions of the Fed are affected. An American bank wishing to invest in a foreign bank or to establish a foreign branch must secure approval of the Fed. At the end of 1978, Federal Reserve member banks were operating 761 foreign banks, and the number of foreign branches operated by American banks has grown steadily in recent years. All indications are that this growth will continue.

In addition to regulating and supervising foreign banking activities, the Fed is charged with administering the provisions of the Edge Act. The Edge Act allows U.S. banks to form corporations for the sole purpose of engaging in international banking operations. These corporations may be located outside the state in which the parent bank is located. For example, a New York or Chicago bank may form an Edge Act Corporation and locate offices in San Francisco and New Orleans. Restrictions on branching across state lines would normally prevent the establishment of such offices. It should be emphasized that these out-of-state subsidiaries can engage only in international banking transactions. The Edge Act also allows banks to own investment companies which, in turn, may invest in foreign financial institutions. Therefore, through the vehicle of an Edge Act corporation, American banks can invest in foreign financing corporations, leasing companies, and insurance companies. Finally, the Edge Act corporations can invest in foreign commercial banking institutions. At the end of 1978, a total of 124 such corporations had been approved by the Fed.

The Federal Reserve Bank of New York acts as the operational arm of the Federal Reserve when the Fed engages in official reserve transactions with other central banks or when the Fed engages in exchange market transactions to stabilize the value of the dollar. In recent years, an integral part of some of the transactions has been currency "swap" arrangements set up with other central banks. Swap arrangements usually involve two related transactions; under a typical swap arrangement, the Federal Reserve might sell the West German Bundesbank $2 billion in exchange for marks with an agreement to resell an equivalent number of marks at some future time. Such an agreement would allow the Fed to obtain a temporary increase in international reserve assets that could be used to "defend" the dollar's exchange value in times of speculative pressure. Swap arrangements, however, do not constitute a cure to more fundamental problems which may be exerting downward pressure on the exchange value of the dollar.

SUMMARY

The International Monetary Fund was a product of agreements worked out by the major trading nations at a conference in Bretton Woods, New Hampshire, in 1944. It was at this conference that the postwar international monetary framework was developed. This framework was characterized by fixed exchange rates and international cooperation aimed at fostering world trade. The IMF was the operational backbone of the system with its primary function being the lending of international reserves to member countries with temporary balance of payments problems so that these countries could maintain exchange rates and avoid measures designed to disrupt either their own domestic economy or the flows of trade across their borders.

The IMF-administered system of fixed rates and mutual cooperation was rated by most observers as an improvement over the prewar system of intensely competitive and unilateral policies by which nations attempted to use the international payments mechanism to promote domestic economic activity at the expense of their trading partners. However, the postwar system was not without its problems; fixed exchange rates proved difficult to adjust at times when adjustments were needed to correct fundamental balance of payments problems. Finding a method of providing for adequate international liquidity in the face of a growing volume of international trade was a constant worry that finally led to the creation of Special Drawing Rights (SDRs).

The creation and growth of the Eurodollar market was an important development of the postwar period. The Eurodollar market grew and prospered, with considerable stimulus from interest rate ceilings in the United States, and has broadened in recent years to become the Eurocurrency market. The result is an international system of making deposits and loans in various major currencies through banks outside the home countries of the currencies involved.

The activities of the Federal Reserve System are influenced by international economic events. As we saw in Chapter 20, the U.S. balance of payments position can affect important domestic economic variables in ways which may be favorable or unfavorable. Thus the Fed must constantly monitor the effects of international transactions on the economy and be prepared to allow for or offset these effects in the process of implementing monetary policy. The bulk of this task falls to the Federal Open Market Committee; hence, Federal Reserve open-market operations are influenced by international monetary developments. The Fed also engages in regulating and supervising the international activities of domestic banks and the domestic activities of foreign banks. Last, but not least, as an arm of the U.S. government, the Fed works with other central banks in trying to work out mutually satisfactory solutions to international monetary problems.

REVIEW QUESTIONS

1. Why were additional dollars not a permanent solution to the international liquidity problem?
2. What type of balance of payments condition is compatible with Federal Reserve attempts to curb inflation? Explain.
3. Is Federal Reserve policymaking made easier or more difficult by fixed exchange rates such as existed under the Bretton Woods system? Explain.
4. How does the Eurobond market differ from the Eurodollar market and the Eurocurrency market?
5. What are the strengths and weaknesses of the Bretton Woods system of fixed exchange rates?
6. What are swap arrangements, and why are they not a solution to fundamental balance of payments problems?
7. Are Special Drawing Rights the solution to the international liquidity problem? Discuss.

SUGGESTIONS FOR ADDITIONAL READING

Cutler, David S. "The Operations and Transactions of the Special Drawing Account." Finance and Development, vol. 8 (December 1971), pp. 18–23.

Dufey, Gunter, and Giddy, Ian H. *The International Money Market.* Englewood Cliffs, N.J.: Prentice-Hall, Inc., 1978.

Friedman, Milton. "The Eurodollar Market: Some First Principles." *Morgan Guaranty Survey* (October 1969), pp. 4–14.

Gold, Joseph. *Special Drawing Rights, Character and Uses.* 2d ed. Washington, D.C.: International Monetary Fund, 1970.

Little, Jane Sneddon. *Eurodollars: The Money Market Gypsies.* New York: Harper & Row, 1975.

Johnson, Harry G. "The Case for Flexible Exchange Rates, 1969." In George N. Halm, ed., *Approaches to Greater Flexibility of Exchange Rates: The Burgenstock Papers.* Princeton, N.J.: Princeton University Press, 1970.

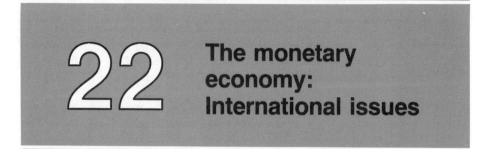

22

The monetary economy: International issues

WARM-UP: *Outline and questions to consider as you read*

Should Eurocurrency markets be regulated?
  The safety of Eurobank operations.
  Eurobank operations and exchange rate insta-
    bility.
  The Euromarkets and domestic monetary pol-
    icy.
  Prospects.
Can the monetary economy cope with the pet-
  rodollar crisis?
  The recycling problem.
  The wealth transfer problem.
  The market power problem.
What does the future hold for the international
  monetary economy?

NEW TERMS

Country risk: the added possibility of loss that arises when the lender makes loans to borrowers outside of the lender's home country.

ECU (European Currency Unit): monetary unit used in official transactions by member nations of the European Economic Community.

LIBOR (London interbank offered rate):   the going rate at which major Eurobanks lend Eurocurrency to each other.

Petrodollars: the dollar holdings of OPEC nations resulting from their petroleum exports.

Recycling problem: the task of channelling the OPEC trade surplus to those oil-consuming nations that need foreign exchange to cover balance of payments deficits generated by oil imports.

When the international aspects of the monetary economy have been considered in recent years, two issues have received considerable attention, and both are introduced in this chapter. These issues are the petrodollar problem and the problem of regulating the Eurocurrency markets. Both issues are complex, and both create a certain amount of apprehension. The third issue raised in this chapter deals with the future of the international monetary economy.

SHOULD EUROCURRENCY MARKETS BE REGULATED?

The Eurocurrency market is an immense and rapidly growing part of the international financial system. Measured in dollars, the Eurocurrency market was a $1 trillion market in 1980, and its annual rate of growth in recent years has consistently exceeded 20 percent. Moreover, as noted earlier, the Eurocurrency market is essentially an unregulated market not subject to control by the regulatory authorities in any country or countries. This lack of regulation is often cited as a primary cause of the market's rapid growth. At the same time, the growth and size of this market have generated concern for the lack of any systematic regulation. In this section, we examine key elements in the argument for regulation of the Eurocurrency market.[1]

The argument for regulatory control over the Eurocurrency market appears to rest upon the following propositions:

1. The Eurocurrency market is characterized by unsound banking practices that raise questions of safety with respect to the major banks participating in the market.
2. The existence of the Eurocurrency market and practices within that market have contributed to greater exchange-rate instability.

---

[1] This section draws heavily from Edward J. Frydl's excellent summary in "The Debate over Regulating the Eurocurrency Markets," *Federal Reserve Bank of New York Quarterly Review*, vol. 4, no. 4 (Winter 1979–80), pp. 11–20; and H. Peter Gray, *International Trade, Investment, and Payments* (Boston: Houghton Mifflin, 1979), chap. 26.

3. The existence of a vast Eurocurrency market complicates, or possibly overrides, national monetary policies, particularly anti-inflationary policies.

Each of these propositions is examined below.

The safety of Eurobank operations

Loans made by banks in the Eurocurrency market are subject to many of the same risks that face banks making domestic loans. Such factors as the creditworthiness of the borrower, adequacy of collateral, and proposed use of the loan proceeds should and do receive careful consideration. However, proponents of regulation cite several aspects of Eurocurrency lending as especially risky. Chief among these is what is sometimes referred to as country risk.

Country risk. Country risk refers to the added possibility of loss that arises when the lender makes loans to borrowers outside of the lender's home country. For example, Eurocurrency loans are being made to borrowers in countries with unstable governments that may repudiate debts or impose restrictions on capital flows and thus prevent repayment of loans and interest. Also, political instability is great in many countries in which Eurocurrency loans are being made. Since such possibilities are usually irrelevant in the case of domestic loans made by Eurobanks, the practices and policies that have been developed to assess the soundness of domestic loans may not necessarily be adequate for assessing the added risk associated with many Eurocurrency loans.

Country risk is not confined to Eurobanks' lending activities. For instance, official institutions of OPEC countries hold large concentrations of Eurocurrency deposits which they may shift from bank to bank or withdraw from the Eurocurrency market altogether. Moreover, most observers see the political situation in the Middle East and the nature of Middle East governments as making such shifts a distinct possibility.

The problem of country risk can be put in perspective by noting that only one third of Eurocurrency loans are made to governments and private borrowers of Western industrialized nations. The remaining loans are being made to borrowers in communist countries, OPEC nations, and some of the poorest of the developing countries. Loan concentrations in some of the latter countries are heavy, and this increased concentration implies greater risk. So far, however, actual losses on international lending have been relatively small, and Eurobanks are constantly improving their procedures for analyzing international loans. Furthermore, the regulatory authorities in many countries have increased their surveillance of international lending by banks subject to their control.

Maturity mismatching and interest-rate risk.   The sources of deposit funds for the major Eurobanks are generally short term in nature; in fact, the weighted average maturity of Eurocurrency deposits may be as short as three months. At the same time, these Eurobanks make many Eurocurrency loans with maturities of several years. This mismatching of maturities can create problems if interest rates are volatile. The cost of funds can rise above loan rates and cause banks to be locked into unprofitable loans. However, a degree of protection is provided by a typical provision which calls for revising the loan interest rates at six-month intervals. Even this protection is not complete, though, since the even shorter maturity structure of Eurobanks' liabilities means that almost all of these liabilities would roll over during a period of six months.

Maturity mismatching and interest-rate risk encompass not only Eurocurrency operations but also the banks' entire asset-liability structures, and the degree of risk varies with the volatility of all interest rates. Nevertheless, proponents of regulation argue that Euromarket rates have, in fact, become more volatile in recent years and that the degree of risk associated with mismatched Eurocurrency assets and liabilities is no longer reflective of prudent banking.

Declining spreads.   During 1979, the spread between the rates earned on Eurocurrency loans and the cost of funds used to make those loans approached an all-time low. The cost of funds is measured by the London interbank offered rate (LIBOR) which is the rate at which Eurobanks lend Eurocurrency to each other. This declining spread was accompanied by a rapid increase in Eurocurrency loans and a rise in Eurocurrency loan rates. The rising rates accompanied by declining spreads are somewhat puzzling, and explanations generally center around possible increased loan competition among Eurobank lenders due to the growing activity of Japanese banks. In any case the lower spreads caused some banks, particularly U.S. banks, to curtail their lending for a time. A major concern is that the reduced spreads will impair earnings and make it difficult for banks to expand their capital (via retained earnings). Hence narrower spreads may be linked to lower capital ratios and a weakening of the banks involved. Greater regulation, it is argued, is needed to control problems associated with the decline in spreads.

The major Eurobanks maintain extensive deposit and lending relationships with each other and with domestic banks. This practice raises the question of what would happen if a major Eurobank failed and was unable to meet demand by other banks for funds on deposit. Would there be a run on other Eurobanks, and could such a run spread to still other banks, thereby producing a worldwide financial crisis? The failure in 1974 of the Bankhaus I. D. Herstatt, a large private bank in Germany, makes such questions pertinent to many observers. While the Herstatt Bank's failure was not the direct result of Eurocurrency operations, the financial community's reaction to its demise demonstrates the fear that could spread among Eurobanks as a result of interbank relationships.

Eurobank operations and exchange rate instability

Proponents of additional regulation of the Eurocurrency market argue that Eurobank operations intensify exchange-rate instability and thus place an added burden on the international financial system. The question of how the Eurodollar market has effected the exchange value of the dollar was discussed in Chapter 21 as a special case of exchange-rate instability brought about by Eurodollar operations. It is argued that the Eurocurrency market makes exchange rates less stable by making it easier for speculators to finance their operations and by increasing the mobility of capital. To date, however, conclusive empirical evidence confirming a connection between the Eurocurrency market and exchange-rate instability is lacking, and debate over this issue seems likely to continue.

The Euromarkets and domestic monetary policy

It is widely believed, especially in the case of the U.S. dollar, that Eurocurrency lending makes the conduct of domestic monetary policy more difficult; in particular, policies designed to curb inflation are the most likely to be circumvented by growth of the Eurocurrency market. The Eurocurrency market grows whenever deposits are shifted from domestic banks into Eurocurrency deposits. As noted in Chapter 21, such shifts may occur without reducing domestic deposit liabilities, although they result in an increase in total (world) deposit liabilities and credit availability. Since the growth of Eurocurrency lending is uncontrolled, a large volume of credit growth can take place worldwide even though monetary authorities in many countries are attempting to curb credit growth within their domestic economies. Some proponents of Euromarket regulation see this world credit growth as a major cause of inflation and, hence, as prima facie evidence of the need for additional regulation.

The fact that Eurocurrency markets allow world credit to expand in an unplanned and uncontrolled manner is not, however, sufficient grounds for concluding that the policy actions of domestic monetary authorities are thwarted. The authorities retain control over domestic transactions balances through the use of traditional central banking instruments. If transactions balances are the key link between monetary policy and the economic goals of the policymakers, then the Eurocurrency market need not cause national monetary authorities to lose control of the means of achieving domestic goals.

Most Eurocurrency deposits are time deposits; hence, they may be regarded as one of several investments that substitute for transactions balances. There is the possibility, therefore, that Eurocurrency activity affects the velocity of domestic transactions balances. If such effects do occur and cannot be reliably quantified or predicted, the consequences would be a less-effective domestic monetary policy. Thus velocity effects are sometimes cited as further need to control the Eurocurrency markets.

Prospects

If the weight of the above arguments is sufficient to justify additional regulation of the Eurocurrency markets, a crucial question remains: Who is to have this regulatory authority? Several possibilities exist, including a new international superagency, an expanded IMF, the Bank for International Settlements (BIS), joint central bank supervision, or some other arrangement.[2]

In April 1980, in what some see as a step toward regulation of the Eurocurrency markets, the central banks of the major Western nations established a standing committee to "monitor" worldwide banking developments. The reasons given were the "risk inherent in the growing rate of international lending fueled by mounting oil prices," and the fact that "transactions channeled through the Eurocurrency market can pose problems for the effectiveness of domestic monetary policy in those countries where . . . differences (in competitive conditions between domestic and international banking markets) are particularly significant."[3]

CAN THE MONETARY ECONOMY COPE WITH THE PETRODOLLAR CRISIS?

The term *petrodollars*, which refers to the earnings of OPEC nations from their exports to oil-consuming nations, arises out of the OPEC price increases of 1974 and has become an established part of

---

[2] For a perspective on the issue of Euromarket regulation see Henry C. Wallich, "Why the Euromarket Needs Restraint"; Bluford Putnam, "Controlling the Euromarkets: A Policy Perspective"; and Robert R. Davis, "Effects of the Eurodollar Market on National Monetary Policies"; all in *Columbia Journal of World Business*, vol. 14, no. 3 (Fall 1979).

[3] *The Wall Street Journal*, April 16, 1980, p. 44.

the international financial vocabulary. The distinguishing characteristic of petrodollars is their ownership by OPEC nations.

The trade surplus of OPEC countries was a healthy $20 billion in 1973.[4] Exports by OPEC nations accounted for approximately 10 percent of world exports in that year, and virtually all of these exports were petroleum related. Following the oil embargo associated with the 1973 Arab-Israeli war, the OPEC nations raised prices drastically. Consequently, in 1974, OPEC exports jumped over 300 percent to almost one fourth of all exports. The OPEC trade surplus for that year was $85 billion, and, of course, this surplus resulted in a massive shift in liquid wealth to the OPEC countries. During the 1975–78 period, the value of OPEC exports grew by only 20 percent. However, in 1979 additional large increases in oil prices caused OPEC export revenues to jump by almost 50 percent, and the total dollar value of the increase was as large as that of the 1974 price hike. It is the size and rapid growth of payments flows generated by petroleum exports that give petrodollars their crisis connotation. If the amounts were smaller, petrodollars would generate no more notice than "bananadollars" or "coffeedollars". Aside from the obvious question of how to pay the high prices for imported petroleum and the possibility of another embargo, petrodollars create several less-noticeable problems for the oil-consuming nations which shall be referred to here as (1) the recycling problem, (2) the wealth transfer problem, and (3) the market power problem.

The recycling problem

The recycling problem has received considerable attention in recent years. The existence of a vast petrodollar surplus on the part of the oil-exporting countries implies equally large trade deficits for the oil-consuming nations. Unless the petrodollars flowing into OPEC foreign exchange holdings are somehow "recycled" back to the oil-consuming countries, the latter group will soon run out of the foreign exchange needed to finance their oil imports, or there will be an unparalleled drop in exchange rates. The challenge of recycling petrodollars was successfully met in 1974 and 1979 but remains a serious hurdle for the 1980s.

The most obvious manner in which recycling could occur would be through increased imports by OPEC nations. While OPEC imports have increased, the growth of OPEC export revenues, especially in 1974 and 1979, has far exceeded the growth of imports. If recycling through additional OPEC imports does not occur, then another

---

[4] All trade figures are expressed in dollars in order to facilitate comparisons.

method of recycling must be found. In fact, the international banking system through the medium of Eurocurrency deposits and loans has accomplished this recycling.

The Eurocurrency market has worked well (thus far) in recycling the huge OPEC petrodollar surpluses of 1974 and 1979. However, signs of strain have appeared (see the previous section on Eurocurrency regulation and country risk), and some experts now estimate the the recycling problem is too much for the Eurobanks to continue to handle. In 1980, Eurobanks may have to provide up to $150 billion in loans to finance petroleum imports.[5] This total is a 50 percent increase over 1979 which, in turn, was a record year. Problems may arise as the Eurobanks are forced to recycle such massive amounts, particularly since loans are becoming concentrated in the hands of borrowers in deficit oil-consuming countries, while deposits are short term and concentrated in the hands of OPEC depositers.

Whether the Eurobanks themselves or their respective regulatory authorities will permit the continued buildup of the loans and deposits associated with recycling petrodollars remains to be seen, but many observers see a pressing need to develop alternative recycling channels. If Eurobanks either turn down further OPEC deposits or refuse additional credit to debt-heavy borrowers in oil-consuming countries, no alternative means of recycling is available as of now.[6]

Proposals for alternative recycling channels center around the IMF (or an IMF-type multicountry agency). For example, the IMF might borrow from central banks in surplus countries or from private borrowers through regular channels in the financial markets and then relend the funds to deficit countries. Two major advantages are cited by proponents of an IMF role in recycling petrodollars:

1. The IMF is better able to handle the attendant risks than the Eurobanks currently involved in the recycling process.
2. The IMF would be in a better position than individual banks to impose corrective measures on deficit countries.

There would, of course, be no reason why the IMF (or a similar facility) could not work closely with the international banking community by, for example, guaranteeing private bank loans in order to stimulate private lending in high-risk situations.

In 1974 the IMF set up a special "oil facility," which was an arrangement to use the IMF to recycle petrodollars. The facility op-

---

[5] Minos A. Zombanakis, "How to Handle the Payments Deficits," *Business Week*, April 7, 1980, p. 18.

[6] For a more optimistic view of the ability of the Eurocurrency market to handle the recycling problem, see Edward Meadows, "How the Euromarket Fends Off Global Financial Disaster," *Fortune*, September 24, 1979, pp. 122–35.

erated in 1974 and 1975 but was abandoned in 1976. Under the oil facility, funds for loans to deficit countries were provided by several OPEC countries and several developed countries.[7] Something along the lines of a new and expanded special oil facility within the IMF is viewed by many observers as the most workable approach to solving the recycling problem during the 1980s.

A particularly worrisome aspect of the recycling problem involves the less-developed countries (LDCs). Burgeoning oil prices inhibit the ability of these countries to import the petroleum they need to finance development. Furthermore, their meager foreign exchange earnings must be used for petroleum imports rather than for capital goods essential in the development process. This situation creates several problems:

1. The rate of growth of LDCs is curtailed.
2. Their ability to buy from developed nations drops, thereby hurting exports of Western oil-consuming nations.
3. The LDCs' ability to service existing Eurobank debt and to qualify for additional loans is seriously impaired which may cause them to be left out of the recycling process in the future.

An IMF role in recycling is seen as essential in handling the needs of the LDCs.

The wealth transfer problem

The very existence of large OPEC trade surpluses implies that the countries involved are not using the funds generated by oil exports to increase imports from the oil-consuming nations. Thus the OPEC trade surplus requires equally large OPEC capital investments in the rest of the world. Recall from Chapter 20 that such capital investments may be in the form of long-term direct or indirect investments or short-term investments. So far, the major portion of OPEC capital investment has gone into short-term financial claims rather than long-term investments; however, OPEC investors are buying farmland, hotels, banks, manufacturing facilities, and other real assets in the non-OPEC world. These purchases, coupled with the tremendous liquid purchasing power being generated by the OPEC trade surplus, have prompted fears that OPEC investors will eventually own a disproportionate share of the world's stock of wealth.

That the huge OPEC surpluses are going to create a wealth transfer problem is certain. What is not clear, however, is when this

---

[7] Robert Solomon, *The International Monetary System, 1945–1976: An Insider's View* (New York: Harper & Row, 1977), pp. 298–306.

transfer will occur. As the relative price of oil rises, OPEC nations will be able to obtain more and more goods and services from oil-consuming nations, since ultimately goods must always exchange for goods. The oil-producing countries have only three general ways to use petrodollars, and only two of these are rational. They may (1) hold their petrodollars, (2) use them to finance increased imports, and/or (3) use them to acquire long- or short-term financial claims.

Holding petrodollars is irrational over the long run since it is equivalent to trading oil for paper. Thus only the last two alternatives are realistic. If OPEC countries use their petrodollars to finance imports, there is an immediate transfer of wealth from the oil-consuming nations in that they must give up more goods and services now in payment for petroleum. On the other hand, if OPEC nations increase their imports at a much slower pace than exports, as has generally been the case, the petrodollars will be invested so as to generate a growing claim on real goods and services produced by the oil-consuming nations. In the latter case, the transfer of real wealth is being postponed.

Observers have cited some advantages of deferring the wealth transfer via capital investments by OPEC countries. As OPEC nations purchase real and financial assets in non-OPEC countries, the economic performance of the latter countries becomes more and more important to OPEC countries; consequently, OPEC countries are less and less likely to take political and economic actions that would disrupt Western economies and, at the same time, decrease the value of OPEC investments in those nations. Furthermore, the OPEC countries themselves know how easy it is to nationalize or take over foreign investments. It is therefore possible that petrodollars used to make long-term investments in Western nations will turn out to be a stabilizing force and will postpone the eventual real income transfer that must accompany the rising relative value of oil.

The market power problem

Market power always carries with it the potential for economic mischief. The OPEC nations' huge petrodollar holdings give them unprecedented power in the international financial and foreign exchange markets. By converting their holdings into and out of particular currencies, they could cause wide and disruptive swings in foreign exchange rates. By withdrawing their Eurocurrency deposits from selected banks or the Eurobanking system in general, OPEC nations could jeopardize the safety of these banks.

Potential disruptions caused by the market power of OPEC may be manageable, however. For example, large OPEC withdrawals from the Eurobanks can be handled if the central banks involved provide adequate rediscount privilege to the affected banks. If Eurobanks suffered massive withdrawals of OPEC deposits, central banks could lend to these banks on the basis of loans pledged as collateral, or the central banks could purchase the loans outright. Extensive use of swap arrangements (see Chapter 21) could be used to counter major exchange-rate movements caused by OPEC activities in the exchange markets. Obviously such activities increase the role and importance of central bank international activities.

WHAT DOES THE FUTURE HOLD FOR THE INTERNATIONAL MONETARY ECONOMY?

A theme that runs constantly throughout this book is that the monetary economy is continually changing. This evolution has occurred at both the national level and the international level, and there is every indication that it will continue in the future. How will the monetary economy change in the decade of the 1980s? There is no way of knowing for sure, but many observers feel that future developments can be discerned from current trends. Probably, the most far-reaching development will be a continuation of the trend toward the *supranationalization* of the monetary economy.

Supranationalization of the monetary economy refers to an international superstructure that encompasses, yet is independent of, individual nations. Thus the term reflects the tendency for the monetary economy to escape the boundaries and control of any single nation. One aspect of supranationalization is the rapid growth and development of financial markets not encompassed by national boundaries but linked together so as to be, in effect, a single market. For example, the tremendous growth of the Eurocurrency market has resulted in a vast and sophisticated financial network with instant links to all monetary economies. We discussed above the extent to which the flow of funds in this market is independent of national government or central bank control, and while attempts to control and limit the markets are likely to occur, the authors feel that such attempts will prove to be essentially futile. The Eurocurrency market is an innovation whose time has come.

The supranationalization of the monetary economy has a second foundation, and that is the movement toward a monetary unit independent of a single national government, that is, a common currency. This movement is certainly not as obvious or as well developed as the financial market evolution, but there are signs of its existence. Of course, for centuries there has always been an international money in the form of gold which, although dormant in recent years, still retains considerable appeal in many quarters. However, events of recent years have moved gold more and more out of the role of international money. If gold is not to function as an international money, what will perform this role? An obvious candidate is SDRs. The nature, role, and development of SDRs were discussed in Chapter 21, where the transition from gold and national currencies to SDRs was discussed. The use of SDRs has not grown in spectacular fashion, but growth in use is occurring.

The movement toward a common currency is not confined to SDRs. The European Economic Community has taken the first steps toward a common currency with the introduction in 1979 of ECUs or European Currency Units. The ECU is to the Common Market countries what SDRs are to the IMF member countries, in that ECUs are used for official transactions within the European Economic Community. The value of an ECU is based on a weighted average of the currencies of the nine member nations of the European Economic Community.

Severe obstacles remain before international money supplants national currencies for domestic transactions. Nations must be willing to give up their national currencies, which means giving up the right to pursue independent monetary policies. According to some observers, nations may be more willing to do this than might be expected since the widespread inability to conduct monetary policy independent of political pressures often results in inflation and accompanying problems. An impartially controlled common currency may, therefore, prove appealing to many nations. However, this development is likely to be slow and controlled, and like most previous important changes in the institutional framework of the monetary economy, a major crisis may be the catalyst that makes drastic change acceptable. With this in mind, all indications are that the 1980s will indeed be a dynamic and interesting period for the monetary economy.

SUMMARY

As the Eurocurrency market has grown in size, it has attracted more attention, which has resulted in some alarm with respect to its unregulated nature. Thus there have been increased calls for some form of control over the activities of the Eurobanks. These calls for control have been prompted by three alleged problems. The first problem centers around the safety of Eurobank operations; a second problem concerns the possible destabilizing effect that Eurobank operations may have on exchange rates; finally, there is the possibility that Euromarkets hinder the administration of domestic monetary policy.

One of the most serious challenges facing the international

monetary economy in recent years is the petrodollar crisis resulting from the huge OPEC trade surplus. The petrodollar crisis has several dimensions including the difficulties of recycling petrodollars to the oil-consuming nations and the tremendous market power that their petrodollar holdings bestow upon the OPEC nations. Of course the very existence of these holdings implies that a significant shift in wealth is inevitable.

The monetary economy is dynamic at both the national and international levels. What lies ahead in the 1980s is of course unknown; however, it seems likely that there will be a supranationalization of the monetary economy as national boundaries succumb to common economic interests.

REVIEW QUESTIONS

1. Explain why the recycling problem is of particular interest to less-developed countries (LDCs).
2. Should the Eurocurrency markets be regulated? Justify your answer.
3. How does the handling of country risk pose problems not encountered in handling normal risks of banking such as default risk and interest-rate risk?
4. Do you feel that recycling should be handled by the international banking system or by the IMF? Discuss.
5. Discuss the pros and cons of a common international currency.
6. How does maturity mismatching create risks for the Eurobanks? Is maturity mismatching a consideration in domestic lending activities?

SUGGESTIONS FOR ADDITIONAL READING

Frydl, Edward J. "The Debate over Regulating the Eurocurrency Markets." *Federal Reserve Bank of New York Quarterly Review,* vol. 4, no. 4 (Winter 1979–80), pp. 11–20.

Gray, H. Peter. *International Trade, Investment, and Payments.* Boston: Houghton Mifflin, 1979, chap. 26.

Meadows, Edward. How the Euromarket Fends Off Global Financial Disaster." *Fortune,* September 24, 1979, pp. 122–35.

Putnam, Bluford H. "Controlling the Euromarkets: A Policy Perspective." *Columbia Journal of World Business,* vol. 14, no. 3 (Fall 1979), pp. 25–31.

Solomon, Robert. *The International Monetary System, 1945–1976.* New York: Harper & Row, 1977.

Wallich, Henry C. "Why the Euromarket Needs Restraint." *Columbia Journal of World Business,* vol. 14, no. 3 (Fall 1979), pp. 17–24.

Westerfield, Janice M. "A Primer on the Risks of International Lending and How to Evaluate Them." *Business Review,* Federal Reserve Bank of Philadelphia (July–August 1978), pp. 19–29.

Index of terms

The following terms are defined in the New Terms section of the particular chapter indicated by the number appearing after each item.

Index

This book has been set VIP in 10 and 9 point Melior, leaded 2 points. Part and chapter numbers are 72 point Helvetica Medium Outline. Part and chapter titles are 18 point Helvetica Bold. The size of the type page is 29 by 46½ picas.